A YOUNG SOLDIER'S MEMOIRS

To Ken Houser,

May you enjoy Adventuring through 1965 Korea with me through the pages of this book

Julio A. Martinez

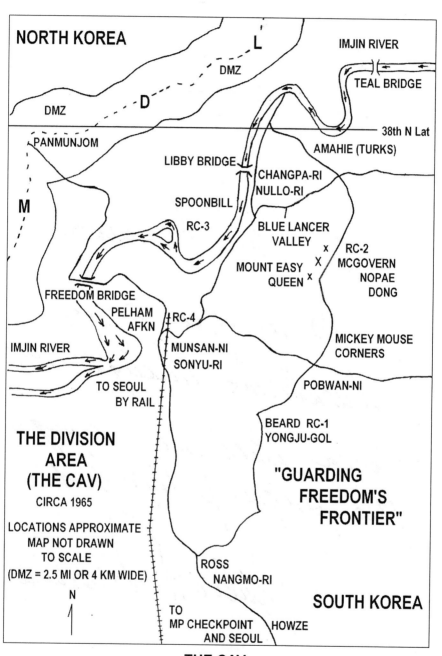

A YOUNG SOLDIER'S MEMOIRS:

My One Year Growing Up in 1965 Korea

Julio A. Martinez

Copyright © 2010 by Julio A. Martinez.

Library of Congress Control Number:		2010914733
ISBN:	Hardcover	978-1-4535-2386-5
	Softcover	978-1-4535-2385-8
	Ebook	978-1-4535-2387-2

All rights reserved. No part of this book may be reproduced or transmitted in any form or by any means, electronic or mechanical, including photocopying, recording, or by any information storage and retrieval system, without permission in writing from the copyright owner.

This book was printed in the United States of America.

To order additional copies of this book, contact:
Xlibris Corporation
1-888-795-4274
www.Xlibris.com
Orders@Xlibris.com

Contents

Preface 13
Acknowledgments 17

Part I Barrio Prospect Hill West, San Antonio, Texas, USA

Chapter 1 Fleeting Childhood Bliss 21
A World outside My House 22
A World outside the Front Fence 26
Kite Flying at the Creek 29
My Backstreet and Bus Ride Adventures 32

Chapter 2 Thirteen Captive Years 37
Battered Childhood 38
Patriotism 53
My Senior Year 59

Part II Eighth United States Army, Korea

Chapter 3 In Transit to Far East Asia 67
Arrival 68
Reception 70
Personnel Duty Station 72

Chapter 4 Camp McGovern, Nopae Dong, Korea 75
Indoctrination 76
Buck Private Rituals 81
Guardhouse Blues 86
Guard Tower Four 91
Motor Pool Guard Post 97

Chapter 5 God and Country 100
The Camp Pelham Branch 102
December 1964...106
My Mission 109

Chapter 6 Early Days at McGovern 112
The Language...112
Money Matters...115
Hiring a Houseboy 119
The Camp Theater 123
The Village 127

Chapter 7 Prostitution, The Main Employment 130
The Teahouse *Josans* 131
Streetwalkers..133
Husband-Hunting for a Ticket Stateside 134
Trade Risks 136
Lucrative Profession 138

Chapter 8 Life outside the Fence 142
Wild Night on the Town 142
Oggie 148
Colossal Buddhas..152
Twilight 158
Nopae Dong 160
Poverty in Korea 163

Chapter 9 To Seoul by Rail and Bus 167
By Rail..168
Seoul...178
By Bus 187

Chapter 10 Transfer! Camp Ross, Nangmo-Ri, Korea 207
Prisoners of War 208
Nocturnal Misadventures...211
Rice Paddies and Vills 214
Reenlistment Dilemma...227

Chapter 11 Impaled! Guard Duty at Camp Ross 231
    Tower One 232
    Personnel Pains at Ross 237
    Ross's Cantina 245
    Peak Dae 251
    Insubordination at Ross 256
    My Princess 259

Chapter 12 Reassigned! Camp Blue Lancer Valley, Nullo-Ri, Korea .. 269
    To the Cavalry! 270
    Orderly Room Blahs and Boons! 272
    Reflagging 275
    Adventures on the Imjin 279
    Birthday Suits 282
    A Momentous Call at a Picturesque Temple 286
    Her Majesty, the Queen 292

Chapter 13 Exploring Queen's Treasures 296
    Ghostly Visitation 297
    Easy Queen Encounter 302
    Nature's Gifts to Easy 306

Chapter 14 Uncovering Queen's Mysteries 314
    Gravestones, Temples, Buddhas, and Bunkers 314
    Skeleton Find on Easy Queen 322
    Instruments of Destruction 326

Chapter 15 Sopping Wet Monsoons! 332
    Monsoon Miseries 333
    Monsoon Guard at the Turk's Compound 339
    A Charming Farmer's Hooch 349
    Monsoon Lull at a Remote Village 356

Chapter 16 September 1965 359
    Kyung Bok Ku 361
    The Capitol 366
    Inchon Adventure 370

Duk Soo Palace 374
Keum Kok Royal Tomb 379

Chapter 17 The Land of the Rising Sun 386

Chapter 18 Camp Blue Lancer Valley 398
My Commanding Officers 398
Our KATUSA Brothers 404
Cavaliers and Tomahawks...408
Mail Call..423
Wildlife of Korea...427
Hi Bob, *Hello, Dolly!* 430
Wonderland by Night..433
The Case of the Slickied Camera 438

Chapter 19 Departing the Pacific 440
Bathhouse Spectacle 441
The Ring 444
Regret at Munsan-Ni 448
Eligible Date to Depart the Pacific..450

Part III Our Korea
The Military Sector 456
Our Crossed Cultures 462
The Camaraderie 467
Camaraderie Lost 471

Part IV Close
Epilogue 477
Glossary...484
Army Rank and Grade 490
About Photographs 491
Testimonial 493
Commentary..495
In Memoriam 497
Index..503

Dedicated to my families

When I was seventeen, my life changed forever . . . I'm fifty-seven years old, but even now I remember everything from that year, down to the smallest details. I relive that year often in my mind, bringing it back to life, and I realize that when I do, I always feel . . . joy . . . This is my story; I promise to leave nothing out.

—Nicholas Sparks, *A Walk to Remember*

I was born an American; I live an American; I shall die an American; and I intend to perform the duties incumbent upon me in that character to the end of my career. I mean to do this with absolute disregard of personal consequences.

What are the personal consequences? What is the individual man, with all the good or evil that may betide him, in comparison with the good or evil which may befall a great country, and in the midst of great transactions which concern that country's fate?

Let the consequences be what they will, I am careless. No man can suffer too much, and no man can fall too soon, if he suffer, or if he fall, in the defense of the liberties and constitution of his country.

—Daniel Webster

Preface

Initially, the objective of my *memoirs* was as a legacy to my children and grandchildren. Because of encouragement from family and friends, I decided to continue writing to its published fruition. I am comfortable that this book is a product of self-publication and although a college graduate and not a professional writer with imperfections notwithstanding, the spirit of this work remains personally original and in my heartfelt voice. My descriptions and personal analyses of Korea are based on my own conclusions. I have not researched any documents or consulted with any historian. I have tried to make the depictions clear to the reader and have attempted to explain life as well as possible, along with the local Korean culture, in this unique situation and the military purpose of the Western Corridor occupied by the U.S. Army.

I had always wanted to share my spirit of adventure, the emotional feelings during my abused childhood, and feelings during leaving home for the first time and departing to the army, eagerly bound for new beginnings in a totally different setting. My tour of duty in Korea was magical in the sense that I was able to divorce myself emotionally from the drudgery of life as a civilian and enrich my cultural heritage with the partaking of a different cultural environment.

Despite all these changes and conditions, religious life was the constant that kept my life from becoming totally hedonistic. My Mormon background helped keep me from going off the edge, and I was able to continue to receive counsel and retain a sense of belonging despite the strangeness of this distant environment. The reader is invited to bear in mind that I was aged eighteen, fresh out of a sheltered household, and five days from high school graduation, thus I was highly impressionable and free of worldly wisdom. That year in the army remained indelibly photographed in my mind, and this is my book with my memoirs about that year. I encourage all brothers to write and publish their memoirs. I invite all readers to open the pages of this book and take delight in my adventures; and I wish you to enjoy venturing with me as much as I did.

Korea, in Far East Asia, was as far as China, and China was on the opposite side of the earth, in the Eastern Hemisphere! As a child, I was wittily led to believe that if I dug a hole in the ground, I would eventually get there! After digging about a foot's depth, I gave up!

Prior to my military duty, I had only known travel via commercial buses. In the mid-1960s, travel abroad was either by ocean liners or by air and limited to those who could afford it. I was not among them. Jet planes were relatively new, so half the time air travel was still by propeller airplanes. A flight across either of the oceans was a matter of a few days or perhaps hours, while a sea cruise took a few weeks, if not months. In those days, a near half-century before today's technology and higher wages, the price of a plane ticket to the Orient was astronomical. Today with credit cards and Internet discounts, all flights anywhere in the world are affordable. Boarding a jet plane bound for the Orient, to Korea in Far East Asia, was thus the greatest thrill of my eighteen-year-old life. Just to experience a stopover in Tokyo, Japan—to know that I had been in Japan—was overwhelming. Then the flight to Korea as my destination and the beginning of all Oriental adventures was a dream come true.

Those were days when communication home was solely by letters. Letters via the Army Post Office were five cents for one month via sea or eight cents for a week's airmail messages. Telephone calls were several dollars a minute and prohibitive at a private's pay of fifty dollars a month.

Thus, the realization sank in that being overseas in Korea *was* being half a world away and totally detached from home. Still, as a young man finally being on my own, with home so far away, I could give full rein to my eagerness to explore the wonders of my new surroundings, study a different culture, and enjoy the comforting sweet patronage of the U.S. government.

"The Land of the Morning Calm" is a peninsula extending from China onto the Sea of Japan. In the ancient times, it was known as "Chosen" (CHO-sun) but also known as Korea, doubtlessly after the Koryo Dynasty. The peninsula boasts a rich but subjugated history since the beginning of recorded time until 1953 with its all-weather harbors and a foothold in the mainland of Asia. Warlords from "The Land of the Rising Sun" (Japan) and "Middle Land" (China) continuously suppressed the Korean people, and until this decade, Korea had no choice but to subsist on a time-tested survival technique—a submissive subjugated agrarian society sowing rice as its staple crop.

Following the Korean War of 1950-1953, the peninsula was divided at the 38th parallel with an uneasy cease-fire armistice that expired in 1963. The North government became a communist dictatorship while the South became a democracy. It was in the year 1964, one year following the expiration of the armistice on July 27, 1963, that I was called to duty at this country. Decades later, I learned that life expectancy south of the Imjin River was fifteen minutes in case of invasion and resumption of the war.

At eighteen, desperately longing to be free of an abusive home and a dysfunctional family, I found every day in this opposite hemisphere to be an adventure. Though Korea was considered to be a hardship tour, I found pleasure in all aspects of duty—from the so-called horrors of guard duty and military responsibility to the delights of wandering all over the mountains finding war relics or gawking in the museums and shrines of Seoul.

In the simplicity of my youthful naïveté and enthusiasm for adventure, I would simply hop on a Korean bus and lose myself by setting off outside the safety net and limits of the military sector for the unknown—blissful and carefree and oblivious to possible threat or hazard that I could disappear in the vast city of Seoul without a trace. I just wandered about as I did within my own neighborhood of my childhood, back in San Antonio. I mixed in with many different personalities and backgrounds, and the magnitude of this experience remained intact in the following four decades.

In my tour of duty, I maximized my time and money. Fortunately, every pass I applied for was granted, enabling my adventuring a positive experience within the allowed limits of The Land of the Morning Calm, during my one year growing up in 1965 Korea.

Note: Military titles in this work are defined in the Army Rank and Grade glossary.

Acknowledgments

I extend my warmest appreciation to Rick, Elsa, Bernadette, and Frank, who very patiently and contentedly bore with me when I ordered, approved or corrected, and reordered full-frame virtually custom prints of Sam's Club #8280 Photo Lab, El Paso, Texas.

I also wish to extend my deepest appreciation to Mrs. Aurora Mendiola for her encouragement when she read my early summaries and encouraged the writing of this book. I thank her for the long hours dedicated to editing my manuscripts, and for all her advice and counsel. Mrs. Mendiola is married to Mr. Abilio Mendiola whose companionship I enjoyed while in Korea and whom I located thirty-five years later via the Net.

Ines
My Eternal Beloved

I especially extend appreciation to my beloved wife, Ines, who heard me out, viewed photos, and her advice in general. Also because of the time she allowed me without objection from the outlining to the book's fruition, a tireless time period of over a decade.

> *The Emperor Augustus was devoted to his wife, Livia Drusilla, and died in her arms on August 29 A.D. 14. When asked how she kept the love and affection of such an important and influential man she replied, "My secret is simple: I have made it the work of my life to please him."*

PART I

Barrio Prospect Hill West, San Antonio, Texas, USA

> *Poverty is the schoolmaster of character.*
> —Antiphanes, Athens 5 BC

Within the little time I had
A moment when my mother's not mad
Though still small worlds of bliss and joy
Alas but few then as boy
From Mem'ry banks since aged five
I felt the stinging quirt alive
Day in day out it was the trend
I told one day would come the end

SNAPSHOT OF AUTHOR ON FIFTH BIRTHDAY

My daughter commented: *"Viewing this little boy's photo I thought, my dad started out so innocent and sweet with so much love and his mother killed his little boy's heart, he faced such horrible things, the kind of life that just makes me cry."*

—Elizabeth Mueller,
Mother and Aspiring Author

Chapter 1

Fleeting Childhood Bliss

The best way to keep children home is to make the home atmosphere pleasant.
—Dorothy Parker (1893-1967)

Prologue

During my childhood, the only happiness and spiritual bliss I ever experienced was in the absence of my abusive mother, who made my home life a living hell and limited my adventures. Limited, because my adventures depended on the few moods that allowed for privileges and escapades. My outings were limited to school, the library, and church, and as I grew older, to downtown and movies, when she didn't notice I was gone. Perhaps her willingness to allow me library privileges centered on the expectancy and selection of a surprise book in Spanish that she had nicely requested. Thirteen of the seventeen years, when relevant memory began, were spent in terror so that any break, insignificant though it may have been, became an adventure in paradise, epic in proportion.

A World outside My House

A world outside my spooky house
Tho spiders bound but naught a mouse
Where greens abound both day and night
I'd play and prowl with sheer delight

My first adventure outside the back door was when I was about four, a preschooler, and I reconnoitered a world outside my house. My world consisted of the space between the confines of the plant-lined backyard picket fence and the house. It was half dirt and half embedded with river rock. My dad had planned on pouring concrete as his pocketbook allowed. Some of the concrete slab was broken up and crumbling, as the combination of poor hand-blended concrete mixture had weathered. There were two shacks: one housed my dad's work area and the other a tumbledown shed that was worn, weather-beaten, and dilapidated. Both shacks were heavily infested and covered with spiderwebs and crawling insects and were not really attractive to me for further exploration. Somehow I became aware of spiders infesting and crawling beneath the floorboards, within the house and the attic. There was a multitude of spiders on the porch rafters, which we'd spray with insecticide.

From a child's perspective, the house was huge and spooky and the backyard boasted homemade wooden steps. I wasn't in grammar school yet, when I first stumbled down those steep wooden steps that my dad had constructed. It was dark underneath the stoop to the "under" house. It was a portal to the pits of hell; mysterious, inviting, and above all dangerous—dangerous, due to my knowledge of spiders lurking the "under" house. After several forays, I discovered other openings along the bottom house leading to the space where sturdy cedar posts held crossbeams holding up the floor of the house. I was oblivious to the smirks of my brother Beau standing by when one day, I tied an empty tin can to a string and onto my waist, and with a table knife in my hand, proceeded to crawl into the bowels of Hades, an underworld of adventure. My brother cracked up laughing, but I continued crawling down some scrap lumber and into the dark pits of hell, dragging the rattling tin can behind me. It was so dark, filled with shadows and so mysteriously quiet. I could not see my hand in front of me. My eyes soon grew accustomed to the darkness with the limited rays that filtered through cracks in the walls. I duckwalked around within the limited confines to investigate the premises. Once, I found a huge white life-size wooden cross, fashioned with discs at each end.

Under the house, my dad had a workbench where he repaired shoes at the southern wall. I noticed that the earth where I stepped was deeply cracked in geometrical patterns formed by the "flood of forty-six" that I'd hear my dad talk about. I crawled through the cedar posts draped in cobwebs stretching between them. I also experienced many spider tunnels in the crevasses among the crossbeams where the cedar posts joined the floor boards. Though the cobwebs heralded the presence of spiders, I never saw any there except once. When I did see a brown spider, I crawled out to tell my brother. However, we never found it, so we never killed it. I remember encountering a huge pile of rocks against the front porch, which I determined counterbalanced the front yard's brick staircase. It is odd that once I had explored and knew what was under the flooring, I never again ventured there. Twice I saw snakes, once, a snake slithering toward the "under" floor through the backyard's rocky walk, and another time a snake in the process of swallowing a frog—quite scary scenes for any child.

I was about six when my entire environment consisted of the perimeters within which sat the house, the backyard, and the picket fence. The yard was overgrown with plants of every kind. My mother had a green thumb and every transplant flourished. I used to love to run, hide, and hop over the immense foliage, as I camouflaged myself within the dense shrubbery. I imagined swinging with Tarzan I had read about in my comic books or venturing through the *Rama of the Jungle's* rain forests, the series I watched on television. I would tie strings of leaves around my head and pretend I was Prince Valiant concealed from my enemies within the brush as in the Sunday paper comic. I was always clipping the evergreens that blocked our windows from neighbors to make bows and arrows, just like in the *Robin Hood* television serial. Once, I made an Indian headdress from oleander leaves that resembled feathers and proudly met the amused postman, wearing my Indian war bonnet. To this day, I wonder what thoughts crossed his mind on seeing a kid in the poverty of the Latin-American barrio with a makeshift Indian headdress of available foliage.

It was within that foliage of the now familiar back, front, and side yards that I, as a seven-year-old second-grader, loved prowling, as the warm summer days turned into balmy evenings. I enjoyed wandering amid the black shadows of the evergreen ivy as the falling night blocked our windows with a curtain of waving leaves. It was a miracle I never ran into one of the many spiderwebs or got bitten by a spider.

One evening, peppy music attracted me to my neighbor's window. The shade was up and a woman was dancing; her shapely body undulated to and fro and round and round to the upbeat music of the saucy, provocative "Mambo Numero Cinco," which was popular at the time. I could not stop staring as she swayed, rotating her voluptuous posterior from side to side, then forward and backward, and then round and round as she seemed to roll all over the room. My seven-year-old eyes danced in unison with each of her movements. I clearly remember I looked forward to the pause when Perez Prado rasped "aaarrrrrRRAAHHHH," so she'd hold her hip still, and then jerk it to the opposite side to his short, but loud "OOH!" Then she'd continue her awesome dancing to the resumed music. The wild music stirred me. I saw something that I enjoyed viewing but could not understand what or why. I kept looking and looking: my eyes opened as saucers until I must have made a clumsy sound. She turned toward the window and drew the shade. I went back several evenings anxious for another look, but managed only to hear the music and imagined what was swinging around behind the drawn shade. Sadly, the scene was no longer mine to enjoy.

There were six trees within the four corners of our property, and there wasn't one that I did not climb regularly. A *nogal* (Pecan) in the backyard was one my favorites. One branch allowed me to view a particularly nice scene of the distant creek. The pecans this tree bore were so tiny they could not be considered nuts, so I used them as ammunition. I pretended that this tree was the mainmast of *The Bounty* and that as an able seaman, I was a top man, climbing all over the yards. I tied many ropes from branch to branch and nailed many crosspieces. Perhaps the tree dried up because I also mischievously sawed many branches off and carved Bounty trivia on the trunk where I chiseled off the bark.

The front yard also boasted pecan trees that seemed to touch the lofty cumulus clouds, scrape the blue sky, and yielded thousands of nuts each year. I would hug the rough bark with all fours and creep up. The tender insides of my arms and legs bled and scraped as I crept upward, but I didn't care—I was a brave Native American Indian (I would worry about the alcohol pain later). Between third and fourth grades for three or four years during the summer months, I loved to climb that front yard tree. There in my fortress, I was surrounded by hundreds and thousands of green leaves amid thick branches. I peeked around the neighborhood through available openings. From my chosen niche, I could scarcely see much outside the foliage because of the many adjoining trees in the neighbors' yards. Still, I managed to make my way out on extended branches into the neighbors' yards or partially over the street. I felt so well hidden within my *hideout* I was confident passersby never knew I was up there. Once, and only once, I jumped from an overhanging branch onto the roof of the house. My dad unfortunately witnessed my jump, and angrily pinched my shoulder saying I would damage the shingles, and so I should stay off the roof.

MY HOUSE WITH FRONT YARD PECAN TREE IN FOREGROUND. VIEW OF CREEK BRUSH AT CENTER OF PHOTO FROM ATOP BACKYARD PECAN TREE LOCATED UPPER OF RIGHT HOUSE PHOTO. RICHARD'S HOUSE (MY KITE-FLYING BUDDY) WAS BEHIND THE TREE AT LEFT ON SALINAS STREET.

It was on those autumn sunny mornings that I loved sitting under the shade of the nogal with its yellow leaves and crack nuts with any rock that was handy. I was nine the fall when suddenly the whole neighborhood was invaded by huge machinery and an army of men was soon climbing all over the trees, with saws making a big commotion. The noise was thrilling to me. I did not mind that they were pruning my tree. I knew that in the spring more thick branches would shoot out—they always did. The workers would hook a wire on a branch, sit on a strap of fabric, and spin left and right, pruning, sawing, and cutting every bit of wood within their reach, all of which rained down on me. Pretty soon the yard was completely carpeted with branches, twigs, and yellow leaves. Once a worker lost a glove and asked me if I would look for it. I accidentally found it and located him down the street later that day. He thanked me by saying, "Attaboy!" The inside of a huge branch, lying on the ground, was an excellent hiding place. I crawled into it, little suspecting that it waited further sawing and shredding. Within my little hideout, however, I found myself totally surrounded by leaves. It was awesome: I peeked out at people and cars and felt myself invisible. Sadly though, my hidey-hole was eventually sawed into smaller pieces and cast into an ugly machine that whizzed as it swallowed every branch and ground up my short-lived sanctuary. I tried to get a close-up view of this machine's monstrous gaping jaw but was immediately run off by the workers. Such was the world outside my house.

A World outside the Front Fence

Outside my comfort zone I sense
A world I saw outside the fence
I stepped outside the gate that day
And wonders new before me lay

One day, I realized there was a whole different world outside the gate that surrounded my playground and my mother's watchful eye. Until then I was limited to the quarters within the four fence walls surrounding my house. I wanted to see what was beyond that tiny space that heretofore was my whole world. I became aware of the constant activity on the street beyond the picket fence. I examined the neighborhood closely. Up until now my outside world appeared as a two-dimensional wall outside my three-dimensional comfort zone. I stared in awe as if I had discovered a whole new world. Previously, I had been confined to walking from the front gate comfortably and trustingly in the company of an adult. At the time, my interest consisted solely of "going, bye-bye" or just going somewhere; anywhere was a joy. Naturally, as with any child, I was completely dependent upon my protector whom I had constantly in full view.

Ever since I became aware of vehicle and pedestrian traffic, I would wave to people and passersby and even greet neighbors from the porch steps. Cars were limited to the rock- and pebble-graded street; back then ours were rural streets without curbs or sidewalks, so that pedestrian traffic was compelled to use the street. Then, I spent time gazing, observing, and staring up and down the street at homes, people, and vehicles from the limited view of the front gate. In the quiet of the day—at a time of a few cars—all I saw were strange people, and to my mind even bizarre people, walk by voicing words I couldn't understand. I must have taken mental pictures as most of my memories were two-dimensional.

Pictures of a man pushing an ice cream insulated cart with many jingling bells on the handle bar and later the ice cream truck playing a chiming rendition of *When Irish Eyes are Smiling* and whose driver smiled and waved at me are clear in my memory. Dime ice cream cups had lids with pictures of movie stars, and twelve lids would get me a large portrait of a movie star. I never had money to buy, but later on I did collect lids as well as ice cream sticks and Popsicle wrappers with coupons for free gifts from trash cans or from the street.

One day I dared to open the front gate and stand in the front lawn. Then I dared to walk to the center of the street. I wondered where it led to. Way north, far beyond the green thicket of the creek, I saw a yellowish house with a green roof that traversed the street. Way to the south, I only saw the pebble-strewn street overhung with tree branches.

Periodically, a short lady in a red, loose dress with a white shawl over her head pulled a red wagon and called out "tama LEEZ, tama LEEZ." I watched her with keen interest and curiosity and wondered what she was up to. Decades later I concluded she was a vendor of homemade tamales.

On Sundays I would see a man with a pushcart yelling "barba-CO-o-a." On rare occasions, my dad would stop him to purchase the head of a calf, teeth and all, and we'd enjoy a treat of "homemade" barbecue meat. I remember how my dad preferred the eyes and brains of the calf. I'd hear the man's "barba-CO-o-a" many times while we were at breakfast or still in bed in the quietude of those early Sunday mornings.

There was another man that walked the street with a wooden carry-box hollering out "a-sol-da-DOR, a-sol-da-DOR," (solderer). Once, I remember my mother stopped him to solder our rain channel that leaked onto the porch during the rains. He charged my mother $3.45. That day my dad had a fit because he could have done the job for materials only—but my mother determined he had procrastinated long enough.

One day a lady came by selling pictures. I told her we couldn't buy anything, but she sat down on a chair on the porch. She kept jabbering about photos, pictures, facial paintings, etc. She finally left. I just listened and listened the entire time.

Mr. Gumercindo, a white-haired old man, was a vegetable and fruit vendor. He had an open-air wagon weathered green, with a flat top. It was powered by a filly, named Shelly Winters. He would stop at the creek where Shelly would feed on the greenery. I watched from within the gate. And times were that a whole flock of the neighborhood children surrounded the wagon and some fed Shelly some of the foliage they'd tear from the creek thicket. As he always needed paper bags, he would reward children with a fruit for a sack full of paper bags. I would take him just one sack for one fruit; I couldn't see the generous offering of so many bags for one fruit when fruit was to be had on a one-to-one basis!

Then one day, I saw a man a long way down in the middle of the street take a bottle out from the front waist of his pants, take a swig as he bottomed it up, and replace the bottle. I assumed it was water. It just seemed to me that the sunny street was quiet and private at times. I associated privacy with the quietude and mental picture taken of each moment or occurrence in time.

I was in third grade when I took to sitting on the front stairs, watching cars. I wondered where each was bound and what adventures the occupants would experience. I promised myself that one day I would own a car and go places. On certain nights, sitting on those steps, I was awed by the multitude of reflections from gigantic lights resembling straws moving all over the sky from the horizon above the front neighbors' trees.

I was about ten, when a man walking down the street suggested I let more string go on my kite to get it to fly higher. I used to run up and down the street happily, contented with my kite at beneath the height of the telephone wires. After this incident, it occurred to me that the spacious scary creek was suitable for kite flying!

One sunny summer day, when I was about twelve, a man walked by saying he would oil any kind of machinery. Immediately, I wheeled out our human-powered roll-type lawn mower, which he oiled with a squeeze can that had a rattail spout as he comfortably sat on one of our lawn chairs. He took out a file and began to strike and file the blades which began to shine. Then he asked for thirty-five cents. I told him that my folks weren't home. He said he'd return later. He never did, to my relief. Such was the world outside the front fence.

Kite Flying at the Creek

T'was a beautiful sunny morn
Windy blue sky with green adorn
By brook's bank, 'neath branches tight
Me and Richard flew my kite

At eleven, now, a fifth-grader, I faced an awesome world just outside my immediate neighborhood. Due to my abusive home life, the times I was able to be carefree and happy were few. So one of the greatest adventures in my childhood, albeit *the* only epic but short-lived adventure, was my visit to the creek.

THE TERRIFYING *ARROYO ALAZAN*. I WAS HORRIFIED THAT MONSTERS WOULD EMERGE FROM THE WATERS AND DEVOUR LITTLE BOYS LIKE ME DESPITE THE PRESENCE OF MY HERO BROTHER BEAU (FOREGROUND WITH BICYCLE). MY ELDEST BROTHER, MOE, STANDS CENTER WITH SHOES IN HAND. AGED ABOUT SIX, I STAND AKIMBO AT THE WATER'S EDGE. MY HOUSE WAS LOCATED AT THE EXACT SPOT OF THE CAR'S HOOD IN THE FAR BACKGROUND UNDER THE BRANCHES OF THE TALL PECAN TREE. OTHER CHILDREN ARE FROM NEIGHBORHOOD FAMILIES.

The chilly wintry months were slowly giving way to the cooling winds of spring, which was just right for kite flying. One-half block from my house, where San Jacinto and Martin streets intersected, flowed the *Arroyo Alazan* (creek). In those days, the brook's banks boasted an abundance of undergrowth that ran the length of the city onto flanking streets. The creek flooded many homes during heavy storms and always smelled of wet earth. Little boys could easily get "lost" in that last half block of thick plant life and high bush that flanked the banks of the six-foot-wide creek. Since my childhood, the Alazan was another world, a mystical forest filled with frogs, toads, snakes, turtles, and perhaps a monster or two, emerging suddenly from the water to eat little boys like me. I always kept my distance although in the presence of my brothers.

It was still cold and windy that morning when I decided to fly my kite. Because of the numerous telephone lines crisscrossing my street, I dared to leave without permission to the only open space around and that happened to be at the creek. However, I did not dare enter the brush leading deeper into to the creek's density but just remained on the street, oblivious of the passing traffic.

An acquaintance, Richard happened to walk by and we began to talk about kites. Richard lived just around the corner from my house. He was a tall, lanky boy, about my age. He sported a huge mop of dark hair reminding me of a burned-out matchstick, an apostrophe, as he always slouched. It always seemed to me he lived so far away from the confines of the fence around my house that I only saw him when he passed by on his way to the corner grocery store. I didn't know much about him, but we struck up a friendship immediately. We found that we both enjoyed flying kites. He confessed he neither had ten cents to buy one, nor another ten cents for the ball of string, but asked if I would let him take turns on "the control," i.e., the ball of string.

He suggested that we would be more comfortable within the creek area, farther down within the brush. I knew his knowledge was greater than mine since he lived across the street from the creek. I held on to the kite as we walked through the foot-high grass along the bank. On our way, Richard picked up a crunched-up paper bag. We finally stopped, coming upon a small clearing under a few short trees that afforded minimum shade. Together with the shade provided by the tall brush on the north side of the embankment, we had a good camping ground.

I couldn't understand why he wanted the bag. As we walked, he was tearing it into large pieces. When we settled under our comfortable canopy, he pulled down on my kite string. As I looked on, he consecutively wrapped each paper, piece by piece on the string length. While he wrapped each one, the wind pushed each paper wad up the string ever so slowly, until it reached the kite. The opening between the trees allowed the kite to fly, leaving us in the comfort of dappled shade as we sat on the exposed tree roots. We stayed there all morning, taking turns to hold the ball of string while gazing at the kite as it floated lazily in the blue sky—its five-foot tail of old cloth swaying left and right.

As the morning wore on, Richard decided that we should eat something and left saying he would return shortly. I recognized my own hunger pangs but going home was out of the question. I knew that if I did go for an instant, my ever enraged parent would thrash me and not let me return to the comforts my newfound sanctuary. He spirited to his house which was a mere block and a half away. To me, his house might have been a million miles away across the abundant brush of the creek. I sat there, quietly, in my new peaceful hideout, devouring the warm sunshine; cold, alone, and oblivious to the Martin Street traffic, which, unbeknown to me, was but perhaps ten feet behind me.

Richard returned presently chewing on a gingerbread cake and brought two flour tortillas, each enfolding two baloney slices. Quickly we devoured the food and with satisfied stomachs, we reclined under our hidey-hole, enjoying one another's company, occasionally breaking the silence by discussing the holdings of our ever-increasing number of Davy Crockett bubblegum cards. We took turns at the control string, and continued observing our kite, fluttering lazily in the windy blue afternoon skies. A cool yellow sun filtered through the tall woody brush under which we lazed, me and Richard, kite flying at the creek.

My Backstreet and Bus Ride Adventures

Down muddy walks I made my way
Where alleys, back streets, pebbles lay
Through arcs of branches overhead
Yards, homes, and trees by moisture fed

Summers were always the best part of the year; no school, just lazy day. The sun was bright yellow and bathing the entire backyard when I stepped out the back door, rattled down the ever-aging wooden steps, and onto the river-rock embedded patio. The whole yard was swarming with the waving shadows of thick green leaves and the crooked branches of our *nogales* (pecan trees) and *alamos* (cottonwoods). I breathed deeply on this summer midday. However, somewhat apprehensively I recalled I would be entering middle school at the summer's end. With elementary graduation still fresh in my twelve-year-old mind, my entire soul took in the beautiful day's sunny atmosphere. I walked down the crumbling sidewalk adjacent to the house, making my way toward the front gate. The entire side yard was overflowing with greenery. I passed by an oleander bush, a dogwood bush, and a clump of ivy that wound around a scrawny cypress—all within the side yard that paralleled a wall of ivy growth that choked the property line. I took in all this fresh foliage along with the smell of freshly watered earth. My mother, with her green thumb, always kept the yard watered when it did not rain. Thus, the entire yard was overrun and climbing with green frondescent growth. This was one of those special days when I was taking the mile-long walk to the public library. My imagination went rampant as I anticipated the upcoming adventure. I closed the picket gate behind me and headed south on San Jacinto Street. I made a right turn onto Travis and outside of my "semi-comfort" zone, where I would infiltrate the maze of alleys and backstreets all overgrown with greenery.

Those were the days before paved streets, so graveled paths gave us thousands of pebbles which littered the streets and alleyways. I pretended that all those tree branches arching over the alleys were a passageway into another world: my domain of adventure. Some residents made a few efforts at leveling the dirt-packed alleyways by filling muddy tire grooves with those pebbles after a good rain. There was also the smell coming from wet leaves, wet wood, and earth lingering and refreshing the ambience for a few days after a good coastal storm. I loved to stroll down those alleys, observing backyards filled with waving laundry, barking dogs, children at play, and old junked cars corroding under the dancing shadows of the *alamos*. The tired-looking wooden frame houses needed paint to enliven their faces, the old paint flakes curling and leaving a wrinkled effect. Some homes sported back porches, others dilapidated storage shacks, and still others open-air earth-floor car ports filled with cast-out furniture and junked cars. The outer wooden walls standing on damp ground showed extended signs of rot. Everywhere was the smell of rotting leaves and wood due to the rains and humidity of San Antonio. Everywhere there was plant life emerging from every rock, between concrete cracks, and anywhere there was a patch of earth. As a child, it was fun to stick out my tongue at other children inside the yards or homes and drag a stick against picket and chain-link fences, making a racket as I went. As I passed, I took pleasure in teasing tied-up dogs and would sometimes throw rocks at the loose ones that came barking at me through the fence. Abandoned toys were strewn over other backyards where some other child had played. The backs of some houses sported windows adjacent to the other alleys, and sometimes I walked really close to the windows to maybe catch a glimpse of the people inside. Perhaps, I thought, by chance I would see something interesting; I mean the thrill of seeing *something* I wasn't supposed to see. Most times I'd hear people talking, yelling at children, or someone taking a look out the window to see the passerby. There *was* life within those rain-beaten wooden shacks. The sun shone with all its brightness through those waving branches of the *nogales* and *alamos* as I leisurely cruised through those alleys and byways of the barrio on my way to the library.

As I exited an alley, I would step onto any side street and stroll down the sidewalk between the overgrown hedges protruding from property lines and other shrubbery on the opposite side at the pebbly street. Sometimes, I'd pluck a sweet-smelling flower from an oleander bush. Some of those houses sported front porches wrapped around a corner. Most sported simple Doric and very rarely the Ionic or Corinthian pillars I had read about after researching Roman and Greek architecture, satisfying my curiosity while reading my *Uncle Scrooge* comic books. Some porches boasted spindle railing and others sported red brick. Old folks, whiling their time left away, swung gently to and fro on bench-type swings. What their thoughts were as they sat there was always a mystery to me. Ivy or foliage covered the ground or crept up fences, columns, railings, and sides of houses. Very few houses boasted well-manicured and mowed front lawns.

A rectangular six-street plot between Martin and Buena Vista streets and two miles from downtown to Calaveras (skulls) Street with my street and the Alazan in between were my stomping grounds. A conglomeration of alleyways and bystreets lay therein. My entire backstreet route to the library doubled as the route to my elementary school and to the chapel where we worshiped. It was Commerce Street that I was familiar with as I walked to school for six years of grade school during the week. On weekends, my sisters Magnolia, Gladiola, and I walked to church through the same route, ignoring the grammar school we passed and focusing instead on worship services. My parents did not attend church. It was during my third year at grammar school that I began to take an interest in the library that was located on the opposite side of our church block, the farthest point of my adventures' trek. In effect, my grade school was only two blocks from the chapel, with the library at the opposite corner by Calaveras Street. I worshiped weekly at the chapel until high school graduation, but visited the library only until the summer following elementary graduation. We always walked on Commerce Street to the school and the chapel and until my solo adventures to the library. I never merged the three walks in my mind.

There were times when I would detour far out of my way and walk away from the library toward town just so I could pass by my little girlfriend's house. How I dreamed that I would get a glimpse of her as I did twice when passing by. The first time, she was standing at the front door glancing out, and the second time, she was watering the front yard plants with a spray can. I would walk down my street and turn left (east) at Houston instead of my usual right at Travis. Then, down about five blocks, library books in my sweating hands produced shaky knees. But as I approached her house, I walked ever slower and then shaking all over, looked into her yard and door. If no one was in sight, I turned right at Colorado Street and right on Commerce Street. I dawdled on Commerce Street and passed my own street, stopping at the drug store for a drink of water and sometimes for a free coke. I meandered by my elementary school, past the store where my sister Rosebud worked, which I ignored, and then hung a left on any bystreet to Buena Vista Street and the library. Although the days were sunny and warm, I did not find it as interesting as the alleys and backstreets, other than my pounding heart and a chance to see Mary Lou again.

There were other times during my mid-teens when my corner street buddy, Joe, and I walked toward town amid the backstreets. I remember I would sit on his bike's handlebars, rest my legs on the front fender as my head rested on his shoulders. We'd cruise up and down the streets—I feeling king of the road with my front row seat. During middle school and high school, these "cruisings" down alleys and backyards became less exciting, perhaps because of my age or because the goal was different and I had outgrown "looking" through back windows in awe, in favor of movies and downtown. Most times we would yell, screech, and playfully shove and push each other all the way downtown. Once, we passed close by Ruth's house, a girl from church, and she waved at me. I felt so flattered! She was very pretty and she noticed me. It was Ruth who later attended the ROTC military ball with me in my sophomore year and whom all the guys in church "adored." I was one of them. Another time, while screeching like banshees as we ran down the street, we met a girl from school who greeted me more enthusiastically than what I cared for at the time. Finally arriving at our downtown fifty-cent theater, we entered into a world of make-believe adventure on the silver screen.

Despite my mother's continued abuse, my spirit of adventure never disturbed me from exploring my surroundings when I had a chance. One rare Saturday, when I was eight and allowed to attend church Primary meetings, I decided to take the plunge and ride the bus by myself. My brother Moe mentioned a bus ride that would take me from the church meeting house to town, double back, and bring me home. That Saturday morning, at the end of the service, I waited at the corner of the street near the chapel and boarded the Prospect Hill bus. I can still feel the adrenalin rush as I excitedly paid my nickel and found a seat by a window.

As the bus rolled down Commerce Street toward town, I recognized my elementary school; Winn's, where my sister worked; and San Jacinto Street where I lived. Several blocks down, I passed by the railroad station landmark—a green dome topped with a Native American statue. I was in ecstasy as the bus then turned left on a side street and right again onto Houston Street, as the driver entered the downtown area. It was a time when downtown was the *Centro*, the center of all business and was bustling with crowds of people, so that the bus was slowed and stopped at every busy corner. All of San Antonio seemed to be out that Saturday morning. All the sidewalks were swarming with shoppers, men, women, and children, complemented by hundreds of airmen in blue from nearby Lackland Air Force Base. From my window, I saw theaters, and I recognized many storefronts and stores that I had passed in the bus or while cruising with my sisters. Everybody was going somewhere, and every time the bus stopped more people boarded and some stepped off. Finally, the bus made a right turn onto Alamo Street and continued toward Commerce Street. I saw the familiar storefront of Joske's Department Store and The Alamo on my left. I always dreamed of visiting there, but my mother was continually in a rush and never showed any interest in the shrine or any other interesting place on our visits downtown. As the bus approached the next intersection, it made a right turn onto Commerce Street, and I knew the ride home had begun.

I recollected the shops and stores I had only rarely viewed from a child's eye-level, parallel to my sisters' waists. Finally, the bus arrived at familiar grounds and approached my street, I sadly knew my stop was ahead. I pulled the bell cord and heard it ring just before my street and got off. I skipped happily as I skimmed the remaining blocks to my home. Nothing could top the nickel spent on this epic adventure, not even a candy bar or a soda pop or a bag of Fritos. One day, after my twelfth birthday, I found out that the motion picture, *The Vikings,* starring Kirk Douglas, was being exhibited at the State Theater in downtown San Antonio. I heard my brothers and sisters talk so much about it that I had to see it. So one sunny day, I just took off on my bicycle, arrived at a parking lot across the theater downtown, and locked it at an attendant's booth. I entered the theater, shaking with excitement at the thought of viewing the most talked about movie of the day! I got so carried away I was still trembling when I picked up my bike. Even the attendant commented on my overly emotional condition. I pedaled back home, and interestingly enough, no one had missed me or questioned my whereabouts during my absence. This first extended escapade led to other times when I would "jump the fence" and disappear heading for the theaters, until my seventeenth year when I simply announced I was going out to a movie. This was a sweet memorable time in my life, my backstreet and bus adventures.

Chapter 2

Thirteen Captive Years

Great spirits have always encountered violent opposition from mediocre minds.
—Albert Einstein

*Children might or might not be a blessing, but to create them
and then fail them was surely damnation.*
—Lois McMaster Bujold, *Barrayar*

My parents only had one argument in forty-five years. It lasted forty-three years.
—Cathy Ladman

Violence is the last refuge of the incompetent.
—Isaac Asimov, *Salvor Hardin in "Foundations"*

Prologue

My parents emigrated from Mexico during the roaring twenties. My mother was eighteen-and-one-half when she married her uncle, who was twenty-three years her senior. That happened following the troubled times of the Mexican Revolution. Their union produced a family of eight, all born and reared in the poverty of a west San Antonio barrio. I was the youngest of this brood. Early in life, I realized that my only escape was the service. My decision catalyzed before my tenth year. Between five and ten, I recognized my suffering under an incessantly abusive mother's whims and sisters' petulance, as I swiftly became "the scapegoat" and victim of the women in my home. This commenced since I was five and continued into my high school years. My dysfunctional home life, such as it was, my spirit of adventure coupled with a lifelong patriotic heart and the promise of higher education under the G I Bill, job skills, and my lifelong dream of travel, were the many reasons I would join the armed services. This goal was realized the week following high school graduation.

Battered Childhood

Slaps and floggings bruises too
Four to teenhood always blue
Patriot travel coming true
Gone away a world to view

In the usual family tradition, the baby of the family is usually a spoiled brat, spoiled by everyone—Mother, Dad, and older siblings. I was the baby, but this was never true in my case. My mother suffered from a "battering parent syndrome."

Our family was doomed the moment my father and mother married as they were too closely related, according to the family. In reality, there may have been some truth in this as overhearing family conversations in my childhood, I learned my first sister, Marigold, was a blue baby; my third sibling, Moe, a learning-disabled brother; my fourth sibling, Azalea, was a permanently bed-ridden, incontinent adult sister; and the remaining five in the family were in good health. Perhaps as result of having to raise two disabled children and the extended family's alienation due to their strange marriage—my father was my grandmother's brother—the extended family denounced my mother for marrying her uncle. This may have caused the emergence of an all-consuming rage producing her ceaseless vulgarity and profanity. My grandparents' portent of "damned children" may have come true in my disabled older siblings. It was always a mystery to me why my mother married her uncle and a taboo subject that hung over our lifetimes. My guess is that she sought a father-figure sanctuary in her uncle in view of my widowed grandmother's abusive mistreatment, only to fall victim to a worldly man's conquests. In those days of our Latin-American culture, a pregnant unmarried girl was an eternal disgrace. The unfortunate girl was frequently disowned and cast out of the family. I would not be surprised if my grandmother beat my mother upon discovering her pregnancy or locked her to starve her to spare family shame. Coupled with the vast difference in the ages of my parents, I, the youngest and most curious of her children, became the family scapegoat. The emergence of an uncontrollable rage, laced with ceaseless vulgarities, beatings, and buffetings by my mother, came to rest on my young shoulders. My mother's rage, plus my sisters' approval of blame, was what I continually lived with from the time I was five until I was seventeen and a junior in high school. Obese, five feet tall and constantly at war with herself during her midlife crisis, my mother became my bludgeon. She was a product of the Great Depression living with an elderly man, with earnings barely enough to maintain a rapidly growing family. By the time I came along, earnings gave way to his retirement and my mother's growing discontent. Limited income from my eldest sisters hardly provided the daily basic needs. This, plus a string of eight children, some of whom were disabled, reared over four decades, and a life with a man twenty-three years her senior, might have overwhelmed anyone. I was her menopausal child and was curious as quicksilver with a loud piercing voice; I might have tried her scarce patience, stressed her out, and became her victim.

My mother suffered my dad's beatings and drunken rages. He was cruel and set in his machismo. She was his property as his "child bride." But he soon grew too old to enforce his cruelty, so she took over and transferred his abuse to her children and made them targets for her wrath. It was this awakened wrath that she released on her children and made living at home unbearable for me after my fifth birthday. The beatings negated any semblance of a loving parent. I never once heard the words "I love you," or "I'm sorry," and neither "please" nor "thank-you." Neither the love of Our Lord Jesus Christ nor of The Holy Ghost could dwell in that house because her barely contained rage, persistently maintained as normal behavior, overruled their presence. I remember she used to talk to herself using senseless Spanish words, not in the dictionary, saying such things as "They don't learn it, they inherit it," or "I want to leave outside of here," and "Beneath the sun and stars only a mother loves and a dog appreciates." She often mentioned how her obese grandmother frequently and accurately smacked her cheek with her favorite wielded back-handed routine of buffetings. Evidently, many of her methods of administering punishment were learned and received from her mother and grandmother. Decades later, I encountered Sister Fountains in church who had visited us during her two-year service as a missionary and heard me out and had responded, "My observation was that there was no love in that house." I can remember as many useless family prayers as fingers on one hand. Curiously, I can still view my mother, wide-eyed in all earnestness, piously staring at the ceiling and praying to the Lord with long drawn-out pleading words. Following these meager prayers, I did notice a measure of peaceful coexistence, so, I guess, she realized she had exceeded what was normal in wicked punishments. However, this was soon replaced by rage and the absence of prayer. For many Sundays, I was the sole attendant at worship services. In all fairness, somehow or other, we were always provided plenty of food and a clean house (sometimes working me until midnight) all under her tutelage and the beatings that I endured. In retrospect, I remember that these torturous memories began on my fifth birthday and continued through my seventeenth year.

It was a time when child abuse was a family affair, and "spare the rod and spoil the child" could be taken to extremes. The more a child was beaten, was reasoned, the better for the child—and that for this reason, my mother claimed that our neighbors told her I was a good child. As we grew to adulthood, strangely enough, half of my siblings agreed with her and refused to acknowledge the role I was given during those tender years. The others understood, sympathized, but simply stood by.

They never acknowledged that I was terrorized each time I'd see her approach me, leather belt in hand, with her consistent rage-filled facial expression—like a tarantula's pounce upon a fated insect. I knew I was about to be in severe pain, all evident by the red welts that became green, black, blue, and purple bruises on my face, thighs, and butt. Going to school, each day I bore evidence of her brutality—bruises on my cheeks. The welts on my legs would have been visible had I been born a girl. She used oleander branches and wood moldings, but her favorite weapon was the belt. I recall her large chubby hands and sausage-like fingers. I remember how she seemed to enjoy bringing her gargantuan arm toward her chest and then swing it outward and crack the back of her hand right on target, my face; and this was for any mumbled or wrong facial expression or gesture. I could sense her satisfaction at still possessing power to exert her buffetings on this last and thus less resisting child.

While she repeatedly flogged my butt or slapped my face with her elephantine paws, my mother's incessant blows accompanied her sadistic pleasure. I remember from her facial expression that her blows were less for my punishment but more for relieving of her frustration or pent-up anger. She seemed to become infuriated for no other reason than seeing me lie face down on the floor, reading. I knew that without provocation and lightning speed she would suddenly pounce and claw me right on my buttocks. My upper arms always bore evidence of the lesions made with her short, thick, razor-sharp fingernails that felt like bee stings. These lesions constantly burned my arms because she broke the skin (much like pinch-pricking a soft peach) and left black or dark-gray bruises and cuts. When friends at school asked what had happened to me on the shoulders, I do not remember what I answered. However, it was only at those embarrassing times that I became conscious of the contusions I bore. Surely my teachers were aware of the brutal mistreatment when I showed up in class markedly bruised. I was probably the talk at conference tables, but maybe it was not, because it was a time when "the more a child was beaten the better for the child," or "a parent who does not love his child will not beat the child." No child protection laws had then been passed. Perhaps too, my low academic achievement was due in part to all this trauma that I might now be classified an "emotionally disturbed" child by today's standards. Then again, what else could be expected of a "Mexican" family from the poverty of the barrio by an all Anglo-American faculty?

I was Simon Legree's battered Tom. Being inside the house was a risk for me as I was within striking distance, and my mother would beat me—demanding that I lie face down on the bed—repeatedly striking with the leather belt in the same body-spot, much as an axe man's experts strikes, and caused severe burning pain and bruises. She never offered explanations for the beatings; I only remember her rabid face, strapping along with a voiced string of swearwords. During my adolescence, she'd clutch my waist above my jeans' top button, pull me toward her like a rag doll, and proceed to strike me repeatedly with open- and back-handed full blows on my cheeks. In high school, she'd simply rush at me lashing at me any place with a switch, belt, wood slat, or whatever she could find. Once, she crashed me with a picture frame breaking the glass on my forearm and causing lengthy superficial cuts, slashes, and gouges. Fortunately for me, I heal rapidly. Once, she slammed me against a wall with one knee angled against my body and her other leg anchored in a braced position, in a frontal attack, pinning me as she buffeted my face while huffing and puffing as if combating a powerful enemy. Each and every time, I remember a face full of hatred and rage with uttered obscenities. I recall she'd go to sleep angry, snore up a storm, and awake angry, striking me saying she dreamed my misbehavior and voice. Perhaps the learning retardation I experienced through my childhood, which lessened in the army, along with the stuttering that resumed well into my marriage was caused by my anxiety or stress from these beatings. During these turbulent thirteen years, it never occurred to me to strike back, and it never once crossed my mind why I was so submissive when she was abusive, as I was old enough to strike back. Suffice it to say that to write of my mother's battering, cursing, and the vulgarity that accompanied each beating would compile a textbook. I have not written one-half of her atrocities. My eternal hope that someone would rescue me, instead of adding to the torment, would have to include my disappointment at my sisters' behavior and their subsequent tragic domestic lives.

MOTHER AGED THIRTY-NINE AND AUTHOR ON FIFTH BIRTHDAY

My mother was judge, jury, and executioner. Her assistants, like lucifer's demons, were my sisters, Magnolia and Gladiola. She was not accustomed to reasoning, logic, or being contradicted, hear responses, or allow her children to be heard. She never addressed issues but flew into rages of madness. However, on the few occasions when we were allowed to express our concerns, she'd tell us to shut up, saying, "You haven't got a face to talk." I never understood what she meant. Her word was law, god on earth, and that law was altered at her will and whim. Much like Amon Goeth's treatment of Helen Hurst in the motion picture *Schindler's List*. She downplayed psychology saying that until she saw a child crap backward she would not consider psychology. Violence was her only response for shutting us up. My father never interfered with her discipline. Unusual punishments included doses of castor oil, a wet detergent dripping finger swirled in my mouth, forced to drink toilet water, and threats to drink my father's urine. One night when I was sixteen, she suddenly flogged me while I was sleeping in my skivvies under the bedsheets. She would create beating situations by asking loaded questions with irrelevant words to trigger confusion so that whatever I responded was incorrect. She was not given to mercy or reconsideration, but carried out her threats and sentences. She was unforgiving, compassionless, and worst of all, apathetic. What maternal mentality could cause so much emotional and physical pain to a defenseless child for almost two seemingly eternal decades, I reflected—it is perplexing!

Once while beating me, she asked me if the beatings were not painful enough to make me cease my "misconduct." I guess she thought that the painful punishment learned in the old country was customary normal practice and acceptable behavior. Her children would eventually forget or overlook her tortures and go on with their lives as if nothing had happened. In fact, my sisters' behavior regarding her abuse proved her right. They never acknowledged the abnormal disciplinary measures she meted out. I believe she refused to acknowledge her brutal behavior and admit that her child could be traumatized, leading to stuttering and learning disabilities or even emotional scars for life, because to do so would confirm a lifetime of error, i.e., my sufferings. She made herself believe that all the pain was forgotten and forgiven when she saw photos where I feigned love as duty, but the truth was in all poses with her during those hurtful years I'd ask myself, "Why do I kiss, or smile with you?" And I reminded myself, "I don't love you." In truth, as I grew into adolescence my thoughts centered on the day of freedom that I could join the service and get out.

Years later, I tried asking for an explanation about her abuse, and she feigned ignorance. She did not understand what I was talking about and made little of my claim. Even decades later, I asked my niece to ask her if she had any inkling of what she had done causing me so much pain and trauma. Her response was, "I don't see that I did wrong!" Much later, I tried again reasoning with her and she repeatedly claimed she did not know what I was talking about, insolently declaring, "I don't care."

I do remember overhearing, as a child, about my grandmother's and great grandmother's brutal and emotional mistreatment of my mother in prerevolutionary Mexico. My mother always downplayed our emotional pain caused by our developing juvenile apprehensions, imagined fears, trauma, and her abuse; but when it came to her sentiments, we were the cause of all her suffering and severe emotional pain. As a preschooler, I would find her sobbing in seeming resignation and deep pain perhaps depression, but when Gladiola and I tried to comfort her, she petulantly blamed us—saying that we were the cause of her crying because we did not mind her. I was the last born, and became not only mother's victim but my sisters' as well. I was their dupe, for what, I never could determine.

Education, academic or spiritual, was not an important part of my sisters' lives. All were grammar or middle school dropouts. Just like my mother, most of my brothers and sisters could not hold a reasonable conversation on any academic topic. Supposedly, my sisters all supplemented the family income. Their earnings began at the time of my dad's retirement, when I was around eight. In those days a diploma wasn't necessary for employment purposes. Their conversations always centered on frivolous, useless, baseless topics and platitudes with no foundation leading to any cultural accomplishments, conclusions, or growth. I cannot remember a conversation with them that did not end in rage, a put-down, or a slap. In their insensitivity, they ignored my pain, belittled my views or opinions, and downplayed my emotions with their opinionated, bullying, or enraged demeanor during the discussion. A few siblings remained neutral or survived by staying out of the way, keeping low profiles, or moved out upon becoming of age, by marriage or employment. To my knowledge no members of my immediate family, except two, ever rose above the first two levels of Abraham Maslow's "hierarchy of needs."

My mother confiscated every nickel or dime I earned on errands and every trivial piece of property I purchased. I was quite an entrepreneur in my childhood. I'd successfully sell nails, nuts, bolts, miniature bars of soap, jar labels, pencils, or just about anything I could get my hands on. Sure enough, like a bloodhound, my sister Gladiola always smelled my sale money out with her huge Macaw nose, pointing it left and right and immediately reporting to my mother.

Once, while strolling home from the corner grocery store I spied a black coin purse lying in the middle of the street. With one swoop of my arm, I instinctively reached down and placed it in my rear pocket. Knowing that whatever it contained would be confiscated and that I could never justify any amount of money, I paused by the side of the house, unzipped it, and pulled out a few bills before I turned it over to my mother. Sure enough, they smilingly welcomed my find. Nothing was ever said of finding the owner or returning the property. Regardless of reward, I was glad I got my share before it was confiscated. I was never rewarded or acknowledged, but I got my share.

One day as I was emptying the trash, I found three twenty-dollar bills in an envelope. I made full use of them and never felt guilty when my mother questioned and wondered what had happened to her money. Additionally, every time I was sent to the *molino* (tortilla factory) for fifty cents of tortillas, I would request two package wrappings: one costing twenty-two and the other of twenty-three, and I would pocket the leftover nickel. I never had the luxury of privacy, so they knew exactly what I owned and took anything from my chest of drawers anytime without asking—I had no rights or respect in that house. One day, aged about nine, I happily purchased a blue Whitman coin holder and began a yearly Jefferson nickel collection from my rare nickel acquirements, which I placed in my chest of drawers. My mother got wind of my collection, and with a sneer at her discovery immediately demanded my "savings." In my panic, I replied that they were not savings but a prized coin collection. She yanked the board from my proffered hands, threw my most cherished possession on the floor, and to my horror and anguish, stomped it under her mastodon feet, angrily mocking me as I openly, loudly, and helplessly (as usual) cried and cried.

I cannot say much about my second sister, Rosebud, as her positive deeds somewhat outweighed the negatives though she played the role of "snitch." As an older sister, however, she displayed immense hatred and anger toward me. Once she pointed to my mother that I had been running around the house yelling the *Jim Bowie* television serial theme song, which as a child I did. But I also frequently yelled the *Superman, Zorro, Rin Tin Tin*, and *Robin Hood* theme songs plus went wild at hearing the *Captain Gallant of the Foreign Legion* bugle calls or William Tell's trumpet sound at the *Lone Ranger* television serial theme intros. Other childhood programs I enjoyed when conveniently allowed to watch television were the *Mickey Mouse Club, Howdy Doody, Roy Rogers*, and *Captain Kangaroo*. For this sin, my mother proceeded to beat me mercilessly with the belt. There was no change in her forceful attack on me when I pulled on the venetian blind cord or ran around the house on a self-burping contest. Yet, my sister Rosebud was also the recipient of my mother's incessant calls for trivial matters. My mother would harass my tearful sister Rosebud at work accusing her of having escaped, while she remained grafted at home. Never mind that Rosebud's paycheck paid for the home expenses. Yet it is Rosebud who holds my sweetest memories, as in my early childhood, within her limited means, provided me with my first Almond Joy and comic books, and the family with candy, cookies, and cake, and if hadn't been for her, we would not have had a turkey on Thanksgiving or a decorated tree on Christmas. At any rate, all birthdays and all holidays were as any other day, never a nickel for a birthday cupcake, but certainly a mother's beating as usual.

My fourth and fifth sisters, Magnolia and Gladiola, respectively, were my mother's demons, who avoided her wrath by monitoring my every move with much zeal, incessantly reporting every misbehavior, slight or imagined, on my part, thus igniting my mother's powder keg rage. This resulted in a triple explosion of irrational anger, culminating in an energetic flogging with her leather belt. Unconsciously, these enablers discovered how to deflect my mother's violence so that I was always the receiver. This twosome, too, had mastered a way to appeal to my mother's vanity as many times I noticed how they ingratiated themselves to her, receiving her smiles for their efforts. Possessed with a superego and irrational hostility so engrossed in finding faults elsewhere, these psychopaths were blind to their own faults and imperfections. They were given to capricious, opinionated, and petulant tantrums. It was Magnolia who once approached my mother with my comic book stack she had seized and ingratiating herself said, "Here, Mother, here are Julio's comic books, sit you down and begin tearing them up," to my mother's flattered smiles from ear to ear and a negative headshake. On another time, she expressed how cute it was when mother brought her arm to her chest and catapulted the back of her hand to smack the victim's face. My sisters appeared to receive sadistic pleasure in witnessing her reactions, which resulted in my howling pain. They had nothing else to do in that crammed five-hundred-square-foot house but spy on my every move.

I remember all had thick, sharp fingernails like my mother and did not hesitate to use them on me. As teenagers, my older sisters and I would scuffle, but there were painful repercussion scars for me as the youngest. Once when I was sixteen, in a fit of anger, Rosebud scratched my forearm leaving painful, deep, lengthy lacerations which almost required stitches. One day, Magnolia, in a usual fit of rage, reached out and gouged an inch long laceration from the bridge of my nose beneath my left eye—coworkers at the supermarket where I packaged groceries commented that my eye was almost hollowed out. Another time, in a fit of madness, Gladiola pulled a camera away from my eye clawing into my lower eyelid and into my eye socket—I painfully shed tears. Once in a while I would see two sisters in a clash, like lionesses that ended with fierce hair-pulling and scratching. These frenzied demons subconsciously formed a foursome alliance; each probably venting their female crises on me: Mother, with her blazing menopause; Rosebud, with a tragic marriage; Magnolia, unmarried with exploding hormones; and Gladiola, probably burning with adolescence and all that it encompassed. I was incessantly bombarded by an all female hysteria. I felt myself considered more as a disposable chattel or a piece of discardable furniture and one step below a dog, which would definitely receive far better treatment as a cherished mascot. Somehow in their collective minds, I was their court fool, whipping boy, and their dog to kick as I would always droop and not strike back, even at seventeen. In later years, I pondered on these reactions and wondered at their gleeful gratification at my pain. To their dying days, these last two sisters, Magnolia and Gladiola, denied my mother's abuse and their participation, flatly worshipping the ground she walked on—upholding her innocence of all mistreatment deeming her a person of worship and never considered she could be wrong or grant benefit of the doubt, though they too were infrequently beaten. What was the family secret, perhaps of female nature, that earned my mother so much loyalty? Once, Gladiola stated that Magnolia was like a second mother to her. What this motherhood consisted of I was never to find out. These two sisters always claimed that I was a spoiled brat with a rebellious nature and a fabricator of tales (insulting my intelligence and criterion), and that I have always been judgmental of my mother, however, I have written the truth—I concede to my Maker, acquaintances, and my reader.

The fourth sister, Magnolia, was an enabler; she behaved as my stepmother, with full beating privileges and added her own brand of violence at times. I could not sit quietly lost in the lyrics of a golden oldie because she would approach, angrily demanding what I was thinking of—she was forever probing my thoughts. Lacking a life, I guess she had nothing else to do but to provoke beating situations. When I received classmates' telephone calls, she would revoke the call and never let me know, and when my next-door buddy whistled our "secret" calls, she would immediately throw a fit saying that my mind was always at play. R.A. was my best childhood buddy. We had a "secret" whistle call and summoned one another periodically to meet at "secret passages" along the property line fence. His parents were well-off by neighborhood standards; all siblings attended private schools, and their summers were spent on the beaches of Mexico. R.'s family was always doing something, and if it hadn't been for his benevolent parents, I would never have viewed *King Kong* at the Texas Theater, learned to ride a bike, or attend an air show at the local air force base. She was always angrily saying that the neighbors controlled their children with only glances, while I would not mind even with whippings. She was relentlessly given to petulance—opportunistically finding fault, so that I stood like a blameless victim before a Spanish Court of Inquisition which had nothing "accusatory" on a blank brandished paper. During my mother's reprimands, Magnolia, her Mephistopheles, interposed angrily, demanding additional information which successfully increased my mother's wrath and beating. Once, I was silently choking, so I hacked to spit. Immediately Magnolia slapped me saying I was being disrespectful to her. Another time, she administered castor oil to me for some imagined infraction. She always barged in on my mother's reprimands, demanding that I bow my head, and once, with my juvenile strength, I physically fought her with my head bowed in traditional submission, but turned away. At the table once, being aggravated by something I had said, she threw a glass of water at my face (a usual by our mother), and I instinctively threw one back at her and ran. Magnolia remained a dutiful daughter to my mother and to my adult third sister, Azalea, both incontinent to their dying days. She never married, and I am not sure that if given the right circumstances, she would have married at all. I guess it never crossed her mind to take up some academic or vocational course or serve in church or find career employment. It was this sister who once menacingly told me never to call home while in the service because charges would not be accepted. Looking back, I wonder if my weapon and my downfall may not have been my submission and my silence because these two things failed their anger. Mentally I responded that I had never considered returning, much less calling home once enlisted. I later learned that my brother Beau once called homesick, bawling *and on his first day in the service!* Once, when I did call because of problems at home mentioned in my mother's letters, she asked why I hadn't called; I replied that Magnolia had warned me not to, which Magnolia immediately denied! Although Magnolia would never admit it, as we began leaving home, she was also beleaguered and increasingly harassed by my mother. Proof of her suffering was the prescription drug she filled which contained narcotics that she was seen taking when she once visited us in West Texas, yet held to the claim that mother could do no wrong.

Somehow somewhere early in my life my fifth and last sister, Gladiola, three years my senior and given to frequent tantrums, decided I was her dog to kick around and wormed her way into my mother's confidence. Gladiola was whiny and petty and had a scandalous nature, made mountains out of molehills creating endless beating situations. She became my mother's informant and her selfishness won her "spoiled brat" status. She was my self-appointed torturer, while to everyone she appeared as a guardian angel or patron saint. She totally dominated my childhood; truthfully she skillfully deflected my mother's temper by igniting it toward me continually. In reality, this perpetrator was Iago personified, continually stoking my mother's already short-fused temper. She was always meddling, intruding, and suggesting endless chore assignments for me so that while I had to do her chores, she'd practice the piano to my mother's intense pleasure, thereby ingratiating herself and winning her approval and pride. I too, played an instrument, but was not well received. One day, during my third grade music hour, Mr. Montoya, a musical instrument professor, dropped in to hear us sing. He singled me out as having a finely tuned voice, a prerequisite for instrument lessons. He telephoned my mother and invited me to take up a musical instrument—a grave error. Little did I know that the following four years would be full of increased beatings and buffetings as I was encouraged to practice the violin that she painstakingly purchased for fifty dollars in payments, which was a lot of money those days. Ever since I could remember, Gladiola followed my mother's example and, in her rage, was always ordering me around to do the chores with put-downs and harassment. I would carry out these instructions, being so "trained" by the required use of my mother's belt. When I complained, my mother replied, "She is not bossing you around. She is only telling you what to do"—granting Gladiola the right to supreme arrogance and authority. Also, Gladiola frequently butted in my decision-making conversations with my mother by making suggestions or recommendations to which my mother always gave credence and acceptance. To make matters worse, Gladiola had mastered techniques to stoke my mother's eruptive violence. When enraged, Gladiola herself regularly threatened to "make trouble for you" if I didn't immediately comply with her wishes. She was the cause of more than 50 percent of all my beatings punctuated with threats and perfected maneuvering and provocations that inflamed my mother. Her threats, her snitching, and connivance appealed to my mother's vanity, her righteousness, or wrath. On one of Gladiola's intrusions, my mother surprisingly took my side telling her to mind her own business; a serious mistake. Thereafter, when Gladiola privately meddled with my affairs and I reminded her of what mother had said—to mind her own business—she at once informed my mother, who, without delay, beat me; a multiple recurrence. Once I was emptying my pockets in Gladiola's presence, disclosing a matchbox that I had by chance carried to school—she straightaway went to tell my mother who proceeded to give me a thrashing. One evening while feeding my invalid sister Azalea, Gladiola observed me playfully tapping Azalea on her butt with a rubber hose. Immediately Gladiola, in her tattletale rabid mode, informed my mother who flogged me with the rubber hose. Gladiola's incessant tattling occurred on a daily basis from the time I was nine, a fourth grader, increasing during my adolescence, and ending at the same time as my beatings, at seventeen. Her rage was a constant, even upon returning from our holiest place of worship. Perhaps she felt doomed at having to care for my incontinent sister Azalea from the time she was ten and took it out on me. Maybe Gladiola also knew that at eighteen I would be free of all the pandemonium at home when I would enter the service, while she remained trapped forever. It was during puberty that possibly her hormones were so overwhelming that she took out her frustrations on me. I must say that only once I really got back to her. About the age 10, I threw a rock at her and bulls eye! The rock struck her between the eyebrows and just above her buzzard nose. That was one rare time my mother did not beat me. I got away scot-free. Curiously enough, in her early twenties (my junior and senior years), Gladiola became more critical toward our mother—at the time our mother was confiscating all her earnings from her lucrative employment. During my stint in Korea, Gladiola married her high-school sweetheart. At that time she began her deprecating remarks toward me. Once when I openheartedly expressed my hopes and wishes a few months into my marriage, she actually jeered at my dreams and with her timeless theatrics and dramatics sarcastically ridiculed my aspirations. Our bishop assessed her as envying my ecclesiastical accomplishments when he heard our taped conversation. I am amused when reminded of Gladiola's theatrics that surface every time I see the woman screech, "The chariots, aaeerrhhh, run, run for your lives!" as the Israelites exit the parted Red Sea at being pursued by the Pharaoh's chariots in the motion picture *The Ten Commandments* with Charlton Heston as Moses. Only once, decades later, did she try to offer an explanation to justify her snitching on a single incident, but I reflected her words were afterthoughts of excuse. Since her contemptuousness lasted well into my married years, I dedicated "My Life" by Billy Joel, which she ignored or was not intelligent enough to comprehend. Then abruptly, all her condemnations ceased in the second decade of our respective marriages saying she might not agree with my claims but would defend my right to speak—a time when our children became teenagers. Is it possible she finally got an insight of her cruelty from her own children? It is perplexing, that although Gladiola witnessed all my beatings and aware of my bruises, she lived in denial claiming they were mere spankings—a continued insult to my intelligence—to her dying day.

My ancient father ignored the abuse and all family problems while filling my head with his adventures as a sergeant in the federalist forces of Mexico during the Mexican Revolution. I cannot remember that he once laid a hand on me, nor did he ever defend me from my mother. As a child I remember hearing that he was a serious man, a macho along with all its ramifications, i.e., the old country ways where men ruled and women were chattels. I sometimes overheard adult conversations in which my mother said my dad came home drunk quite often and at times even brought women—that he was a womanizer, and that he always called her *puta* (whore). In their arguments my mother would consistently insist to him she was not one of his *soldaderas* or revolutionary camp followers. Perhaps in later years, she became the aggressor and he the powerless victim. I can never remember any tender moments between them: kissing, hugging, holding hands, or chivalrous behavior; although they did share the same bed and sat side by side when watching television and at the porch swing. It was a time when divorces were unknown and couples stuck it out. I do remember that my sisters mentioned that mother never allowed him to discipline us. My guess is that she relished the pleasure of being the executor of discipline with beatings and whippings, and as he grew older, he did not have the strength to contradict her. About the time he died, following my sixteenth birthday, the abuse abruptly ceased.

AUTHOR'S CONSCRIPT FATHER, JOSE, AGED TWENTY-TWO, 23RD INFANTRY, A SERGEANT IN THE FEDERALIST FORCES DURING MEXICAN REVOLUTION, 1906.

It is beyond my comprehension what part I played in Almighty God's celestial plan or purpose of being delivered to lucifer's lair on earth. My feelings hurt and I suffered because of the abuse and subjugation my spirit received from dysfunctional parents and siblings. Nothing was more wounding to the core of my soul—the quality, innocent, subservient, docile spirit duly conceived in God's birthing primordial heaven—than to have the essence of my mortal conception delivered to the abusive undeserving recipient, the incessant instant evil and cruel violent vicious exploitation by my parent, and sisters, yet . . . *Lord, Thy will be done*. It never once occurred to me of course—that I could voice a *no*, or refuse physical or emotional abuse or run off—I was a lamb being led to the slaughterhouse during my battered childhood.

Epilogue

My mother's abuse and incessant floggings, coupled with my equally vindictive sisters' provoking constant fear in my tender years, magnified a certainty that the future held unrelieved pain. However, sometime during my sixteenth year, for no reason and to my great relief, the violence abruptly stopped. At that time, I was testing and requesting her signature to enlist in the armed forces reserves. I began to enjoy freedom of leaving the house to enjoy my escapes: viewing motion pictures at the low-priced theaters downtown and dating girls from school or the girl next door. I have no idea why she quit victimizing me. She might have realized that in two years I would be graduating and leaving for the military.

Decades later, I asked myself why I was so compliant to the abuse. Why did I lie face down on demand to be flogged? Why did I obediently stand still to receive her buffetings? Why did I not raise my arms to block her? Why would I comply with her orders to drink body fluids? Was it that I was programmed or was the fear of more pain powerful enough to obey without question? I believe I was programmed to Moses' *"Honor thy father and thy mother,"* (Ex 20:12) or Solomon's: *"My son, hear the instruction of thy father and forsake not the law of thy mother,"* (Prv 1:8), even though our spiritual life was nonexistent. But no one ever bothered to quote Saint Paul, *"Fathers provoke not your children to anger, lest they become discouraged,"* (Col 3:21). I must say that my anger was awakened; however, as angry as I got, I never expounded on it as I was immediately overpowered physically and verbally by my sisters and mother. Perhaps she realized my developing body and awakening strength at seventeen were becoming a risk. I could very well retaliate at any moment. Perhaps she sensed black thoughts of matricide were more frequently crossing my mind at that age. More than likely, it might have been the realization that I was no longer the scapegoat, the helpless child she always victimized. I guess my sisters made their peace

with God, never considering reconciliation or restitution with their brother. And my daughter commented: *"Dad, you bore thirteen years with your mother, but Mom more than made up for it plus an eternity to look forward to."*
—Marisol Iris Drawe, U.S. Army, Mother

STUDIO PORTRAIT OF DAD AND MOTHER TAKEN AROUND 1937

Patriotism

In daylight bright or darkly dim
At the sound of our country's hymn
I'd stand up tall through thick and thin
At sounds of brass and drums and din

It was the year 1964, when the draft was still in effect, that I enlisted. I was RA (Regular Army) all the way. Because of my ROTC background and performance, I was appointed squad leader both in basic and AIT (Advanced Individual Training). The commanding officer in basic nominated me for the American Spirit Honor Medal. As a gung-ho ex-Boy Scout and strike HS ROTC cadet, I was *ready* for a thirty-year military career. Army life; the military life? No problem, I felt I had been *born* a military man ever since I listened openmouthed to my dad's battle experiences of his conscript years as a federalist sergeant during the Mexican Revolution. I felt I would easily adapt to any situation. Hardship tours? Never knew they existed. War? Never gave it much thought. If I died, I *died*! In the innocence of my patriotic childhood, I was *ready* to die for my country! Hey, I would get up from my bed regardless of room temperature to stand on the cold, splintered floor at respectful attention when the Star-Spangled Banner was sung but more so performed by some military band at the end of the television broadcast day.

My first soldierly exposure was ten years earlier, in 1954, when I had attended the Primary church program for youngsters, and I earned awards that I pinned on my shirt such as the Top Pilot (class) wings that I proudly wore. Later, we wore a "banlo" (a green felt necklace-like sash) round our necks on which other plastic achievement badges were attached. How I loved to parade to and from Saturday church meetings with my banlo wrapped around my neck (which along with my earlier wings in my boyhood mind were my first military-like medals)! Then one day I happened to enter the Boy Scout meeting room. A whole world opened before me. I looked forward to the day when I turned twelve and became eligible to join the Boy Scouts of America—I would be eligible to wear my first army-like uniform. In due course I registered, attended meetings, and began earning my ranks and merit badges. I worked hard selling crafts I made from vegetable wood crates in order to pay my fees and dues! However, because of the abuse, my Primary and boy scouting dreams were short lived as my mother not only seized my every painstakingly earned penny, but rarely allowed me to attend meetings, much less field activities, so crucial to advancement. Still, I was proud of my long-sleeve official shirt, which I purchased with my own hard-earned money, and I wore it even on the hottest days to show off my achievements.

Then, in my fourteenth year as I entered high school, I was awed at the ROTC, program with authentic rifles (WWII M1s) and army uniforms. I felt very special and wholeheartedly signed for the class. I could not get over the fact that such a junior military program existed. I would be wearing a genuine army military uniform! Medals and stripes could be earned! *Finally*, I was in a situation where my mother could not control my activities because the ROTC course group was part of the school curriculum. I had graduated from Boy Scouting to a junior military training program! The time I spent in ROTC was perhaps the one light in my daily torturous childhood and adolescence as the beatings did not stop until early in my seventeenth year, while a junior in high school.

I was to be a Cadet Private! I mean a *Cadet*, something like the Space Cadets of Tom Corbett's television series! I was so proud that I would wear my starched skin-tight khakis even as a buck private with no awards other than the school and military shoulder patches. Then, after the first semester, I was advanced to Private First. I shone my single yellow stripe on the black folded epaulette, which was wrapped on the shirt's shoulder flaps. I even flattened them more with cardboard inserts to make them look like those of the naval officers. Aahhh! but I was in princely pictured paradise, all at the expense of the school district taxpayers! Some kids laughed at me and smirked behind my back, but I could not have cared less. That same semester I was awarded the Highest Grade Average ribbon that I pinned one-eighth inch above my left pocket seam. It was in that same freshman year I qualified with the small bore 22 mm rifle as a sharpshooter. I pinned this badge also to flaunt all my achievements. It was during the second semester of my freshman year that I was assigned student traffic-director duty. A string of cadets stood at the halls' centers, ensuring that no student would cut across the flow of student traffic on the two-way halls. We stood in parade dress, and when an officer walked by, we snapped to attention clicking our heels and slapping our hands on our trousers seams. It was a steady beat down the halls above the controlled student chatter, as each cadet in turn was heard to click and slap at his appointed time at each officer's passing. Oh, but it was a time when patriotism was in its heyday and this was continually a thrilling experience!

I loved to march, so I immediately joined the Second Drill and added the corresponding royal blue fourragere that draped down my arm from my left epaulette under my Private First slat. The Second Drill Team consisted of basic marching called "straight drill," preparatory to joining the First Drill Team. It was during this year that the Second Drill Team was honored with guarding the queen of the Battle of Flowers Parade during Fiesta Week downtown San Antonio, that April of 1961. Our post was to march behind the Queen's float to prevent any possible well-wishers' mischief. How proudly we marched *in a parade*! We wore a simple undecorated uniform but with mirrored sunglasses, blue cravat, and white spiderweb-laced jump boots. One girl from school later told me that we "looked sharp, very sharp." This added greatly to my military ego.

My sophomore and junior years passed in a blur of activities. It was during my sophomore year that I was nominated for color guard and approved by the commandant. The Color Guard was always in demand at school assemblies, during parades, festive holidays, on the streets of San Antonio, graduation, football games, and anywhere that the Colors were required. I had joined the elite yearly foursome guard of bearing the Colors—the American flag along with that of the school. In my sophomore year, I carried the school flag and was privileged to grace my uniform with a white fourragere and entitled to wear a second honored award, the color guard ribbon. Then, during my junior year, I bore the Colors, and in the latter part of the year, I was elected Head Color Guard by the other three guards who were—*Seniors*! Me, a junior in charge of seniors! Oh, how proud I was those last two years—to wear the only special uniform uniquely distinguished with my first of two senior fourrageres. I proudly flashed not only my white fourragere, but also my glazed ribbons, and my color guard only six "master sergeant" stripes on my audience. To don my starched khaki dress uniform with my choking blue and white cravat, my white helmet with the letter L for Lanier, white gloves along with white spiderwebbed lacing on my mirror-shined bloused combat boots, and a white pistol belt gave me the greatest of thrills. Of course, part of the appeal of appearing in this regalia was the attraction and anticipation of the girls eyeing me in my finest.

I will never forget how during assemblies at the Sidney Lanier High School auditorium (especially at the downtown Municipal Auditorium during graduation), once the student body was seated, we color guards performed our ceremony. One flag bearer and one rifled guard stood at the very back of the auditorium, each pair at a side aisle. We flag bearers mounted the flags on our harnesses while the guards shouldered their rifles. At this time, the drummer beat the cadence and we marched in place.

♪ *Ta-RA-tat-tat*
Ta-RA-tat-tat
Ta-RA-ta-ta-ta-ta-TAT-tat-tat ♪

At the head color-guard's signal—careful not to jab the low ceiling—we marched forward on respective aisles toward the stage as the entire student body rose in respectful silence to the continued drummed cadence. My heart beat in unison with the drum's resounding strokes during the ceremony that sent blood rushing to my temples each time. (I remember how I felt goose bumps on my very first experience at viewing the passing of the beloved Colors, as a freshman, newly arrived at the school.) Each pair entered at our corresponding door located at opposite sides of the stage and climbed the steps, while backstage, the drum still beating cadence, we again marched in place, unseen by the audience. At my signal, we marched forward across the stage so that the flags crossed at center stage, the Colors toward the audience. The flags were positioned in their respective floor mounts, the Colors at its own right, with all guards now facing it. At this point, the drummer ceased the marching cadence and drummed the roll, signaling the drum major to strike up the band.

♪ *Thr-r-r-r-r-r-r-r-r-r-r* ♪

Again at my signal, the flag bearers came to the hand salute, and simultaneously the rifle bearers came to "present arms" (salute with rifles). The majestic thunder from the school's senior band reverberated the national anthem clear across the auditorium and back to me. Although I had performed this ceremony for two years, each time I felt the adrenalin rush up my temples as the band in the orchestra pit immediately below struck the overpowering rumbling waves of the anthem that ascended to us.

Each of these ceremonies brought me to the grandest moments of my life thus far in my "military career." The guard remained at "present arms" as the music came to an end. The audience stood at respectful ceremonial observance, when the silence was broken with my words, "Now we shall say the Pledge of Allegiance," inundating the entire auditorium as I spoke into the microphone. This was one of two momentary times that I was absolutely in charge of a ceremony. My entire tenure I wanted to say, "Now we shall pledge allegiance to the flag," but I was told not to by the commandant. The whole student body pledged to the flag followed by my "order arms" (end salute) signal and the exiting of the stage.

Ah, but the first of two epic crowning ceremonies was my experience at the San Antonio Municipal Auditorium when we performed at the 1963 commencement which was not only attended by the faculty, but made exceptional with the presence of the San Antonio Independent School District superintendent, mayor, civic dignitaries, parents, and graduates—with standing room only. Although accustomed to announcing the pledge at the school auditorium, I heard my voice in higher magnification on that graduation night. The second was the flag-raising ceremony during Veteran's Day on campus. The entire student body was present, and the ROTC brigade stood at attention in full respectful salute while I rapidly raised and then slowly lowered the Colors to half-staff. The firing squad saluted with four volleys and the bugler sounded off *Taps*. I was in complete control, as only after lowering the flag to half-staff and securing the halyard, followed by my unlimitedly timed salute, and calling the "order arms" command did the brigade and the entire student body come to "at rest" position.

One special treat was when we were invited to present the Colors at David Crockett Elementary, my grammar school. Following the field flag-raising ceremony we performed an auditorium presentation in the cafeteria. There was the added bonus of introducing ourselves. I waved to Mrs. Gerodetti who had put up with much of my hyper behavior seven years earlier, and who was very much aware of my abusive plight. It was impossible not to flirt with the impressed wide-eyed exceptionally pretty sixth-grade girls—the boys were no competition.

These two years also found me as a member of the First Drill Team and authorized to wear my blue and white speckled fourragere the second of two. The First Drill Team performed at public functions with straight and demonstration drill. My favorite fancy drill was when the squads faced one another and performed a prearranged manual-of-arms, which also included an exchange of rifles. When I wasn't performing the color guard ceremony, I could march with the drill team. We would march in the downtown parades during Fiesta Week, Veteran's Day among others, and at the school spring festivals and competitions. How I loved to march with such an elite troupe on those exceptional city celebrations—there was magic in the air those nights. I remember a city-wide celebration during each April when there was always something going on all over in commemoration of the Battle of the Alamo and the Battle of San Jacinto. San Antonio is after all, a city of "fiestas" year round! I thrilled as all of San Antonio watched us drill. I loved to watch the illuminated floats, experience the afternoon turn to evening, twilight, then dusk and the cheers we earned from our schoolmates below the downtown city lights, the neon signs, all under the black starlit sky deep in the heart of Texas.

It was during the Federal Inspection that the First Drill Team was called out to perform when the color guard First Drill Team members were reprimanded by the visiting army officers for leaving the flags unguarded, while we rushed to the drill team's formation for exhibition drill. Needless to say, thereafter, I assured substitutes in place while performing momentarily elsewhere away from the Colors. I truly enjoyed my three years in High School ROTC though I did not take the class in my senior year. During my last year in school, I spent my time in enjoying other elective classes, attended all senior activities, graduated, and walked out the door to perform my patriotic duty in the new military life the army offered to fulfill my patriotism.

My Senior Year

In poverty where I was caught
Money for school for me was naught
The skills and touring that I sought
Three years of army life I bought

1964, my senior year. I was eighteen and one month. The radio airwaves were filled with military service proposals. It was a time when all four-year military branches announced attractive offers in order to divert volunteers from the three-year enlistment of the U.S. Army. The Vietnam War was in its infancy. Throughout my junior year, I had researched all military branches for incentives. All said that following enlistment, I would be placed in a job subject to the requirements of the branch service and based on a battery of tests. All my life I had planned on a commercial career requiring office skills. The army recruiter at the ROTC armory at my high school announced that all graduates would be granted their choice of schools dependent on the Armed Forces Qualification Test (AFQT) required for all draftees or volunteers prior to being sworn in. Upon passing the entrance test, the recruiter handed me a document that guaranteed me Pay School at enlistment. This was gratifying because it was my career of choice. All along I had wanted to join the navy because my head was filled with childhood sea stories and travel to distant ports of call while at sea. I had always sung the "We join the navy to see the world" recruiting jingle. The fact that Payroll School was guaranteed prior to joining the army facilitated my enlistment in that branch instead of the navy. I knew that at Pay School I would learn office skills that would open doors for employment following my discharge if I did not decide to make the army a career. It was also explained to me that at my release from active duty I was entitled to GI Bill benefits leading to a college education. These career blessings were far greater than what I could ever hope to achieve at home under a devastating situation, even with a high-school diploma!

Because I lived in constant fear of being flogged or abused, I created my own escapes, of which one was losing myself in reading the classics. Although my favorite reads were boy's books of colonial naval America and the fighting sails of the British Navy, I further indulged in hero worship. I was "Marco Polo" in his journey from Venice across Asia and his travels in China, and "Ferdinand Magellan" in his circumnavigation of the earth—all epic biographies. I ran off to sea with Roger Byam in HMS *Bounty* (a trilogy). I adventured with John Smith as a slave in North Africa and then under his leadership in the New World. I lived in England where I suffered with Silas Marner and his stolen gold and shared Oliver Twist's happiness when he is adopted by Mr. Brownlow. I detested the unappreciative Heathcliff, and in France, I sword-played with Dartagnan when I wasn't hunting treasure with Edmund Dantes on the Island of Monte Cristo. Then I joined the French Foreign Legion and wore my white kepi in the North African sands with Corporal Victor, after traversing another scorching desert with Allan Quartermain while departing King Solomon's Mines brimming with jewels. I loved sailing all over the Agean Sea in the Argos, being with Calypso, and I cried when Hector was dragged by Achilles at Troy; and when I wasn't with Nemo in the Nautilus exploring some seafloor and dreaming of treasure, I swung to board the Natividad with Captain Hornblower (eleven volumes). No other memorable closing of a book tore my heart from my chest as Roger Byam's return to Tahiti after a two-decade absence and he finds his daughter by his beloved deceased wife Tehani, and a mountain breeze at the seashore fills his surroundings with ghosts of blissful times past, and his own among them.

One of my favorite childhood passions was reading comic books. I loved lying on the smooth time-worn planks of the front porch reading of my heroes. I would enter the comic and be right there with them. Those summer days were so sunny that I was oblivious of the humidity and heat of the day. I loved to swing through the jungle within each picture of Tarzan's comic books when I wasn't treasure hunting and traveling to far off exotic places with the rich Uncle Scrooge McDuck, or fighting villains with Batman, Superman, and Captain Blackhawk. I devoured the Junior Woodchuck adventures of Huey, Dewey, and Louie—always outwitting Donald and rescuing McDuck. Other favorites were Little Lulu, Tubby and the gang, Bugs Bunny, and Andy Panda with Charlie Chicken, when I wasn't involved with Tom and Jerry. I remember comics cost five cents, then ten cents and I could not afford them. Somehow I managed to purchase those of Walt Disney's *Uncle Scrooge*. Since my earliest childhood, I remember he had a huge money bin filled with coins and some dollar bills. Lying around his office floor and as bookends were bulging money bags tied up and boasting huge dollar signs. How I loved his dollar sign and his stuffed money bags. I told myself that when I grew up I would also have such moneybags. When I made these feelings known to my sister Magnolia, she responded with a curt putdown saying that I was "money hungry." What impressed me most about Uncle Scrooge McDuck were his travels all over the world, which fascinated the adventuresome spirit in me. He was always finding hidden treasures or valuables under the sea, in the deserts, underground, and in space. Everywhere he went he got rich, especially one time when he took along Gander Goose. I wanted so much to travel around as he did and find treasure or just have a good time visiting all those fascinating places. I'd walk around the house with my head whirling with the adventures and perhaps the treasure the world had out there, waiting for me. I was afraid that by the time it was my turn, there would be nothing to see of what I had read. How I wanted to join the navy and travel all over the world. However, I sensed that my comic-reading moments would be short lived as I lay face down on the floor—sure enough as expected, my mother would pass by and claw me on the buttocks for some trivial reason or other.

Since childhood, I had wandered around the San Antonio backstreets and alleys devoting my preteen life to dreams of adventure. As a youth I was enchanted by the television travel series *Bold Journey* and *I Search for Adventure*, and I felt a personal pride as the host addressed his audience, "Ladies and gentlemen, boys and girls," I knew he was speaking to me. Having been brought up in a west-side San Antonio poverty-ridden barrio, I realized that my high-school diploma was not only my passport out of an intolerable home situation, but would open the door to my choice of duty in the service. What better occupation would hurl me to distant lands without professional or basic skills? What far-flung realms were out there waiting for me to discover and explore? I subscribed to the *American Geographical Society's Around the World Program*. I devoured those booklets with their colorful stickers along with the travel brochures I'd collected from downtown travel agencies. Each booklet visited a different country, and for some unknown reason, the Orient fascinated me along with the South Pacific. Pirate movies at the local fifty-cent theaters of San Antonio were my way of vicariously assaying my adventuresome spirit.

I was a fourth-grader when my travel dreams were further enriched with the navy. With *Don Winslow and the Navy* I felt my adrenalin pumping with the theme music: navy anthem. A favorite movie was *Anchors Aweigh* with Frank Sinatra and Gene Kelly. Ah, but the navy band in that anthem sent my blood rushing up to my temples. Ten years from my birth year, I viewed the movie *Around the World in Eighty Days* with David Niven, Shirley McClain, and Mario Moreno Cantinflas. Needless to say, I was in ecstasy. I was fascinated by the Paspartout's train ride across the India countryside and of his stroll by Daibutsu, the giant Buddha in Kamakura.

During my middle-school years, I happened to see what would become my two life-long super special movies about sailors and hula dancers in the South Pacific of the late 1700s. I'll never forget my visit to the South Seas with Benjamin Blake (Tyrone Power) and how I fell in love with Gene Tierney in *Son of Fury*, and also how I worshipped Debra Padget in the classic movie, *Bird of Paradise*. Such were my escapes from the daily terror-filled horrors at home.

In my later teens, I'd frequent the three-movie fifty-cent theaters countless times to again live within story plots. Among many sea sagas, I sailed with Henry Morgan when he captured gold-laden Spanish galleons along with his capture of Panama in Steve Reeve's epic movie, *Morgan the Pirate* and with Ragnar when he and his Vikings invaded England and their ingenious shield wall successfully assaulted Ayala's castle in *The Vikings* with Kirk Douglas and Tony Curtis, I witnessed Walter Drake's (Rod Taylor) adventure and Spanish treasure raids in *Seven Seas to Calais*. I read *The Bounty Trilogy* seven times and could hardly wait for the movie premier of *Mutiny on the Bounty* starring Marlon Brando of 1962. How I craved to be a sailor on a voyage to the South Seas. In my naïveté, I imagined visiting some remote island and meeting up with a saucy hula dancer under swaying palm trees, with the sunset's reflection on a golden ocean turning into the blue night. I further dreamed myself gorging on coconuts, bananas, and breadfruit, all amid mountain greenery with perhaps a backdrop of a volcano or two. Then to swim amid the coral reefs catching and eating fish and perhaps present my grass-skirted girl with a strand of pearls. How I yearned to sail the sea, to fulfill my childhood dreams by joining the navy, visiting foreign places, and exploring all the ports where my ship would anchor.

I always felt assured that the armed forces would be my sure ticket to adventure and travel to distant lands. However, because of the payroll promise, my final decision was the army. Thus my fate was cast. I was finally going to make my travel dreams come true after a childhood nightmare at the end of 1964 my senior year!

Epilogue

It was the fifth day following high school graduation. I could not have left house sooner due to the weekend. I was sworn into the U.S. Army on the morning of Monday, May 25, 1964. I remember the recruiter had agreed to come for me that morning. The day I had waited for since childhood was finally here! No more verbal abuse, no more harassments, I would be a free man with all the hell of home left behind.

It was still dark when the recruiter's car arrived. As soon as I heard it, I ran out the door, but my mother called me back in a voice I had never heard before. Annoyed for stopping me in my tracks, I turned to face her. For the first time in my life, I saw her eyes glazed with, what I guessed, an expression of held-back anxiety. And with what I recognized as a knot in her throat, I heard her utter some faint words. With a new life beckoning, I had neither the time nor the patience to listen to her—it was too late, not ever again! I jubilantly ran out the door toward the world of freedom and welcomed the adventure awaiting me, never looking back at the conclusion of my senior year.

Afterthought

Remember young Beethoven in the motion picture *Immortal Beloved* escaping through a window from his father's rabid wrath and running, running, running through the forest under the starry skies? You picture me. I saw myself running and as I ran, each pace was a step away from my mother's abomination. It was her ghastly voice I heard in the movie that chilled the marrow in my bones and rasped through my memory of thirteen years' horrors calling me, but as with Ludwig, I no longer listened or cared. I enthusiastically ran and ran and ran with him under those jeweled skies as he tirelessly trotted in rhythm to the spirited music. I was away, alone, floating, partially submerged in the water's quietude—elated with my newfound free will in the army as I became one with Beethoven under the myriad of celestial gems within the millpond sanctuary while cognizant of his choral composition, the thunderous "Ode to Joy." Freedom, I was gone! No more monsters.

Hallelujah, for The Lord God omnipotent reigneth . . .

> *You gain strength, courage and confidence by every experience in which you really stop to look fear in the face. You are able to say to yourself "I have lived through horror. I can take the next thing that comes along."*
>
> —Eleanor Roosevelt

PART II

Eighth United States Army, Korea

I will! I am! I can! I will actualize my dream. I will press ahead. I will settle down and see it through. I will solve the problems. I will pay the price. I will never walk away from my dream until I see my dream walk away: Alert! Alive! Achieved!
—Robert Schuller (1926-)

Long to tour a far off land
A soldier went to join a band
Of brothers and treasures to discover
Pagodas, shrines, temples to uncover

Chapter 3

In Transit to Far East Asia

Go confidently in the direction of your dreams.
Live the life you have imagined.
—Henry David Theoreau

Prologue

If you can picture a smiling, wide-eyed child going out somewhere, anywhere, all wild with excitement, you picture me. Countless were the times I had anticipated world travel with its wondrous adventures, all being realized. Arrival at a new land, and preparation for a new way of life unfolded before me.

Arrival
November 10-12, 1964

Boarding a jet bound overseas
My day my soul my heart did please
Things to do and places to see
Asia is mine or soon will be

As a graduate of the elite Payroll School, a soldier in U.S. Army wearing my dress greens on that Tuesday, November 10, 1964, bound for duty in the Orient, was infinitely exciting for me. The military lifetime of travel and adventure was about to begin and this was my first horizon. The flight from San Francisco and stopover in Seattle was uneventful other than a little nausea. On the flight from Tokyo, once over the Pacific, I immediately took note of an Asiatic gentleman seated close to me. I was fascinated by his attire consisting of the traditional bulged whites and black mini stove-top hat. To me, he seemed to have materialized from the Department of Defense (DOD) pamphlet cover that introduced Korea to the military. I noticed that the airline stewardess too, was of Asiatic descent and that her name tag read Miss Kim. Asiatic facial features with sloe eyes immediately introduced my mind to Far East Asia. I was oblivious to all other passengers, including my numerous military companions. I was euphoric about witnessing my introduction to a different culture, a different race, and greedily I took in all the sights and sounds of a whole new world to immerse myself wholly in Korea.

Only two months earlier on a hot, sultry, and humid day in August 1964, while assigned at Company H Fourth Training Brigade at South Fort Polk, Louisiana, I asked a sergeant regarding my next duty station. I happened to be in the orderly room assigned to charge of quarters as a squad leader during Personnel School. He rattled off military jargon which ended with Korea. At those final words I went ballistic! Traveling overseas, just as I had always planned! I had lived for this news since childhood, and now I had it all for free! I completed Personnel School in early October 1964 and flew to Fort Harrison, Indiana, for Payroll School. Following school at Fort Harrison, we flew to Oakland Army Terminal in California. A few days later, we boarded a Northwest Jet with Korea as our destination. After an extended flight across the Pacific Ocean, we had a brief layover in Tokyo, Japan! Excitedly, I roamed all over the airport. The first of my many dreams come true. I walked into a curio shop and purchased post cards to send home to prove I had been in Tokyo, Japan. After a few memorable and exciting hours, we reboarded the same jet that delivered us at Kimpo Air Force Base, Korea! In my naïveté, I marveled that our mimeographed military orders on plain white paper were all we needed to board our airline to and from Asia. I was impressed by the liquidity that our uniforms afforded: how easily we boarded airplanes and flowed through the airports without passports or presenting ID cards, and at times not even showing a copy our mimeographed orders. I later realized that the government had made all of these arrangements.

I WALKED INTO A CURIO SHOP AT THE TOKYO AIRPORT AND PURCHASED POSTCARDS TO SEND HOME.

As the jet descended at Kimpo on the morning of Thursday, the twelfth (having lost Wednesday the eleventh crossing the International Date Line), I viewed a noticeable difference in the geography from my window. This was mountainous country, doe-brown with tiny scattered patches of green. I knew I had entered my anticipated adventure in another land, another world, another dimension.

Upon deplaning on that cold and chilly, sunny November morning, the bustle of busy Oriental people arriving and leaving the airport followed by Asiatic writing on signs, streets, and businesses brought the Orient to a reality. Excitement bubbled over! This was Korea! So this was Asia! I had arrived! My first adventure half a world away from home! I was so excited at viewing the beginning of new horizons that I must have likened a raccoon, with my eyes as big as saucers, and probably flared nostrils trying to take in everything and everyone at once! My anticipations from what I read in the DOD pamphlet—the imposing mountainous landscape and the Korean gentleman as pictured on the cover—and seeing so much in so short a demanding time, made it impossible to remember everything, with more at every turn. Tucking away memory after memory like pictures, I vowed I would pull them out to examine later at my leisure, a practice I followed during my whole time there.

Abruptly, the receiving officer returned me to the present as I listened carefully to instructions for departure to duty. Transported from the Kimpo AFB to the Army Support Command (ASCOM) installation took all my attention from noting the Korean environment. However, upon arriving at the nearby ASCOM, the introduction facility, I was taken aback when reality snuck in to present the true military purpose that had brought me to this Far East corner of Asia.

Reception
Friday, November 13, 1964

Stripping dress greens and coats and ties
Donning long johns with groans and sighs
Fatigues, jump boots, and baseball caps
Elite we were but Army saps

It all began at the Indoctrination Center at ASCOM near Seoul where we arrived the day before, Thursday, November 12, 1964, after deplaning at Kimpo Air Force Base. All the marvels of travel and civility vanished as we were bussed to a deployment station and ordered to remove our greens and "get into your fatigues." Fatigues are green khaki base uniforms usually worn for manual labor or nonpublic duty. As personnel specialists, we recognized we were to undergo a ghastly, nasty turn of events. The base uniform brought back dreaded memories of Basic Training and again of Advanced Individual Training at Fort Polk. Only a week earlier we had graduated from Payroll School at Fort Benjamin Harrison in Indianapolis, Indiana, where the green woolen uniforms had been the dress, the ticket to special treatment, and we had got used to being treated special. It had been a nice-looking scene to see so many soldiers in a sea of greens accentuated with gold buttons, like at a military academy. Our duty had been trouble-free and undemanding so the post was nicknamed "Uncle

Benny's Rest Home." Now, however, we were being herded into a dark, gloomy room and given a lengthy indoctrination sermon on what to do and not to do in Korea. More was said than what my brain could register. Tired and still recovering from jet lag and disoriented with so much change, I have no recollection of what was said. We were then most emphatically ordered to shower before we hit the sack.

After reveille and breakfast that Friday morning of the thirteenth, we were herded into a Quonset for supplementary clothing. Supposedly, once a man didn't shower the night before, so the supply dressing area was permeated for an extended period of time with his body odor. The governmental shower was to avoid similar incidents. We were lined up and ordered to strip down to socks, drawers, and T-shirts. We were supplied with temporary local winter clothing. Two pairs of long johns were issued to each man. After this, we were all issued two olive green heavy woolen shirts and as many olive green trousers of fine thick woolen fabric. These "olive greens" substituted the dress greens within the division during winter (While the uniform to Seoul consisted of the (winter) army greens and overcoat; or (summer) khakis). Then came a field parka that extended all the way down to the knees and sported a fur-lined hood. The field trousers that matched the parkas were oversized balloon-like pants that along with the parka, shelled warm detachable liners. These field pants also included suspenders that comfortably held them in place. The leather-palmed mittens that extended to the forearm, sported only one cloth finger for the weapon's trigger. The thermal "Mickey Mouse" boots I received were a godsend during the snows of December and January. They were completely made of gray rubber with a white smooth interior. I chuckled as Private Lee attempted to slip the thermals over his jump boots. A pair of calf-high rain boots and a poncho was issued for the forthcoming monsoons. The last item was the fur pile cap which could be folded down to warm the neck and ears. However, only the pile caps available in the village sported a furry visor. This extra clothing was an added fascination to the place itself.

By noon when the uniform issue was complete, we were herded onto a chocolate-brown army bus for a long ride north to Camp Ross to be in-processed at Personnel. We were interviewed by providing information for insurance and gratuity pay in case we were "killed in action" (KIA). It was then that we were marched to the arms room where we were issued an M14 rifle, a steel pot with liner, a harness with mess kit, and a protective mask. As buck privates, we were further indoctrinated on the honors of guard duty. That Friday night, our second in Korea, later burned brightly in my spring '65 memory when crushing beetles and lamenting my fate at Guard Tower One. Rapidly, surely, and with discouraged countenances, we came to the realization that Uncle Benny's "partying" was over with and army reality was sinking in. I was now an officially functioning army soldier in this Far East corner of Asia.

Personnel Duty Station
Saturday, November 14, 1964

Wide eyed, cross eyed, mesmerized
As north we rolled viewed and sighed
Vills, and fields, and campsites too
Much to take the mind it blew

I recall the extreme culture shock I experienced during the transport from Camp Ross to McGovern in the exhilarating chilliness of that calm morning twilight. We were ordered onto the beds of the deuce-and-a-halfs and trucked to our assigned Personnel Service Centers on the light foggy morning of Saturday, November 14, 1964. Extreme fatigue set in as I hauled and loaded the additional clothing and equipment. Up until this day, I had experienced instruction at ASCOM and a night of hellish guard duty at the indoctrination compound, Camp Ross. As the trucks rolled through Ross's main gate and onto the road, a whole new world of medieval countryside opened before me. I was fascinated by the quietude of the imposing mountains flanking the road on both sides in contrast to the Texas Plains where I grew up. As a youth I felt as if I was entering one of those intriguing fog-bound movies where the characters enter mysterious unknown lands with fantastic dreamscapes. I had traveled back to the Dark Ages, or perhaps was privileged in witnessing ancient Asia live. This new world could be likened to the landscape and villages of the Greek city-states in the readings of my youth.

My attention was attracted to a row of soaring derrick-like towers of electric power on the left planted in the calm and cold landscape. I asked a second-tour veteran regarding the flanking towers along the road. He replied he remembered them from his former duty year and that they were supposed to have been wired since then for civilian electricity to *our* North Country.

As the trucks rolled farther north, the stench of fecal matter became more apparent. It permeated the entire ambience, clogged the nasal passages, stifled the throat, and intoxicated the very soul. The agricultural fields extended to distant brown mountains at either side of the road. There were mountains and mountains and fields and fields everywhere, and between mountains and fields in this North Country I saw tiny settlements of conglomerated shacks "termed" villages amid army camps. I saw countless enclosed U.S. Army compounds confirming that this country was more like a war zone frozen in time rather than a U.S. Army stateside fort. All camps were surrounded by eight-foot-high poles attached with huge coils of barbwire and mesh. All compounds' perimeters were strategically dotted with structures, being the guard towers, and a main gate that displayed unit titles with respective colorful crests and emblems.

The busy villages with Asiatic writing and swarming GI's, the Oriental population and rice paddies and mountains, and the diesel exhaust compounded by the everpresent human fecal stench, seemed one huge busy live picture-puzzle—everyone and everything just seemed to belong and had a purpose. It was later explained to me that I was passing through a segment of the U.S. Army's occupation of the Western Corridor, which was the traditional invasion route from the Asiatic mainland as far north as China all the way down the peninsula through Seoul. This was the lowland that allowed for majority of the rice fields—or dense population—no where found as plentiful as in this segment of the corridor.

The trucks continued rolling north. Villages with numerous shops squeezed tightly side by side; no space spared. Those greater "city-villages" such as Yongju-Gol, Pobwan-Ni, and Munsan-Ni bustled with denser indigenous population. The overall shanty-like appearance of their homes and the mud-packed trails incessantly fascinated the novice in me as did the many GI's that swarmed the roads and shops. I was continually met with Asiatic stroked writing and a bit of lettering everywhere I cast my eyes. My attention was unavoidably drawn to the friendly female population with their welcoming smiles and shy demeanor. Then, the truck turned off the road and through the main gate of Camp Beard. Here, at Personnel Service Center Number Two, were dropped a few of our Payroll School graduates—we never thought we would ever see them again and for an extended period of the time did not. Bewildered as we were, the rest of us were continued out the main gate and back onto the road. I realized later that these fortunates were quartered by this greater village of Yongju-Gol. Had I not been quartered farther north, I would not have become aware of remote epic adventures, but would have focused on the soft "city life" of Yongju-Gol

Finally, after more countryside with its continued stench of human fecal and fluid waste, hamlets, and camps, our truck entered the main gate of

Camp McGovern where we were dropped off at Personnel Service Center Number Three. I calculated we had traveled an approximate length of a county within the state of Texas. We were all dumfounded and disoriented as we were finally marched to our receiving Quonset for Personnel indoctrination at this Far East corner of Asia.

Chapter 4

Camp McGovern, Nopae Dong, Korea

November 1964-March 1965

Prologue

    Korea was not only my first permanent duty station, but was also to be the first of many exciting world tours in the U.S. Army. I knew that somehow I would make use of every opportunity beginning with exploring the camp, then the local village, followed by the major villages, the alluring and finally grandest dream of touring *Seoul*, and the impossible dream: *Tokyo*! I was overwhelmed, and to think that it began at Camp McGovern, Korea.

Indoctrination
Saturday, November 14, 1964

A sunny morning calm with haze
As diesel, feces cause a craze
A dark and gloomy room with spiel
Of warning talks both true and real

We arrived at Camp McGovern, Korea, on a chilly Saturday, November 14, 1964. The sun was a pleasant light yellow as it covered the calm land on this hazy morning. The shocking overpowering stench of human fecal matter greeted us as it permeated the entire ambience. It offended our olfactory senses mixed with the stacked-up fumes of diesel exhaust. I remember that I was overwhelmed yet curious, as I assumed my first overseas duty station in the U.S. Army.

We were trucked in through the main gate and dropped off at the Personnel Quonsets. We were then politely ushered to an unlit and gloomy Quonset at the far left of the Personnel Service Center Number Three offices flanked by a barbwire fence under what became my favorite Guard Tower Two. This scene was to later remind me of Messala's somber quarters in *Ben Hur* and the grave atmosphere of the recruiting office in *Legionnaire*. My curiosity overcame me, so I stepped through the darkened Quonset to the backdoor and peeked at a diesel tank, the colonel's residence and his guard tower, and Guard Tower Two beside me; but what caught my attention was the imposing mountain, Easy Queen. Since we had not yet been assigned quarters, we were still burdened with the newly issued inclement-weather clothing and field equipment. I was still stunned with our weaponry that was neither a school supply nor office instrument other than in basic training; it was as if we were preparing for war. We all trooped in and sat bewildered, as we waited for the indoctrination lecture. As I settled in my seat, I laid my M14 with the barrel unintentionally pointing forward. No one corrected it. (I later learned that all rifles in Korea contained a pin in the trigger mechanism, enabling bullets to be fired so that we indeed were in a war zone!)

I STEPPED THROUGH THE DARKENED QUONSET TO THE BACKDOOR AND PEEKED AT THE DIESEL TANK, THE COLONEL'S RESIDENCE, AND HIS GUARD TOWER; AND GUARD TOWER NUMBER TWO BESIDE ME; BUT WHAT CAUGHT MY ATTENTION WAS THE IMPOSING MOUNTAIN, EASY QUEEN. (SEE PHOTO P. 299)

Presently, a multi-striped soldier entered and sat in the center-front of the room facing the taboo position of the rifle. He introduced himself as Master Sergeant O. I later learned he was nicknamed "Mother" because he had a mild way of touching the troops.

"Make yourselves as comfortable as possible," he said, as he began his lengthy spiel.

At first, I listened attentively as this was my first duty station in the U.S. Army! However, as a novice, my curiosity overcame me, and my mind wandered—the words forgotten until thirty years later—as I first surveyed the building. The entire barrack seemed to be constructed of corrugated sheet metal resembling a gigantic lengthwise-bisected cylinder. It reminded me of a grounded UFO without the flashing lights. There was an unscreened door at either end. Its length was lined with small protruding windows allowing limited sunlight. The lackluster color of the walls and sterile furnishings did nothing to stir my senses. In fact, because the outside was so different, it seemed drab and dreary by comparison.

"North Korea and the enemy are one point six miles in that direction," the sergeant continued pointing to the left of the barrack.

Behind "Mother" was one of the projected windows. It was through there that the outside world beckoned. I sat absorbed in thought as I stared at the wire mesh fence topped with menacing dull-gray galvanized concertina barbwire so prevalent in the morning sunshine. How long I pondered, I don't know, but eventually, my ears returned to "Mother's" speech.

"These people are professional thieves, do not play their game," he droned on.

However, my attention was quickly glued elsewhere focusing repeatedly from the sunny scenic distance through the window and back to the sergeant's subdued face. I was eventually rewarded by the action of a huge silver Korean "Kimchi" bus with a horizontal red stripe noisily making its way beyond the fence. The bus, different from American models, was my first Korean view of this country's rural transportation. I felt an overwhelming eagerness to mingle in fellowship with the Asiatic people within. However, the bus just seemed to noisily zoom by, trailing a cloud of dust.

"There are stripes to be made," continued the sergeant.

Beyond the fence, I could just make out the endless rice paddies like those on the cover of the DOD pamphlet. Ascending mountains beyond the fields on the horizon provided a brown autumnal backdrop to the scene. For an instant, a sense of adventure overcame me and swept me back to my childhood. I remembered as a child, how many times I had longed to explore outside the yard, beyond the picket fence which surrounded and confined my house—to explore the mystifying street extensions, back alleys, and the *beyond*. I craved to explore, clamber, and reconnoiter this irresistible terrain too. I remembered being awestruck at having read somewhere of the many Buddha statues that were scattered all over these mountains. I yearned to inspect this foreign soil and wander all over it, and maybe discover one or several Buddhas—alluring and fascinating statuary, like hidden jewels—waiting for me to be found and sent home as a prize or souvenir! It never occurred to me that these were not mine "just for the taking." The lecture ended abruptly. As newly deployed troops, we hurriedly collected our considerable gear. After racking our rifles and steel pots in the arms room, we were marched to our assigned quarters.

I can still recall this lovely, crisp November morning on my first day in Korea as an impressionable youth. It turned out to be one of my favorite memories. When we exited the dreary building, that whole unfamiliar camp and incredibly stinky landscape beyond the fence again opened up before me under the cold Korean sun. I scanned the Quonset-lined hills and military buildings with unit crests or the division emblem enclosed within the impressive and extensive barbwire sector. My eyes again contrasted and reinforced the sight of my duty station inside this prominent Asiatic rugged environment and the awesome and delightful but smelly terrain outside the camp. No matter what warnings "Mother" had issued regarding the inhabitants of the area, my sense of adventure overrode any danger that I was sublimely oblivious to.

A whole new world was beckoning. I felt as encumbered by the surrounding barbed cobwebs, which separated me from adventure, as the picket fence of my childhood home. Silently, I marveled at my good fortune. The Land of the Morning Calm with its Oriental mysteries was waiting. It was all mine to discover and explore as soon as I could escape these confines in search of adventure. I vowed to myself then and there that I would create ways to ensure I would welcome with open arms what lay ahead for me in the way of adventure in this Far East Corner of Asia.

BUCK PRIVATE IN FIELD DUTY UNIFORM

Buck Private Rituals
Monday, November 16-20, 1964

Easy tease the newly arrived
Faces and words simply contrived
Time alone experience derived
Then teasing others, now survived

"Who did he kill?" asked Private First Wain of no one in particular as he continued swinging his pick and at stabbing the stone-stiff ground. We were all digging our foxholes in the hard Korean frozen earth that early Monday morning of November 16, 1965, and as newly arrived buck privates, we were being teased mercilessly by other privates. There was an on-going mania among all soldiers regarding the number of days remaining in the tour of duty in Korea. The army termed this a hardship tour. Responding, I answered "three hundred and sixty-five days." Upon hearing the response I gave, all the senior privates laughed uproariously and simultaneously called out "lifer!" Later I learned the secret of their merriment. An unwritten rule universally held that a lifer had duty remaining in the three digits days, a "short-timer" in double digits days, and a "short," in the enviable single digits days.

I was an enlisted man, a volunteer, and I *wanted* to go to Korea, but I immediately realized others, actually most of the other guys were draftees, and considered this assignment really a hardship. Despite the fact that these draftees were better off in Korea than in Vietnam, they considered being sent half way around the world to a peaceful country, a hardship. These men had left behind wives, jobs, and families, while the enlisted volunteers joined up to avoid the draft. It was the draftees, titled Army of the United States, who "suffered" the most. We, the enlisted, or the volunteers, were titled Regular Army of the United States. I guess it made a difference only on paper because we were all equally affected by culture shock and duty. In my case, I was jubilantly free from dysfunctional circumstances where any life away from home was upgrading, and I would grow. Some privately confided to me that they too experienced delight at knowing Korea was their assignment until they arrived, understood what the duty entailed, and timely joined the teasing crowd. Still there prevailed a general spirit of patiently awaiting the day for a flight back stateside. As for me it was just the beginning of a year full of fun.

Our group of new arrivals had just departed "Uncle Benny's Rest Home" in Indianapolis, Indiana five days earlier. Titled "Uncle Benny's" because of the privileges and comforts we assumed would be constant wherever we were stationed. We were so "spoiled" wearing our greens with coats and ties as the daily uniform as we went about our classes. We secretly considered ourselves the elite of the army because we were *payroll specialists*. We were *finance*!

What a letdown! Arriving at our duty station that Saturday, there fell upon us the reality of our true overseas duty on Monday. We were crestfallen and disappointed. Gone were the days of "rest home" privileges and comforts. Bad humor and grumbling were rampant—and my feet were freezing. We all dreamed we'd be working in permanent offices, with a professional environment, with nice office machines, and perhaps cubicles for privacy, and the continued aura of specialized office workers. Hello! Like having ice water dropped from above, we awoke to the realization that we were just ordinary soldiers with duties in the field—just like in the U.S. Army. Loading all of our personal, cumbersome field equipment plus all the office field furniture and machines as we would be fully operational in the field as at the camp office was the first dog-tiring segment of my initial field experience. I could not understand why the field file cabinets were so weighty, if all they were to contain were folders. Later I discovered they were loaded with veterans' private stores of goodies and cans of softdrinks. Once, in the field I glanced around, Private McC had been ordered to dig a trench around the oversized office tent. His face was redder than usual as he bent to his work, jabbing at the earth in dissatisfaction. His face had taken on a permanently disconsolate expression. Interestingly enough, I never wondered what faces I might be making that my peers were keenly observing. Having drunk my canteen dry, I proceeded to the army dark-green ovular-shaped water trailer for a refill. The big swig of the processed potable water I swallowed tasted like something out of a sewer, which further added to my miseries. That evening, however when we each finished our foxholes, a coworker, Private McG, and I were so dog-tired that when we pitched our two-man tent, we slid into our sleeping bags and with our rifles and field gear between us, conked out immediately. Curiously enough, I guess the senior privates pulled guard that night.

The following morning after a good night's sleep we all slipped out of our mummy sleeping bags and our pup tents in our long johns, and dressed as rapidly as possible under the freezing Korean sun. We eagerly lined up for a hot breakfast of either eggs or "shot on shingles." After a lifetime of oatmeal for breakfast and beans and rice for lunch and dinner, I loved it and wolfed it all down. Our camp was suddenly invaded with Korean youngsters, boys standing around for a morsel of our food. I beckoned one over and gave him of my food and had him drink out of my cup.

OUR CAMP WAS SUDDENLY INVADED WITH KOREAN YOUNGSTERS, AND BOYS STANDING AROUND AND WITH THEIR A-FRAMES FOR A MORSEL OF OUR FOOD.

As the newly arrived buck privates, we were saddled with the worst of the camp duties. We hand-carried a five-gallon diesel can from the fuel trucks to the office tent, then we dug a company latrine over which we placed a wooden box with a hole on it, then we took over the graveyard guard duty shift, and during the day stood ground or held the perimeter with our M14 rifles or M60 machine guns, while the rest of the troops went to chow. On my first day after arrival, we unknowingly filled the five-gallon diesel can with gasoline for the stove that heated the office tent. As we trooped in with the gasoline, the sergeant chewed us out. We had to do it all over again and return with diesel. Little did we realize we could have blown up the entire Personnel office camp!

As newly graduated payroll clerks when we arrived, we had probably acted snobbish or arrogant due to our assignment in Personnel. I noticed, however, since our arrival, the rest of the camp personnel viewed us with suspicious, excluding, and dismissive side-glances as if saying, "You haven't seen anything yet," or "You don't know what you're in for." We all felt the anxiety that came from the stonewalling soldiers resulting in our plight of being pointedly ignored. None of the senior privates bothered to talk to us or befriend us. Most would just glance at us and literally turn and walk away without a word. We were not given a smile or even an unfriendly sneer. Our forced landing into the "real world of soldiering," resulted in disappointment and a broken spirit, until we became acclimated to our situation. Little by little we made friends among the seniors and were introduced to the dreariness and monotony of camp life and duty. Office life was no problem because the officers and sergeants got us down to business, and we found ourselves immersed in office work. I found that self-indoctrination was the key. We had to accept the hardship spirit of the duty of the country and doubly so as new arrivals instantly indoctrinated by harshest experience: the week-long field duty. We understood that no explanation could express the situation. We each had to go through this difficult experience alone. I then understood what the Kingston Trio lyrics meant when they sang, "You gotta walk that lonesome valley, you gotta walk it by yourself." We became resigned to the duty, and the definition of hardship. We came to terms with reality and simply accepted our plight—that we, "the elite of the army," were just plain army soldiers and infantrymen in a hardship state of affairs, with freezing feet, yet we had to make the best of it.

 The senior privates sporadically teased us all that eternal week, which finally ended Friday the twentieth. They were "short" and we were "lifers." A few weeks later, our entire role changed when we received new arrivals straight from Payroll School. This was especially educational since most soldiers, we in-processed infantrymen, were trained for war. So we did not necessarily explain to the new payroll clerks what they were in for. We had a vision of ourselves a few months earlier just as our senior privates had viewed us. We understood: the senior privates were acclimated to the duty and the country and had acquired a life, while *our* army life was still in its infancy. Like the others, we teased the new arrivals and knew that one day those new arrivals would do the same: tease other arrivals to this Far East Corner of Asia.

THE GUARDHOUSE AT CAMP MCGOVERN AS AT ALL CAMPS WAS JUST ANOTHER BARRACK. AUTHOR IN GUARD DUTY UNIFORM: FIELD JACKET WITH AMMO AND FIRST AID POUCH ON WEB BELT, FIELD PANTS AND PILE CAP.

Guardhouse Blues
November 1964–March 1965

Quiet was the guard house hall
Silence echoed wall to wall
Sleep there was for one and all
Death to life at sergeant's call

My first exposure to guard duty was in Korea. In the States, I had been exempt as a squad leader in Basic Training and Advanced Individual (Personnel) Training. Guard duty consisted of three units: *first guard, second guard, and third guard* and each guard posted *two walks*—twice a week and every other weekend. During the *first walk*, first guard posted the fence or the tower, while second and third guard slept. Then second guard relieved first guard, so that first and third guard slept. Consequently, when third guard relieved second guard, first and second guard slept. Thus first walk ended, and the repetition was known as *second walk*. In effect, each soldier walked two and a half hours twice during his ten-hour night and slept for five consecutive hours.

I preferred and always selected first guard as all sentries of second and third guard were still awake from the daily routine and the guardhouse was already alight, so it was impossible to rest so early during normal daily "wake" time.

The guardhouse at Camp McGovern, as at all camps, was just another barrack with the sergeant of the guard's quarters located at the entry. The sergeant's quarters were partitioned from the guards' bunks and had the only permissible light after first guard's first walk. Each guard bunked on its own side (row) of the guardhouse so that the sergeants easily located the next guard for the next walk.

The First Battalion Seventh Cavalry augmented our guard duty at McGovern. They always came in late during first guard, and with first and second guard taken, they were assigned third guard. It was during their arrival on first guard and "wake time" that they would hit the PX and were always munching on candy bars, sipping cokes, and reading magazines. All lights were on, so no one slept.

The cold-weather clothing, consisting of woolen olive greens, thermal underwear, windproof parkas and pant shells with liners, gloves, and insulated boots was crucial for winter duty. I quickly found the field jackets and thermals sufficiently comfortable for the November cold. The windproof parkas with liners were vital protection for the December through February wind and snow. The Korean pile cap had a furry wrap fashioned with extended earflaps that fully and comfortably sheltered the nape of the neck and the ears to the chin when folded down. These caps made us appear like Asiatic soldiers from the mainland. Wool socks and jump boots did little to warm my feet, thus the thermal (Mickey Mouse) boots were a Godsend for guard duty.

One night, a sleepless newly arrived buck private, sitting zombie-like, observed me as I arrived from first walk. I remember removing my parka and loosening my belt. I spun the pile cap backward so that the lengthy nape-flap covered my eyes up to my nose, and ears. I was thus assured darkness with all stray sounds muffled and free breathing. Finally, I dropped on the bunk, boots on the foot rail, parka as cover, and head on the pillow in this mummy-like position—accustomed to in-field sleeping bags. As I was fatigued, sleep immediately closed in on me, and I heard the faraway onlooker say, "Well, I'll be damned." I did not realize until decades later that the observer was addressing my sleep prep. Sleep was broken only by the sergeant's kick on the bunk for next walk.

The only time I can remember ever regretting joining the military was during a turn at the guardhouse. I was burned out, exhausted, and on overload. I was resigned to the never-ending outdoor duty during inclement weather including the tedium of guard duty and field maneuvers, the unaccustomed living quarters, and all other drudgeries that were building up on me. From the recessed darkness, I remember gazing at the sergeant's lit quarters as I lay on my side sullenly lamenting, "Why did I join this man's army?" Yet I was proud of being a soldier in the U.S. Army, and I had expected duty somewhat of this nature since my childhood—all part of the job. However, after a good night's sleep, all my regrets were left behind with my exhaustion, and I was ready for another round of adventure.

The only guard duty blessing was the privilege of sleep-in the entire next half day. Some sergeants allowed us to go directly from the tower or walking post to quarters without customarily reporting to and sleeping in the guardhouse following second walk. Once when I was assigned third guard, the magnanimous sergeant allowed me to go see "Kissing Cousins," the featured movie at the camp theater across McGovern Boulevard from the guardhouse.

One night, we, the dead to the world, were returned to life by the medics. They were on a surprise "short arm's inspection," a medical examination for venereal disease. Not yet fully conscious, I had a difficult time finding myself through layers and layers of inclement-weather clothing. Fortunately,

I succeeded, was examined, and was excused. I vaguely remember, however, that two sentries from my walk were cited, confined to quarters, and required to report to the dispensary.

I found great comfort in reminding myself that throughout my childhood life I had expected worse from the military, and that if sub-zero guard duty was the worse the army required, it was a cut-rate price for whatever wonders lay ahead for me. Of seasonal guard duty, it was the winter station that impressed me the most as we rarely experienced snow in central Texas. Despite the fatigue of this tedious duty, the guardhouse duty hours were the only place and time that assured sound, quiet rest and immediate deep sleep. While we all detested guard duty, we all slept in relatively comfortable luxury in direct contrast to the brothers at the DMZ (demilitarized zone) at this Far East corner of Asia.

In the words of a medical corpsman:

> "During April 1973 I was a medical corpsman with 1st Battalion, 15th Field Artillery Regiment, and went with an advance team to the DMZ, prior to our Battalion Operational Readiness Training Test. We received orders to patrol in search of North Korean infiltrators. Some fired their rifles into the darkness believing they had targets, but no casualties. No one slept really well through the night. Toward early morning we heard more rifle fire, and then at least one extremely loud explosion—a North Korean artillery round that hit the edge of our camp. Almost immediately one of our howitzers fired in response. I realized that I had better get around checking for casualties. Several men of one howitzer crew had suffered bruises, cuts, etc. After cleaning and dressing these injuries I drove some to Camp Greaves. I had not extracted any shrapnel, but the physician did; these men remained at Camp Greaves. Next morning I saw a ROK Army truck—in back were two dead bodies covered in canvas. The ROKs grabbed the bodies by their ankles and dragged them into the ROK camp. These were North Korean infiltrators killed by the ROKS during the previous night."
>
> —SP4 Michael Witmer, Medical Corpsman,
> Attached to 1st Bn, 15th Arty Field Regt,
> Korea, 1973

DMZ MILITARY POLICE JEEP MOMENTARILY PARKED AT NCO CLUB, CAMP ROSS.

I STOOD FACE-CHILLED IN THE EIGHTEEN-FOOT-HIGH OPEN-AIR GUARD TOWER NUMBER FOUR THAT WAS CONSTRUCTED OF WOOD POSTS AND SLATS.

Guard Tower Four
November 1964–March 1965

To reach the rise through many crawls
By climbing slides with icy falls
Then bitter gales through open walls
That sliced the guard through open stalls

How could I ever forget Guard Tower Number Four! It was located at the farthest northwest corner of Camp McGovern by the ammo dump and hidden by the only prominent landmark at McGovern, the water tank. This godforsaken place required a steep crawl with slipping, sliding, and falling at climbing up the icy downstream to reach the desolate post. The boxed-in duty station faced Easy Queen with the charge being to prevent unauthorized trespassing via the barbwire fence.

As newly arrived buck privates, innocent of its isolation, we were promptly initiated to this abhorred outpost. I stood silently, my face chilled, in the eighteen-foot-high open-air watchtower constructed of wood posts and slats. It was meant to keep the sentry awake without the luxury of a seat. Without the benefit of a telephone, but wired for one as were others, I felt like a sitting duck, an easy target—the prime victim of certain death in case of infiltration. It had once boasted a mint green color, but after years of service it was dirty, weather-beaten; and the carved graffiti vouched for its many occupants. The chilly November wind of 1964 blustered mercilessly right through the open posts. However, my Korean fur pile cap and windproof parka made the duty physically bearable. Most of the time, we were armed with a shotgun, but this day I carried a baseball bat (although the purpose of the bat was anybody's guess). There was nothing else to do but maintain vigilance on my two-and-half-hour "guard-walk."

From atop Number Four, I examined my initial charge at McGovern. Number Four faced west, and Mt. Easy Queen towered before me. The curved fence offered the only semblance of motion on the mountain groundswell alongside the path within, worn smooth by countless walking sentinels. What appeared to me a procession of webbed unsharpened pencils in a lineup was in reality a fence of square posts connected by stretched barbwire mesh topped with concertina at the base and on crosspieces. North and to my right was the ammo dump comprised of tiny houses, all secured by tiny doors to mark their entrance. Panning right, northeast and partly behind Tower Four, I spied faraway Koom-Shi, Camps Coursen and Paris, which appeared as misty mirages (silent apparitions with little or no visible life) on the calm cold land. The hill on the east and southeast behind the tower was completely blocked by what could have been the only notable view of McGovern peaked with its highest structure—the water tank, a prominent landmark. Guard Tower Number Three due south, was visible distantly from Number Four along the fence. I had turned full circle back to Easy Queen with its doe-brown sloping foothills in all its bare majesty, where warfare had raged a decade earlier. Later in my experience, I would discover a burial mound beyond the fence.

Because of the nature of guard duty with nothing but time on my hands, one afternoon I made a phenomenal observation. I became aware of the lazy sunshine as it progressively lit the contoured landscape.

NUMBER FOUR FACED THE QUEEN WITH THE CURVED FENCE THAT OFFERED THE ONLY SEMBLANCE OF MOTION ON THE MOUNTAIN GROUNDSWELL ALONGSIDE THE PATH WITHIN, WORN SMOOTH BY COUNTLESS WALKING SENTINELS. LATER IN MY EXPERIENCE, I WOULD DISCOVER A BURIAL MOUND BEYOND THE FENCE (AT FOOT OF POLE). (SEE PHOTO P. 299)

Queen's foothills cast looming shadows as the light crossed my field of view. As the sun lethargically rose to its zenith, all of her eastern secrets slowly opened to me—her every nook, corner, cranny, crag, crevice, jutting protrusions, minor curves, and vegetation gradually teased me as she revealed herself all the way up her skirts and bluffs to her peak. She exclusively taunted me when twilight darkened her skirts. I vowed then and there that before I departed Korea, I would ascend and claim her lofty bluff for me and me alone! At 6:00 p.m., it got quite cold on Number Four. The setting sun behind the immediate towering Queen brought in the chill and increased shadows very early in the afternoon. As lampposts lit up, it facilitated night viewing.

Alone, on one of those icy, chilly, and calm Korean evenings while observing from my post, I caught sight of a tiny faraway fuzz ball creeping along the mountain foothill outside the fence. It entered from the far right of the mountain skirt above the ammo dump and into my field of view. Soon the bundle developed a little body that resembled a white layer-clothed doll. It was a *papasan*, an elderly family gentleman bearing his burden of brushwood on his A-frame. I marveled at the *papasan's* stamina as he bore his top heavy load

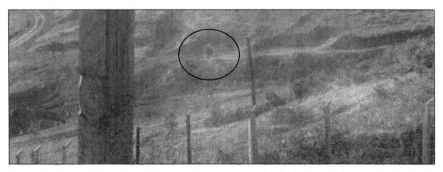

A *PAPASAN* BEARING HIS BURDEN OF BRUSHWOOD ON HIS A-FRAME BROUGHT LIFE TO GUARD TOWER FOUR.

on his back and with an even pace, drew closer and closer to the camp before the tower, outside the barbed wire fence. The quiet, calm, and chilly day with the wood bearer in transit appeared to me a perfect setting for an Oriental mural. I became intrigued by this third world mode of existence and the determination with which he passed by the military area, in *his homeland*, not pausing or turning right or left. He was aware of the sentinel in the *pocho* (guard) hooch (the hovels they had as homes) but gave me as much notice as required—none. Since I was new in Korea, other than my readings, I knew next to nothing of the actual culture. I concluded though, that the brush on his back would either supplement his income or warm his hooch. As he crossed Number Four, I wondered about the *papasan's* life. How did he come by the brush? Where was he going? How many children did he have? Was he a grandfather? I hurriedly drew my instamatic 126 camera from my magazine pouch and snapped a shot just as he trudged into range. As he advanced toward the tower's left pillar (my view), his back fully displayed his huge bundle on two seemingly small white legs. At that instant I realized my position was somewhat part of the *papasan's* life, perhaps an American intruder in *his domain,* yet the *papasan* as a person would never be part of my world.

This was the most dreaded and shunned post. Still, it was at Number Four where I was provided time for deep thought and contemplation. Also, it was in this isolated and quiet corner that I became one with my queen as my tinnitus increased in loudness accompanied by the sounds of silence. Distractions were rare and as such were welcomed. The Korean November scenario became an etching in my memory. Those Korean days, although bathed in yellow sunshine, were cold and icy. I, a proud fresh-faced, green-clad young soldier (dreaming about this manly military duty at eighteen since boyhood) stood at a lone tower by the foot of the quiet dusky mountain. There I patiently awaited tomorrow's wonders in my first army overseas assignment in this Far East corner of Asia.

NORTH, AND TO MY RIGHT WAS THE AMMUNITION DUMP COMPRISED OF TINY HOUSES ALL SECURED BY TINY DOORS TO MARK THEIR ENTRANCE.

PANNING RIGHT NORTHEAST BEHIND TOWER FOUR, I SPIED ON FARAWAY KOOM-SHI; AND CAMPS COURSEN AND PARIS THAT APPEARED AS MISTY MIRAGES ON THE CALM COLD LAND. IMMEDIATELY AT PHOTO RIGHT WAS THE (LANDMARK) WATER TANK.

I ADMIRED THE MILITARY EXACTITUDE AND ALIGNMENT OF THE PARKED DEUCE-AND-A-HALF-AND THREE-QUARTER-TON TRUCKS, JEEPS, AND TANKS.

Motor Pool Guard Post
January 1965

Dark and black 'mid icy white
Chill and freeze with frosty bite
Midnight clear 'neath lamp post bright
'Round a wonderland by night

The Motor Pool was a preferred post as it was located in the center of the compound where the sentry could find shelter and comfort between the vehicles. The sentinels in the towers surveyed the first line of security at the barbwire perimeter that enclosed the camp.

I remember walking into an icy winter wonderland of snow that January of 1965 from the warm comfort of the cozy guardhouse. The whole earth was covered with a blinding blanket of glowing white that sharply contrasted with the black shadows and dark buildings in the deathly quiet atmosphere. The cracking of the snow crunching under my Mickey Mouse boots was loud and broke the freezing night's sounds of silence as I made my way to the Motor Pool guard post. My feet were toasty warm snuggled within my thermal boots as I walked on the frozen ground. This warm experience, unlike my previous freezing feet of November and December, turned out a cozy misadventure.

After successfully responding to the guard's challenges, I relieved the sentry who handed me a shotgun and three shells. I recalled my orders that I was not to chamber a shell until challenging an intruder three times. Only then, could I chamber a round in the weapon and call out three more challenges. Finally, after another two challenges, I could shoot to kill. It was a dragged-out process which would certainly lead to the soldier's demise if the intruder was determined. At that time, I did not consider that this procedure was to avoid a "trigger happy" mistake that could lead to disaster. The general order was "To walk my post in a military manner observing everything within sight or hearing," and it echoed in my brain and reminded me of basic training. There certainly was much to observe at the vehicle post.

The numerous lampposts lit the Motor Pool as clear as daylight beneath the jet-black sky. I admired the military exactitude and alignment of the parked deuce-and-a half- and the three-quarter-ton trucks, jeeps, tanks, and the commander's helicopter. All were topped with about a three-inch layer of snow that contrasted with the dark recesses and corners where the snow could not reach. I was reminded of a story we had read in Mrs. Ruth Robinson's literature class as a sophomore two years earlier. It told of a mechanic at such a motor pool in Korea who made use of his ingenious capability to replace his general's jeep engine with another from a civilian sedan. During a bombardment, the speed of the higher-performing engine confused the enemy and the general's life was saved. I chuckled at the Korean memory I was experiencing and made a mental note to write to Mrs. Robinson and relate this recollection I had while walking guard at the Motor Pool.

THE MOTOR POOL (LEFT) HOUSED ALL VEHICLES INCLUDING TRUCKS, JEEPS, AND TANKS; WITH NEARBY HELICOPTERS (CENTER).

As I walked my charge, the glare under the intensely lit post limited my observation beyond the pool's perimeter. Under the blinding incandescence, my eyes had difficulty repeatedly focusing and refocusing from the bright snowy outlying area to the shadows of the nearby vehicles. I decided to withdraw and mingle within the safety of the shadows and lingered between the transports. Thus I inconspicuously secured my charge and simultaneously observed the snow-white area *within sight or hearing*.

Pausing a few moments, I quickly realized that walking increased my blood flow and warmth. At first my steamy breath formed an icy frost on the furry hood that stung my nose. The cold froze my trigger finger. The bulky mittens afforded the option of the immediate transfer of the index finger to the only fabric flange. Concealed elastic bands fastened the leather (palm) and fabric extension of the windproof mittens at the middle of the forearm. The windproof parka and shelled liners maintained my growing eighteen-year-old body warm to my very bones in the frosty, stinging calm of the night. I remember shaping the wired furry hood opening to accommodate my nose and eyes to increase my peripheral vision. In my ignorance, I had no idea that my warm breath formed mini vapor clouds in the scant light as I walked between the monstrous tanks disclosing my presence. The accumulated vapor settled and gelled on the parka's fur beneath my nose while my breath melted it again and caused a trickle around my lips. Periodically I readjusted and wiped the wired hood as the soggy fur tickled my nostrils.

Having nothing to occupy my two-and-a-half-hour walk but observing the silent landscape, I moved out onto a snowy hillside on one of those duty nights. I scratched out a horse's head with the useless baseball bat (alternately assigned as a weapon). I had learned to sketch a horse head with the least number of strokes while in high school. (I was dubbed "Horse" by Henry, the class comedian, who had decided to get at me before I got to him.) On a second walk, I noticed the added words *"Mule."* The previous guard had taken note and qualified the etching.

A HELICOPTER LANDING BY MOTOR POOL. NOTE WIDE PATH TO NOPAE AT UPPER RIGHT.

The Motor Pool was considered high risk as it was not enclosed with barbwire and all vehicle parts were at a premium in the third world country and thievery was quite common. The military transports remained a prize doubly secured at this Far East Corner of Asia.

Chapter 5

God and Country

Prologue

Where there are groups of men far away from the structure of family and home with sinful pleasures overwhelmingly and openly available below wholesale prices, despite the presence of ecclesiastical guidance, the best well-bred person could very well succumb to the decadent environment. As a practicing Mormon, I had to admit the need for spiritual guidance in the life of the serviceman.

**EIGHTH UNITED STATES ARMY RETREAT CENTER
PROGRAM COVER**

Note: It is traditional to address the men and women in our faith as brother and sister, respectively, as it is to shake hands. The association of the membership for worship or recreation is known as fellowship. To magnify, means to righteously practice.

SERVICES WERE HELD AT THE CHAPEL LOCATED IMMEDIATELY TO THE LEFT OF THE MAIN GATE OF CAMP PELHAM BY THE GREATER VILLAGE OF MUNSAN-NI.

The Camp Pelham Branch
December 1964–November 1965

To lay before Him feelings rent
Recurring soldiers came and went
Seniors and juniors all had bent
The knee, bowed head that He had lent

"Brother Martinez, I am unable to serve today," one of the brothers quietly advised me, and I silently understood the walking of wayward paths. No one ever questioned with *whys*, since one of the church's prime objectives is to "perfect the saints" (members) in due course. He and many of the brothers were treading on wayward waters, and I was no exception. The return missionaries—those who had served two years of full-time service away from home and generally the draftees—were always primed for Sunday service and for performing the Sacrament. They were the quorum instructors and group leaders, and Brother (Private First) Fountaine was one. I always cherished the moral standards Brother Fountaine magnified.

Called to serve as Second Counselor in the Camp Pelham Branch of the Church of Jesus Christ of Latter Day Saints (The Mormons), I held the stewardship of conducting services in the absence of the branch president. Brother (Staff Sergeant) Jeffords, then Brother (Captain) Galbraith, and lastly Brother (Specialist Fifth) Brittain were consecutive branch presidents during my tenure in Korea. Brother Fountaine was called to serve as First Counselor. That one time the branch president was an enlisted soldier while a commissioned officer was his counselor—confirming that all brethren were equal in church—was not surprising.

Services were held at the chapel located immediately to the left of the main gate of Camp Pelham by the greater village of Munsan-Ni. Attendance was low due to the nature of the service: guard duty, field problems, maneuvers, charge of quarters, and any numerous details the service required.

One of the greatest blessings after services was that the bretheren convened at the Camp Pelham Mess Hall for lunch. All ranks, the officers and the enlisted men, fellowshipped at the same table. I observed that the Specialist Fifth brother respectfully addressed the Captain, as I respectfully addressed the Specialist Fifth *and* the Captain. Nevertheless, a warm glow and spiritual unity bridged the ranks, which was the respect for the Priesthood—as all were ordained ministers with respective stewardships (ecclesiastical assignment). A Korean brother that lived in Munsan-Ni attended services with us. He could not have lunch at the mess hall with his military brothers, and it pained me to watch him walk toward the main gate and home.

POSED WITH BRASS TEMPLE PLATE ARE BROTHERS FIRST COUNSELOR (SP5) BRITTAIN, SECOND COUNSELOR (PFC) MARTINEZ, AND BRANCH PRESIDENT (SERGEANT) JEFFORDS AT RETREAT CENTER, SEOUL.

Every Sunday Brother Galbraith, the branch president, sent his jeep to McGovern for me, and at times he showed up unexpectedly to personally wake me. I was overwhelmed to have a commanding officer of an artillery unit checking my presence even at my warm bunk in the Quonset. Other times a sleepy runner from the telephone hooch trotted to my hooch announcing that the Captain was at the main gate and would be at the Quonset presently. The best times were when the jeep arrived without the Captain, and I rode shotgun (front passenger) with all personnel saluting the captain's bars posted on the jeep's grill. (Decades later, I realized that although duty precluded the captain's Sunday attendance, he *was there* for me—a lesson for me to learn and eventually be there for others—an action totally unrelated to military duty.)

There were times when I felt awkward in Brother Galbraith's presence, especially while fellowshipping at the pastry shop or the PX—the rule in the army being "no fraternizing between the ranks." At first I was apprehensive that a captain would regard me so brotherly, and I asked if I should salute first and then shake hands or vice versa. Brother Galbraith replied either way, but in reflection I knew better: the regulation salute would precede the time-honored handshake. I never once forgot, knowing all too well, that I was a private in the U.S. Army—in this case the Captain doubled as my military superior and church group leader in this Far East corner of Asia.

RETREAT CENTER ENTRANCE, SEOUL

December 1964:
Joyous Christmas-A First

The note, the pass, the bus to Seoul
To worship Him with heart and soul
Three lovely dolls but not for me
A brother from across the see

On an early December morning of 1964, being my fifth week on overseas duty, I was pleasantly surprised with a letter from the branch president of my church. A three-day pass to Seoul was enclosed. Staff Sergeant Horn, my section chief, approached me and asked me to sign it, that I was going to Seoul to attend a church service. Bewildered, I signed the mysterious document in English with Korean script, and in due course set out on my first "official" but "purposeful" adventure to . . . *Glorious Seoul!* I never wondered how the church discovered me so soon after my arrival far-off overseas; I just accepted it as church standard.

This Christmas conference was where I met Brother Galbraith and other military members from all over Korea. For the first time since my arrival in Korea (in the army for that matter), I felt I was *home*, once more within my element. During a moment between sermons I, along with some brethren, visited the Yongsan PX and walked the chilled streets of Seoul to Pagoda Park, but we visited only a few other places because worship services prioritized sightseeing.

AUTHOR ON CHRISTMAS WEEKEND, 1964, WITH YONGSAN PX IN BACKGROUND. WE WALKED THE CHILLED STREETS OF SEOUL TO PAGODA PARK.

The Christmas activities included the joint servicemen's and missionary's conference with the Korean congregation at the Sam Chung Dong Branch in Northeast Seoul. I was pleasantly surprised when the voices of our Korean sisters outshone our strong masculine voices while singing the Christmas carols and hymns. The greatest significance of these conferences was that the military from all branches and both civilian genders from all cultures meant they were well-attended. It was neutral turf at its greatest spiritual magnitude. During the customary fellowshipping following the conference a number of young women approached us servicemen and engaged us in short, limited conversation. Not until years later did it cross my mind that these sisters could be prospective eternal mates.

That evening after the conference, soldiers and missionaries congregated at the Mission Home for a Christmas party. There was much laughter and gaiety and everyone was in good spirits. The food was superb with five-gallon jugs of eggnog or punch. Following the plentiful feast, we sang Christmas carols. That was the best Christmas I had enjoyed thus far in my life. To have enjoyed it while far from my homeland made the memory more precious.

OUR KOREAN SISTERS OUTSHONE OUR STRONG MASCULINE VOICES WHILE SINGING CHRISTMAS CAROLS AND HYMNS.

I had met Brother In Soon Lee, a Korean brother in Texas, and fellowshipped with him my entire high-school senior year. I mentioned Brother In Soon's name to the mission president. I was pleasantly surprised the following morning when family, Brother Choong Kil, and Sister Koom Ja arrived at the Mission Home. Their friendship was open and gracious while they cordially led me on a two-day tour, taking in the highlights of Seoul. I always seemed to end up sitting in the taxi's rear seat with the very pretty sister, Sister Koom Ja. It never occurred to me in my naïveté that perhaps I should have taken serious note of her. During one part of the two-day tour, Brother Choong Kil exited the taxi by the capitol at the northern end of the Seoul Boulevard, leaving me alone with Sister Koom Ja for the remainder of the long ride down the Seoul Boulevard to the USO. It took me thirty-plus years to realize that Brother Choong Kil might have done this on purpose because Sister Koom Ja could be a potential eternal mate. However, my youthful free spirit was seeking adventure, and I was not ready for any serious consideration regarding any serious relationship at the time. Forty years later, I learned that the entire family had migrated to the United States and settled in San Francisco.

One evening, following the Christmas servicemen's dinner at the Retreat Center in Seoul, two beautiful and "dolled-up" Korean young women glided toward me. One handed me a postcard from Brother In Soon in San Antonio. The message was in Korean script with my full name in letters. I was taken aback by the two girls' radiance and especially by their "forward" manner. There was a well-known rumor that two girls had made it plain that they wanted to find American husbands in church, and to my surprise, these were they! I suddenly realized it was one of those two girls who had dated my buddy Brother Fountaine back at the Cav and of whom he had once raved about! However, I was too stunned. Just then an air force sergeant rescued me from this uncomfortable situation. Relieved, I quietly slipped away leaving the sergeant to flirt with them and if he wanted, he could follow up on their husband hunting. All was fair in love and war I reflected, they had the right to the pursuit of happiness, and these were beautiful sisters. I never gave the girls (or any other girl) any serious thought. I learned at the next retreat that that particular air force sergeant was advanced to Elder and remained in Korea to serve a full time mission. As a two-year missionary, he would live the strict life of a recluse and of closely supervised service—so much for the girls' chances with him to marry and migrate to the United States, I reflected during my service at this Far East corner of Asia.

My Mission
February 1965

Far from camp was church of choice
Still there was the still small voice
Tears of sadness, tears of pain
Tears and pleas at His feet lain

I began my first unofficial missionary labor by searching for members of the Church of Jesus Christ of Latter Day Saints in all the Personnel records in my charge, while at McGovern. I dared not search other records outside my charge but requested of Lieutenant Daniels, the Personnel Commanding Officer, if he could order such a monumental hunt for me. He replied that Personnel did not have the time, but he did authorize me to search the records of the entire division by myself! Because of the overwhelming duty with the Form 20s, I never got around to it. I did locate two members right there in camp, Brother (Private First) D.G. and Brother (Specialist Fifth) R.B. Brother D.G. heard my invitation to church but related that he did not want to attend services. "... at least not while I'm in the army," he said. Brother R.B. was a middle-aged soldier who expressed concern, but his faraway look did not convey interest in attending. Then, to my dismay, I finally found Brother (Private) R.S. (whom I had a terrible time locating) in the stockade! I always felt a certain responsibility, though far from my control, to visit Brother R.S. Later, I reflected that I had no right to search official military records in my care for personal use. Still, as a member of the church, I had both the spiritual and moral obligation of seeking out the brotherhood and perhaps some brothers would not appreciate being found. Also, all members know that the church is always there for us and that one way or another someone will find us—as Brother Galbraith located me less than one month into my arrival in Korea. In the end, I found great consolation that the commanding officer approved the full search thus pacifying my conscience between God and country.

Perhaps I experienced conflicting emotions about God and country. Because of my adventurous spirit and due to the fact that the military assured and facilitated travel abroad, I had always planned on a military career. Yet, I also knew I had always wanted to serve the Lord a full-time two-year mission. My subconscious was regulated by Divine Providence. As a full time missionary, I would preach the gospel anywhere in the world as assigned. At the PX, I ordered two topcoats, one of camel hair and another of cashmere. I also purchased five suits, four of tweed and one of sharkskin. The total expenditure was $265, a little over five months' pay. I mailed them home with the forethought of serving a mission following my military discharge if I did not reenlist.

I could not have known that a certain return sister-missionary with sparkling green eyes, who was foreordained to honor me and capture my heart, awaited me at El Paso. My plans were ambivalent: reenlistment with world travels or a full-time mission? As Divine Providence would have it, a third mission prevailed—a Celestial Marriage. Twenty-five years later, significantly, my son sported my cashmere topcoat on his mission to Germany. Thus my "either" plans were dissolved with family commitment.

ATTENDANCE AT CHURCH AND CONFERENCES MADE ALL THE DIFFERENCE DURING MY "HARDSHIP" TOUR OF DUTY IN KOREA.

It never occurred to me (until forty years later) that perhaps an additional reason for being so miserable during my three-month assignment at Camp Ross was the lack of my own church involvement. Although I attended nondenominational services, I was unable to attend services and fellowship at the far-off Camp Pelham due to the lack of transportation. Camp McGovern, Camp Pelham, and later Camp Blue Lancer were located in the northern sector of the division and thus within close proximity for church services. Camp Ross, however, was one of two most distant camps located in the far south at the division's entry and thus out of the way. That the Korean bus service was unavailable from Ross to Pelham did not help either. A taxi was not available or affordable either. Apart from this, the twenty-four-hour-a-day Personnel duty precluded my attendance with the brethren. However, once at Blue Lancer, and again within my own warm element, Brother Brittain somehow or other acquired a jeep that facilitated attendance.

How could I forget the one particular Missionary and Servicemen's Conference in Seoul during a testimonial service with a few score of soldiers in attendance where I was prompted at public confession? This conference was presided over by a General Authority, Elder Gordon B. Hinckley. Little did I dream that thirty-plus years hence Elder Hinckley would be the Presiding Elder of our church, headquartered in Salt Lake City. The general authorities in suits and ties, along with the sympathetic group leaders of the mixed military ranks and branches in dress uniforms, listened to the penitent GI among others with great sympathy and pained eyes—or was it empathy? I wept to my ♪*"Master, with anguish of spirit,* (I) *bowed in* (my) *grief* (that) *day. Torrents of sin and of anguish swept o'er* (my) *sinking soul, and I perish, I perish dear Master. Oh, hasten and take control."*♪ Tears rolled down my cheeks as a sympathetic air force sergeant proffered me his handkerchief. A transparent ambience of rock-solid mercy reigned over the military congregation and nothing accusatory ever surfaced, for all acknowledged that *only* the *blood* of one *Man* stood between all and God. All recognized that it was a matter of time before voluntary due process redeemed the *wayward* to church standard—and in my case, growth had begun with the leadership position of responsibility at the Camp Pelham Branch where I served at this Far East corner of Asia.

Epilogue

I have to admit that it was the attendance at church and conferences that made all the difference during my "hardship" tour of duty in Korea. It was heartwarming to see and cross paths with the brothers in the course of duty in the Division area. There was an inner church brotherhood within an already existing military brotherhood that brought the *brethren* to common ground. Forty years later, I reflected that I had enjoyed life in a threefold family world: the church, the military, and my *indigenous family* of this Far East corner of Asia.

---

* Mary A. Baker, "Master the Tempest is Raging" (1874)

Chapter 6

Early Days at McGovern

Prologue

These early days at McGovern were a lighthearted awakening of camp environment and the Korean culture. Once settled in my quarters and broke into the military routine, I began to investigate the street jargon and camp resources and privileges. Additional money was to be earned, and I discovered the delightful absence of domestic chore drudgeries as I continued in my favorite pastime, the theater, where I felt right at home.

The Language
November 1964

Curves and lines, rounds and squares
Strokes and scrawls everywhere
Back and forth, up and down
Perplexing, all around

I was bewildered when I first overheard a soldier rattle off what appeared to be a foreign language. Puzzling sentences and distorted English words mixed with foreign words blew my mind. I was impressed that most of the soldiers spoke and understood one another in that parlance, and this furthered my determination to learn the lingo.

Familiarizing myself with this new "dialect," I realized it was a simple, uncomplicated distortion of English with a mixture of Japanese and Korean words that formed a universally understood language, commonly spoken by the military and indigenous population at large.

Eventually, I concluded that most conversations fell into one of six identifiable categories: (1) *proper grammar*, (2) *street language* (distortion of either language), (3) *colloquial*, (4) *slang*, (5) *a GI lingo* (a combination of Korean and English), and (6) *Japanese*. Interestingly, I detected an absence of Chinese words. Soldiers used a separate vocabulary of universal military jargon. Only three remembered words fell into almost all of five of the first five categories.

The first word "good:" (1) proper: *CHOT seem-nee-da* (good is), 2 street: *numba HAna* (first quality in quantity), (3) colloq: *ch'eh EEL* (number one quality), (4) slang: *CHO-ta* (good), and (5) GI: number one (first quality).

The second word was "give" or "gift": (1) proper: *KA-joo-wah o-SHIP shee-oh* (give please), (2) street: *pre-ZEN-to* (give, more as recipient), (3) colloq: *Ka-joo-wah* (gift for me, or give me), (4) slang: *ka-KWAH* (give to me), and (5) GI: *pre-ZEN-to* (give, more as presenter).

The third word was "unimportant": (1) proper: *KEN-CHAN seem-nee-DA* (doesn't have importance), (2) street: No big thing, 3. colloq: *Ken cha-na*, (4) slang: *Ken cha-na*, and (5) GI: no sweat.

Not satisfied with day-to-day jargon, I was determined to learn the native Korean language, Hangul. At first, I was ecstatic to attend a language class at Brigade Headquarters. However, I became discouraged as time after time—although the instructor tried to be fair—the officers and senior sergeants monopolized the class. Realizing that a first class private would not stand a chance, after only two sessions, I withdrew from the class. I decided I was better off on my own. However, I did learn two very basic points: that my accented Spanish facilitated pronunciation; and declarative and interrogative sentences were dependent upon the verb at the end of a sentence—punctuation being nonexistent in Hangul. For example: *I love you*: **(1)** *Nanun tangsheenul sarang hamneeda (NA-nun tan-shee-NUL SA-RANG ham-nee-da)*, meaning, "Love is/exists between you and me." The literal translation is: "I you love is *or* I you love have." **(2)** *Sarang hamneka(?) (sa-rang ham-nee-KA(?))*, meaning "Does(Is) love exist(ent) between you and me?" *or* "Does love exist from you?" The literal translation is: "Love is? *or* love have?"

I purchased an English-Korean dictionary and an everyday language guide, with an extended glossary, and with Hangul meaning written in English-worded phonics following English sentences. These sentences in turn were followed by the meanings in the Korean script alphabet. Needless to say, I was fascinated by the stroked alphabet. I was elated as I turned to the appendix and located the pronunciation key of the strokes, that is, of each consonant and vowel. Trembling with anticipation, I read the strokes cross-referenced and joined on a graph to form syllables—each with its own sound. By joining syllables, for the first time I spoke as well as read words in Korean! An added elation came when I also recognized that proper pronunciation was only possible by proper knowledge of script phonics. It was then I also understood why the language was written vertically. It is that the flow of the brush creates syllables with symbols left to right but with the third and fourth symbol below. It made sense that the syllables made for better clarification in descending flowing order rather than the horizontal order.

I BEGAN RECOGNIZING AND READING SCRIPT WORDS ON SIGNS AND BUSINESSES, ALTHOUGH NOT UNDERSTANDING THEIR MEANINGS. SIGN READS: NANG HYANG, EE BAL KWAN.

Suddenly, as I first learned to read, a whole world lay open before me. As I went about the villages or went touring, I observed all written words and unceasingly asked about the syntax, vocabulary, and more of any native Korean within reach, but especially of the KATUSAs. I then began recognizing and reading words on signs and businesses, although their meanings were then unknown. I reached further clarity when I noted the difference between Korean and Chinese writing. Heretofore, it all had appeared alike to me. Chinese inscription consisted of concepts written in single characters with greater stroke complexity—two or more joined to broaden or change meanings. With this discovery, I was not only able to differentiate between Korean and Chinese, but to my amazement, I recognized Japanese characters by a simple process of elimination. As I practiced my Korean, my efforts, especially in public, were laughed at, but I was oblivious to all mocking. My reward came when the natives and people outside the military sector expressed wonder that an American soldier would take interest in their culture at this Far East corner of Asia.

Money Matters
November 1964–March 1965

Walking guard or lending cash
Money earned or paid from stash
Ten today or twelve pay day
Five to lend plus two to pay

The whole purpose of the military occupancy of Korea was to "Guard Freedom's Frontier," and guard duty in any form was the rule. While at Personnel at camps McGovern and Ross, everyone was scheduled to walk guard twice a week and every other weekend.

It was during the first month in Korea that I discovered the first of two money-making opportunities. The first was the "purchase" of guard duty, and a little later I learned that the second was money lending. Cash loans and guard substitution was quite lucrative as there was a less than a thirty-day wait for payment, with the sky being the limit for these supplementary earnings.

Purchasing guard duty was especially attractive for buck privates as we came straight from basic training with vanished dreams of pay school and were freshly introduced to hardship duty. Walking guard was abhorred by all. However, the prospect of earning an extra ten dollars made the substitution of guard duty a lot less painful. The going rate for guard was ten dollars in hand or twelve on payday. Ten dollars was about 20 percent of a private's monthly pay! For the first time in my life I was earning money that was mine alone to spend as I wished. No snitching by my sisters, no losing by a seizure to my mother. It was a blessing for me to be in the army.

There were many reasons why guard duty was up for sale. At times there was special entertainment at the EM Club or the soldiers wanted to take a date to the movies that night. Other reasons included the tiresome walking posts or the tedium of standing guard in the towers, especially during the snows and the monsoons. Again, perhaps the soldier was unhappy with the shift (first, second, or third guard) he was assigned to, or he just plainly did not want to do the duty and would rather pay the money.

When agreement was reached both, the buyer and the seller approached the duty sergeant and announced that the buyer would walk the seller's guard duty. The buyer would just show up for guard mount, and perform the duty as if it was his own. The sergeants made it plain that what we arranged among ourselves was our business alone. Payment was always due and payable on payday outside the pay hooch. I cannot recall of anyone reneging on paying for a guard job because of the hardship—it was really money earned. Most sellers kept their word and paid the two dollar payday bonus.

I had many takers. One week I grossed fifty dollars, a month's pay! At times there were last minute requests from GIs who had some pressing business. I recall only one minor loss on guard recompense. Private First G. got last minute word that his village *josan* (prostitute) wanted to see him on a night he was scheduled guard. He immediately contacted me and we contracted for a payday adjustment. That payday, G. refused to pay me the two dollar bonus at the pay hooch. Then and there I aggressively demanded the difference, but he just walked away. I had no recourse but to accept the loss. I wanted to chase him, which would have resulted in a physical confrontation, but two dollars wasn't worth a punch in the nose. In a way, I was glad to have ten dollars, but the two additional dollars were always useful.

Then there was Private First R., a successful moneylender. I remember that R. was always walking guard duty and earning his twelve dollars on payday. However, he would also sell his guard duty when necessary. In keeping with his opportunistic behavior, I had heard of his foul business practices. As a new arrival and new at hiring myself, I learned of his deceptions the hard way. Once, we contracted guard as he was clearing for rotation back to the States. He was to come in late that evening, so he had third guard. I stood the guard mount inspection, and stayed the first two walks in the guard house. He arrived as I exited the guard house to walk the post and approached me saying he was walking and would not require my service. He kept saying that the night was beautiful, and I guessed that meant that the walk wasn't a hardship. I told him we had a contract and I would walk it and get paid. He turned and walked toward the post. I then realized one more reason why he was "hated." I then understood why the sergeants said that what we did among ourselves was our business—there was nowhere to go for justice.

This R. always carried a wad of MPC (military payment certificates). Upon my arrival in Korea we were required to surrender our currency and change. In return, we received paper certificates in denominations of greenbacks and coins. It was my understanding that the designs on these paper certificates changed periodically. Anyway, R. always sat at the back of the office yelling out "batta ejee." Batta ejee was a Korean mispronunciation of "better easy," or rather "take it easy." My guess is he was attempting acceptance in the camaraderie by casting words into the air.

    R. was detested by all I knew though he charged the same going rates as anyone else in money-lending. However, I never knew of anyone else as sought after as he; somehow he cornered the money-lending market. He once advised me he'd lend me five dollars anytime for seven dollars on payday. I actually saw sergeants borrow fifty dollars for eighty dollars. I remember seeing R. standing outside the pay hooch every payday making sure he got his money with the interest. I overheard some soldiers once say that if they ever saw R. down they would stamp him further underfoot because he had made a small fortune from them. I did hear of only one soldier, who rotated to CONUS (continental United States), get away from paying R. the loan and the interest, although I never knew how much.

    I wondered what caused soldiers to borrow money at such usury rates? One day, I noticed that a borrower took his loan and made tracks for the village. I guess he had a kept-girl or a hot date or perhaps some desperate need that required immediate payment. Once I saw a borrower who proceeded to the PX, purchased a case of beer, and shared it with his bunkmates. I guessed each soldier had his own requirements, whether physical or emotional (need of esteem from his fellow soldiers). Whenever I saw guys carrying a case of beer into the hooch, I wondered and could never understand why anyone would drink and not share the expenses. I had far better use for my money

    R. always argued with the cooks, especially during the field problems, over the bread rolls. He always demanded extras. I never saw R. purchase any goods from the PX, never knew he drank with the troops at the EM club, never knew he had a *josan* in the village. He was always seen in the teahouse standing by the same pillar with a beer bottle in hand. Never saw him spending any money on private snacks during field problems. Whenever any of us purchased goodies at the PX or from field vendors during maneuvers or when someone opened his private goodies locker for a treat, he always stretched his hand for a handout. As detested as R. was, it was beyond me why we were all so complacent and placed goodies in his hand.

    Very rarely (once or twice), I also lent five or ten dollars, but only to trusted and proven soldiers. I pulled my share of purchased guard and earned an equivalent of about two, perhaps three months' pay during my entire duty tour. As abhorred as guard duty was, these purchases were the only times that guard duty proved to somewhat "sweeten" this duty in this Far East corner of Asia.

I CHUCKLED, AS WOULD A YOUNG GENTLEMAN AWAY FROM HOME AT THE PROSPECT OF HIRING A MANSERVANT. AUTHOR IN OLIVE GREEN UNIFORM AND MR. COE, OUR HOUSEBOY.

Hiring a Houseboy
November 1964–November 1965

Scrub scrub scrub, the houseboy hard at work
Brush brush brush, before the dawn they lurk
Shine shine shine, apply and polish wax
The foot, the bunk, ne'er a moment lax

I first heard wonderful stories about the houseboys of Korea during Advanced Individual Training at Fort Polk. Staff Sergeant Teti, a highly decorated soldier and Personnel Instructor, related that all the drudgeries of Basic Training chores were taken care of by the hard-working houseboy. At the time, I had no knowledge or concern regarding my first Permanent Change of Station so I had dismissed the houseboy story. My mind was involved in the upcoming Pay School in Indiana and all the adventures to be had in Indianapolis! I would continue considering travel as a priority. I never remembered the houseboy perk even when I received orders for overseas close to the end of Pay School.

Then, on my arrival in Korea, at the indoctrination center at Camp Ross that November of 1964, I noted about twenty pairs of low quarters and boots lined up next to two squatting Korean gentlemen. They were involved in soft phonetic chat as they systematically and skillfully applied polish and brush to the foot apparel. I became aware of the possibility that in my quarter's assignment I might hire my own houseboy.

Life was hard for unskilled or nonprofessional work. The houseboy was not a youth, but an adult man. He lived in a world where any job with the U.S. government was preferable to Korean earnings; wages close to a private soldier's pay were a prince's ransom. I once noticed that a Korean mess hall worker set aside leftover steak from our scraps. In this case our table scraps were possibly a feast for him and his family. The barbershop, recreation center, bartenders, laundry, as well as being a PX employee were the better paying jobs and always provided quality service. I found that the Korean privates augmenting our army earned a meager $1.60 a month. I only noticed one professional employee in my entire year. He was a Korean dental assistant at the dispensary who sliced at my gums after cleaning my teeth and then tortured me with an acid, saying I wasn't to swish for a few hours.

"Mr. Coe will polish your boots and low quarters, fix your bunk, and clean your field gear for five dollars a month," Specialist Fifth Riley informed us newcomers at Camp McGovern. We cast side-glances at one another with raised eyebrows. After all the drudgeries and GI parties of Basic Training and AIT, these words were music to our ears. I chuckled, as would a young gentleman away from home, at the prospect of hiring a "manservant."

As soon as I received my bunk assignment at the Personnel Quonsets, I was introduced to Mr. Coe. Mr. Coe was a middle-sized man by American standards whose facial features did not appear Oriental but were more closely arranged as the caricatures in Walt Disney comics. The veteran GIs immediately informed us newcomers that although the commanding officer had set the houseboy salary at five dollars a month, all were paying eight. I immediately reflected that eight dollars a month was almost 20 percent of my salary and the five dollars was a mere 10 percent. The vets made little of three dollars saying, "What's three dollars?" *But*, I thought, three dollars were three dollars that represented six haircuts, or thirty-six pictures, or nine movie tickets. Well, having to choose between the drudgeries of Basic chores or freedom, I would just have to cough up with the extra three dollars. What, eight dollars a month received from ten soldiers, that would be eighty dollars, thirty dollars more than a Private's pay for a month, and for half days' work!? Later I found that Mr. Coe also swept and took out the trash of the Personnel Quonsets for another few dollars per month from the Personnel coffers. Private First Abilio Mendiola, a buddy, and I once volunteered to take on the work for the meager salary when it was reported that the houseboys were not doing a good job. The houseboys shaped up so we were not hired.

The houseboy's duty also included general cleanliness of the Quonset. One predawn morning when I returned from the guard shack I noticed that the Quonset was as freezing with cold as outside. The stove was out and I thought that perhaps no one had bothered to go to the diesel tank for fuel. In the darkness I did notice something white at the stove. Later I awoke to see Mr. Coe upset with an added chore of cleaning all the chemical foam from the fire extinguisher that enveloped the entire stove and part of the floor. Evidently the stove had caught fire, and the GI's had put it out with the fire extinguisher.

Mr. Coe decided to remain at McGovern when we relocated to Camp Ross that March 1965. We all encouraged him to relocate with us, because the transferring units that would replace us and occupy our Quonsets would bring their own houseboys, but he said his family was settled at Nopae Dong. This was a grave mistake because the First of the Seventh in effect, relocated their houseboys with them into McGovern.

One day, Mr. Coe appeared at Ross looking for a job. By that time we had swelled Ross's population and were welcomed by our hired local houseboys, so Mr. Coe was out of a job! I did see him polishing shoes later on though; he had probably been subcontracted.

One day during lunch break at Blue Lancer, I returned to my hooch to find my bunk overturned. Captain Baker, commanding officer of Headquarters Company First of the Twelfth, had conducted an inspection and the houseboy's work was unacceptable. I had contracted the houseboy for seven dollars a month. When he asked, I informed Captain Baker of the seven dollars, which sent the CO into a tizzy. The pay rate was five dollars a month.

I later overheard the houseboys at the orderly room reporting to the CO that they expected at least "six dollars a month or we quit!" Needless to say, all the troops still privately coughed up the eight dollars and in some cases nine dollars a month.

The houseboy was a nice bonus in the Korea *hardship* tour of duty. They knew what was expected of them and they did their job all in a day's work. Their invisibility made the soldiers take their work for granted. However, they did relieve the troops of some grunt work at a nominal fee and afforded a decent wage to the Korean folk. In retrospect, I really could not recall ever grumbling or even exchanging more than a hundred words with all the three houseboys hired at all three camps during my tour of duty at this Far East corner of Asia.

THE TWO MOST MEMORABLE MOTION PICTURES SHOWN WERE *CLEOPATRA,* WITH ELIZABETH TAYLOR AND RICHARD BURTON; AND *QUO VADIS* WITH DEBRA KERR AND ROBERT TAYLOR.

The Camp Theater
November 1964-November 1965

Into a world of make believe
Where I would lose and then retrieve
Myself from plots with shades and sounds
Of scenes in time that knew no bounds

"WHHREEEEEEE," the shrill whistling grew louder along with frenzied yelling and catcalling in the already noisy theater. Anyone and everyone was talking, yelling, paralleling words to the movie script, mimicking sounds, and laughing. Nothing was greater than the whistling as when an airplane appeared on the screen, and sure enough someone always yelled out "Short!" There was general gaiety all around, and no one ever complained, or cared.

THE MCGOVERN THEATER, CENTER OF PHOTO

The McGovern camp theater was an oversized Quonset-shaped building. The box office and the foyer were like any theater elsewhere, with a ticket window and concession stand. Admission amounted to thirty-five cents and the popcorn cost a nickel. It was the only treat at the concession stand and about the size of a small cereal box. Most theaters had one showing normally scheduled at 7:00 p.m. and a matinee on weekends. The wide middle row of seats was flanked by narrower rows at either end.

I entered the Blue Lancer Playhouse and sat and noticed a crowd of children at the front row softly chatting and laughing. They were guests from the local orphanage. Some GIs busily walked up and down the aisles providing them with free boxes of popcorn. There was always a smattering of village *josans* escorted by their GI boyfriends plus a few KATUSAs (Korean soldiers serving with the U.S. Army) in the audience.

THE CAMP THEATER WAS THE BEST OF THE ARMY'S MODES OF ENTERTAINMENT.

The entire production began with the national anthem so that everyone stood at attention in full respect. The lights went out and the screen lit up. A ribbon inscribed with "Army and Air Force Far East Exchange" flowed across the screen. It crossed a globe at the center, and hugged the globe at the third quarter of the screen. The music sounded something like the 20th Century Fox prelude. The introductory military ribbon was always followed by news of the day. I remembered one news clip where the Queen of England visited a ship at sea and accepted a tour below deck. She was being helped as she descended by means of a narrow ladder. The clip that remained engraved in my mind was that of Peter Tchaikovsky's Piano Concerto in B-flat Minor being played by a pianist named Van Clyburn who had visited Moscow and performed at some major symphony competition. Van Clyburn was specifically invited by Prime Minister Nikita Khrushchev who also awarded him first place. I remembered how Van Clyburn's busy fingers blurred on the keyboard, as the music flowed flawlessly by, and the rush of adrenalin I felt at my temples as the music swelled. The cellists and violinists were all wearing black tuxedo jackets with white shirts and tiny buttons—all was set in elegance. I was so caught up in the concerto that I was disappointed when it gave way to the next clip.

For a split second I flipped back to earlier theater adventures of my late teens. I had always been a movie-goer. As a child I remember the unique darkness and subdued lighting of San Antonio oversized theaters. The outside foyer always displayed a marquee with huge letters announcing the movie. Along the walk were pictures depicting great moments in the film. I enjoyed walking by the neon signs, and I loved the one-inch clear-glass blinking light bulbs circling the marquee and the theater title on the facade. There was a thrill to approaching and stepping up to the front glass-enclosed box office and paying the admission of twenty-five cents to the ticket lady. Just pacing the few steps from the ticket box office past the glazed color-contrasted tiled walls on my way to the theater doors was exciting. My anticipation knew no limits as the red-uniformed doorman swung open the heavy glass doors just for me. The unique aroma of over-priced fifteen-cent theater popcorn, seasoned with hot butter, pleasantly greeted me. As I approached the ticket-taker I bypassed the concession stand with its tempting and price-inflated fifteen-cent Hershey's candies, and Dreamsicle and chocolate covered ice cream bars, along with the equally priced fountain drinks (twenty cent without ice), while carrying my paper sack filled with cookies, bananas, peanuts, and a quart-size grape soda. It was awesome entering that quiet immense theater and selecting a seat within the multitude of rows. It was a big thrill for me to count the rows as I left for the boys' room or the concession stand and returned to my same seat. I would become ecstatic when there chanced to be a girl sitting next to me. And once for a moment of about two minutes, I gathered the nerve to actually place my arm around a girl's shoulders, and we were consensually cuddling when her friends announced they had to go, leaving me all frustrated. The Texas and the Majestic Theaters, both bragged lower-priced balcony seats with Greek architecture on the walls opposite the screen, and a starlit ceiling. The Aztec boasted walls seemingly of an Aztec temple's stone interior, carved with glyphs. By the time of my late teens, the aging Empire had seen better days, and was reduced to three running movies for fifty cents. The Prince was one rectangular room as was The Joy, while the Empire still boasted a balustrade, clear across the theater's balcony.

Back at Camp McGovern, the newsreel was over and the motion picture began. The two most memorable motion pictures shown were *Cleopatra* with Elizabeth Taylor and Richard Burton, and *Quo Vadis* with Debra Kerr and Robert Taylor. My eyes were glued to the screen during Cleopatra's arrival at Rome, when a skimpily clad female dancer waved herself all over the screen to the loud catcalling of the captive GI audience that activated some of my eighteen-year senses and awakened others I did not know I had. The worst movie I remember was *Bye Bye Birdie,* with pretty Ann Margaret, that in my opinion was a waste of my time and money. *Kissing Cousins* with Elvis Presley wasn't so bad, because I had always loved and enjoyed his music and songs. I remember a Frankenstein flick where the defrosted monster was beckoned out of frozen waters by the welcoming gestures of a young woman. Many of the guys called out "hooch-hooch" to the roaring laughter of the crowd. How could I forget *Mutiny on the Bounty* with Marlon Brando, my super favorite for three years? My brother Moe had taken me to view it at the Broadway Theater in San Antonio during the premier two years, earlier in 1962. I followed it all through Basic and AIT viewing it at each post theater. Finally, I got to see it one last time at the McGovern Theater. I remember my *josan* date kept saying that Percy Herbert resembled Vain. Who was Vain, I kept asking, and after a few repetitions I guessed she was referring to an office coworker named Private First Wain! It was this same Wain who had initially teased us, regarding our tenure back in the field last November as buck privates. While I was comfortable with army life and Korea, this motion picture had made me fall in love with the South Seas, imagining all those nymphs of my earlier youth that I could have visited if I had joined the navy!

To me, the camp theater was the best of the army's modes of entertainment for the troops. It afforded a full view of movies that were featured back home so that one was sort of up to date with current hits. I continued to escape into a world of make-believe involving plots, situations, places, and lovely actresses for several hours from the rigorous military duty of this Far East corner of Asia.

The Village

A peek, a peep, a stolen gaze
A glimpse, a glance, a hovel maze
A glare, a stare, a mental daze
To seek, to see, a final craze

The village: everyone spoke about *the village*. I had only known of villages as picturesque miniature cities in fairy tales. I envisioned cottages with thatched roofs and brown wooden cross braces on white walls built into tree trunks under a mystical shaded dark-green forest. Perhaps I also imagined scantily clad nymphs in white sheer gossamer with long flowing light-brown hair prancing around the forests. Yet, there in Korea, my fellow clerks raved about the wonders within *the village*. Mystified as I was, I could hardly wait to uncover what the mystery was within *the village*.

So it was a week or two after my arrival at Camp McGovern that my attention was drawn to the sunbathed village under the cold Korean sun. Because of the great landscape approaching any village, the atmosphere reeked with human fecal matter from the rice paddies always fronting it. Needless to say, outhouses or a similarity thereof was not part of the cultural architecture. Those first days, I glanced toward the village as the chilly late-autumnal wind blew into my face. Staring at the only semblance of Korean life, I could see in the settlement right outside the main gate; I was curious about what lay beyond. The morning was chilly and sunny, as I stood dumbfounded, observing the perplexing shacks and hovels that were the homes of the local Korean people. There, facing me was the indigenous population I "had lived for" to mingle with, in this first opportune overseas assignment. Underlying my curiosity was the anticipation of exploration and travel in this foreign country. Military buddies talked of interests entirely contrary to all my anticipated travel expectations. I went about, in continuance with my military duties periodically glancing toward the village in The Land of the Morning Calm, waiting for my opportunity to explore further.

Through the snowy months of December 1964 and January 1965, I periodically paused in the course of my duties at Personnel or on guard duty and found myself gazing toward the white-layered village as the stinging cold bit my face. The icy wind filled my lungs through my cold nostrils, thwarted in part by my windproof parka. Once I saw a thick white cloud that just seemed to hover above and across the entire length of the village, perhaps the steam of living warm bodies living there. Later that month, I noticed that the rice paddies between the village and Camp McGovern were frozen solid and stretched across the panorama like translucent glass. One morning, I made out several tiny black inverted Y's running, sliding, falling, and freely and carelessly gliding all over the frosty and seemingly icy stubbly fields. Skaters, I realized. The faint smoke from many protrusions all over the village made an odd picture. Each hovel I could discern housed a group of people laughing, eating, drinking, and going about the daily business of living, snugly protected from the bitter Korean winter. The biting cold that stung my face as I climbed the downslide toward Guard Tower Four, continually reminded me of the Korean elements. Sadly I realized I was on the dreary outside "looking in."

The month of February, 1965, brought about a warm thaw, resulting in a pleasant and welcoming atmosphere. The weak sun became stronger and brighter and the days were more comforting, as the yellow globe warmed the chilly air. Within the security of the compound, I still gazed over the Quonsets, across the recreation buildings, and beyond the barbwire fence toward *the mysterious village*. The distant conglomeration of stacked-up hovels seemed to call and beckon me, as they ascended the mountain slope behind. I could now discern the box-like structures overlapping one another, some with overhanging straw roofs and others with tiled structures. Some appeared to be made of plastered adobe and others of scrap wood. In my imagination, some developed eyes, mouths, and hair, calling out to me personally. It just seemed to become more familiar; and I became more at ease, the more I observed the village.

I FOUND MYSELF GAZING TOWARD THE WHITE SNOW-PATCHED DISTANT VILLAGE FROM OUTSIDE MY QUONSET AS THE STINGING COLD BIT AT MY FACE.

It was during these two months that I made a friend of Private First N.E. who spoke a bit of Spanish. We talked about our parallel lifestyles in the Spanish "barrio" and the Afro-American ghetto and quickly understood one another as we had much in common. We attended the theater, talked about home, and shared boyhood adventures; in effect, N.E. and I became good friends. Then one day our conversation turned to *the village*. It was time, I thought, to make that long overdue visit. The baffling village would be mine on smoother conditions under the tutelage of N.E. Thus, one Saturday morning in mid-February, when we were both off duty, we donned our olive greens, picked up our passes, exited the main gate, crossed the road, and sauntered up the wide dirt-path that led to *the village*. With flared nostrils and oversized eyes, and wild for adventure, I casually strolled into *the mysterious village* of Nopae Dong, at this Far East corner of Asia.

Chapter 7

Prostitution, The Main Employment

> *Girls blush, sometimes, because they are alive, half wishing they were dead to save the shame. They have drawn too near the fire of life, like gnats, and flare up bodily, wings and all. What then? Who's sorry for a gnat or girl?*
> —Elizabeth Barrett Browning

> *We say that slavery has vanished..., but this is not true. Slavery still exists, but now it applies only to women and its name is prostitution.*
> —Victor Hugo

Dolls here, dolls there, dolls everywhere
Hundreds of cuties sweet and fair
Patrons and girls without a care
Have tricks and treats at wholesale fare

Prologue

At the library in Fort Benjamin Harrison, Indiana, on October 1964, I remember reading an article about prostitution in Korea. It reported American soldiers delightfully tilting the faces or chucking the chins of prostitutes who abounded and responded cheerfully with "Please come to my hooch." I did not give the article further thought, dismissed it, and continued admiring the last of the 1964 silver half-dollars, advertised with the new John F. Kennedy effigy. However, once in Korea, I was astounded by the article's veracity. I came to realize that in war-torn Korea poverty was rampant. Until its democratic government, Korea was an oppressed civilization under the emperors of China or Japan. Lucrative employment was unknown in this twentieth century feudal culture. The population needed immediate revenue, and education afforded a meager salary. Men turned to burglary while docile young women turned to prostitution for survival. The northern sector of South Korea, occupied by the American Army, offered high recompense for sexual favors and became quite attractive to starving women from as far south as Pusan.

The Teahouse *Josans*

The teahouse girls
With fancy swirls
But naught with curls
Worked tricks with whirls

Brothels or "teahouses" were inky dark or dimly lit by clear or small multicolored bulbs like those on Christmas trees of the fifties. The barmaid served OB beer and played American songs of the sixties. The walls were usually black, plain or with geometric designs in dark colors. Some walls were lined with benches, sometimes tables or booths, to accommodate the teahouse *josans* (prostitutes) and patrons. The club was heated by a stove in the very center and was fired by a cake of white fuel in winter and opened doors in summer. Soldiers could only frequent establishments approved by the Office of the Provost Marshall, and these were periodically inspected by both the U.S. Army and the Republic of Korea Military Police—though a blind eye was turned at the illegal operations, and undocumented prostitutes fled the premises when warned by lookouts.

Teahouses were crammed with lovely sloe-eyed young women, either seated on the surrounding benches or dancing with soldiers. Touch-dancing was still the style of the day. Some sported makeup that further enhanced their already pretty faces—others simply went all natural. Some showed off nice "Americanized" elaborate hairdos such as beehives and bubbles while others simply boasted lovely, long, straight, ebony hair. Most of them kept the local beauty shop in business and were probably the beauticians' only source of income. All were nicely groomed and dressed. As in the fashion of 1964, they all wore "body" sweaters or blouses but above-the-knee skirts. A few afforded two-piece suits with side slits. One buddy excitedly reported that while seated cross-legged, some slits strategically opened revealing legs and corners above dropped skirts that further displayed fair and lovely thighs even in the dim light—once in a while a flash of white V-shaped fabric was visible within the deepest, darkest recesses. Supposedly there was never an awareness of store-bought perfume, but all held a slight uniform scent perhaps due to their staple diet, rice. Very rarely did I note a trace of the expected yellow complexions of the Mongoloid Race, and to me their skin color so likened my own that it increased my comfort among the populace at large. I heard complaints that the teahouse had its minute share of homely prostitutes that although rejected, were persistent—that they could not be improved upon with any amount of makeup or nice dresses. Needless to say, they were not as successful in their chosen profession and oftentimes ended up working the streets.

As a company administrative clerk, I learned that these women were quite adamant about their names. I supposed that their birth names, background, and age must have remained universally personal and privileged. It was enough to debase themselves in catering to English-speaking foreigners; many refused English names. These prostitutes assumed a Korean alias and only on rare occasions, such as marriage or for identification cards, would reveal their true names. Others indifferently accepted an English name such as Betty, Connie, or Katy.

I chuckled when I heard the guys grumbling that while *The Wedding* was playing a rendition of *Ave Maria*, the entire conglomeration of *josans* wailed the lyrics to the melody in unison, followed by *Good-bye, Jimmy, Good-bye*—that the whole teahouse reverberated with what sounded like a few covens of howling sirens in stereo. I guess they all had a remote hope of love and marriage unnerving the guys as they were likely candidates! While these women were professional prostitutes or "business women" as they termed themselves, they were human, with human hopes and dreams, and had the right as anyone else on earth to seek happiness. These teahouse *josans* stood a far better chance of marrying a soldier than the chancy streetwalkers. Evidently, many soldiers passed through their lives with whom they had hope for marriage, thus the universal popularity of these two songs.

The teahouse *josans* displayed competition with one another only by their appearance, personality, and special "skills." Reportedly, many of the "better" prostitutes in the teahouses were really pretty, younger, unusually well-endowed, and these did not have to walk the streets or push themselves. The attractive *josans* were always sought after and never lacked business; they just sat attractively and patiently, awaiting clients or regulars. The most lucrative and easiest way to earn a living in 1965, as anywhere where severe poverty was prevalent, was as a *josan* in this Far East corner of Asia.

Streetwalkers

A splash of red,
A spray on head
A few words said
A splay on bed

Prostitution was widespread north of the Military Police checkpoint located a few miles north of Seoul clear to the DMZ through the American Army occupied sector. *Josans* swarmed all over the Cavalry area, especially in the greater villages. Unlike the teahouse prostitutes who did not walk the limited paths of the village, the streetwalkers shamelessly wandered about, around, and everywhere in complete confidence and in full acceptance in their "business" attire and makeup with or without a soldier or *mamasan*. To be seen with a soldier was an obvious mark of a prostitute. Conceivably, *josans* were the supporters of many houses and businesses which were perhaps dependent on their industry. These streetwalkers stood the least chance of finding a husband among the military patrons.

The greater villages of Yongju-Gol, Munsan-Ni, and Pobwan-Ni boasted a greater number of brothels and streetwalkers. However, on these streets prostitutes freely walked up to a soldier and placed a hand under his forearm saying *"hooch, hooch,"* meaning "come to my room." Once, I was passing by a few *josans* congregated outside their hooch, and all of them sang out in chorus to the tune of "Clementine," ♪*"Yobo-seh-o, yobo-seh-o, yobo-SEEEH-O gee-e eye,* money *oop-so cutta cho-gie,* money *ee-so, ee-dee-wah"*♪; its closest translation would be as follows: "Hello you there, hello you there, hello you there GI, don't have money go a far way, have you money, come right here." I could not help but chuckle at the mode of their invitation as I walked my way. Most of these streetwalkers were homely, older, overweight, not well-endowed, and more than likely, diseased. Their thicker application of rouge, lipstick, and eye-makeup could not make them any more attractive. It was sad how some of these desperate women clung and meandered a short distance to the soldier's arm for business. Once in a while, an older woman, a *mamasan,* or perhaps a procuress, approached a GI saying, "cherry girl," or *"chuh-nia,"* meaning "virgin." I had heard of some GIs purchasing these *primus coitus* upstarts. That these girls were sold and resold numerous times as virgins did not occur to them.

Although most streetwalkers worked independently, some had a *mamasan.* Most of them appeared clean, neatly but less than casually dressed, and did not boast of professional grooming. Mostly all sported clean straight short hair or simple hairdos while others simply showed off their natural, lovely, long, ebony hair. However, it was difficult for me to tell some of them apart from other young women while strolling in Seoul because they did not make themselves as obvious as in the military sector. Perhaps the difference was in the style of makeup. These streetwalkers were mostly interested in earning a living rather than investing in better clothes or hairstyles. So were my observations of the streetwalker *josan* at this Far East corner of Asia!

Husband-Hunting for a Ticket Stateside

A man was sad
Became a cad
No more a lad
A wife and dad

The teahouse *josans* stood a far better chance of landing a husband than the streetwalkers. These post-teenagers had everything to gain and nothing to lose. Sooner or later a lonely soldier, perhaps one who had never experienced his first lay succumbed to their Oriental charms. Perhaps reaching out from our American military's seemingly affluent lifestyle with the thought of rescuing her from a life of prostitution in a third world country appeared appealing and stroked an ego or two. At times the practiced and knowing *josan* tuned in and accurately pushed the soldier's "buttons." I suppose a soldier felt he could never find a girl back home and here he could afford to choose. He might have felt homely, unattractive, and above all, lonely. He lived amid a candy store generously overflowing with unlimited sexual encounters and amid completely affordable live dolls, all instantly willing to fulfill his most basic and passionate needs. That these young women's love and fidelity might not be really genuine was unimportant. The urge was overwhelming, and he could allow himself, by means of reenlistment, the luxury of being their plane ticket stateside.

Perhaps a lovesick soldier yielded to his *josan's* expertise as well-acquainted were they with the tricks of their trade. I learned of one very attractive and enterprising prostitute who serviced three different soldiers in three close-proximity hooches on one payday weekend night. Each soldier had paid her for a full night of pleasure and was unaware of the others. The following morning, two soldiers compared their nocturnal adventures at the PX pastry shop and discovered the duplicity. They decided to return and confront her. To their surprise, they caught her in the third hooch with the third soldier! So much for memorable nights of passion!

Many requests for marriage crossed my desk at the Headquarters Company Orderly Room. Perhaps these soldiers, after listening to a repeated tale of his girl's circumstances for entering this trade, were prompted to rescue her. Private First C. advised me that he proposed marriage to his fiancée within a few days of meeting her because she had responded accurately and favorably to his lifelong feelings and wishes in a wife. I overheard a conversation once between two GIs discussing the possibility of marrying a *josan*. The older GI advised the lovesick soldier to consider finding a girl back home—that the local prostitute was "used up and all rotted." Far away from the influence of family, parental restrictions, peer or public criticism and disapproval, and society, in a live-and-let-live environment, a soldier easily could succumb to women's wiles. Many soldiers arranged to bring home a Korean wife from the sea of prostitutes.

However, back in the United States, though—I worked in Personnel—most of those same GIs I processed from Vietnam who had formerly served in Korea, related stories of infidelity. These men had reenlisted for six years to afford their Korean wives' passage to America, thus fulfilling every Korean prostitute's dream that "he is just my plane ticket stateside." Once here, I learned of mostly failed marriages. In the course of my work as a public official following my discharge, I supplied legal data to some divorcees who with existing entrepreneur skills opened bar-and-strip establishments, while very few others found gainful, decent employment upon learning vocational skills. As a result, my educated guess would be to place in the single digits the probability of successful marriages with *josan*s from this Far East corner of Asia.

Trade Risks

Down the vill
Love from thrill
Some with ill
Cured with pill

The profession was not without risks. That pregnancies occurred during the American occupation in the sixties was evident by the number of mixed racial non-Korean-looking children—a common sight playing in the village. Although I heard of pregnancies, I never saw an expectant *josan*.

Once, I saw a prostitute carrying a baby of an obvious Afro-American father, and I am sure there was another share of Latin-American and Anglo children running around. On another occasion, a beautiful, light-complexioned little girl with blue eyes, at McGovern, surprised me when she communicated with me only in Korean. Later I found out that she was the daughter of a Korean employee. Only once did a prostitute advise me she knew of a pregnancy that was terminated by making a scissor sign with her hand. Once in Yongju-Gol, I came across a beautiful "business woman" with long, dark brown hair and hazel eyes, probably an offspring of a Korean War soldier.

To my knowledge, altercations were rare. I do, however, remember one night of great excitement as we entered the village. One soldier was bent over a jeep, bleeding from his bandaged head while an MP attempted to control the gathered crowd with his .45 pointing in the air. I never knew what actually happened, but decades later I learned that about that same time, a village prostitute had been stabbed.

I only heard of a two-*josan* brawl in "The Alley" at the greater village of Yongju-Gol. "The Alley" was taboo for Caucasian GIs as the prostitutes catered to our Afro-American brothers. A Caucasian medic attended the stabbed *josan*, with Caucasian MPs present, to avoid any unauthorized intruders or confrontations. I never heard of two soldiers fighting for one girl, for no woman was anyone's chattel, she simply boasted multiple clients. Out of mutual respect among buddies, no soldier would supposedly patronize his pal's girl.

There were a few cases where bullies harassed virgin soldiers by questioning their manhood until the soldier succumbed. It was obvious that these older aggressors had a few manhood problems of their own and found easy targets in the inexperienced and naive younger upstart warriors. I was privy to a situation where a female barber addressed a soldier as "cherry boy," an appellation by the indigenous female population to virgin soldiers.

Unlike streetwalkers, all the *josans* who worked out of the teahouse received frequent medical attention and were required to carry identification cards (termed VD Cards) to prove they were free of disease. Once, I heard of a prostitute who had just returned from convalescing from a severe attack of venereal disease. She had to be certified "clean" to continue in the profession. Before signing out on a pass, all soldiers were required to carry a prophylactic. It was common to see a box filled with contraceptives by a sign that read "No enlisted man will be allowed on pass without a prophylactic in his possession" at the sign-out desk. Seldom did the officer or sergeant in charge of quarters ever enforce this, but woe unto the soldier who contracted the disease. Still, despite all precautions, I knew of at least one close friend among others who contracted gonorrhea. He was restricted to camp and underwent a series of penicillin shots and checkups at the dispensary until he was cured.

Supposedly, the *josans* retained half of all earnings, less their indebtedness to the *mamasan*. The *mamasan* (in this case the pimp) in turn washed their clothes, cooked, and provided for all their needs. Somehow, the *josans* always ended indebted to their *mamasan* until they paid up or some lovesick soldier "purchased" them as a "steady." Reportedly, *josans* consumed three meals a day, and I once heard that a *mamasan* beat up a *josan* because she had consumed more than what she earned. In effect, the *josans* were enslaved by their *mamasan* until redeemed. Conceivably, most supported their parents and siblings who must have known or ignored how their daughters worked. Another story circulated about a prostitute who had had enough from her *mamasan,* and while the *mamasan* was about, the *josan* ran off after stealing all monies from the premises. I understood that Korean law prohibited these prostitutes from marrying a Korean National, so one of them explained to me about opening and operating a bakery in Seoul at her "retirement." With the exception of the independent streetwalkers, all *josan's* passion (along with the risk of disease) was negotiated with the *mamasan* and sales and services took place like bargaining at a bazaar at this Far East Corner of Asia.

Lucrative Profession

Bought and sold
For some gold
Slave to be
Slow to free

I must say that I was pleasantly surprised when, upon my arrival at Korea in November 1964, I noticed Korean men and women employed in the business establishments within the camps. I never noticed any Korean nationals employed at the Yongsan PX in Seoul. Anglo-American women, probably military dependents, had the cashier, bookkeeper, and clerical jobs. In the division area, Korean women worked as barbers, manicurists, and masseurs at the barber shops. Each PX within the division area also hired Korean women as sales clerks. I also noticed a troupe of about 100 Korean women heading toward the laundry facilities located within Camp Blue Lancer early every morning. They did the laundry for all the camp and probably for other camps as well, judging from the size of the building. Women could have served cleaning offices, polishing shoes and boots; as well as houseboys, fixing bunks; or as kitchen police hirelings and cooks in the military compounds. This might have led to relationships not approved by the military. The presence of limited vocational women and the lack of professional women in the military area made prostitution a lucrative profession around the camps. I was surprised once with the company of four female university students, who attended a picnic sponsored by the Service Club in Yongsan, Seoul. They participated in all activities and as the day came to a close, hinted at extra activities for the evening and night. We soldiers were stunned at their forwardness and had considered them elite women, though bold enough to attend an army picnic. I do not believe they were full time *josans*, but perhaps prostituted on the side for college money.

Rather than attending financially inaccessible higher education and still earning such a meager living while witnessing their families starving to death, the postwar poverty and the U.S. military occupation of Korea made women's roles in prostitution attractive with the otherwise impossible opportunity of marrying a soldier and migrating stateside. Many young women from all over Korea sought their fortunes up north at the military sectors, with the certainty of a better income. In conversation with a young prostitute, regarding how she came into the profession, she explained that one day, hungry and strolling the streets of Seoul seeking employment, a nice woman walked up to her. After a short introduction, the conversation turned to the availability of a job. The compassionate woman bought her a meal and offered her a job. She was told about American soldiers in the North Country seeking companionship, and all she had to do was provide them with sympathy and her presence. She said the woman never told her she was expected to engage in sexual intercourse. The woman then bought her a toy whose description I never understood, but my interviewee said she was comfortable and secure. She was then brought to the military sector, sold to a *mamasan* who in turn sold her virginity. Considering her sexual experience, she could not return home in shame. Also, for the first time, she had substantial money of her own and the prospect of more, so she entered the world of prostitution. Every woman had a story to tell, and it was probably repeated to every inquiring and curious GI.

The prostitute lived by an unwritten code. The village *josans* with *mamasans* who worked out of the "teahouses" considered themselves the elite because of their health ID cards and expected the standard fee. This identification was required to enter military facilities but only while escorted by a soldier responsible for them. These were the pretty, pampered, well-groomed, and nicely dressed *josans*. They would not allow themselves to be seen nude—modesty was their self-requirement.

The teahouse *josans'* favors were available for two to three dollars a trick. Five dollars would purchase one night's passion. The more stripes on the soldier's sleeve, the greater the price. Payday's sex was costlier, other times, it was highly negotiable. Reportedly, the village was prohibited to senior sergeants and especially to officers—though everyone turned a blind eye. Still, there were other means and ways for these gentlemen to find and pay for their pleasure. Some soldiers went "steady" or "kept" *josans*. They paid from thirty to fifty dollars a month depending on her attributes and the soldier's rank. Needless to say, their faithlessness with other soldiers was additional income when the troops were away on week-long field problems or on guard duty. The independent prostitutes who roamed the streets without a *mamasan* or teahouse privileges would do just about anything for money from a variety of nude dancing to oral sex. The possibility of contracting a venereal infection from these streetwalkers was extremely high. They too, insisted on a standard fee but were more amendable, open to negotiation. Then there were those residing at a brothel known only as the Turkey Farm. Reportedly, these prostitutes were so vaginally diseased that they had been reduced to performing oral sex exclusively, because no soldier would otherwise patronize them.

I guess the despicable work of a *mamasan* (pimp) and the ignominious procuress was a lucrative profession itself. The moneylenders were another story. I do not know who was the worst offender, the despised GI moneylender, the mamasan, or the procuresses. I never learned much about procuresses but the *mamasans* openly lived as the queens of the village, each with a group of three to five *josans*. The *mamasans* bargained for their girls' favors and these behaved as the sweetest and most amiable women around. I remember one *mamasa*n who took her girls to the theater in Pobwan-Ni periodically. Her *josans* looked happy with the outing. On another occasion, I spied a well-known *mamasan* inspecting a sack of rice from a farmer before her purchase. A *mamasan* and her family shared living quarters. Once, by coincidence, I came across one of a *mamasan's* biological daughters (who was not in the business) at a pastry shop in Seoul. She was exceptionally well groomed and clothed—at the expense of the *josans* of this Far East corner of Asia.

Epilogue

It could be argued that postwar-Korea was a single man's paradise. Yet, I remember limited or stray comments under restrained whispers about this phenomenon from perhaps one or two senior sergeants, prior to my duty overseas. However, in the Korea of 1965, during my tour of duty, the information in this chronicle was common knowledge. The profession of teahouse *josans* or streetwalkers was accepted in the military sector by the resigned local population as a way of life in the poverty status of postwar-Korea—it was a truth, it existed! Although the subject of sex and prostitution was always taboo stateside, I would still classify the *josan* as a soldier's best-kept secret of this Far East corner of Asia.

In the words of a fellow veteran:

> "As I read this book it brought back vivid memories. I could not help but wonder in what light I would have viewed this chapter if I had not been there myself. I ponder how one can grasp the shocking realities of such open prostitution without experiencing the environment that bred them. The Koreans are a marvelous people worthy of our respect for their hard work and the hard lives many endure. In the United States we think of prostitutes as women willing to sell their bodies in order to enrich themselves, to make a living without an education and hard work, or to support a drug habit. Many of the Korean prostitutes were very young and turned to the profession to support grandparents, parents and siblings. They had no option for welfare, food stamps, or government assistance. Most had no hope of an education or

employment beyond bare subsistence. It breaks my heart to think of a father giving up his child in this way so the rest of the family could eat. I am told these girls earned more money in a month than their fathers would gross in a year. Their world was one in which they either worked or starved. I find I cannot judge them and leave that to a higher power."

**—Command Sergeant Major Jay Fidel,
United States Army (Ret)**

Chapter 8

Life outside the Fence

Prologue

My adventuring outside the camp included associating with the indigenous population. Discovering available transportation and Service Club perks, my ventures extended outside the community to include souvenir shopping, the culture and poverty of Korea.

Wild Night on the Town
February, 1965

A China doll I met that day
Who walked with me along the way
A ride, a show, a dance, a sway
Somewhere I lost my runaway

It was one of those sunny but cold mornings, sometime during the late winter of 1964-1965, that my buddy Private First N.E. decided to wander within the village of Nopae Dong and invited me along. Then as the balmy afternoon gently flowed into night, little did I anticipate it would become a wild one. He told me to just be cool and enjoy the tour. We spent the entire balmy afternoon, wandering around Nopae Dong, visiting several hooches, and dropping by on many a *josan*. I saw many people that I paralleled to the people in my barrio back home. I had no memory of where within the village we strayed, only that the stench, hooches, and especially the prostitutes blew my mind. Since it was my first time gallivanting all over the village, and having dropped by many a hooch, I became slightly disoriented, and I had no idea where we were. It was late in the afternoon when N.E. decided to pay his current *yobo* (girlfriend) a visit, so we cruised through the rice paddies and proceeded to her hooch by entering a patio somewhere in the nearby village of Koom-Shi. I felt pretty lost in a foreign hamlet in a foreign land somewhere in East Asia. N.E.'s *josan* was hanging out on the porch and greeted him profusely. Well, his girlfriend had a girlfriend who introduced herself as Yung Su. She was my first date in Korea, and I instantly took a liking to her. All village *josans* were willing dates, so I was aware that perhaps I was not attractive or special or necessarily her first or last. Yung Su was petite, very feminine, and so short that her head barely reached my neck. She was a quiet person; her voice was soft and mellow. Her long, black hair draped her shoulders. Her brown, sloe eyes shone softly as she smiled sweetly. Her small mouth parted, displaying a pair of full lips that only exhibited her two front teeth. Her pixie-like face was free of makeup, which was a norm for pretty village *josans*. Yung Su spoke a little English and my Korean consisted of the word *ne,* meaning yes, and *ku-mop seem-nee-da,* thank you. N.E. and his *yobo* were engaged in a GI lingo conversation while Yung Su and I managed a forgettable conservation of sorts.

It was dusk by the time N.E. and his girlfriend finally decided on a movie at the greater village of Pobwan-Ni. As we left the dimly lit village of Koom-Shi and walked into the night, I couldn't tell exactly where we were, but since I was so involved in the evening, location seemed unimportant. N.E. was a veteran of thrills and knew his way around, so I trusted his judgment and knowledge of the area's amusements and entertainments. All the distantly placed lampposts were brilliantly lit along the road, as were all the lights at McGovern, in contrast to the dimly and randomly lit village. I barely remember boarding a Korean Kimchi bus, which was always crowded and crammed with passengers. I remember that Yung Su deliciously clung onto me with her arms fully around my waist, as the bus rolled and wobbled about the uneven Korean rural road. N.E. and his girlfriend were as carefree as I was uneasy about getting lost. However, due to my height, I was able to always pick him out among the tops of the many heads in the crowded bus. It was nightfall when we reached Pobwan-Ni, and I was wild with excitement. Pobwan-Ni's lighting along with the entire heavens was a combined smear of non-memory.

When we finally got off at Pobwan-Ni, the theater was featuring a live stage show. We entered to find a comedy in progress. I remember the actors were Korean people dressed in colorful native costumes, playing pranks on one another. A couple involved in a dialogue kept the audience in laughter. I was in high spirits. The young woman sitting next to me was my date, and not there by coincidence, as sometimes at the San Antonio theaters of my youth. In the available subdued light, I could see Yung Su's smiling sloe eyes focused on the comedians as she enjoyed the show and how she blinked just before each smile. Each of her sweet smiles revealed her parted lips that displayed her twined front teeth. Placing my arm around her and clasping her close to me, I kissed her cheek. She turned to me with the sweetest smiling eyes and parting lips. Suddenly something tan colored flashed by me. It smelled like something between dead fish and dried shrimp. A vendor was selling dried, pencil-thick, stinky, flattened frogs uniformly dangling from a coathanger-like wire. A girl close by bought one, tore at it one piece at a time, and chewed it like taffy or fruit leather. She looked at me and chuckled. I can only guess what facial expression I was producing as I wondered what her breath would reek like. After the variety show was over, we fought our way through the crowds and proceeded toward the exit. We boarded a bus heading back to the camp where N.E. assured me of continued entertainment. Yung Su again hung onto me for dear life during the bus ride, while I grasped the overhead rails. I guessed that because of her height she was afraid she could easily become wedged among the *taller* people and become "lost," and this was an acceptable way to stay close.

THEATER AT THE GREATER VILLAGE OF POBWAN-NI

We arrived safely at McGovern and N.E. headed for the clamor of the EM Club. I had never been in a nightclub, and curiosity rampant, followed to see what kind of amusement he anticipated. Heretofore, I had nonchalantly bypassed the club since it held no interest for me. As we entered, the noise was deafening, with loud boisterous talking, laughing, yelling, and the merrymaking environment unfamiliar to me. I saw some of my Personnel buddies and many from Third Brigade and others I didn't recognize, probably from the First of the Seventh—all drinking beer from bottles, or cans, or from glasses at the bar and at tables. I could see the surprise in their faces when they saw me. It was as if I had just grown three heads or something unnatural. However, no one said anything or seemed to care about anyone else—all were involved in their own business in this live-and-let-live far-from-home situation. There was a dance floor for dancing to live music on the stage. I saw many neatly dressed and over-painted prostitutes, all caught up in the gaiety as they partied with their GI dates. Later, I realized these *josans* were enjoying and living in the moment. N.E. moved easily through the crowd and found us an empty table. As we sat down, he ordered a round of beer, but I requested a coke since I did not drink alcohol. I absorbed my surroundings. I saw Private First P. on the dance floor having a great time spinning and dancing to a rock-and-roll song followed by a *Cha cha cha* with his guest. As we were the new arrivals to Korea, I was naïve enough to believe that they had discovered this type of life way before me. Later, I realized their experience in this type of environment had begun stateside. As the evening progressed, a few guys asked me about Yung Su, and all I could say was that she was from Koom-Shi. I guessed that she must not be one of the local *josans*. Perhaps her clientele were the guys from Camp Coursen, Paris, and Johnson (an adjacent "community" to McGovern), which bordered her village.

After a while, I got to know Yung Su a little better and we danced. I took some pictures of her and with her. The evening grew late and my unaccustomed ears were popping and buzzing to the deafening music and loud noise of the people "having fun." Soon I was yearning for peace and quiet. I wanted to get back to the quietude and calmness of my warm quarters and check my mail. Finally, N.E. took pity and we decided to take our guests back to Koom-Shi.

This was my first night out on a date. For the first time in my life I dated a girl of my choice without being shamed or ridiculed by my mother or sisters, whether she was a girl next-door or a prostitute of far-off Asia. I found it exciting because of the dazzling lights, the dark, cold night, and all the events which made up the kaleidoscope that seemed to whirl me round and round distorting scenes and disorienting me, and especially the heady pleasure of having a warm body clinging to me.

I was indebted to my bosom brother N.E. (who later EDDPAC'ed at Ross) for his patient and empathetic ear that period of my naïveté during my early days in Korea. I never saw Yung Su again. I never looked her up. She never crossed my mind. I never understood what happened to my first date; my Yung Su at this Far East Corner of Asia.

PHOTO CREDIT: (SP4) L.R., PERSONNEL, 15TH ADMIN CO, 1ST CAV DIV, KOREA, 1964

AS WITH ALL GIS, I EXPERIENCED AN INSTANT CRUSH ON OGGIE.

Oggie
February 1965

Within the Land of the Morning Calm
I met a world with never a qualm
The care for her I could not feign
Over my heart this doll could reign

It was in the winter of 1964-1965, following the freezing snows, that I again accompanied my bosom buddy N.E. on a picture-taking outing away from the confines of "our community." I departed the community and entered the mysterious "outer" world in the Land of the Morning Calm. Before this, most of my experiences were limited to the privileged access to the outside world under the auspices of a supervised church retreat or service club sponsored tour, but N.E. assured me that there were many other wonders beyond the barbwire threads. I had looked forward to this since childhood—I had lived for this very day, and all the marvels of the world were waiting for me, when I exited McGovern's main gate and boarded a Korean bus.

Our first stop was at Pobwan-Ni, where I first experienced a whirled, blurred night-out with N.E. and Yung Su. N.E. assured me that this village boasted more shops and facilities than Nopae Dong. Time passed in a bustle of sights and sounds with nothing recalled except a gorgeous chilly and bright sunny day with the underlying eternal stench of human-body waste. Through it all, I managed to take a really bad picture of the main drag with my "Mickey Mouse" instamatic 126 camera. N.E. was surprised at the kind of camera a buff like me was using such that he proceeded to advise me on the power of the single-lens reflex camera. It did not take me long to understand picture quality, so I immediately prepared to purchase a higher quality instrument. We were off on another adventure.

Our next stop was at the greater village of Yongju-Gol. The cold, sunny afternoon warmed my adventurous spirit such that even the fecal-smelling ditches that lined the dirt streets momentarily ignored my nostrils. I was awed by the whole "commercial district" which bustled with GIs and Oriental people along the series of colorful slap-dash shops. This was more like the *Downtown* we had passed by on the truck the night I was on air guard on our return to camp from the November field problem, when a buck private. I felt that I had found the place where I could shop for genuine mementos.

At Miss Lee's Variety and Souvenir Shop, N.E. introduced me to Oggie. Oh, Oggie! One glimpse at Oggie and I knew I'd have ♪ *"to stand in line to get a dance with sweet pea,"* and that *"underneath the stars (I'd say) to sweet pea: Oh, sweet pea, I love you can't you see?"* ♪ as in "Sweet Pea" by Tommy Roe and like in the song "Jo-Ann" by The Playmates: ♪ *"And if you saw her you'd understand-Ann, JO-Ann."* ♪ As with all GIs, I experienced an instant crush on Oggie. Then N.E. asked Oggie to don her traditional Korean dress, so we could photograph her. At that point, I could have traded my soul for Oggie. My legs weakened, my jaw dropped, I went mute, and moaned. She posed with all her majestic poise and manner. She was so feminine, good-looking, and charming. Oggie had a Hollywood-quality beauty as a well-endowed *ten* in my book. She always wore a sweet smile and went out of her way to please all her customers. Her warm personality never ceased to cause fierce pounding of my heart.

Years later, I admitted and confirmed (to myself at least) that of the many women I came across in my entire year in Korea, even the gorgeous women in church, none could compare to Oggie. She was an all-natural beauty. She needed no makeup to enhance her looks. It was no wonder that I faithfully shopped at Oggie's while stationed at McGovern and Ross. I ordered a custom-made photograph album, purchased silk, woodcarvings, and souvenirs for the family. For the remainder of my tour of duty it was at Miss Lee's Variety and Souvenir Shop that I confidently purchased 90 percent of my keepsakes, trusting Oggie without fear of being taken. At times, she trotted down the streets of Yongju-Gol to find a particular article I wanted: a silk robe, a square of black velvet—she always succeeded. Anyone who met her knew she was a prize catch, and blessed was the man who would win her heart.

PHOTO CREDIT: (SP4) L.R., PERSONNEL, 15TH ADMIN CO, 1ST CAV DIV, KOREA, 1964
THEN (PFC) N.E. ASKED OGGIE TO DON HER TRADITIONAL KOREAN DRESS SO WE COULD PHOTOGRAPH HER. SHE WAS SO FEMININE, GOOD-LOOKING AND CHARMING.

Once I had my film developed, with Oggie as my star model, I mailed my mother Oggie's picture. I informed her that I had found the love of my life and that, as soon as convenient I would baptize her in the church in preparation for marriage. I forgot all about the message until a week or so later when I received, a shocking *cablegram*, expressing, *"Don't marry, mailing detailed letter."* I immediately replied saying that the whole story was a joke and for her not to worry. In a succeeding letter, my upset sister wrote that my "marriage announcement" blew mother's mind and sent her into a flying rage. Ironically enough, my niece had picked up the last sheet fallen to the floor where I had stated that all was in jest. Still, my mother ordered the cablegram. Eight months later, I chuckled as this whole incident was brought to mind during guard duty, while walking the fence behind C Company, beneath Radio Hill, at Blue Lancer Valley (BLV), during the November 1965 chills.

Once I relocated from Ross to Blue Lancer the summer of 1965, the Blue Lancer PX (that rivaled the PX in Yongsan, Seoul) provided for the remainder of my shopping requirements. Although I frequently returned to Yongju-Gol during the remaining five months of my duty year, stationed at the BLV, it was not until thirty-plus years that I was amazed I continually bypassed Oggie's shop. How soon I forgot my infatuation! I never again paused to feel her *music* or "rekindle" her enchantment. As I sit back and reminisce of Oggie, my new "Runaway," my "Sweet Pea," my "unrequited flame," I hope she eventually received the best that God had to offer at that Far East corner of Asia.

THE KWANG TAN MIRUK OR MERCIFUL BUDDHAS

Colossal Buddhas
Early Spring 1965

A pair of statues touch the skies
Of sculpted stone with half closed eyes
Command the peak to far-flung hills
And fields and glens and peopled vills

It was on one of those chilly mornings under the Korean early spring sun of 1965 that troopers of the First Cavalry Division assaulted Mount Chan Ji. As the troops swarmed up the foothills, some were compelled to drop to a crawl through the thick brush. Running high on adrenalin, I maneuvered along the greenery on my first "live action." I remember wriggling on my belly around the brush and boulders like a snake through pebbles and over twigs, when I encountered the dreaded barbwire that secured our objective. As I squirmed through to avoid entanglement, I was sighted, and at that moment, I became aware of the droning whistle of an approaching missile. I instinctively flattened on ground level and successfully dodged the flying object whizzing through the bushes and heard one of the troopers behind me go down. In instant reaction, I took aim and got a few crack shots. Many fingers simultaneously squeezed many triggers all around me, but confident of my aim, I witnessed one go down—*on my first shot*!

I exulted over the power of my trigger finger. I was blown away by the thrill that my first *snapshot* was of kowtowing worshippers, and of the monk who had stoned us off from the Kwang Tan Miruk religious ceremony.

The trip to the Kwang Tan Miruk or Merciful Buddhas at Mount Chan Ji was my very first tour, and the Camelot Service Club of Camp McGovern's Recreation Center had sponsored it. I really had no idea where we were going, or what the Kwang Tan Miruk was; all I knew was that this was my first guided adventure of the Korean rural culture.

I INSTINCTIVELY FLATTENED ON GROUND LEVEL AND SUCCESSFULLY DODGED THE FLYING OBJECT WHIZZING THROUGH THE BUSHES. MONK AT RIGHT BEHIND TREE HURLING A STONE.

MY FIRST SNAPSHOT WAS OF KOWTOWING WORSHIPPERS THROUGH BARBWIRE THAT PROTECTED THEIR SANCTUARY.

As the deuce-and-a-half approached the mountain, my excitement accelerated when I caught sight of the colossal Buddha trio at the summit. I remember that my life nearly ended as I jumped off the truck before it came to a complete stop, but I did not care. Intoxicated with delight, I charged toward the six-story-high sculptures like a bull at a red flag with wide-opened nostrils exhaling smoke. I was in ecstasy and in such a wild state that I must have slid, slipped, and slithered about, around, over, among, and between these authentic Asiatic objects of worship. The sculptures commanded a panoramic view of the valley and the rice paddies below. Here I was, not only mingling among *genuine existent Buddha statues*, but the memorable moment in time was among sculptures of *monumental proportion* on a stunning mountaintop of a remote Asiatic country such as I had only seen on filmed documentaries. Excited by these ancient treasures, I could hardly take it all in as I took pictures everywhere. I was a crazed madman, fulfilling one of my dreams beyond my wildest imagination! I could not believe this fortunate episode that a childhood dream was realized. Aahhh! but I was picking up the pace toward nearby ninth Nirvana—all as I had anticipated in my boyhood when I would join the U.S. Army! Thirty years later, I visualized myself as this young soldier, eyes huge as saucers and which were probably crossed by the time I descended that remote mountaintop.

The heads of the two Buddhas were about three times a man's height, each about one-body-length across, and about twelve times as high from the ground. One had a square top hat and the other a wide rounded brim. They were constructed of three parts: the hat, which sat on the head, which in turn rested on the chest and body. They both appeared in meditation with their Oriental eyes half closed. All were sculpted from the gray seemingly porous stone common to Korea. I reminded myself that these colossi were exactly what I would visualize in a *National Geographic Magazine*.

THE BUDDHAS' HEADS WERE ABOUT THREE TIMES A MAN'S HEIGHT.

THE SCULPTURES COMMANDED A PANORAMIC VIEW OF THE VALLEY FROM THE RICE PADDIES TO THE FAR MOUNTAINS.

A nine-hundred-year-old legend held that King Sun Jong (1084-1094) caused these two immense Buddha effigies to be fashioned out of two enormous mountain boulders at Mount Chang Ji. They represented two Buddhist monks who had advised his childless queen in a dream. They thirsted for water, and after she satisfied their thirst, they promised her a son. The king built an altar at the site and prayed for an heir. Soon Queen Won Shin presented him with a son and the next king of the Koryo dynasty. A third tiny Buddha was installed in 1953 by President Syngman Rhee. Childless couples are known to worship there in petition for children.

At the foot of Mt. Chang Ji, Miss Chang, the hostess had a group picture taken at an altar. As we lingered around, we came upon an incense-manufacturing hooch, surrounded with intensely Oriental spicy but pleasant fragrances. A second quaint and picturesque hooch with a straw roof, plastered walls, papered windows, and a raised porch caught my attention. It seemed to materialize out of a medieval picture book. I photographed it as a memento of Korean culture, thinking to perhaps share it in conversation with friends back home.

MISS CHANG'S GROUP PICTURE TAKEN AT AN ALTAR WITH AUTHOR AT UPPER RIGHT CORNER.

Once back and seated in the departing truck, I gazed back. The colossi optically appeared to loom progressively larger as we drove off. The grand sculptures, in all their majestic dignity, appeared magnified amid all the wooded greenery, crowned with a magnificent aura of royal blue. This, my first tour, in all its abundance of color and detail, would remain forever etched in my memory of this Far East corner of Asia.

THE COLOSSI OPTICALLY APPEARED TO LOOM PROGRESSIVELY LARGER AS WE DROVE OFF.

THE BUDDHA'S FACE WAS AS TALL AS THE AUTHOR'S SIX-FOOT HEIGHT.

Twilight
Spring 1965

A father close, a father far
Un padre al cruzar el mar
Two fathers with a single son
Nauy abogee, papasan

One evening at twilight, I happened to be seated on a porch at a hooch at Nopae Dong. Observing the setting sun and the approaching dusk waning into darkness on an early spring evening in 1965, I felt comfortably at ease, carefree as the wind, and lost in the sunset phenomenon.

I HAPPENED TO BE SEATED ON PORCH AT A HOOCH AT NOPAE DONG.

An elderly Korean gentleman, with a faraway look, happened to be seated next to me. He also seemed to be taking in the amazing transition from light to dusk on this balmy evening. Unconsciously, I took the *papasan's* hand as I used to take my dad's when we were seated on the front-porch bench-swing in my boyhood. I was taken aback when I felt that his hand, like my dad's, was as rough as coarse sandpaper and broken in some places, marking his life's work in this still agrarian third-world country. His face, hardly discernable under the fading light of the dark porch, revealed a wrinkled weathered countenance. It reflected the unforgiving life of hardship and poverty he had lived. It was clear he had handled the plow, sowed and reaped his field, and bent his back under the A-frame throughout his long life.

I broke the silence and in my poor Korean quietly said, *"Nauy abogee catago yogie eeseemneeda."* (My father had same hands), *"Nauy abogee Mexican namja eemneeda,"* (My father is a Mexican man).

The gentleman did not say a word. He never withdrew his hand. His eyes were also fixed on the distantly lit horizon.

There was quietude in the air. The faraway sky turned light blue, clearly defining the skyline of the distant Easy and Queen.

For a moment, just one moment in time, I again felt my dad's hand. For that moment too, perhaps this gentleman felt in me the presence of an absent son, or one that he never had, or one he may have lost in the war. How could I let the *papasan* know that my deceased dad had suffered similar experiences during his early life in Mexico, or of his impressment, and of his advancement to sergeant in his turbulent service in the federalist forces during the Mexican Revolution? The communing moments enveloped us silently.

The sky directly above us quietly turned a navy blue, discernibly contrasting with the blackness of the porch posts and overhanging straw roof.

The atmosphere remained still and calm. We jointly became one with the quiet land. We sat thus, silent in contemplation, enjoying the last of the disappearing soft blue twilight that touched the mountaintop in the distance under a progressively darkening sky.

The blackness of the night closed in. The clapping of the village generator broke the stony silence typical of the land and hooches were randomly lit all over the dark village. Somewhere, a girl sang, ♫"Yo SO so soo."♫ Our merged spirits parted, and I bid the elderly gentleman farewell saying *"a nyang hee ka ship shee yo, abojee,"* meaning "farewell, Father."

In the years that passed, I pictured the Asiatic gentleman still seated at his porch *with ghostly me* in this remote scene in faraway Asia, much like my own dad sat *with ghostly me* at our porch, if only in my imagination, during the last years of his life at my San Antonio home on the opposite side of the earth.

Memories of that evening's communion when a *Hanguk abogee* (Korean father) and my *soldado padre* (soldier father), via an occupying American GI, touched spirits, were everlasting for me in this Far East corner of Asia.

Nopae Dong
March 1965

Distant shacks and earth paths too
Plastered walls, tiled roofs a few
Sticks on legs stir to and fro
Mid stench at fields where reapers sow

Standing at Number One, McGovern's preferred guard tower and gazing toward the village of Nopae Dong one of those early spring afternoons, the scene just begged for McGovern to be immortalized by photographing the camp from each guard tower. The village, along with the ever-present rice paddy stench that doubled in the warming temperatures, attracted my attention. My eyes remained fixed on the distant panorama. In the distance, it appeared quaint and picturesque. Although I had daily viewed the village, it suddenly took on a different aspect. Unexpectedly, the whole accumulation of hooches that ascended the sloping mountain backdrop took individual distinctiveness, a mural. I had already gotten up close and personal by walking through the village, but I had never viewed it from this perspective.

For the first time I stared at the Korean *dong* (settlement) and frame by frame, I viewed it with objective interest. I noticed that some hovels were roofed with tile and others with straw. Walls of painted clay and others of earth-brown appeared like tiny stacked-up brown cardboard boxes of different sizes and shapes. Although a far cry in culture and construction, these hooches reminded me of the Native American Pueblo Dwellings of the southwestern states of Arizona and New Mexico. Both communities could be representative in their respective continents during The Medieval Era. Closer inspection revealed porches at recessed patios. I thought I saw a shadow within an open door. I noticed roofed chimneystacks and separated outhouses with slanted makeshift slat-roofs. Two white prominent structures identified the teahouses.

One spring morning, on one of our many village adventures that my buddy Private First Abilio Mendiola and I were traversing Nopae, I experienced a need to use the restroom. Feeling much at home and among my own people, I decided to casually stroll through a side path that led to the private dwellings. Perhaps I would catch sight of some interesting female secret within the opened paper doors, as I had once purposefully slowed my stroll through the San Antonio alleys close to open windows. At the corner of a neatly swept dirt-yard, I found what I was looking for. Meticulously scanning the approximate vicinity from Number One, I finally located the outhouse. It would not have mattered, if I had contributed to the already smelly environment at any corner or tree, but I decided on a little discretion. The small patio was abandoned, and no one seemed to be home or around at the outhouse I had encountered. Without invitation, I swung open the outhouse door, and a five-gallon drum sunk at earth level greeted me. The increased stench of human feces further assaulted my nostrils within the warmed-enclosed structure. A generous concoction of solid and fluid fermented matter lifted its fumes and bombarded my olfactory glands from between two time-stained parallel slats. As a six-footer, I practically had to fold my head under the tiny coffin-size structure. Maneuvering, by the grace of God, I narrowly missed falling between the slats into the brewing mire. I found it difficult to get my business done, missing the narrow opening every time within the cramped quarters.

At the guard tower, with restrooms in mind, my thoughts flashed back to December 1964. I recollected the unisex restroom at the church Mission Home in Seoul. An oblong arched and concave-ridged ceramic "toilet" projected from the center of the tiled floor. It was about eighteen inches long, six inches wide and about four inches at the high arc. At the tug of a handle, water would flush from one end and would drain at the other. The Asiatic anatomy easily enabled squatting for evacuation. Taller westerners would just have to make do with the accommodation. On the door was an approximately eighteen-by-eighteen-inch plain-glass window that allowed for occupant observation. Korean protocol, as elsewhere in Asia, does not call for toilet or gender privacy as in Western or European cultures—the "busy" occupant was considered invisible.

Then, upon noticing a chimney at each hooch, I recalled the construction of the typical rural home, exactly as described in the Department of Defense guidebook I had read prior to my arrival in Korea. The floor of the Korean home, constructed of earth or concrete, was honeycombed with embedded tubes fashioned from soft-drink cans. These ducts ran past from one side of the hooch to the other, with one end at the chimney and the other at an outside circular concrete pit. This cavity was about nine inches in diameter and about one foot deep. It accommodated a white-charcoal cake that warmed the floors during winter—eliminating the need for shoes—and doubled as a cooking stove. In summer, a damper blocked the ducts while still allowing for cooking.

All the while on Guard Tower One I fixed my gaze toward the village, occasional random movement assured me that life continued as usual in the community. I became aware of white dots and sticks moving purposely all about bringing my picture to life. Tiny white dots that progressively filled a backyard in a straight horizontal line caught my gaze. Then those tiny dots appeared wavering to my strained watering eyes. From my vision's left, I saw a white "stick body" dot entering my picture mural through the rice paddy, with a small bushy bundle on its forward-leaned back. Approaching it, another "bulkier," smaller white dot, but with another tiny white dot on its head from the opposite direction, entered the scene. I watched curiously as the two dots approached one another on collision course, briefly merged, and then resumed in opposite directions. My glance slowly traveled to my right where I spied the main path of the "commercial district" that led to the village from McGovern. I detected minute dark "sticks" with legs moving about hurriedly across the road and in circles. Larger "sticks" with legs emerged from business doors and either traversed the road or continued up the wide path. The people were going about their business of living!

I noticed that some of the empty rice fields displayed the beginnings of the planting season with emerging water. I marveled as the slowly flooding paddies mirrored the cumulous clouds amid the blue-sky heavens. I found myself again awed by the pleasure I felt at observing this typical Korean agrarian village from afar.

ALTHOUGH I HAD DAILY VIEWED THE VILLAGE, IT SUDDENLY TOOK A DIFFERENT ASPECT. SEE PHOTO P. 215 FOR OPPOSITE VIEW OF THIS GUARD TOWER ONE FROM VILLAGE COMMERCIAL DISTRICT.

As I stood captivated, observing the humble homes of this third world country, it occurred to me that there was a distinct similarity between these hardworking Koreans and my own west San Antonio barrio home, a modest wooden structure in a poor section of town. Here too, people lived, worked, and played—myself among them—under very similar circumstances. However, much as this moved me, I climbed down Number One and in my naïveté merrily resumed my picture-taking from each of McGovern's guard towers at this Far East Corner of Asia.

Poverty in Korea
Entire Tenure

There is nothing so dreadful
as a great victory—except a great defeat.
—Wellington at Waterloo

I was first introduced to the poverty of Korea when some young Korean boys infiltrated the bivouac camp during chow at my first field problem back in November 1964. The boys stood around expecting scraps of food. I always shared my food and remember one time when I shared my milk with one boy by tilting my mess cup on the boy's mouth, allowing him to drink. While these boys were nuisances, most GIs willingly gave them what we did not eat or candy from private stores. It was at these field camps that women came around, selling apples or sweet bread; and peddlers sold cookies or Korean goodies. Curiously enough, though, I never saw girls, although decades later some veterans reported they had seen them. These veterans also commented they specifically took goodies for these children.

Private First N.E., my best buddy and "mentor" upon my arrival in Korea, once pointed out an older man who ceaselessly roamed the streets of Pobwan-Ni, describing him as a "professional beggar." Thereafter, every time I entered Pobwan-Ni, I noticed this same beggar panhandling all the *josans* and GIs for money. It was at the villages that some men approached GIs selling *skivvy* (pornographic) pictures

163

Upon catching sight of soldiers in the mudpacked streets of Yongju-Gol, or Pobwan-Ni children would run up asking for money with *"TONG CajuWAH,"* meaning, "Give me money." The soldier normally responded, *"OOP SO,"* meaning "Don't have," whereupon the kids' response was *"EE SO"* meaning "Do have." These kids panhandled by walking alongside in stride, stretching their arms with cupped hands across the GI's waist. They surrounded the soldier so that he had trouble shoving or pushing them away, as they paced in unison with him. The kids would not tire and at times attach themselves for extended distances. Once, I saw a GI toss a few ringing coins on the ground to be rid of them. Needless to say, the children jumped at the coins like a flock of fowl at feed.

One chilly, winter afternoon, N.E. and I were comfortably seated in a warm village quality restaurant, enjoying a hot cup of herbal tea. A student in his black school cap and tunic proffered me an apologetic note, asking for a donation. I gave him a one hundred won note (approximately forty cents) whereupon the student gave me two maroon pencils and a courteous bow. In retrospect, I hope these children would always harbor a pleasant impression of an American soldier.

I WAS NEVER GOING TO BE ABLE TO GET OVER FREQUENTLY OBSERVING THE TIMELESS PRACTICE OF THE OX AND (RAKE) PLOW.

MEN CARRIED HEAVY BURDENS ON THEIR BACKS BY USE OF THE ANCIENT A-FRAME, HIS PRIZED PLOW SHARE IN THIS CASE. NOTE FARMERS HIP-DEEP IN RICE PADDY BACKGROUND. WOMEN WASHED CLOTHES IN MUCKY STREAMS OR BY USE OF LATHERED WASTEWATER FROM CAMP LATRINES.

I experienced the continued poverty of the Korean countryside, which was more evident during train and bus rides. Still, as an impressionable soldier from the 1965 United States, I was culture-shocked: the grooving of the rice paddies, men carrying heavy burdens on their backs by use of the ancient A-frame, farmers knee-deep in the rice harvests, and horse-drawn wagons, both in the countryside and in Seoul, which I thought was over with the Middle Ages. I saw women washing clothes at mucky streams or in lathered wastewater from camp latrines—it was all part of my year-long mural.

One day, while walking down the Seoul Boulevard on my way to the USO from the Seoul Station, I came across a bedraggled, filthy man lying on the sidewalk with an equally unwashed child by his side. The little boy was quietly and slowly inspecting a corncob that had been already stripped of its kernels. I walked up to them with the intent of waking the man or handing the little boy some money. However, in a moment, a crowd of children who had observed me and the unfortunates surrounded us. Fearing that the observing children would take any money from the little boy, I slowly walked away. Decades later, I recalled my mother's whisperings to one of my sisters. She related that as a starving little girl walking the streets of revolutionary Mexico City rummaging for food scraps, she came upon corn kernels in an alley somewhere. She picked up the food and popped into her mouth and immediately spit it out when she found it to be undigested fecal matter.

Some men turned to burglary. A "slicky boy" or a slick hustler plagued every GI at one time or another. "Mother" warned us at indoctrination not to engage in business with the population, and sure enough, I had my camera taken right under my nose. It was these slicky boys, these professional thieves that successfully burglarized military compounds, without leaving a trace of evidence.

A SMALL SLICE OF STATESIDE AFFLUENCE WAS VISUAL AT EVERY MILITARY CAMP; AND PERHAPS THE TROOPS IN VIEWING THE POVERTY OF KOREA COULD GREATER APPRECIATE OUR COUNTRY! NOTE THE PLOWSHARE AND FRAMEWORK PULLED BY THIS OX.

Whether the poor of Korea included children old enough to beg, *josans*, or job-hunting adults, the GI was looked upon as a sure source of money especially at the beginning of the month. The soldier's monthly salary, although below American standard, was nonetheless a princely sum in this poverty-ridden postwar third-world country. Thus, the American soldier was also a prime game for thieves. Perhaps this small slice of America, personified by the U.S. troops, who represented a controlled or limited American lifestyle, was enough to cause a glimpse of affluent America (the camp), or, at the very least, it afforded a handy potential piggy bank to increase their own standards of living in this Far East Corner of Asia.

Chapter 9

To Seoul by Rail and Bus

November 1964-November 1965

Prologue

My rolling adventures to and from Seoul consisted of a great circle of travel. From my camp at Blue Lancer Valley, my northernmost point of travel, I walked or thumbed the half-mile ride northward to the village of Nullo-Ri. Because GI bus service was unavailable from the camp to the train station at Munsan-Ni, I caught a silver *kimchi* bus at Nullo-Ri heading west, toward the Imjin River that curved south to the greater village (almost a city) of Munsan-Ni and Camp Pelham, to Recreational Center Number Four (RC#4) at the village of Sonyu-Ri. The bus continued to Cultural Center Number Four (CC#4), where I also worshiped. At the Munsan-Ni depot I caught the train which let me off at the train station in Seoul. From there I would walk to the USO or take a taxi to Yongsan, a military shopping center and GI bus depot.

My return trip began with bus number twenty-five at Yongsan, my southern most point of adventure, and headed north through downtown Seoul and to the northward countryside. The MP checkpoint followed and we were in the Cavalry Division area—a conglomeration of villages, military compounds, endless mountains, and stinky rice paddies. Camp Ross, then Camp Beard, and the bus depot within, at the marvelous greater village of Yongju-Gol, followed. Continuing north was the busy commercial minor village and *hopsan* depot of Pobwan-Ni. Then Camp McGovern followed, and after a westward turn to Nullo-Ri, I returned to Camp Blue Lancer Valley, completing a circumvention of the Cavalry Division, area including far-off Seoul.

In the words of an army bus commuter:

"I took a bus to Seoul, sort of like a school bus but military color . . . we had to go to RC #1 (Camp Beard, Yongju-Gol) to catch that bus. I only recall that the trip to Seoul was slow and long. Seemed like the bus took 1 1/2 to 1 3/4 hours for the 35 (?) miles to Seoul. Part of the route was a dirt road, then pavement into Seoul. The bus stopped along the way and in the villages. Doubt the speed was more than 30 or 35 mph over the dirt roads, and a bit faster on the pave ones. There was another bus route in our immediate area. Seemed like this bus did not run too often and made a huge circle that included RC#4 (Munsan-Ni), Camp Pelham, and several places in the direction of the DMZ or in a direction of camps where we did not normally go. Our small unit had a Dodge deuce-and-a-half truck and we used it around the First Cavalry area mostly. Often on personal trips we took a taxi . . . a small car like a Datsun or the like."
—SP4 Michael Brown, AFKN Radio Cavalier,
Eighth Army, Sonyu-Ri,
Korea, 1963-1964.

By Rail

Sights by rail to other zones
Things to view at sites unknown
Scenes and folk and wonders see
Of daily life all just for me

I loved the picturesque Korean countryside that one could see while traveling from Munsan-Ni to Seoul by rail. When I heard about the rail service, I immediately made my way to Munsan-Ni via a *kimchi* bus from Nullo-Ri, and easily found the train station. Once, before the war, rail service ran north beyond Munsan-Ni, across the Imjin River, with probable connections to China and to all of Asia. I took pictures of the river before the train pulled into Munsan-Ni. From Munsan-Ni, service connected to the Seoul Train Station and on to the interior of South Korea. During the conflict, the tracks were blown up at the Imjin River, and I once saw a picture of the damaged tracks. Somewhere, I managed a snapshot of the rails, with Charlie Block in the far background.

RAILROAD SOMEWHERE IN THE CAVALRY AREA, WITH CHARLIE BLOCK MOUNTAIN AT HORIZON

THE IMJIN RIVER, JUST BEFORE THE GREATER VILLAGE OF THE MUNSAN-NI RAILROAD DEPOT

I remembered walking up to the Seoul ticket window, where I simply paid the fare, presented the ticket, and boarded the coach. I made myself comfortable as I scanned the countryside. On each trip, I chose opposite window seats to assure me of all available viewing. Each of those memorable summer or fall days of 1965 was bathed in generous sunshine. I was selfishly exultant while indulging in these happy-go-lucky moments, forgetting my military duty, or any other obligation in the world, of home. Aahhh! but I was careless, caution less, and carefree, all at fifty dollars a month! I was touring every corner of this Asiatic country as I was of many more to come, which was my sole purpose for having joined the U.S. Army.

The countryside was stunning in its own season of the year. Contoured tiers of flooding rice paddies extending to the distant mountains reflected seasonal clouds that announced the coming of the monsoons or the time after the monsoons. I took note of the darker greenery that contrasted against the rich blue sky as the train wove its way among the mountains. I noticed the timely green foot-high rice shoots waving with the wind. According to term, farmers were either opening lumpy furrows, plunging shoots calf-deep in their paddies, or harvesting the rice. I was forever fascinated on viewing that the ox and the plow, which I thought was obsolete and went out with the Middle Ages, were still alive and well in the distant muddy rice paddies. Women carried water jugs or baskets balanced on their heads. Oxen towing farmers' loads and men carrying heavy burdens on their backs by means of A-frames were a common sight on the worn side paths. A farmer and wife team made full use of the ancient threshing method of whipping rice seed from the chaff. The train passed families at lunch, with mothers nursing their infants under shady trees. *Mamasans* slapped their wash at streams and girls washed their hair at creeks. At a pond, children of both genders splashed, naked as the day they were born. The train passed by stops on roads by general stores paralleling the rails with rural folk waiting for the *kimchi* bus. I was reliving the panoramic *India Countryside* motion picture segment observed by *Cantinflas* in the epic film *Around the World in Eighty Days.* Until 1965, I had seen and enjoyed this movie but only once at the Majestic Theater in downtown San Antonio back in 1956. Somehow, I discerned that I had witnessed these splashing children, hills, river, and country folk before—my heart leaped as my memory banks surfaced these recollections. I remembered being overwhelmingly taken-up by this color movie and inspiring musical score, especially on full theater screen—somewhat like my favorite black-and-white travel series: *I search for Adventure* and *Bold Journey,* limited to the small-screen television of the fifties. It was this motion picture I reflected that had awakened and brought to life my dreams and hopes of the otherwise impossible travel outside the service.

CONTOURED TIERS OF FLOODING RICE PADDIES EXTENDING TO THE DISTANT MOUNTAINS REFLECTED SEASONAL CLOUDS THAT EITHER ANNOUNCED THE COMING OF THE MONSOONS OR A TIME AFTER THE MONSOONS.

I WAS FOREVER FASCINATED ON VIEWING THAT THE OX AND PLOW, WHICH I THOUGHT WAS OBSOLETE WITH THE MIDDLE AGES, WERE STILL OPENING FURROWS FOR PLANTING IN THE DISTANT RICE PADDIES.

WOMEN CARRIED WATER JUGS, BASKETS, BUNDLES, OR WARES BALANCED ON THEIR HEADS. FARMERS WERE EITHER PLUNGING SHOOTS CALF-DEEP IN THEIR PADDIES OR HARVESTING RICE. MEN CARRIED HEAVY BURDENS ON THEIR BACKS BY MEANS OF THEIR TIME TESTED A-FRAMES.

A FARMER AND WIFE TEAM MADE FULL USE OF THE ANCIENT THRESHING METHOD OF WHIPPING RICE SEED FROM THE CHAFF.

THE TRAIN PASSED BY A FAMILY PROBABLY ENJOYING LUNCH UNDER THE COOL SHADE OF A TREE WITH THE BABY UNDER THE ADDED PROTECTIVE COVER OF AN UMBRELLA.

A MOTHER NURSED HER INFANT UNDER A SHADY TREE. A GIRL WASHED HER HAIR AT A CREEK.

MAMASANS SLAPPED THEIR WASH AT FAST-MOVING STREAMS.

CHILDREN OF BOTH GENDERS SPLASHED AT A POND NAKED AS THE DAY THEY WERE BORN.

THE TRAIN PASSED BUS STOPS BY COUNTRY GENERAL STORES ON ROADS PARALLELING THE RAILS WITH RURAL FOLK AWAITING THE *KIMCHI* BUS.

Inside the coach, a young girl sang a song loud and clear. I noticed the indifference of the passengers who ignored her. I pulled out and handed her a one hundred won note. She rapidly bowed very low in gratitude. A vendor came around selling ice cream sticks. I purchased about twenty (W100) and passed them all around. The people eyed me, showed a semblance of a smile, then slowly unwrapped and enjoyed.

Once, I saw a pretty girl with a mole on her cheek, reading my nametag. I said to her, "Yes, my name is Martinez," in Korean. I read the surprise in her face as she smiled. I asked her where she lived, and she replied, "At a nearby village." In small talk, I mentioned that I regularly visited and toured Seoul.

I once entered a coach with no available seats. A ROK soldier immediately got up and in deserving mode, I readily took it. I was to eternally feel regret and shame. Years later, I realized that the ROK soldier was far more of a refined gentleman than this uncouth "ugly American" GI. Curiously enough, I never encountered other GIs on the train. I mostly saw a younger crowd, probably commuting to work in Seoul.

I would never be able to express enough how much I enjoyed the rail rides. The gliding flow of the coach on the rails was a far contrast to the bumps and sways of the crammed *hopsans* and kimchi busses on the roughly graded rural roads. Sometimes I excitedly imagined myself inside a space capsule zooming through a subterranean conduit to adventures in parts unknown, as I remembered in the space flicks or *Flash Gordon* television serials during my childhood. In my own world I just floated from one adventure into another from the Munsan-Ni depot. Each excursion seemed a passage into another dimension that uncovered more sight-seeing, extended mysteries, and unknown marvels of this Far East corner of Asia.

ELDERLY GENTLEMAN AND LADY IN TRADITIONAL WHITES

Seoul

Loved the structures, loved the sites
Loved the temples, loved the heights
Loved the people, loved the lights
All in daylight, or the nights

I remember my first solo tour of Seoul. I bunked at the USO, located across the Seoul Boulevard from the train station. By public transportation, bus or taxi, I toured just about every subdivision. However, I also took tours sponsored by the USO and the Service Club at Yongsan.

One of these visits was at Walker Hill. We rode up on a cable car, and at the top, I took photos of Seoul and the panorama from and of the resort area. We drove over the Han River where we stopped, and I took some photos on the Han River Bridge. Once, with a church group, we visited an immense Buddhist temple. We walked in and tiptoed all around the perimeter and took many photos of worshippers. The Buddha behind a glass case appeared of polished gold. On a solo tour, I sought and found the Pul Guk Sa Temple, which had seen better days and where worship was seldom. One tour visited a horse race-track. Some of the officers remained at the track because they had placed bets and awaited their outcomes. On another solo tour, I visited East Gate, a pagoda-like Medieval structure that was once the eastern entry to walled Seoul. Nearby was East Gate Market with a vast open store of goods where one could buy silk, gold, fish, or just about everything necessary. All the vendors were very friendly and good-natured; I guess they were rarely visited by a lone American soldier. At a park somewhere, I saw two men playing a game on a board resembling checkers. A cosmetic factory was filled with hundreds of female employees, and we could not help but cast flirtatious eyes at them. We were rewarded with a bag full of weakly-fragranced fluid lotions. We were provided with a free soft drink at the Seoul Cola plant, where we toured the bottle-making room, the bottle-inspection belt, and a yard with thousands of stacked bottles. At a park somewhere, I came across an elderly gentleman who allowed me to photograph him and his wife in full traditional whites. I think these folks were carrying on the tradition and possibly the last of a vanishing culture, as most wear was westernized. Korean people rarely allow themselves to be photographed, much less pose for the camera.

The USO and Yongsan became my focal points of destination prior to wandering off. I greatly enjoyed all my time wandering around and locating the interesting sites of the city of Seoul, in this Far East corner of Asia.

SEOUL PANORAMA FROM WALKER HILL RESORT

VIEW FROM WALKER HILL

WALKER HILL SWIMMING POOL

WALKER HILL ACCOMMODATIONS

SCENE FROM HAN RIVER BRIDGE

HAN RIVER BRIDGE, SEOUL

WORSHIP IN SESSION AT A MAJOR BUDDHIST TEMPLE IN SEOUL

WORSHIPPERS, ONLY THE ALTAR REMAINED AT THE PUL GUK SA TEMPLE

AT THE RACE TRACK, SOME OFFICERS REMAINED TO SECURE THEIR INTERESTS.

JOCKEYS IN FULL GALLOP ON TRACK

EAST GATE, THE ANCIENT ENTRY TO SEOUL

EAST GATE MARKET, VENDOR OF DRIED FISH; AND ALL KINDS OF FOOD AND DRY GOODS WERE AVAILABLE

PHOTO TAKEN WITHIN A FISH STALL

MEN WERE PLAYING A CHECKER-LIKE GAME

STOREFRONT OF A COSMETIC FACTORY

ASSEMBLY LINE OF NAIL-GLOSS-LIKE BOTTLES

COLA BOTTLE INSPECTORS AT SEOUL COLA PLANT

COLA BOTTLE-FILLING MACHINERY AT SEOUL COLA PLANT

ENTRY LANDING TO USO, SEOUL, KOREA

By Bus

Choice of buses from Seoul to Beard
Traffic, people, buildings appeared
Vills with shops, and fields with smell
My camp, my bunk, I rest all swell

After a good weekend lost in exploring the wonders of Seoul via the USO or the Yongsan Service Club, but mostly on solo tours, I prepared to return to camp. I made my way to Yongsan, where I located the appropriate bus—number 25—bound for Cultural Center Number One (CC#1), Camp Beard at Yongju-Gol. All the buses, resembling chocolate Tootsie Rolls without the flared front and end, were stamped with numbers on small white metal tags at the front and rear. Singling and boarding my intended bus among numerous others at the bus depot, I patiently waited among the few seated mute travelers. At the appointed time, the driver simply entered, occupied his seat, and drove off! Sometimes, number 25 was empty, or occupied by a few soldiers, but rarely ever full. Because GI buses were slow, unreliable, and inconvenient, given the circumstances, I preferred Korean public transportation which ran faster and more often.

BUS DEPOT AT SOUTH SIDE OF YONGSAN SHOPPING CENTER. I WOULD JUST BOARD NUMBER 25, PATIENTLY AWAIT THE DRIVER WHO AT HIS APPOINTED TIME SIMPLY ENTERED AND DROVE OFF.

The silver Korean buses, known as *kimchi* buses, serviced the Cavalry (division area), while the *hopsans* traveled all the way to Seoul from Pobwan-Ni. A *hopsan* was a tiny Volkswagen-like van, modified to seat about twenty passengers. These depots were located at Pobwan-Ni (in the First Cav, at Mickey Mouse Corners) and at the Seoul Station. I simply checked the stroked destinations in Korean, boarded the *hopsan*, found a seat, paid the sixty won fare (roughly sixty cents) to the roaming hostess, and headed for Seoul. This mode of transportation waited for no one and was so hurried that entry or exit was determined by harried passenger control.

Once the northbound GI bus exited Yongsan, it made its way north through the main Seoul Boulevard. I enjoyed the gorgeous chilly calm, mornings; the hot, humid middays; and even the cold afternoons and evenings of December 1964 through November 1965. Gawking at the multitude of busy Asiatic people, I observed the bustle of traffic amid the odor of diesel exhaust. The few horse-drawn wagons that cantered about the boulevard were fascinating and lent a quaint air to the scene. I noted concrete buildings with open-air windows and Asiatic, stroked writing.

The bus rounded the South Gate (Medieval entry to walled Seoul), and then past several statues of seated or standing Korean warriors prominent in oriental armor, buildings, and general infrastructure. Looming up on us was a high Arch of Triumph, which appeared even greater as we passed by it. The Seoul Station on the left faced the USO across the boulevard. At the very end was the capitol. It boasted a semblance of Greek architecture built by the invading Japanese. It was constructed by the Japanese to purposefully obstruct the still existing Medieval Korean capital buildings of Kyong Buk Ku behind it, and further humiliate a historically conquered people.

Toward the outskirts of Seoul, thatched roofs and poorly constructed homes extended all the way up and completely covered the adjacent mountains.

CONCRETE BUILDINGS WITH OPEN-AIR WINDOWS AND ASIATIC STROKED WRITING LINED THE BOULEVARD. NOTE POSTWAR *KIMCHI* BUSES, *HOPSANS*, BIKE-RIDERS, AND PULL-PUSH CARTS.

ASIATIC SCRIPT ON BUILDING FACADES. NOTE ELECTRIC CAR AT RIGHT.

APPROACHING SOUTH GATE, ENTRANCE TO ANCIENT SEOUL AND ONE OF KOREA'S NATIONAL TREASURES

SOUTH GATE, NOTE *HOPSAN* TRAFFIC. THE SEOUL BOULEVARD WAS FLANKED BY STATUES OF WARRIORS.

TWO-WAY TRAFFIC BYPASSED THE ARCH OF TRIUMPH. CLOSE-UP OF THE ARCH.

SEOUL STATION. TRAINS FROM MUNSAN-NI AT CAVALRY AREA SERVICED TO THIS STATION AND INTO THE INTERIOR OF SOUTH KOREA. THIS STATION WAS ALSO THE END OF THE LINE FOR *HOPSANS* FROM POBWAN-NI IN THE CAV.

THE CAPITOL BUILT BY THE JAPANESE WAS THE ONE-TIME CENTER OF BUSINESS DURING OCCUPATION.

As the northbound bus exited Seoul, a different atmosphere was evident. Here I was able to breathe fresher air, with less diesel exhaust. The buildings were sparse, scattered and recessed.

A yellowish rectangular-shaped theater on the right with numerous announcements in Korean strokes featured movies. A flatbed composed of rear wheels with rubber tires was pulled by an ox. Another driver sat himself between his horse and would-be load so that the poor beast bore his master's weight on his fore feet and shoulders—and not the weight-bearing wheels of the flatbed. A potter's yard displayed huge clay urns that reminded me of the flowerpots on my mother's front porch. In the distance, a flock of white birds was in full flight above the smelly rice paddies. Villages with tiny general stores appeared as the bus approached the country. A man carried a huge load of brassware on his A-frame. I was impressed by a very neat home, unlike the hovels we were accustomed to seeing in our communities, probably the property of a successful farmer. A *mamasan* on a hillside lowered her balloon pants, about to do her business, exposed her generous posterior just as the bus rounded the hill, leaving her behind (double meaning).

A THEATER AT SEOUL'S OUTSKIRTS COMPLETE WITH HUGE ANNOUNCEMENTS AND NEON STROKE SIGNS

A LOAD BALANCED ON THE BED'S WHEELS POWERED BY AN OX

A HORSE BORE HIS MASTER'S WEIGHT ON HIS SHOULDERS AND FORE LEGS.

A POTTER'S YARD WITH HIS *KIMCHI* JARS

A HIGHER QUALITY ABODE PERHAPS OF A SUCCESSFUL FARMER

As a lone GI on Korean public transportation, I noted that the people did not ignore my presence, but displayed more of a quiet appreciation. I always felt accepted as one of them and was extended the respect of the culture. I noticed most wore traditional whites; the *ajoshees* or *papasans* (elderly gentlemen) with their black, mini, stove-top hats, and the *ajemas* (elderly ladies) with their tight vests and long bell-shaped dresses. One lady wore a pin with a double heart. They were friendly with smiling kindness when I addressed them. In retrospect, I noticed elderly people only on the *hopsans* but none on trains. It appeared only the younger working crowd commuted by rail.

Eventually, the stinking rice paddies took over the open country extending from the road to the far mountains. In the fields, farmers tilled the mucky earth by use of an ox with a rake-like plow. As we drew near the military district, an MP checkpoint marked the entry to what is known as Freedom's Frontier, where all traffic stopped for inspection. The MPs never once glanced at or asked me for orders or passes when I traveled on GI or Korean transportation.

As the bus entered the Cavalry area, the U.S. Army's presence was more recognizable with the numerous U.S. compounds and the GIs swarming all over the roads, village paths, and establishments; and I felt once more within my element. The greater village of Yongju-Gol sported many general stores, portrait studios, jewelry stores, eating houses, and shops. All were decorated with Asiatic, stroked writing and stood side by side as they trooped down both sides of the road. People just seemed friendly, sociable, and conversational in these greater business villages, perhaps because it was a business district, in slight contrast to the remote village folk. Camp Beard in Yongju-Gol was the GI bus depot. I dropped off here and transferred buses on to Camp McGovern and later continued to Camp Blue Lancer Valley, or hopped on public transportation.

FARMERS TURNED OVER THE MUCKY EARTH BY USE OF AN OX WITH A RAKE-LIKE PLOW SUNK IN THE KNEE-DEEP MUD.

THE BUS PASSED BY THE MAJOR VILLAGE OF MARVELOUS YONGJU-GOL THAT SPORTED MANY GENERAL STORES, PORTRAIT STUDIOS, JEWELRY STORES, EATERIES, AND SHOPS. THE BRIDGE TRAVERSING THE RIVER T-BONES YONGJU-GOL AT LEFT, OUTSIDE PHOTO. CAMP BEARD, (CC#2) WITH A GI BUS DEPOT WITHIN, IS LOCATED AT ABOVE LEFT OF PHOTO.

STREET SCENE AT GREATER VILLAGE OF YONGJU-GOL. *HOPSAN* IS AT T-BONE STREETS WITH RIVER AND BRIDGE ON STREET ENTERING FROM RIGHT OF PHOTO. CAMP BEARD (CC#2) IS LOCATED BEHIND SIGN ABOVE *HOPSAN*.

GENERAL STORE, JEWELRY STORE AND SHOPS LINE THE STREETS OF YONGJU-GOL

PHOTO CREDIT: (SP4) L.R., PERSONNEL, 15TH ADMIN CO, 1ST CAV DIV, KOREA, 1964
SALES ASSOCIATE AND OGGIE. FRIENDLY GENTLEMAN; PEOPLE WERE FRIENDLIER AND SOCIABLE IN THESE GREATER VILLAGES. NOTE TRADITIONALLY DRESSED GENTLEMAN WEARING WESTERN HAT RATHER THAN MINI TOP HAT.

    On the open road from Yongju-Gol to Pobwan-Ni, I could not help but notice another quality home, perhaps of another prosperous farmer or of wealthy country folk. Along the way, an elderly man carried a plow on his A-frame while the ox followed, and sometimes a young calf trotted along. We passed children pulling and pushing at a cart, full of scrap wood. Men transporting upside-down pigs tied to the backs of bicycles and others carrying numerous vertically bundled soda pop cans that had been soldered into tubes, were common sights. Once, I waved out of a Korean bus window to a sentinel at a tower and was flicked a birdie in return greeting. A girl in the bus threw an apple into a deuce-and-a-half full of GIs and they almost killed one other for it.

The road was lined with more and more minor villages. The stench of human fecal matter plus body fluids—an increased common smell to these rural hamlets—initially offensive, was repugnant to live with. It permeated the whole Cav area and was overwhelming even as the bus approached the minor business district of Pobwan-Ni and bus depot.

A QUALITY HOME ALONG THE ROUTE FROM YONGJU-GOL TO POBWAN-NI

A MAN CARRIED HIS YOKE AND HARNESS ON HIS A-FRAME WHILE FARMERS WORKED BEHIND IN KNEE DEEP RICE PADDY. CHILDREN SMILED AS THEY HAUL CARTLOAD OF GOODS.

THE *HOPSAN* DEPOT AT THE VILLAGE OF POBWAN-NI, ALSO KNOWN AS MICKEY MOUSE CORNERS, WHERE I WOULD SIMPLY READ DESTINATIONS ON THE WINDOW, BOARD, AND TRAVEL.

A short drive beyond Pobwan-Ni by the ever-reeking rice paddy countryside, the bus approached my community of Camp McGovern by Nopae Dong. While stationed there the first three months of my duty tour, I would just hop off and head for my barracks. However, during the last four months of my duty tour, being stationed at the Nullo-Ri community few miles farther, I would continue on either of the two available bus services all the way there and to Camp Blue Lancer Valley.

THE STENCH OF THE RICE PADDIES PERMEATED THE ENTIRE CAV AREA AND WAS OVERWHELMING AS THE BUS APPROACHED MY COMMUNITY AND MY COMPOUND.

THE BUS THEN PASSED BY THE VILLAGE OF NOPAE DONG AND EITHER ENTERED OR BYPASSED CAMP MCGOVERN ON ITS WAY TO CAMP BLUE LANCER VALLEY. NOTE ROAD ENTRY FROM RIGHT OF PHOTO, SNAKES UPWARD TOWARD THE VILLAGE, THEN LEFT ACROSS THE CAMP NORTHWARD AS IT EXITS AT CENTER AND LEFT OF PHOTO.

NULLO-RI AT T-BONE, WHERE THE GI BUS ARRIVED AND TURNED LEFT INTO CAMP BLUE LANCER VALLEY (BEHIND BRUSH), WITH ROAD WHERE ONLY THE *KIMCHI* BUS CONTINUED WESTWARD TOWARD MUNSAN-NI. NOTE IMJIN RIVER BELOW MOUNTAINS AT HORIZON THAT TRAVERSES THE PHOTO. THE VILLAGE OF CHANGPA-RI IS AT THE FIRST-THIRD OF THE RIVER WHERE THE LIBBY BRIDGE IS ALSO SITUATED.

COUNTRYSIDE VIEW OF THE ROAD TO MUNSAN-NI FROM NULLO-RI

The bus then continued northward from my initial (hometown) community of Camp McGovern and the village of Nopae Dong, and curved left, heading west toward my final destination of Nullo-Ri and a good walk south to the secluded Camp Blue Lancer Valley. It was from this community that I made my way to Seoul via rail by heading west toward the major village (city) of Munsan-Ni, a bustling major village where Camp Pelham was situated and where I would board the train to Seoul, thus circumventing my touring zone.

GIRLS PUMPED WATER AT A PUBLIC WELL AT MUNSAN-NI.

BUSTLING TRAFFIC AT MUNSAN-NI, LOCATION OF RAILROAD DEPOT. NOTE OLDER TRUCK MODELS, *KIMCHI* BUS, AND BOY WITH A TOY GUN.

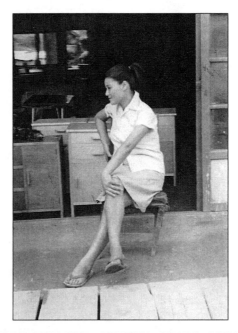

A FURNITURE STORE DISPLAYED *EEDEEWA* STANDS POPULAR AMONG THE TROOPS FOR SUPPLEMENTAL STORAGE BESIDE TRADITIONAL WALL LOCKERS AND FOOTLOCKERS.

During my four mid-months, while stationed at Ross, I would jump off the Korean Kimchi bus at an inconvenient stop and walk about two miles to camp. One night, the bus broke down in the middle of nowhere. All fifteen or twenty of us GIs got off and pushed until the driver got it started. That was the one justifiable night that it did not enter a compound as scheduled.

Our driver waved greetings at oncoming GI bus drivers. Korean Nationals employed by the United States and Turk soldiers enjoyed GI bus privileges. Once I saw two Turk soldiers laughing and teasing a young Korean lady, a U.S. government employee, seated behind them. They hurriedly turned and wiggled their hands on her knees. She promptly rewarded them each with a slap. On another time, I met a Turk soldier who spoke Spanish, and we conversed without a problem about I cannot remember what. I saw a soldier rapidly shuffle and pass his *josan* into the bus past the driver, saying she worked at the PX but had just forgotten her pass.

THE GI BUS DRIVERS WAVED GREETINGS ONE TO ANOTHER ALONG THE KOREAN ROADS.

The bus stopped (as did all traffic) to let pass the GI or ROK trucks or tank convoys that had priority in this military zone. Tank convoys rapidly and majestically "clanked" by, with the ridged track clicking as it gripped the road. I reflected that a tank convoy on full roll was an impressive spectacle that commanded respect and attention. Once, I wandered across a ROK truck convoy, with marathon runners catching up. I saluted the officer in each truck and received a return salute. In all cases, a convoy was a big attraction to large masses of the local population and as such was treated with respect and awe.

Missing any bus was no problem. I would hitch a ride with anything on wheels in the Cavalry area that rolled from filthy Korean trash trucks to greasy oil tankers. GIs could effortlessly catch rides anywhere with the complacent populace. It was a time when the Korean people embraced the U.S. military since the conflict with the lapsed armistice was still fresh in their lives. This whole roadway was a segment of the Western Corridor or Bowling Alley, direct low-terrain access from Pyongyang in North Korea all the way to Seoul, the traditional invasion route.

Via bus, I became infinitely acquainted with much of the people's daily life, where they lived, how they traveled, and the surrounding countryside. These rides were almost as exciting as my spine-tingling memories of my very first lone bus adventure from the church bus stop to downtown San Antonio, around the Alamo, and home at eight years of age, like my Korea touring zone. The whole wealth of culture that I felt privileged to observe and thoroughly enjoy on the way to Seoul by rail and bus from the BLV was a once-in-a-lifetime experience at this Far East corner of Asia.

Chapter 10

Transfer! Camp Ross, Nangmo-Ri, Korea

March-June 1965

The mind is its own place, and in itself,
can make heaven of hell, and a hell of Heaven.
—John Milton, *Paradise Lost.*

Prologue

Just when one settles in and experiences a comfort zone, change occurs. I was content in my community for four and a half months, when we got word that the entire Personnel section was being relocated to Camp Ross, a troop transfer depot. McGovern was home, Nopae Dong our hometown, and to be uprooted was heartrending.

Prisoners of War
Spring 1965

The troops alarmed lost all their worth
When thunder claps shattered their mirth
Struck, shoved, and queried was their plight
To live amid a foe in site

"Under normal circumstances you would try to es*cape*," the sergeant yelled, "but at this time you *will* not try to es*cape*. However, make every attempt to resist as a group. Mines have been planted all over the area, but you *will* not try to es*cape*," he emphasized again. We were all chuckling and smiling when suddenly three grenade-like explosions literally shook the ground. Our grins were smeared away, and our chuckles died an early death.

Only a few days before, Personnel at Camp Ross had been ordered to attend a Code of Conduct class at the demilitarized zone on a nice spring morning in 1965. The road north of the Imjin had loosened a chalk-white nontoxic powder that literally enveloped us, as we rode within a convoy of open trucks. Breathing was difficult, but we survived. Although some of the guys said we crossed a wide river, I cannot remember, the white dust was blinding and afforded no respite to see much. I remember that it seeped into all our orifices and folds exposed to air. At the end of the journey, we all looked like chalky, ghostly-white apparitions. As we scrambled off the trucks spitting out white chalk and dusting ourselves off, wiping the chalk off our faces and blowing our noses, we became aware of the spectacle we presented. Specialist Fifth Scott's face, an Afro-American, was covered with dust over his dark skin, and we knew we looked about the same so that it brought even greater mirth. We all laughed at one another good-naturedly, as we scrambled off and were called to formation.

When the earth trembled, three men in yellow khaki outfits with insignia on their red collars, resembling soldiers from North Korea or China, emerged from a shack.

"Look at your officers," they yelled as they roughed them up and dropped them to their knees on the damp earth. At this point, a stony silence fell upon the formation and we all got serious—this *was* serious! I was not afraid, but perhaps angry and confused as to what was going on. No one in his right mind would ever dare rough up an officer.

"You have surrendered, you are our prisoners," the aggressors barked, as they pushed the troops downward, repeatedly attempting a kneeling position. They proceeded up and down the ranks attempting to force us too, to sit on the mud, but as a group, all resisted.

Imbecile, I'm talking to you," the North Korean (NK) yelled at a GI, while another held his arms back with his knee pressed into the GI's arched spine. For a split second the greatest amount of Spanish filth that poured from his mouth took me back to my childhood, echoing my mother's customary words. They kept yelling for military information: number of troops, unit location, officer's names, etc., and demanding accurate responses.

I noticed that a NK, with gold insignia on his red collar and saucer hat, strolled up and down the files calmly asking questions. His demeanor identified him as their officer. A young GI broke down and cried. I knew he was divulging information, because he was whimpering and responding to the officer's mild-mannered interrogation. We considered silently that the young GI was somewhat of a coward because he had easily succumbed with insufficient resistance. I reflected that it was only a matter of time and buffeting before even I or anyone would break.

Private First Abilio Mendiola stood at my immediate right, and about to be harassed—got the same treatment. One questioning soldier grabbed him with both hands at the collar and yanked at him to-and-fro. Abilio would not respond and took it with a very serious face. I was upset and somewhat angry because my buddy was being mistreated. My thought processes were interrupted as the NK forced my buddy to his knees and flogged him with a black billy club. Though I saw him wince, he did not show pain. Then I momentarily experienced flashbacks to my childhood where my abusive mother flogged my butt and thighs with her thick, black, leather belt or cracked my face with her elephantine hands. This time I was not restrained from striking back as instructed in church. I recalled that we were taught not to strike back when surrendered, but to await the opportunity for escape. Then my thoughts returned to the present. The differences or grudges that Abilio and I may have had once, suddenly seemed trivial. Abilio kept up a straight face such that I reflected if he could take it, so could I.

I felt a twinge of fear crawl up my temples. I quaked as an enemy soldier approached me, and thought, "*Dang*, here it comes." As I reflected my mother's buffetings, I recalled the pain I had suffered for those thirteen years so I knew pain. It was the fear of the upcoming unknown torture or interrogation processes that terrorized me. Still fear and anger stirred within me. I realized that this was the fitting time to legally strike back (perhaps kill) at the opportune moment and attempt to escape.

"Hey, here is one of our comrades from Castro's Cuba," a NK said, tapping my nametag. Terrified, I shivered at the aggressor's words and at what my Spanish surname implied. To my relief, the officer called out and the harassment ceased. I saw Abilio dragged off.

As prisoners of war, we were shoved to close formation, body-to-body, spoon-like, front-to-back with hands cupped behind our heads—walking and stumbling over each other. All this time the enemy continually harassed, pushed, and tripped us, yelling obscenities and that we were beaten. During this drag walk, I noticed through the corner of my eye the Personnel sergeants and senior specialists behind some trees observing us, so I determined this really was some kind of training. Finally, we were herded into a stockade flooded with mud, resembling a bog. We were pushed downward into the watered soil and ordered to sit down. Evidently, we all had remembered the instructions to resist as a group, as we all just refused despite, increased harassment. I saw Abilio in a hutch across the stockade subjugated by kneeling on all fours beaten by what seemed a club, but which was a black sock filled with another sock. It looked real enough, though.

The now bareheaded blond officer stood on a guard tower and, with a NK soldier interpreting, lectured in a foreign language. We all stood in two-inch mud and water listening to what amounted as propaganda—basically repeating that neither our army nor our country was as good as theirs. To add to our misery, a squall passed us overhead. Some of the guys had had the foresight to bring ponchos while the rest of us got soaked to the skin.

Finally, the class began. We were allowed to find comfortable spots and listen. There were too many of us, about one hundred men, and limited dry spots, but I found mine. The lesson instructed on resistance, escape procedure, environment awareness, foreign language phrases, etc. All this was a necessary part of training. As army office personnel, we had little contact with this type of training, since we were not in the front lines, the DMZ, or on the Imjin; but the army felt that all personnel, even the administrative people, had to go through some sort of survival training to meet any emergency. At last, we were trucked back to Ross where the drudgery of overtime work greeted us. We chuckled when the following class returned the next day with their butts muddied, and I especially teased Private First Fabrin whose butt was particularly caked, smeared with dried-up muck. Thus ended our Code of Conduct class experience in this Far East corner of Asia.

Nocturnal Misadventures

Lost in the thick of night
Ne'er left ne'er right ne'er sight
Lovely girls, cops with stripes
Drains, trucks, and dusty wipes

One late, almost starless and moonless, night during the early spring of '65, dressed in my greens, I was on my way back to McGovern from an escapade in Seoul. A thumbed ride from a deuce-and-a-half had just dropped me off somewhere in the cavalry area, I reckoned by the village of Kumkok. The unlit road darker than an unlit cave was so black that I could not see two steps in front of me, so I was afraid of veering off the road. When my eyes became accustomed to the dark, the sparse starlight barely illuminated the countryside. I gazed skyward and immediately located the belt of Orion so that in the least I reckoned the four compass points. As I very slowly and carefully stepped my way on the road, a distant fuzzy illumination progressively appeared followed shortly by a pair of approaching lights. I quickly thumbed a ride. The headlights belonged to a cab. As it hesitated, the back door opened to reveal a drop-dead gorgeous *broad* in the backseat. She was clad in a green, skin-tight, sequined Shanghai-style dress with a slit clear up to her thigh. Her jet-black hair neatly pulled back sported a bun at the top of her head. Her makeup was not exaggerated as that of the *village josans*, so I deduced she must be an important passenger. She produced a delectable smile and motioned me in by patting the seat next to her. Her presence caused all kinds of sparks to fly as my body reacted to this specimen of womanhood. I never knew I could get this excited over a mere invitation. However, sanity returned and I respectfully shook my head and turned down the ride. I was no fool. In this upside down world I correctly so assumed that she was probably an officer's high-class call girl. I watched the cab speed away with the headlights piercing the black curtains of night as two red taillights followed dimly in the distance. I thanked my lucky stars the next two headlights miraculously belonged to a military bus driven by my chauffer buddy who safely drove me directly to camp.

MY BUDDY BUS DRIVER WHO DROVE ME ALL OVER THE CAVALRY AND WHO PICKED ME UP ON THAT DARK MOONLESS NIGHT IN THE MIDDLE OF NOWHERE.

"What do you think you're doing out here at this time of the night?" Sergeant Gibson, an MP, demanded of me at Yongju-Gol late one night, a few weeks later in mid-spring of 1965.

Producing the document, I replied that I was on pass. It was the weekend night of our relocation to Personnel Center Number Two. The Top of Camp Ross had earlier advised me that the evening carried the late weekend curfew. Because I had newly arrived at Ross, I could not remember Sonnier, the first sergeant's name. After a short interrogation, the MP relaxed and confided that many of his fellow MPs were always properly cared for by Personnel including flights home, and he would forgo any report. It appeared that the Military Police sergeant, despite his outranking me, was displaying his nervousness with hugely rounded eyes and wide smile on his dusky face, evident of his Afro-American birth as he spoke. However, I was entirely innocent of the impact of my rank. It wouldn't be until thirty-seven years later that I realized that the nervous police sergeant had actually ceded to a low ranking Personnel clerk fearing repercussions from Personnel. He courteously escorted me to Camp Beard and dropped me off at the main gate. I was nervous and a bit frightened but somewhat agitated that my night on the vill was cut short.

A few days later when all the clerks were out at lunch, I sneaked into the MP record clerk's empty Quonset and removed Sergeant Gibson's Financial Data Records Folder. I misfiled it at the back within the same drawer where eventually an inconvenient search would find it. As chance would have it, my buddy Specialist Fifth Alex Moya who maintained the pay records for the Military Police in jest informed me thirty-seven years later, "It's still there." I had experienced Personnel-wide record searches for "lost" financial files requiring thorough hunts and they always showed up. Otherwise, we'd experience an inquisition under the steel-gray eyes of the commanding officer. Still, this misdeed trust of such important documents serving under the Adjutant General Corps haunted me such that I felt sorry later.

Another moonless late spring night found me riding on a Kimchi bus back to Ross from an escapade at McGovern. There was no direct public transportation to Ross, so I was deposited in the middle of nowhere. For some unknown reason I began to "double time" on the nearly invisible road. A pair of headlights flashed my eyes just as my right foot slid on the embankment causing me to fall into a ditch. I rolled to the bottom.

Almost immediately, Korean troops were in the ditch and dexterously pulled me up. Everything happened so fast. Stunned, I remembered a female voice as I was carefully and gently lifted into the open bed of their deuce-and-half. A few more authoritative words in Korean got the truck going again. I was all shaken up and disoriented but glad to be alive. The truck belonged to the Republic of Korea (ROK) and the troops were all in white outfits. One ROK soldier in broken English said the truck lights happened to flash on me just as I went down.

Everything happened so fast; I was still restoring my equilibrium when we arrived at the Camp Ross Main Gate. It was then that I realized they had dropped me to where I was going without a word from me. Still unstable, I thanked them, jumped off, and stood dumbfounded in the middle of the road. A ROK soldier thumped the cab and the truck drove off. Seeing my confusion, the main gate guard recognized me and asked if I was OK. I replied absently and proceeded to my barrack. It was as if nothing had ever happened. I arrived prior to curfew with my buddies or anyone else none the wiser. I truly thanked my lucky stars after this misadventure!

A few weeks later Private First Wain from another office hooch grinning at me, explained that his *josan* (who lived at far, far Nopae Dong at McGovern) coincidentally happened by and recognized me. It was she whose voice I had heard and who had informed the ROK soldiers where I was bound. It never occurred to me to ask him how she had happened by at the middle of the nowhere road, late in a black night, not with him, and instantaneously recognized me.

I chuckle again, as I did thirty-seven years earlier—I had had the last laugh on an MP. I again thank my bus driver buddy and the Korean soldiers for my safe passage. Raising my eyebrows, I smile slyly thinking back on the multiple fantasies inspired by the *josan* in the cab's back seat at that Far East corner of Asia.

Rice Paddies and Vills
Summer, 1965

Over the mountains and through the vill's
We cross the dales and climb o'er the hills
The ever-present fragrance from the earth
Of fecal matter spoils the mirth

One gorgeous morning in the early summer of 1965, Abilio, my best buddy and I decided to return to McGovern from Ross and visit our *raza* (countrymen) at the First of the Seventh by Koom-Shi. We chose to reminisce our way through the village of Nopae Dong, which necessitated the traversing of the adjoining rice paddies.

When we approached the well-remembered road from McGovern to Nopae, we began the long trek on the wide earth-packed path to the village. The green flourishing rice paddies on either side of the path attacked our olfactory glands, the closer we approached the vill, with the strong odor of human fecal matter used for fertilizer. Once in the village, the stronger stench of humanity overlay odor due to open pit toilets and randomly dispersed body fluid and *other* waste. From what I remember, the defecation and urination of humans was not a matter of privacy, but of whenever and wherever the need occurred. I once saw a man dip his honey bucket into a pit toilet and withdraw a generous amount of feces. What this was used for was beyond me. It might even have been used to water a plant. The stench was at its very height due to the summer heat. It seemed to bother no one.

THIS PHOTO CLEARLY SHOWS THE EARTH-PACKED PATH TO MCGOVERN FROM VILLAGE COMMERCIAL DISTRICT. SEE PHOTO P. 162 FOR VILLAGE MURAL SCENE FROM GUARD TOWER ONE.

We passed by the familiar tiny commercial district consisting of the grocery stores, shops, and eateries, all of temporary makeshift construction where we once hung out, and of which I now had a mural photo from Guard Tower One. Feeling right at home, we ambled through the many earth-packed side paths that led to private family dwellings and made the usual stops at any pit toilet at will. We made our way by the numerous windowless hooches, fashioned of earth-plastered walls with papered or wooden sliding doors and straw roofs. All the hooch-backs faced the road so that the front with the porch afforded the privacy of a family courtyard. Provisional fences of discarded wood separated the road from some hooches by mere centimeters, in an effort to discourage loiterers, street vendors, and the posting of bills on hooch walls. Still, some hooch walls managed to become plastered with faded, weather-worn announcements of movies at the Pobwan-Ni theater. Here and there someone claimed an unfenced hooch wall and posted their calendars. Despite the squalor, the village was quite picturesque, considering its overall poverty and scrap wood improvements. The only imposing and seemingly permanent structures were the brothels, better known as the teahouses. I noted that all other structures appeared of a temporary nature.

Children of obvious biracial parentage played along the feces-stinking ditches by the tree-lined roadside. A crowd of boys surrounded a man crystallizing tiny candy amber-colored guns from sugar, with a hot iron. Village folk barely glanced at us, two passing soldiers, and gave us the attention we merited—none.

CHILDREN AT PLAY BY POSTED-CALENDAR FENCE

FRIENDLY LITTLE BOY ON ROAD LEADING TO RICE PADDIES, KOOM-SHI, AND CAMP COURSEN. NOTE PROVISIONAL FENCE OF DISCARDED WOOD.

Abilio and I made our way up to the center of the village. As it seemed a picture-taking opportunity, I wanted some shots of McGovern from Nopae, so we continued on and climbed the mountain behind the vill. Upon our return, we took the dirt road north, heading for Koom-Shi.

VIEW OF CAMP MCGOVERN FROM HILL BEHIND NOPAE DONG. NOTE (LANDMARK) WATER TANK AT TOP AND MOTOR POOL AT CENTER AND FLOODING RICE PADDIES AT BOTTOM OF PHOTO.

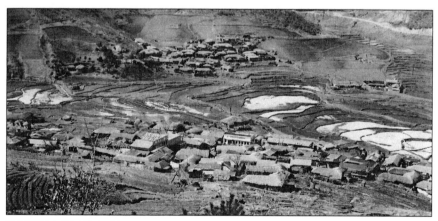

THE VILLAGE OF SHOSKI NOPAE SITS IN THE DISTANCE, NOPAE DONG IS SITUATED IN THE FOREFRONT WHILE THE WHITE TEAHOUSE WITH WHITE PILLARS IS PROMINENT.

As we finally exited the village, the whole view of terraced rice paddies opened before us. The village road narrowed to eighteen-inch-wide paths, separating the contoured fields as they tiered from the mountains at our right, extending all the way toward the main road at McGovern to our left. I always enjoyed the peaceful quietude on these scenic treks. Every few yards or so, anciently tested diminutive waterfalls calculated the descent of flow from the upper flooding-field to the lower one. I marveled at subtle music emanating from the continual water overflow, as it gently poured and faintly bobbed and bubbled at the lower paddy. The fields themselves were myriad shades of greenery, with shoots sprouting two or three inches above the water. During the monsoons, the far-reaching rice fields would shoot up and wave with feet-high greenery.

WE PHOTOGRAPHED ONCOMING BUSINESSMEN CARRYING ATTACHES. I ALWAYS ENJOYED THE QUIET SCENIC TREKS BETWEEN THE RICE PADDIES. I SQUATTED ON THE EIGHTEEN-INCH-WIDE PATHS, WITH RICE SHOOTS SPROUTING INCHES ABOVE THE RICE PADDY FLOOD LEVEL. EVERY FEW YARDS OR SO, ANCIENTLY TESTED DIMINUTIVE WATERFALLS CALCULATED THE DESCENT OF FLOW FROM THE UPPER FLOODING-FIELD TO THE LOWER ONE. (SEE PHOTO P. 339)

WE ENCOUNTERED A MAN WITH A BALANCED LOAD OF LONG LENGTHS OF LUMBER ACROSS HIS A-FRAME. HIS LITTLE BOY REMAINED BEHIND THE SCENE.

Pedestrian traffic was minimal, but brisk. Considering the lack of vehicles on the paths, I supposed it was safer than the main road. As we traveled this common path, Abilio and I encountered a man with a balanced load of long lengths of lumber across his A-frame. We photographed oncoming businessmen carrying attaches. *Mamasans* carrying jars or bundles on their heads and *papasans* bowed under A-frames loaded with merchandise passed us, but with a glance.

During the chilly winter, these fields froze solid, allowing children to skate on homemade crate sleds. In early spring, as we cruised, I was awed at observing the use of the ox-drawn plow opening furrows at other fields amid huge clumps of earth. I noticed the use of a grader that further broke down the lumps, as a man stood on a rake-like plow drawn by oxen.

PHOTO CREDIT: (SP4) L.R., PERSONNEL, 15TH ADMIN CO, 1ST CAV DIV, KOREA, 1964
THE FROZEN SOLID RICE FIELDS ALLOWED CHILDREN TO SKATE ON HOMEMADE CRATE SLEDS.

PHOTO CREDIT: (SP4) L.R., PERSONNEL, 15TH ADMIN CO, 1ST CAV DIV, KOREA, 1964
CHILDREN PLAYED ON THE ONCE FLOODED, NOW FROZEN, RICE PADDIES BY THE EIGHTEEN-INCH-WIDE PATHS. NOTE (LANDMARK) WHITE WATER TANK TOP OF PHOTO.

The dazzling morning was warming up when we approached the sunny village of Koom-Shi. The narrow rice paddy path opened a wider pathway, where we came across a tumbling waterfall that looked so refreshing that I felt like standing under it to cool off. We entered that little village, which is etched in my memory because it was far more picturesque than Nopae with a bustling but hushed population. We continued our way, observing a barbershop and other businesses run in shackle shacks, some with stroked writing, all, as at Nopae Dong, of a seemingly temporary nature. I smiled, secretly enjoying the more all-expense-paid escapade, courtesy Uncle Sam. A hooch that appeared cool and cozy, hung on a hillside from which a *papasan* poked out his head to catch a glimpse of the chatting GIs. Here was a man who was sporting his hunting dogs. Abilio pointed out a man who rolled up a dead dog in a mat and carried it off saying, "He's going to make hot dogs." We passed by a yellow cow that just stood there, secured by its master.

My mouth would not stop smiling, with probably flared nostrils, as we strolled through all of the dirt paths amid slap-dash hovels, among Asiatic people—all under the sunshine of Korea. I could not get over the fact that I was again enjoying another of those lifelong dreamed adventures I had expected upon entering the service. Aahhh! but I was treading on God's golden glory, all at Uncle Sam's gold metal standard! The sun was a beautiful bright yellow orb that bathed us gently on our way.

It was at this village, I reflected decades later, where months earlier Private First N.E. had introduced me to Yung Su, my very first sweet date in Korea; and it never occurred to me to look her up.

WE CAME ACROSS A REFRESHING WATERFALL AT APPROACHING THE VILLAGE OF KOOM-SHI.

I SMILED SECRETLY ENJOYING THE MORE ALL-EXPENSE-PAID ESCAPADE COURTESY UNCLE SAM WHILE PASSING THROUGH THE TINY COMMERCIAL SECTION OF THE VILLAGE OF KOOM-SHI.

THE HOOCH HANGING FROM THE MOUNTAIN BECKONED TO BE PHOTOGRAPHED. NOTE SCRAP WOOD STRETCHED TO MAKE NEAT-LOOKING FENCE.

A MAN WAS SPORTING HIS HUNTING DOGS.

YELLOW COW, BECAUSE OF YELLOW HEAD IS INDIGENOUS TO KOREA. ALL BEASTS OF BURDEN WERE REFERRED TO AS OXEN.

Abilio and I arrived at the First of the Seventh to find a beer party in full swing. The place was packed and overflowing with GIs, mostly Latinos. A lot of rowdy jokes, laughter, and loud singing of Mexican "macho" tunes reverberated within the Quonset. Everyone joined in on the unknown celebration, crying, in heartfelt emotion, the words to traditional Mexican music. These guys were seriously homesick puppies. Their rendition of our romantic Mexican ballads in chorus was hilarious. An older GI was staring into the air, half-smiling in a zombie-like trance. Even Abilio got into the act by beating a rhythm on a handy footlocker. This definitely was not one of the ways I wanted to spend my time! Nope! I had things to do and places to see.

After a few minutes of observation, I was ready to go. I signaled with a side jerk of my head to Abilio for us to leave. He seemed ambivalent and hesitant. However, I had had it with this circus; I was up and out of there before he decided. I made my way toward the exit, and as I reached the Gary Owen main gate of Camp Coursen, I heard Abilio behind me catching up. How could people even think of being cooped up drinking and carousing to oblivion when there was this beautiful day, with its superb sunshine, just waiting to be enjoyed? Aahhh! but the day was like a beautifully bowed birthday box waiting to be unwrapped to reveal its free hidden treasures and adventures.

My son commented: *"Dad, joining the army was a few steps up from the abusive life you lived while growing up at home; as for the camaraderie, a few steps down!"*

—Marc Martinez,
General Contractor, Personal Trainer

During my days at Camp Blue Lancer Valley, I continued to wander and traverse other panoramic rice fields at the bivouac field and at Mt. Easy Queen by Nullo-Ri. I traveled the byways blissfully because truthfully, I really felt very much at home. While I mingled with the Korean people, I felt as one of them—and when my path crossed one of the elderly *papasans*, I felt closer to my own father. Both the poverty and the cadence of the Korean language felt familiar to me as a barrio-bred Latin-American; I was at home among the Korean People. It seemed that our spirits touched a time or two during my contact with them

As I reminisce, I am transported back in time. I again stroll through villages and fields in a medieval or ancient feudal setting and society. I remember strolling the narrow paths, observing the water-filled rice fields and the waving foot-high rice shoots amid the fecal stench. I feel privileged that for a brief period, at nineteen, I had lived and witnessed this Asiatic daily life, as I lived with these gentle country folk. For a moment at least, my thoughts fly back in time, lost in time, as I relive my youthful love affair with mother Korea on whose earth I tread and rambled in her Far East corner of Asia.

IT WAS PRIOR TO MAY 24, 1965, THAT I CONSIDERED REENLISTING.

Reenlistment Dilemma
May 24, 1965

*"When we are discharged from the army
 we'll enlist again,
 we will like hell we will."*
 —*The Last Time I Saw Archie*

"Re-up," someone yelled in the theater following a touching military motion picture incidence. It was a time of great commotion in the spring of 1965, especially among the recruits who were about to complete their first year in the service. The army had just made a proposal, known as "short reenlistment." This meant that following one year of service, one could ETS (Terminate Service) conditional upon immediate reenlistment for three to six years for a new school option or some other trivial privilege. Some of the guys were really considering reenlisting, and I was one of them. Still, curse words and oaths quickly followed the reenlistment comment in the theater.

One of soldiers took the army up on it, reenlisted, and received his four hundred dollar reenlistment bonus. He planned on flying to Mexico and visiting family with the thirty-day leave as an added reenlistment privilege. However, he continually enjoyed good company and a fine time at the EM Club. After buying uncounted rounds of drinks and paying off gambling bets, the entire bonus of four hundred dollars was exhausted. Every night for a month, he walked around whining and visiting our bunks, lamenting his plight. He bawled, saying he missed his family and regretted ever having reenlisted. He continually cursed the army and his added year. I last heard that he was shipped to the DMZ to pull fence-walking duty.

It was prior to May 24, 1965, that I seriously considered reenlisting. This would be the first of continual reenlistments where I would accomplish one of four goals anticipated in my childhood. World travel! This reenlistment would assure me of another overseas adventure rather than some mind-numbing station. Since my military goal was to travel as much as possible at Uncle Sam's treat, I talked to the recruiter about a possible assignment to Europe. He bade me to return in a week. At the end of the week, I was handed several papers to sign and upon affixing my signature, I was handed orders to report to Bremerhaven, Germany, on January 4, 1966, plus an authorized forty-five-day leave en route. I enthusiastically signed all papers. It was so easy! Upon receiving my orders, I smiled once more, triumphantly—just like when I had received my guaranteed enlistment orders for Pay School, exactly one year earlier. I saw myself wandering all over Europe, and eventually the world. *Europe!* I silently celebrated; the opposite end of this very ground! What new and exciting adventures, what epics awaited me, as I would stand on the two worlds of Marco Polo?

Suddenly, the daydream was interrupted by the orderly, when he asked me to report to finance and receive the overlooked four-hundred-dollar reenlistment bonus and very amenably added, "You're in the army now." "Four hundred dollars!" Reality set in and I desperately reflected, "four hundred dollars!" "Do I want four hundred dollars?" Four hundred dollars? Europe! No, my mind replied, not even the prospect of eight months' pay up front appeared alluring. At this point, for some unknown reason *definitely beyond me*, I panicked and with heart thundering in my chest, I announced that I did not want to reenlist. In my alarm, my mind went blank; despite my lifelong traveling goal, I was not ready to reenlist for another tour of duty. Unexpectedly, the boon of touring Europe became insignificant. I was thunderstruck!

"What?" the sergeant quietly asked, viewing me with a puzzling glance, not believing what he heard. He then calmly arose from his desk behind the orderly, approached me, and serenely added, "The army has given you what you wanted!" Nevertheless, that was no consolation for me, and in my desperation, I couldn't be convinced otherwise, and I reiterated that I wanted out. All this time the orderly silently continued with his work, oblivious to our dialogue.

"But I haven't been sworn in, and I didn't raise my hand to be sworn in!" I pleaded desperately. Then the considerate sergeant calmly turned around and asked the orderly to destroy all the documents, including the orders for Germany and the pay voucher for the bonus. Then, almost paternally, he continued addressing me saying, "OK, I understand, you're not sure you know what you want. When you do, come back and see us." He returned to his chair where he and the orderly resumed their work, as if nothing had happened. I walked out with an unsteady gait, feeling as though I'd just escaped the guillotine. Man, was I relieved and thankful! Almost in tears, with a lump in my throat, I hurried across the compound toward the main gate and marveled at the close call.

Leaving the Recruiting Office behind and now approaching at Camp Howze's main gate, I suddenly realized I did not regret missing out on Europe. I was a free man! (At least after the next two years!) For some unknown reason, Europe's possible adventures faded from my mind. Still a bit unsteady, I sighed as I approached the main road to thumb a ride back to Ross. Shaking but relieved, I nervously smiled as a deuce-and-a-half picked me up, and who would I encounter as the driver? It was none other than my buddy, Brother Fountaine! Was it coincidence, or Divine consolation? I didn't care at this point. Here was someone who would help me through this *almost* catastrophe! I literally poured out my heart on his shoulder. With a puzzled brotherly smile, my return missionary brother heard me out sympathetically, almost paternally, as I practically sobbed away my reenlistment caper at this Far East corner of Asia.

CAMP ROSS HEADQUARTERS OFFICES WITH PAVED PARADE FIELD IN FOREGROUND AND WATER TANK AND GUARD TOWER AT UPPER RIGHT CORNER. IT WAS ON THIS PARADE FIELD THAT WE HELD REVEILLE; OUR DOGS' FIGHTS TOOK PLACE AND WHERE WE ALL SANG A FALSETTO JODY DURING A MARCH.

Chapter 11

Impaled! Guard Duty at Camp Ross

March 1965-June 16, 1965

Prologue

It was one of those sunny and warm weekend afternoons that I *again* stood guard at Tower Number One near the main gate at Camp Ross. Number One faced a road that ran north and south and paralleled the western boundary of Ross, secured with a barbwire fence. The day had advanced to a temperate and amiable evening. Hues of blue streamed across the vast skies, as the twilight followed with an ideal mood (under given circumstances) for a romantic escapade, but it found me rabid with anger and frustration. Personnel Service Center Number Three had only last month relocated to Ross from McGovern, and already I abhorred the camp and the despised circumstances at Personnel. To top it off, I could not seem to adapt to Ross! All the troops were granted passes, following an eternally long week of overtime duty, and as fortune would have it, I ended up on guard duty. The night closed in, and the lampposts lit up.

Tower One
March–June 1965

Up the tower, down the tower
So it went, hour by hour
Time to think and time to reflect
A duty post ne'er to neglect

I gazed north and south, being right and left, again and again as I observed my post all along the fence. My mind bitterly resented this duty. It was so monotonous! My eyes grudgingly rested momentarily on the distant floodlit main gate at the northern part of the fence that buzzed with night insects. I glanced frontward, toward the lamppost-lit road beyond the barbwire fence, and then left, toward the southern limit of Ross. Nothing was happening, nothing moved! I envied the guys having a good time on their passes or sleeping, and I couldn't help but feel dissatisfaction with my plight.

DURING DAYLIGHT, I GAZED NORTH LONGINGLY AT THE ROAD TOWARD MARVELOUS YONGJU-GOL WHILE MY EYES GRUDGINGLY RESTED ON THE DISTANT FLOODLIT MAIN GATE AT NIGHT.

I GLANCED FORWARD TOWARD THE LAMPPOST-LIT ROAD BEYOND THE BARBWIRE FENCE AND THEN LEFT, TOWARD THE SOUTHERN LIMIT OF ROSS.

  This abhorred evening reminded me of the very first guard mount I had encountered as a transient last November, five months earlier. From Number One Tower, I glanced behind me across the compound toward the fence-walking-post by the water tank, only to find it obstructed by trees and the night's darkness. I recalled the challenging orders the officer of the day demanded during guard mount. The guards were to shout "halt" three times, followed by "*chamkansola*" another three times. Then, if necessary, chamber a shell in the shotgun and fire in the air, then aim for the intruder's legs, then after chambering a third shell "shoot to kill," but only if life or government property was in jeopardy. I reflected that by that time I would certainly be dead!

  "What is the nomenclature of the M14 rifle?" the officer of day asked me as the guard mount continued. I had no idea in Hades what "nomenclature" was. "United States rifle thirty caliber M14, air cooled," I ventured out as I racked my brains for the supposed answer. I had remembered my ROTC training regarding my old M1. Since I was not selected super numeral (standby substitute), I concluded my answer was unacceptable. Later I realized that it would not have mattered what I answered because as a rookie transient, I needed to be indoctrinated to the nightmares and guard of Korea. I was assigned the fence-walking-post next to the water tank.

  I recalled that bitterly cold and frosty night of that last November. As I had readied for my duty, I reached for my Korean pile cap pausing to remember how I had admired it in my boyhood army comic books of

Sergeant Rock during the 1950s. I donned it with such secret childish delight because it made me look as Asiatic as the other GIs and like those in my old war comic books. The pile cap enabled me to fulfill a youngster's fantasy of soldierly pride. The Korean winter chills compelled me to wear my parka and the woolen olive green duty outfit for the first time.

THE NOVEMBER CHILLS OF 1964 COMPELLED ME TO WEAR MY FIELD PANTS, PARKA, WOOLEN OLIVE GREENS, GLOVES, AND PILE CAP FOR THE FIRST TIME IN KOREA. PARADE SUMMER DRESS AND GUARD DUTY UNIFORM ON SPECIAL OCCASIONS FOLLOWING FIELD MARCHES AT ROSS AND BLUE LANCER.

Because I was a squad leader in Basic Training and in school, I was aware that I had never walked guard before. However, I took this duty seriously; carefully surveying the fence, the path, and all that was visible under the water tank and lampposts that were my area of responsibility: I was a walking duck. I walked up and down the path by the barbwire fence, and I assured myself nothing, no one was going to infiltrate my post. However, it was from this guard tower that I gazed longingly southward at the road that led toward wondrous Seoul, and as I gazed northward, I spotted the guard tower where I again escaped military discipline, while listening to the radio during review by the band officer a few weeks earlier.

While continuing my walk, I reminisced of how I had felt a certain self-importance, knowing that I was a soldier in the U.S. Army, performing my duty on the other side of the world. I gladly acknowledged this assignment abroad when first advised of it—I knew my world tour had started. I knew I would be a good soldier. I took pride in my soldiering, and began by observing my first soldier's assignment, this post. I held that nothing could unnerve me, as I monitored my first place of duty. After what seemed an eternity, I observed a short apparition in military fatigues approach my post. Filled with adrenalin, I flung off my rifle and took a bayonet stance and challenged the intruder. The bewildered Korean soldier (KATUSA) halted each time, as required.

"Advance to be recognized," I called out, and the poor KATUSA slowly advanced. "Ojin," I whispered, with the shotgun barrel aiming above the KATUSA's head. "Out," the short figure responded, and added, "T'ake it eegee, s'throll, just s'throll."

I was unaware of the Korean Augmentation to the U.S. Army (KATUSA) and I thought that the Korean relief soldier could have been the enemy. Back at the guardhouse, the sergeant of the guard told me not to worry; it was a common mistake of all transients on initial guard duty at Korea. A textbook incident, I reflected, unlike probable reality such as duty at the DMZ. However, I still reflected, I could have killed the friendly soldier in my ignorance and could have been tried for murder. I chuckled momentarily and then a thought horrified me—instantly dismissed—that the KATUSA could have been set up for elimination!

I WALKED UP AND DOWN THE PATH WHERE I CHALLENGED THE POOR KATUSA BY THE BARBWIRE FENCE EAST FROM THE WATER TANK TOWER.

FROM THE WATER TANK TOWER, I GAZED PENSIVELY SOUTHWARD AT THE ROAD THAT LED TOWARD WONDROUS SEOUL. THE VILLAGE OF NANGMO-RI IS AT THE LOWER LEFT.

PARTIAL VIEW OF CAMP ROSS NORTH FROM THE WATER TANK GUARD TOWER. NOTE DISTANT TOWER AT CENTER OF PHOTO WHERE BAND OFFICER NOTED MY RADIO FULL BLAST. THE WATER TANK WAS IMMEDIATELY TO THE LEFT OF PHOTO FRAME.

Something else happened at the Water Tank Guard Tower earlier that spring. I would periodically step down to break the monotony and pace the fence path. All was well, so I ascended the tower. This tower, unlike Number Four at McGovern, had a telephone and the luxury of a seat, so I sat down. The next thing I knew was that I opened my eyes to the presence of the Officer of the Day (OD) who was about to use the telephone. He was the same OD that I had encountered back in November's guard mount. *I had fallen* asleep, *face up, in the sitting position!* The OD gave me but a glance and said nothing as he reported the overflowing water tank. It was only then that I noticed the tank's tidal overflow and heard the splash at the huge puddle below. The OD silently departed the tower leaving me horrified, thinking of the grounds for a court-martial. Quite shaken, I climbed down and continued walking my "post in a military manner observing everything within sight or hearing." I never knew why the OD hadn't said anything about my lapse of duty as I crushed the thick caramel out of the black beetles below Ross's Number One at this Far East corner of Asia.

Personnel Pains at Ross

North of Howze and by a vill
Lone, midway, remote and still
Ninety days of hellish loss
For this clerk at hated Ross

I first noticed the ground carpeted with hundreds of black creeping beetles under Number One's lamppost, one night on guard duty. They were about an inch long, each with a huge pair of what I found to be harmless pincers that crunched and splattered their caramel-like insides under my jump boots. I walked northward, along the length of the barbwire fence toward the main gate, then back to the tower, then continued south to Ross's southern limit, and then returned to the tower, again, again, and again.

"Lifer," one of three camp dogs, playfully lumbered up, wagging his tail. I knelt, patted his head, and ran my hand along the length of the dog's back and slid my curled hand around and along his lengthy wagging tail. The dog snuggled into my cupped hands, all along wagging his tail. Then he wriggled free, and shook himself by rapidly rocking sideways from head to tail, progressively alternating his left and right legs. It was common for the camp dogs to approach and accompany the guards at any time. As we walked under the lamppost, Lifer caught sight of the beetles and began a battle on a one-to-one-thousand basis. I was amused as I noticed that he aimed for a beetle only to momentarily lose it when it stopped moving. I guessed that at times his color blindness could not detect them against the black ground. Although he nosed and teased them, they were not bothered and crept one over another. Lifer soon lost interest and trotted away.

It was quite common for all companies to have a dog for a mascot. Camp dogs were playful and friendly and had free-run of the camp. Chingo (friend), Lifer, and Dagger were Personnel's. Although these mascots were fed and lived in their initial master's hooch and under his bunk, they seemed to know and therefore responded only to company soldiers. When their "owners" relocated to the States, they responded to any one who addressed them and cared for them. Although mascots may have become masterless and perhaps lonely among so many soldiers, their lot was much better than those ending in a stew pot in the village. For that, I suppose, they were grateful and became loyal to the company. I imagine they were good company for the dog lovers.

Dagger gave birth to Lifer's pup, which the Personnel clerks named Lucky—probably after the *Lucky* beer. One day, in the course of my work, I happened to enter the Quonset where Dagger was billeted, and having had the pup, she lunged at me snarling, showing huge and deadly fangs. I literally ran out, terrified!

DAGGER POSED WITH HER PUP LUCKY BY (PFC) NICHOLS

Lifer was a mild-mannered dog and Chingo—always ready for a dogfight—seemed to have it in for Lifer. One day, Lifer lay next to my desk and would not budge. Then a clerk approached Lifer and asked him what the matter was. We all knew that Chingo was on the prowl outside and Lifer was afraid to go out. Lifer seemed to understand and just lowered his head to the concrete floor and slowly wagged his tail.

Chingo always waited outside the mess hall to see what surprise awaited him. I could not remember ever having brought him a morsel or a bone. I recalled that after one week-long field problem, Chingo accidentally got left behind, as he always went with us. No one remembered to bring him back to camp, or perhaps he temporarily wandered off. Somehow or other Chingo still made it back to the safety of the compound, but for a long time would not cuddle up to anyone. It was a wonder that he had not ended up in someone's stew pot.

Every morning, at reveille formation, the band's dog and Chingo, Lifer, or Dagger growled into a fight. Everyone ignored it and no one did anything about it until after one good dogfight, the commanding officer had all dogs removed from the camp. End of story.

In my opinion, Camp Ross was a desolate godforsaken dump between marvelous Yongju-Gol to the north and the wonders of Seoul toward the south, via the road that faced me. For most soldiers like me, the compound was simply a stepping-stone to paradisiacal parts unknown. I felt that the only use for the words "Camp Ross" was as an entry on a blank space or empty box for a three-day pass. It stood as an indoctrination depot where transients continued deployment to the division units.

Camp Ross was my initial horror as a transient upon my indoctrination last November, and the terror resumed upon relocation from Personnel Service Center Number Three (PSC#3) at Camp McGovern by the village of Nopae Dong. Personnel Center Number Two (PSC #2) at Camp Beard by the village of marvelous Yongju-Gol had preceded PSC#3 to Ross, and were especially resentful because Camp Beard was *the* major recreation center as well as being located in marvelous Yongju-Gol. Yongju-Gol was a coveted spot to be stationed. The great plan—Personnel Service Division, Camp Ross—was to eventually materialize when PSC#1 from Camp Howze (farther south from Ross) moved into Ross.

PSC#3 CAMP MCGOVERN, NOPAE DONG, NOVEMBER 1964-MARCH 1965

PSC #2 CAMP ROSS, NANGMO-RI, MARCH-JUNE 1965

The PSC#3 troops and I from McGovern were settled and fully contented with Nopae Dong as our "hometown" because we *felt* very much *at home*. McGovern was also a recreation center with related comforts—in effect, McGovern *was* home. That February of 1965, the shocking and unwelcome news of relocation was met with company-wide resentment, especially by certain village rats. The following month the monumental grunt work of gathering, carrying, and loading all the PSC#3 Camp McGovern office furniture, field equipment and armament, and personal gear added to the already flaming emotions. I remember suffering the further agony of unrequited passion at departing my yet unravished Queen who continued her successful defiance during the last four months, and at whom I gazed longingly from the truck's bed. I sulkily rode away along with all the pay and personnel clerks on that spring March morning, flushed from a dream camp into the bitter sewer life of desolate Ross. I watched enviously as my fellow clerks in khakis approached the distant Main Gate on pass.

Camp Ross became our nightmare. The normal routine-flow was interrupted by coincidental and seasonal chores requiring extended duty and loss of accustomed privileges to already spoiled clerks. "This is a madhouse," commented the sergeant I was processing, as he surveyed the organized stir. Everyone seemed to be talking at the same time. Only last month, two shiploads of replacements had invaded Camp Ross for in-processing. The processing agenda was scheduled in eight-hour shifts, twenty-four hours a day for two weeks—with all passes again cancelled. I petulantly recalled this in-processing period as I again paced the fence at Guard Tower One. "Even the enemy would not bomb this place and end this confusion," I replied. The in-processing Quonset was overwhelmed with the uncommon commotion and boisterous bustle of multiple processing. The incoming soldiers were directed from the pay to the personnel clerks or vice versa. Although I never raised my voice while interviewing a transient, there seemed to be an air of *organized confusion* that reverberated all over the office Quonset. The transients—bewildered, newly arrived, and culture-shocked—blurted out answers as best they could. Dozens of Underwoods clicked away in the temporary overcrowded typing pool as the newcomers responded to information regarding leave, Soldiers Group Life Insurance beneficiary, gratuity pay, etc. The Personnel sergeants raised their voices to maintain order and simultaneously assure a smooth-flowing operation. To top it off, because of the poor acoustics within the crammed Quonset, all sound echoed, giving us an aura of chaos.

These bewildered GIs, new to Korea, asked the same questions about the duty, the cameras, the Oriental people, the mountains, the stench, the KATUSAs, and of the stroked writing that fascinated them. By then I had learned to write Korean, and I stroked their girlfriends' names in script. They liked the idea about the houseboys they could hire for a few dollars a month and no KP (kitchen police), but the guard duty that was pulled twice a week and every other weekend, shocked them all.

UPON RETURNING ON A SUNDAY FROM A RARE PASS TO SEOUL WHILE AT ROSS, I WAS ORDERED TO REPORT DIRECTLY FOR WORK, TYPING THE DESPISED 20S FROM 201 FILES, IN NON-DUTY UNIFORM.

I remembered that every available hooch was crammed with the newly arrived soldiers. All troops were detailed guard duty, as I too had been, last November. The ambience of Ross during those evenings was uncommonly filled with increased commotion and excitement. All guard posts were manned with fresh GIs spilling over onto the fence from the towers, which in effect singularly relieved Personnel of this detested duty during this in-processing instant. I could see that they, just as I had, were taking their duty seriously as they walked their posts with the added luxury of flashlights. I reflected that no slicky boy (thief), as professional as they were, would venture a theft because of the nervous, probably gun-happy, transient guards. After their initial evening, the newcomers crammed the *cantina* (saloon) nightly with larger than usual crowds—the sounds of merriment reached out even to the most remote guard towers.

I descended from my musings to become aware of the slower late-hour traffic under the brightly lit entry of Ross's *cantina*, a stone's throw away from Number One at this Far East corner of Asia.

In the words of a fellow clerk:

"At Camp Ross (we used to call it the armpit of the world) I pulled guard duty 154 times in fourteen months. In the winter I remember walking guard or sitting in a guard tower in the freezing darkness, trying to keep awake. I will always remember one Christmas Eve on guard duty, that the speakers at the camp were playing "I'll be Home for Christmas" by Frank Sinatra—that was a sad day. We hardly ever got passes, but when we did, I managed to hop on a *kimchi* bus or *hopsan* to Recreation Center #1 (Camp Beard) at the village called Yongju-Gol. I did make some good friends while spending time in Korea, one in particular was Julio Martinez."

—PFC Edward Fabrin, Personnel,
2nd Admin Co, 2nd Infantry Division,
Korea, 1964-1965

ROSS'S CANTINA (NCO AND EM CLUB) WAS LOCATED A STONE'S THROW FROM THE BARBEQUE PIT AND AT TOWER NUMBER ONE'S HINDQUARTERS.

Ross's Cantina

For just one flash in frozen time
A fantasy, a pantomime
Elated joy worth every dime
For just one flash in frozen time

Tower Number One lacked a seat and phone, so after a few moments of observation, tedium bade me descend and walk the fence. My eyes rested on the barbecue grill at Number One's hindquarters. I remembered an earlier and happier experience at the barbecue pit.

After we had settled in Ross with personnel routines when newly assigned at the camp, we began exploring and wandering around; my best buddy Abilio and I had wandered into the picnic area. We were both in party mode and pantomimed *asando chuletas a parrilla* (grilling steaks) while fantasizing a great *fiesta*. We imagined dancing to *polkas Mexicanas* with a couple of *senoritas bonitas* at their *jacalitos* (homes) in south central Texas. Perhaps colorful cut squares of tissue hung across the *nogales* (Pecan trees) and *alamos* (Cottonwoods) that added Mexican flavor. We boasted that the cuisine of San Antonio and La Joya was superior to none—talking about Mexican food; we especially missed refried beans and salsa de *chile*. Abilio was an accomplished dancer and once sang a *fandango* tune that I constantly repeated, until it eventually drove him insane. It was fun to laugh and frolic as we enjoyed a twinkle of "happy times" at the isolated Camp Ross.

JUST ENJOYING ONE CAREFREE MOMENT OUTSIDE MY OFFICE QUONSET. ANOTHER MOMENT RESTING ON GRAVEYARD GUARDIAN. ONE MOMENT OF DELIGHTFUL AMUSEMENT AT THE PICNIC AREA.

I glanced toward the EM Club from behind the isolated Number One and the music within became apparent. I had been totally oblivious of it as I was not usually attracted to nightlife. I rarely frequented the clubs, but one night I made an exception. Abilio assured me that the evening's performance would be worth my while.

(PFC) MENDIOLA, MY BEST BUDDY AT ROSS, ASSURED THE EVENING AT THE CLUB WOULD BE WORTHWHILE. NOTE HIGH GUARD TOWER NEXT TO THE BARELY VISIBLE WATER TANK AT EXTREME UPPER RIGHT CORNER OF PHOTO.

It was an evening of live entertainment at *Ross's Cantina* (EM Club). I was quite uncomfortable, but I attended and eventually got caught up in the excitement. There was an unusually larger crowd at *Ross's*. The audience included numerous transients and Personnel's clerks relaxing after a series of overworked evenings. There was rowdiness and loud merriment in anticipation of the evening's highlight. I hurried back to my barrack and returned with my faithful 35 mm camera. I made sure the battery was functional, as I blinded the guys with the electronic flash and synchronized the aperture and speed required within dark settings. I found myself a perch at the edge of the dance floor with an unobstructed view of the stage, by Abilio's table. This was going to be fun!

Two lovely ladies, dressed as flappers, appeared on stage dancing the *Charleston*, when suddenly one of their ivory-beaded necklaces broke. What a riot! The newly arrived troops stormed the stage for souvenirs, overwhelming the Master at Arms, but I got mine! The dancers quickly retreated upstage until the Master at Arms threatened to stop the show if we didn't settle down.

In the next number, the flappers brought out two bamboo canes that rested on crosspieces at either end. Two flappers kneeled and rhythmically clapped the canes lengthwise, alternatively once on the pad and twice together. The third flapper began skipping and dancing between the clapping poles, displaying synchronization skills. As the music accelerated, she increased her speed, and began cartwheeling between the clapping canes, all the while cheered on by the two clappers with "Wheeeee!" The crowd cheered with increased approval as her cartwheel splayed (spread wide) toward the audience. I was supplicating my stars that this picture-perfect pleasure would not too soon end.

Then the small band chimed out the Moulin Rouge *Can-Can* prelude. Three smiling ladies attired in Parisian "oo-la-la," dresses swung on stage, waving their skirts, and the crowd started up again. The ladies raised their skirts all around from their waists, revealing all kinds of lace and fishnet delights. I forgot all about my camera when the high kicking followed up with waving ruffles and flying skirts, rising to shoulder level, below wide smiles. I was unaware of my own yelling and catcalling, blending in with the rest of the troops. The Master at Arms had to intervene again, but the show continued. Then, when three legs went up for a joint three-legged hop and whirl, the crowd stood up, raising their drinks, and that is when I remembered the camera. The flash could not reload fast enough to catch the remainder of the eye-goggling dance. It did not dawn on me that the flash acted with split-second lighting, illuminating the darker, recessed delights, even though the optics of one eye on the viewfinder and the other on the girls should have brought me some excitable viewing. My fast reloading flash may have caused a blinking psychedelic effect, common to the Roaring Twenties' stages in the dimly lit club. It was during one of these boisterous moments that one lady rode around in a unicycle, much to the cheers of the audience.

The best moment of this evening was when one lady, attired in an evening dress, sang on the dance floor, and since I was at hand; she summoned me to dance. Excitedly, I handed my camera to Abilio and rushed up to her. Following the dance, she rewarded me with a kiss on the cheek, amidst loud catcalling. I could not have thanked her more for her already generous poses or Abilio for holding the camera, while I was touch-dancing with my model.

FOLLOWING THE MOULIN ROUGE *CAN CAN* DANCE, THE FLAPPERS DANCED AND CARTWHEELED BETWEEN CLAPPING CANES.

THEN THEY DANCED, SANG, AND RODE A UNICYCLE

It was between one of my picture-taking breaks that I was approached by newly arrived troops, asking how much my camera cost. I mentioned that I actually had three pieces; the camera, and the strobe, along with the oversized, high-speed battery charger that powered it. In my excitement, I flashed back within my memory banks to the similar question I had once asked of another shutterbug upon my arrival in Korea.

My buddies and I returned to our hooch in high spirits, gratified with the evening's activities. Abilio kept repeating in fine jest that anyone hearing my Mexican yells and conduct that night would for sure know that I was *un hombre perdido* (a lost soul). For one evening, and just one evening, I forgot all about hellish Ross. Aahhh! but I hit the sack that night in utter ecstasy with my camera's pleasant promising prints, all at the cost of my absence from Aunt Ross's guard tower. That night was the zenith of my entire stay at Ross. As rapturous as that incident was, I argued with myself that the evening's entertainment could never have made up for the abhorred duration at Ross. However, responsibility interrupted my recollection of high spirits, as I resumed duty and ascended Number One, at this Far East corner of Asia.

TWO MENACING DRAGONS' HEADS GUARDED THE MEDIEVAL GATE TO PEAK DAE PARK.

Peak Dae
Spring 1965

Darkened skies then twilight blue
Trident peaks a threesome few
Pearly crowns a moment true
Wiped by dawn that left no clue

As the earth turns on its eastward course, radiant light reveals the darkest recesses while racing in counter direction. Golden rays gleam on blue, ruffled waves and rouse The Land of the Rising Sun (Japan) as they advance to the Asiatic mainland. The rays illuminate The Land of the Morning Calm (Korea), a peninsula extended from Middle Land (China), on their eternal pursuit of morning twilight. Owing to the earth's curvature, these earliest rays of dawn claim the loftiest summits centered within the rugged headland of Korea, before outlining its coastal contours. It is on this mountainous landscape where a trio of crags greets these first beams of dawn. At a faraway guard tower by the village of Nangmo-Ri, I stand: a lone sentinel, gazing to the southeast at the barely discernable points of Baekje (Anglicized Peak Dae) amid the sunrise haze.

It was under one of those predawn, black skies that I again stood guard at Tower Number One, near the main gate at Camp Ross. Although the fatigue of lost sleep was catching up with me, I was fully caught up in enjoying the freshening coolness of dawn in anticipation of the approaching daylight, that early summer of 1965. I gazed northward over the main gate as the twilight progressively lit and defined the surrounding distant mountains and nearby rice paddies under the scantily lit, distantly placed lampposts. I glanced westward to see if I could yet trace the road that traversed my field of view. I scanned the road. It ran to my left, heading south, as it disappeared behind mountains on its way toward wondrous Seoul. My gaze continued half circle toward the far horizon to the south-southeast. There, my weary eyes rested on the three distant and barely visible crests of Peak Dae, barely outlined in the horizon's emerging light. The resplendent twilight profiled the peaks, resembling inverted gray icicles with pink vertices against the pale blue sky in this overwhelming still scenario. I recalled the story of King Onjo (18 BC-28AD) who had climbed to the top and claimed them within the capital of his kingdom. The king had built his palace in this rugged zone, with a surrounding wall.

HARDLY VISIBLE IN BRIGHT DAYLIGHT, THE DISTANT CRAGS OF DAE WERE BARELY OUTLINED ON THE HORIZON'S MORNING TWILIGHT.

I smiled as I recalled my visit to Peak Dae in the spring just the month before. The cherry trees were covered with white blossoms, all along both sides of the road. For a moment, and only a moment, I imagined myself blessed within an enclosure, purified by the white flurries. As the chocolate tour bus approached the ancient gate, the three vertical colossi of Dae appeared as wide as mountains and seemingly towered to the sky. I recalled reading a brochure that on a clear day, both coasts of Korea were visible from the loftiest pinnacle. I wondered what it would be like to fly up there as a bird and see this miracle for myself.

Presently, we arrived and I was disappointed to find the ancient structures and the crumbling walls that once surrounded the kingdom were now in ruins and in disrepair. However, the remaining scattered towers attested to a once well-built fortification. The main gate boasted a double-tiered tile roof, with upturned corners and two menacing dragons' heads at the arched entry. All the ceilings, posts, rafters, and crossbeams bore predominantly green, geometric, Oriental patterns. Everything was constructed of the gray stone common to Korea.

ENTRANCE GATE TO PEAK DAE PARK

ALL THE CEILINGS, POSTS, RAFTERS AND CROSS BEAMS BORE PREDOMINANTLY GREEN GEOMETRIC ORIENTAL PATTERNS.

    As our tour group proceeded into the grounds, we came across more fruit trees with the same captivating white flowers. I saw whole Korean families picnicking and children playing among the numerous gigantic stones. Many men were boisterous, drunk, or had passed out and were lying on flat stones, or reclining on boulders. I realized that Peak Dae served as a recreation area: a public park. Groups with microphones played musical instruments under colorful canvas canopies, others simply played in the open—there was much merriment. At such a group, I happened to notice a woman singing. Then my attention was attracted to a GI from the tour group who was singing *Michelle,* a cappella. To my surprise, upon my curious approach, a Korean man handed me the microphone, as I watched the singing soldier run off. The well-attired multitude eyed me expectantly, half-smiling, but with curious eyes and bobbing heads, all happy with drink. Impulsively, I sang *El Rancho Grande,* along with a couple of Mexican yells. As I sang, I noticed all eyes and faces showed increased attentiveness at what, for sure, was their first exposure to a Mexican song in Spanish and the related yell. Upon my last yell, I handed the microphone to the master of ceremonies and ran off to my group, amid a weak applause. Decades later, I realized that a talent show was underway at that canopy.

GROUPS WITH MICROPHONES PLAYED MUSICAL INSTRUMENTS UNDER COLORFUL CANVAS CANOPIES, OTHERS SIMPLY PLAYED IN THE OPEN.

As we departed the park, I could not help but remain impressed by the gate's architecture. Gates were always of superior design, perhaps to promote the sovereign's affluence. My dreams of this escapade amid this morning spectacle were abruptly interrupted by the peal of the bugle call, heralding reveille, and I returned to reality.

EXIT GATE FROM PEAK DAE PARK

THE KING HAD HIS PALACE BUILT IN THIS RUGGED ZONE WITH A GATE AND SURROUNDING WALL.

The shapes of the distant, pale, gray peaks gradually vanished in the aurora's brightness. I chuckled with immense gratification at my facility to readily identify the Peak and relive an adventure on this awakening dawn in this Far East Corner of Asia.

Insubordination at Ross

You're in the Army now, you're not behind the plow
you'll never get rich, by digging a ditch (or son of a witch)
you're in the army now
—author unknown

"Shut up!" Specialist Fifth Canyon shrieked at me in his emotional, almost feminine, voice and with unusual confidence in the presence of the Personnel lieutenant and senior sergeant. I had again sassed back, regarding some minor correction, while typing away at the hated, yellow Form 20s late one evening. My words could have been judged grounds for insubordination.

"Whip me out another Form 20," commanded Canyon in his high-pitched voice.

Once more I found myself standing guard at Number One Guard Tower, thinking back to certain occurrences that brought me close to a court-martial and possibly, time in the stockade.

"Take those stripes off," I menacingly challenged (meaning the Specialist Fifth arch).

"This is not the way of the army," Staff Sergeant Gilliam calmly interposed, "return to work, Martinez."

"Yes, Sergeant, if you say so," I meekly responded, whereupon the sergeant patiently responded with a quiet "OK."

"Because *I* say so," shrieked Canyon, breaking the silence in his shrill voice, having to have the last word.

After a few moments, the sergeant and Canyon stepped out. What transpired between them after that outburst is unknown.

Lieutenant Bollini, a former *Private* soldier, then coolly asked one of the clerks to go to the pastry shop and buy him an éclair and (with an air of what I realized as empathy, in later years) to get the clerks "whatever they want." Bewildered, all the clerks and I glanced at one another and quietly ordered an equal value éclair. The lieutenant's kindness managed to change the bitter atmosphere to a rare blissful moment at hated Ross. Glancing up and down Number One's barbwire fence, I remembered the day Canyon claimed "insubordination," because I had heckled him the entire morning.

"What's this?" Lieutenant Daniels demanded, rising from his chair as his eyes radiated infuriation. Without hearing either side of the issue, as we were about to pass through his office door, he gave us a lawful order, "Get back to work, both of you."

The commanding officer of Personnel, in an authoritative voice, literally threw Canyon and me out of his office. He did not bother to hear more from either of us, and we both quietly returned to duty. The lieutenant's usual, kindly, fish-gray eyes instantly shrunk and contracted to frozen, steel gray that seemed to spurt fire, hell, and brimstone at both of us. For the rest of my life, I never forgot the lieutenant's stern countenance, or the killer eyes that seemed to pierce right through me to my very soul, as if through an M14 viewfinder. Although at first I seemed to find humor in the whole episode, I dared not once glance at Canyon, but sat terrified, and shuddered quietly the rest of the day. Perhaps the lieutenant was fed up with the childish behavior he witnessed one time too many. I guess the combination of Canyon's effeminate voice and pettiness unconsciously reminded me of my mother's abusive nature. Conceivably, I was retaliating against Canyon's behavior, which paralleled my mother's.

"Yes, he's here. He'll be back shortly," the Chaplain said and hung up the telephone. It was Sergeant Gilliam, looking for me. I had no earthly idea of what I wanted to see the Chaplain about as I sat in his office, unless it was to tell him I was fed up with my duty station and needed a sympathetic ear. I chuckled as I continued guard duty in Number One, while recalling the incidents a few weeks back.

"Do you want to go to jail?" Sergeant Gilliam angrily barked at me, as I returned from the pastry shop.

"No, Sergeant," was the only reply I could muster.

"Have you got a problem?"

"No, Sergeant," I responded meekly.

"Then get back to your desk," blasted the sergeant, as his bushy eyebrows merged with anger that shocked me. This was not like Sergeant Gilliam, as he tended to be a fine, patient, senior soldier. Evidently, there were other factors at work here.

"Yes, Sergeant,"

"Any questions?"

"No, Sergeant."

"Get to work."

"Yes, Sergeant," I responded, with my head lowered, as I halfheartedly sat at my desk and resumed typing the hated new Form 20s.

I sulked, as I concentrated on the forms with the intimidating sergeant standing by. I had only earlier been ordered out from the gym by the sergeant, where I was attending my karate class, instead of returning to the office after chow. I was playing hooky from work because I was fed up with typing the new 20s in duplicate from the obsolete greens. Personnel was again working late into the night, until 10:00 p.m. and all passes had been cancelled for what seemed the millionth time. I allowed myself to wallow in misery, as I continued pecking at the Underwood typewriter.

After walking the fence, I felt the back of my waist ache, so I ascended the tower to lean within the enclosure in order to momentarily relieve the discomfort. I glanced toward the parade ground, now obstructed by the trees, and recalled another incident a few weeks back.

"You ladies bitch about the duty, but you cannot sound off like men," were the words Specialist Fifth Riley roared as he reprimanded the men he was drilling. As I walked my post, I envisioned the incident of a month earlier at the Command Support Headquarters parade ground from Number One. Riley had stopped the Personnel platoon long enough to regain our respect. He knew the troops were exhausted and demoralized with the extended work-schedule and on that one occasion, to liven things up, called out a jody (marching song). The entire platoon, in high-pitched, falsetto voices, shrilled in slurred unison an unplanned *"One, two, three, four; one, two, three, four."* Being in the center of the platoon, the eerie and stereo shrilling sounded somewhat like several wailing covens of *lloronas*, banshees, or witches at a funeral pyre. What followed was like an omen. The troops, except for a few unfortunates, were granted passes. I, one of those unfortunates, ended up on guard duty. However, when I applied for the weekend pass anyway, the benevolent Sergeant Gilliam bade me report in the morning without the usual sleep-in. He saw to it that the pass was granted without query.

As I continued with the monotony of guard duty at Number One, I glanced back toward the brightly lit Personnel Quonsets. I visualized the detested duty my peers were still performing late into the night at this Far East corner of Asia.

My Princess
June 1965

I glance upon her lovely hills
Traverse her valleys and her rills
And freely clamber, crawl, and scale
Her boundless curvy endless vale

From the mountain tributaries near the *Ilbon* (Japan) Sea, the Imjin River descends and flows on its westward course across the rugged peninsula of ancient *Chosen* (Korea) and exits at the waters of *Chungu* (China). It has witnessed countless military onslaughts since the dawn of existence. In this environment, I could easily envision warriors in chain mail, waving banners brushed with perplexing strokes, while wielding razor-sharp *katanas* and lances. Led by silk-clad samurai and warlords from countless kingdoms, these hordes ceaselessly overran its eternal waters. The river glides past the hollow eyes of Buddha sentinels that guard ancestral bones interred beneath sacred burial mounds. Glistening, streaming waters, it seemed to me, observed the sentinels who maintain vigilance for occasional infraction on the opposite banks of recent, man-made boundaries. As the river curves and winds across this rugged and mountainous landscape, it passes a lowland known as The Western Corridor. At this locale, nestled between Easy Queen and Radio Hill just across the Imjin from Spoonbill, reigns Princess Blue Lancer.

As a Personnel clerk, I visited the Third Brigade troops north of the Imjin River, near the Demilitarized Zone—whose 210 Personnel Records I maintained—to review their new demographic Form 20s in the summer of 1965. To keep up to date, the army had decided that typing a new form in duplicate for each trooper in the Cavalry (division area) would enhance Personnel. "EASIER TO WORK WITH," the banner on the Pacific Stars and Stripes newspaper read, with some dork smiling as he viewed a Form 20. The only problem was that neither the dork nor the newspaper reporter ever had to type them up. Thus for a few months, Personnel's workday ended at 10:00 p.m., despite guard duty and all passes cancelled.

PERSONNEL CLERK, PERSONNEL SERVICE CENTER NUMBER TWO

I HANDLED THE RECORDS OF ALL THREE BRIGADES' HEADQUARTERS INCLUDING FIRST OF THE TWELFTH CAVALRY AT BLUE LANCER VALLEY.

I was exhausted from lack of sleep, and my head involuntarily nodded, as I now and again dozed to the rhythm of the rolling truck. I maintained the personnel records of all three brigades and First of the Twelfth Cavalry. Heretofore, the troops whose records I maintained only existed on paper to me. These Personnel visits opened my awareness to the actual life and world of the line soldier. It was only then that I began to grasp the magnitude of the military occupation of Korea.

Returning from the DMZ sector while crossing the Imjin at Teal Bridge, I was impressed as I scanned its panoramic grandeur. Heading south, the river, with its blue water, peacefully flowed from my left, under Teal, and to my right toward the Yellow Sea. As we "centered" the river I found myself surrounded by gloriously smooth waves between two coasts with mountains on all backdrops. My heart leaped as I digested this circle of blue water surrounded by distant greenery, all under warm, bright, yellow sunshine. For an instant, and only a split-second, I was in the U.S. Navy, on board a ship sailing toward those islands in the South Pacific, with those elusive grass-swaying Polynesian girls of my dreams. However I observed girls neck deep in the river who pulled up at my wild gestures to satisfy my curiosity! Instantaneously, my delusion ended as we reached the southern bank, where I immediately caught sight and was highly impressed by the menacing bunkers that stood watch on mountaintops facing North Korea, all along the Munsan-Ni road. I promised myself that one day I would examine the Buddha statues (those hidden jewels I dreamed at the indoctrination spiel), reportedly scattered all over the mountains, that at this moment, I imagined were staring and beckoning to me alone. How I craved to extend my adventures to this alluring locale. Duty, however, drove me south from the T-bone at the notorious Blue Diamond Store by Nullo-Ri to the First of the Twelfth at Camp Blue Lancer Valley. I sleepily readied the 201 Personnel Files on my lap with the new yellow "20s" for revision. "Back to the salt mines," I grumbled under my breath, "no nonchalant wonderings today."

ENTRY TO TEAL BRIDGE FROM EASTERN BANK. APPROACHING IMJIN RIVER.

AS WE CENTERED THE RIVER WHILE RETURNING FROM THE DMZ, I FOUND MYSELF SURROUNDED BY GLORIOUSLY SMOOTH WAVES BETWEEN TWO COASTS WITH MOUNTAIN GREENERY ON ALL BACKDROPS.

ARRIVING AT THE EASTERN BANK, I IMMEDIATELY CAUGHT SIGHT OF THE MENACING BUNKERS THAT STOOD WATCH ON MOUNTAINTOPS FACING NORTH KOREA ALL ALONG THE MUNSAN-NI ROAD.

Princess Blue Lancer immediately captivated me when I first laid eyes on her. From a distance, I caught sight of her majestic beauty, as I entered a beautiful valley surrounded by high mountain greenery. As we approached the main gate, I saw two Blue Lancers, opulently uniformed in snug-fitting coats of fine, blue, broadcloth with gold-brocaded swirls on their sleeves, standing on opposite sides. They both came to attention, bringing their gleaming sabers to the "present arms" salute, bearing the sword's glinting gold hilt at their noses, with the mirrored silver blade extending well above their tall, black, plush, bearskin helmets. I was made to feel as if I was a guest of honor, in review of their military bearing. I blinked, momentarily blinded by the sparkle of their gold buttons, ribboned medals, and heavy bullion epaulettes with braid that resplendently glittered in the sun's rays. I caught a flash of the gold-textured patterns on brocaded stripes along their trousers' lengths that disclosed mirrored shoes, as they returned to the "parade dress" position, and as they both simultaneously sheathed their shiny sabers, after three clicks of sharp movements. The graded road I tread seemed like a carpet of fine, scarlet plush. I was awed by the cascade of white waters, silently descending from the distant Alps, vaporizing, and faintly bubbling at a blue lagoon below. A brook poured from the pool and flowed through the length of her realm toward us. I observed a fine equestrian guard and carriages with footmen at my immediate right. Hundreds of green-liveried cavaliers swarmed all over her vale in attendance.

PRINCESS BLUE LANCER IMMEDIATELY CAPTIVATED ME WHEN I FIRST LAID EYES ON HER. FROM A DISTANCE, I CAUGHT SIGHT OF HER MAJESTIC BEAUTY AS I ENTERED HER SOVEREIGN DOMAIN SURROUNDED BY HIGH MOUNTAIN GREENERY.

As I trampled through her breathtaking glory, I immediately noticed she was secured from all quarters. Company A and B stood guard on her left mountain slopes along with the recreational buildings at the far left. C Company protected her on the right declines, while the 702nd Battalion patrolled the far-right, rear corner of her stately, enclosed sector. Her Blue Dragoons of Headquarters Company constituted her rearguard—responsible for defense from all flanks. Colorful military coats-of-arms on banners and shielded crests that proudly emblazoned each regiment added to her royal pageantry. Only three emblems of staffed freedom fronted the brigade offices at the very center. From her throne (the division icon) Her Royal Highness comfortably scrutinized her sovereign domain. It encompassed the parapets and battlements that surrounded her realm and all else across the parade grounds to the far-flung Quonsets and main gate—all amid the alpine greenery. She reigned over her court and the Blue Lancers in all her regal dignity.

A double line of Blue Lancers came to attention, as I approached her royal presence. I gasped in awe at the aura that enveloped her, and that mesmerized me. The light pink blush on her dimpled cheeks softly complemented her fair complexion, and her pixie-like face was all aglow. Her wavy dark brown hair sparkled with twinkling blue accents as it swirled around her radiant, creamy neck and shoulders. Her lustrous, long-flowing, white gown of sheer gossamer, with a shimmering, bluish effect at the slight folds also randomly sparkled at her slightest movement, as it graced her tall and slender statuesque poise. It bore two blue ribbons, the length of the gown, from shoulder to hem, that simulated flowing waters at her every motion. Her bare arms that emerged from a body garment of baby-blue silk with exquisite wrists and dainty hands were free of opulent ornament. A fold from her knee to her hem revealed a slipper that appeared made of the finest-crafted iridescent fabric resembling *mother of pearl*. Her affectionate gaze revealed a pair of soft, blue eyes that liquefied me. Her rose-petal-pink lips parted, as I approached closer, to reveal even and symmetrical pearly teeth. I was further overcome by the intoxicating fragrance of the lilac *parfum* she wore. The fragrance activated every pulse sense I had, together with those newly discovered. On her golden-brown noble head rested a platinum tiara with a trident of sparkling emeralds on a yellow setting. Her left hand rested on a shield, bearing a green trident on a yellow field, while her right fingers clasped a lengthy scepter, wrought as a lance. Her entire fragile composition gave the impression of the finest porcelain ever fashioned by specialized Oriental craftsmen, requiring divine attention. "Come here," she said in her soft sweet, melodic voice. My heart pounded as I drew before her. She was surrounded by officers in different colored uniforms who further blinded me with greater gold brocaded swirls on their coats, trouser seams, heavier gold braided epaulettes, swords, and with a multitude of gleaming honors, ribbons, and medals on their chests.

 Her sentinels simultaneously faced one another and in three quick motions drew their flashing sabers, presented arms, and crossed their weapons overhead to form a gleaming canopy. I reached my exhilarated zenith, as I passed under the shimmering, crossed, silver sabers and knelt before my princess with unconditional adoration. Reciprocating my very passion she rose from her throne, blinding me with all her radiance as her man-at-arms took custody of the shield and as she handed her scepter to a lady-in-waiting. My princess then placed one hand, in seeming respect, momentarily on my head, as I took her opposite hand in my Neanderthal, tremulous fist and kissed her pink fingertips with all high regard. Then with trembling hands, she instantly ennobled me by anchoring a rather heavy gold and jeweled crown on my head. With her dainty hand, she bid me rise and summoned me to attendance at the forefront of her entourage to share her throne. Then, her angel-like, sweet, melodic voice softly whispered, "Turn around." I turned to partake of her breath-taking glorious spectacle as her respondent vassals' cheers echoed my name all through the entire valley: *"Martinez, Martinez!"*

THE FIRST CAVALRY DIVISION ICON AT BRIGADE HEADQUARTERS OFFICES WAS THE NUCLEUS OF CAMP BLUE LANCER VALLEY.

I MAJESTICALLY MADE MYSELF COMFORTABLE AT THE BRIGADE HEADQUARTERS ICON, NOW REFLAGGED AS SECOND INFANTRY DIVISION.

VIEW FROM BRIGADE HEADQUARTERS OF THE ENTIRE CAMP BLUE LANCER VALLEY, A AND B COMPANY QUONSETS AT RIGHT AND 702ND MAINTENANCE WITH C COMPANY QUONSETS AT LEFT.

"*Martinez!*" The driver's faraway voice broke through and brought me back to life, "*What the hell . . . ?*" I heard him say, as I was abruptly thrown back from my daydream. Affectionately, through clouds from dreamland to reality, echoed her last words that were to remain implanted in my youthful, love-sick brain forevermore, "*I will always love you . . .*" I sleepily and painfully extracted my embedded head from the bobbing truck's dashboard and looked around. Awakening from my dreams of tenderness amid bleary clouds, still in a stupor and with my heart pounding I witnessed the whole of the Blue Lancer Valley, in all its grandeur, unfolding before me, in full anticipation of yet another adventure.

"*Martinez!*" It was Sergeant Gilliam's voice that brought me back to actuality. I had paused, dreaming wide-eyed in full daylight of Camp Blue Lancer Valley, while tediously typing away on the Form 20s. I slowly looked up at him, blinked and slowly returned to my Underwood, and continued typing. He walked away, mumbling I don't know what. I then looked around and heard my fellow clerks say, "Man, you were really out of it this time." I was on overload, exhausted, and worn out, not only from the dread of guard duty, but from working overtime. I had slumbered off into oblivion, but with memories of a sweet dove at a dream camp in a daydream adventure in this Far East corner of Asia.

Epilogue

Bitterly lost in reflecting the negative side of the past three months, I realized I could still not make the best of a bad situation. Just when I thought things could be worse, they got worse! I was disillusioned! I forever wondered what genius had selected this penal complex for Personnel! It was then that I decided on a transfer—to the infantry with all its miseries—even as a target at the hazardous DMZ would at least provide *some* adventure. There had to be a better life than Personnel at Ross with its dreaded overtime, guard duty, and no passes. Little did I know that my fortune was about to change.

THE SEMPER PARATUS FIRST OF THE TWELFTH CREST FRONTED THE BULLETIN BOARD WHILE OLD BILL STOOD BY THE FIRST OF THE TWELFTH'S ORDERLY ROOM AT CAMP BLUE LANCER VALLEY.

Chapter 12

Reassigned! Camp Blue Lancer Valley, Nullo-Ri, Korea

June-November 19, 1965

> *In Xanadu did Kubla Khan, A stately pleasure dome decree . . .*
> *With walls and towers were girdled round . . . Enfolding sunny spots of greenery . . .*
> *Through wood and dale the sacred river ran . . . It was a miracle of rare devise . . .*
> *To such a deep delight 'twould win me . . . And drunk the milk of Paradise.*
>
> —Samuel Taylor Coleridge, *Kubla Khan*

Prologue

I had an excellent view of the compound all the way to the main gate from my new hooch number one located catty corner to the PX and immediately behind the brigade education hooch. I stood quietly, slowly savoring and drinking it all in—complacently surveying my soon-to-be conquered new world that morning of June 16, 1965. To my right, beyond the headquarters' hooches, was the towering Easy Queen. Panning left, were the recreation buildings, the theater, the gym, the endless line of Co A and B hooches, the remote mountains of *North Korea* above the main gate, the POL (Petroleum, Oil, and Lubricants or the Motor Pool), the Co C and 702nd Quonsets, the well-provisioned PX, and finally, the message center being the Battalion Headquarters at my left completing the semicircle of my periphery. This was my Shangri-la; a spectacle, another dream coming to life, a wish realized coming true upon my arrival at Camp Blue Lancer Valley.

To the Cavalry!
June 16, 1965

The sun will rise another day
With New horizons on my way
Streams to cross and hills to scale
Suns to set and stars to hail

Upon my return from my visit north of the river and of the immediate military sectors, I remember walking around like an angry worker ant, unappreciated and overworked by my employer. My moodiness was due to several factors. I was fed up with Personnel, the detested overtime duty, lack of three-day passes, and the complete absence of allocations for promotion. I longed for a transfer to the DMZ and company-level clerical duties. I kept daily tabs with the line company orderly rooms, and one by one, each reported no vacancy.

I couldn't believe how taken I was by my recent visit to a charming compound named Camp Blue Lancer Valley near the Imjin River far north from Camp Ross. I wanted to be part of this compound and become a Blue Lancer. Some of my buddies at Personnel (and some at Blue Lancer Valley) expressed disbelief that I would leave the comforts and prestige of Personnel in exchange for the infantry—and because there was nothing at the BLV! However, I knew better, and I had other interests there. I remembered a major theater (BLV Playhouse), a fully equipped photo lab, a woodcraft shop, and a well-stocked modern PX that only the one in Yongsan, Seoul could rival! I could almost taste being there!

Finally, on one of those fine mornings in early June, I chanced to see Staff Sergeant Coffey walking past my Personnel Quonset. He was the Personnel Staff Noncommissioned Officer from the First of the Twelfth and I sensed that before me was my opportunity. Thinking no further, I called out to him.

"Sergeant Coffey, do you need a clerk typist at the First of the Twelfth?"

"*Shoot yeah*," replied the sergeant with a serious face, his thick eyebrows merging, "are you interested?"

"Yes," I lied, "and I can type eighty words a minute."

When I received my transfer orders I danced in front of Canyon, my immediate supervisor, directing and waving two birdies at his face, chanting, "—you Canyon,—you Canyon, I'm going to the DMZ." Where upon Canyon angrily responded in his thin effeminate voice, "Get working or you're going to the DMZ as a Private E-2." I immediately withdrew to my desk quite shaken and terrified.

The next morning I loaded my equipment on a jeep and headed for the First of the Twelfth. The memorable day was June 16, 1965. I relished the late morning sunshine as I rode toward my coveted duty station. I smiled wildly to myself as I passed through the main gate of Camp Ross as a Personnel clerk for the last time bound for the Camp Blue Lancer Valley assignment.

Enthusiastically, I looked forward to my new station with the glee of a newly found treasure. Happily, I welcomed and bade greeting to the familiar shops of Yongju-Gol, and then as I passed Pobwan-Ni I viewed the *hopsan* depot, the gateway to wondrous Seoul. Reaching McGovern, I glanced toward Nopae Dong, my "hometown" still with bygone wild adventures and sweet mischief, now being left even farther behind with newer anticipated bold DMZ goings-on. My eyes gleamed eagerly toward Easy Queen at the left knowing fully well that she was finally mine to surmount and with resignation that she knew what was awaiting her. And in my emotional involvement I pictured she winked at me. As the jeep continued north, I was filled with delight in expectation of new adventures ahead at Nullo-Ri and Blue Lancer Valley. Suddenly, I realized that the BLV was in the proximity of the Turk Compound and an added source for possible adventure. All those secret Buddha statues, bunkers, and temples scattered all over this North Country that I had long dreamed of locating, would now be mine to discover.

Upon arrival at the BLV, Private First H. met me. He helped me unload and transport my gear to quarters (Hooch Number One), and we both proceeded to the orderly room.

"You can type eighty words per minute?" Captain Baker smilingly asked me.

"That was when I was in high school," I lied again, smiling back.

"This is my Top, First Sergeant Ch, morning report clerk Private First G., and you've met H.," the captain said.

Immediately G. demanded that I type a morning report. I did my best and in minimum time whipped it out with only three acceptable errors. No one was impressed though. I could not have cared less; I was where I wanted to be and oblivious to all. The clerks, the recreation sergeant, and Top took an instant dislike to me because I proved even less interested in socializing, thus bickering ensued. I guess I was further disliked because of my independent spirit that demonstrated I had purpose, a life and not tied down to the daily grind. Despite orderly room status, the commanding officer took kindly to me.

I was assigned a familiar Underwood typewriter, a field table, and a place next to the captain's door under the only protruding window at the south wall of the orderly room. My teeth chattered as I shivered excitedly fully pleased with myself resuming the remainder of my tour of duty in the cavalry. Little did I know that this change would bring about new lifelong anticipated wonders of this Far East corner of Asia.

Orderly Room Blahs and Boons!
June 1965

If looks and stares and eyes could kill
If files of tasks there were to fill
This unmoved clerk the extra wheel
Would make the best of any deal

As an orderly room clerk, I was overwhelmed to finally be away from all the hell of my former job in Payroll and Personnel. The sun, a bright golden yellow globe, beckoned me as it bathed my days at my coveted and beloved Blue Lancer Valley duty station.

I could not believe the numerous Personnel Request 1049 Forms that would come in for transfers to Vietnam. Most of the troops felt lucky and were content with the hardships of a Korean assignment, and refrained from even talking about another hostile duty assignment, although some talked about the hostile fire pay being attractive. The commanding officer used his own criteria as he approved some requests but denied others. One of the sergeants drew up such a fantastic self-recommendation that it was approved by the CO but denied at the division level.

As I worked at my station, I became aware of the lives of many soldiers at First of the Twelfth. Some would dream of married life in the United States but others considered other options. There were so many complacent Korean prostitutes, so that might have been a reason. I do know that the urge to marry a U.S. soldier seemed to be an inborn trait of *josans* who saw this as a door to a much better life. It was amazing how many soldiers would consider marrying a professional prostitute. Many marital applications passed through my desk, but only one was memorable because of the soldier's colorful and varied life. Private First T. was underage, so he requested, received, and submitted a notarized parental permission to marry. I later received a letter disaffirming his mother's permission, but it arrived after the marriage ceremony. I guessed that, as with many other such marriages, T. must have reenlisted in order to fly his wife with him to his next PCS (Permanent Change of Station). Because of regulations, soldiers could not cohabitate with their wives in the village. However, T. threatened to jump the fence and go AWOL (Absence Without Official Leave) in order to be with his wife. Finally, the CO had him sign in every hour at the orderly room in order to keep track of him. Then T. would not write to his mother, so the CO had him sit at the office and write home. Subsequently, word came one day that T. had backed a deuce-and-a-half in the village and killed a little girl, and I never knew what followed. What became of him or of his Korean wife, I never knew.

One sunny day, while typing away, a loud bang was heard in the company area. When we ran out, we found Specialist Fourth Tomzak from the commo shack on the ground—between the orderly room and the mess hall—below the telephone pole from which he had fallen. He had received a high-voltage shock. His fatigues and visible body were black and burned, and he was rushed to the hospital. Three decades plus later, I learned that the commo specialist (promoted to sergeant) had requested a second tour of duty in Korea. According to Specialist Fourth Pechtold, Sergeant Tomzak still bore huge visible burn scars across his chest and ribs because of the electrical burn he suffered while I was at this compound.

Many times the officers had the clerks type personal material. I remember typing songs for the officer's choir on purple stencil and running copies at the brigade offices. "Jamaican Farewell" was a favorite. Although I made many typing corrections, the CO was unconcerned. In fact, he was down on all fours collating the song sheets with me.

One evening, two troopers ripped off a radio from the commo shack and were caught hauling it off to the village. As a result, the burglars were thrown in the stockade and then court-martialed. In the ensuing charges, I was assigned the task of transposing the witness statements onto legal documents. The CO either again overlooked or did not seem to mind my numerous corrections. These individuals were eventually imprisoned at Fort Leavenworth.

Once I was assigned to accompany a certain Private W. from a line company and clear him at Personnel. W. was a prisoner but I had no idea what he had done. I was also issued a .45 caliber automatic pistol with which to guard him. Ironically, it was W. who instructed me (gun in hand) how to load the .45. Consequently, he begged me for a village stop before his departure to Leavenworth. I was tempted to comply with his last request, but I had to decline. Suddenly, the infantry private disappeared from my sight. After a good deal of searching, however, I finally located him in the latrine. When I mentioned my fear that he had run away, he calmly informed me he was not about to escape and jeopardize his free flight back to the United States.

Most of the troops I came in contact with were friendly, and because of my job as their former payroll clerk, I was respected. I still maintained communication with my buddy Abilio and other clerks at Personnel, and these connections enabled me privileged information. Specialist Fifth Brittain, my church brother, learned of his next Permanent Change of Station long before his orders were cut. I could also be sneaky. Sergeant Ha, who had harassed me all along in the orderly room, had his 201 Personnel File "lost" along with his departure flight delayed by two weeks. During these two weeks, Sergeant Ha paced around the orderly room like a demented caged lion, ceaselessly cussing. Although Top was fed up with me, strangely enough he never reprimanded me. The two clerks, who worked with me, were not too charitable toward me either—especially when the CO approved my 1049 request for a ten-day Rest & Recuperation leave to Japan and Hong Kong, and the coveted five three-day passes to Seoul, *and* of my promotion to Specialist Four. Sergeant Ha and the clerks accused me of arrogantly walking around the orderly room, thinking I, was "too good for them," and according to rumor, Top was overheard saying he was shipping me to a line company. I had no idea what my office mates were talking about, except that perhaps it was due to my not socializing with them after duty hours—perhaps a drink at the EM club. My informer was none other than W., the prisoner quartered in the orderly room. When I approached Top, he flatly denied such hearsay. He said, however, that some of my "work had to be done over again" but nothing else. It did not dawn on me until decades later that word must have gotten around of my "connections" at Personnel!

Perhaps being the third and newest clerk, I was constantly delegated (detailed) with the "unpleasant tasks" as the orderly room representative. However unpleasant, this gave me a chance to be away from the office and the monotony of ceaseless typing. I was uncaring and content with the shunned chores. I always turned each detail into another adventure—like when I was assigned to fill sandbags and redirect the monsoon flood that yearly threatened the compound. Aside from compound guard, some details carried me to the Imjin River and the Turk Compound. I took the opportunity for a closer look at the enemy, and a sample of Imjin waters—plus a chance to fraternize with soldiers from Far West Asia at their environment within their forbidden compound. This time, away from the scrutiny of my office coworkers, felt like freedom despite having to carry out shunned details. I knew I was under no one's specific scrutiny and that all major and final official decisions were handed down from the commanding officers, not the subordinate sergeants. I concluded that if this duty was the worst the Cavalry had to fling at me in exchange for all the excitement it derived, plus being far away from Personnel, I was ready to take on all of them. I knew a good thing when I had it. Aahhh! But I was in high hog heaven, with a little monthly pay voucher to brighten up the duty! I philosophically accepted all duties, one unpleasant task at a time. Far from being unhappy about this, I felt spoiled and pampered within the BLV in my new assignment at this Far East corner of Asia.

Reflagging
July 1, 1965

Under the burning sun that day
In full dress khakis marched our way
To witness flags, and jeeps, and guns
When drinks were last I fled with wons

It was a hot sweltering day on July 1, 1965 that there was much excitement in the camp. We were reflagging units which necessitated a flag ceremony and a parade followed by celebration and merry-making. The First Cavalry flag was being replaced by the Second Infantry Division flag at Camp Howze. This simply meant that the Division name was changed along with respective replacement of all crests and patches. Our unit, the First Battalion Twelfth Cavalry was replaced by the Second Battalion Thirty-eighth Infantry at Camp Blue Lancer. Thus a BLV meridian occurred by unit changes that forever altered the compound's identity. It was a monumental task not only to replace division patches on all uniforms, but also of exchanging unit billboards and replacing the symbols, crests, and lettering with that of respective battalions from that of the Second Infantry. I recalled my share of excitement in high school when our ROTC First Drill Team participated in school festivals, downtown parades, and competitions, but somehow I did not sense all the enthusiasm on this day as I had in high school gala. I guess I had advanced from youthful naïveté and exhilaration, now preferring exploring Korea rather than marching under the July sun.

Our ceremony included a parade composed of all Headquarters and Headquarters Company (HHC) troopers. We were ordered to dress in khakis and assemble under arms (rifles), in front of the mess hall that morning. After our fall-in inspection, Captain Baker marched us to the parade ground before the flags at Brigade Headquarters. We stood there in company formation like fools performing the manual of arms under the scorching sun. Then we finally observed the ceremony.

UNKNOWN PHOTOGRAPHER

WE WERE ORDERED TO DRESS IN KHAKIS AND ASSEMBLE UNDER ARMS IN FRONT OF THE MESS HALL THAT MORNING. THEN CAPTAIN BAKER MARCHED US TO THE PARADE GROUND BEFORE THE FLAGS AT BRIGADE HEADQUARTERS. AUTHOR IS THE SECOND TALL FRESH FACE LEFT OF COMMANDER.

I saw the battalion officers and sergeants march to the center of the parade ground with a lengthy spiel about what I could not understand and could not care less. Prominent were two color guards bearing unit flags, one with our Semper Paratus crest and the other with the Rock of the Marne crest. Another senseless speech followed, I guessed about each unit's history. Finally, the reflagging began. The color guards and color bearers faced one another. Sergeant Camp advanced and exchanged the battalion flags from one flag bearer to another. Under the increasing heat of the sun, for one moment my mind flashed back to my years as color guard at Lanier. I recalled how proudly I carried the school flag in my sophomore year and the American flag in my junior year. Like an accelerated slide show, I relived my flag-bearing activities at the spring festival, downtown San Antonio Fiesta Week parades, football games at the Alamo Stadium, school assemblies, and graduation. I remembered how stiffly I stood at attention or held on to the flagpole from my harness during windy field days. I held myself just as still now, as I saw Sergeant Camp mechanically march from flag bearer to flag bearer. I noticed the mirrored helmets of the guards and recalled my own white helmet with an L on it for Lanier. This wasn't like me who always enjoyed the Colors, marching, and the fanfare of ceremony, but for some reason under this normally Korean glowing sun, July was a scorch, and the pomp wasn't as enjoyable as my experiences in high school ROTC. What I missed most was the absence of the band that in my days stirred the spirit with the national anthem. After the reflagging ceremony and the exchanging of flags, I saw senior sergeants appear in ecstasy at inspecting the new flag in the presence of the officers. We were dismissed to attend the festivities.

UNKNOWN PHOTOGRAPHER

SERGEANT MAJOR APON GRIPS THE SECOND BATTALION THIRTY-EIGHTH INFANTRY FLAG. CAPTAIN BAKER (SECOND FROM LEFT FACING FLAG) WAS THE COMMANDING OFFICER OF HEADQUARTERS AND HEADQUARTERS COMPANY SECOND BATTALION THIRTY-EIGHTH INFANTRY.

I was roasting under the hot searing sun. The celebration consisted of M60 target competitions, jeep maze contests, and vehicle mechanical inspections—all for which I had no interest. However, I could not escape as no passes were authorized, and the day progressed uneventfully and ever so slowly. I was ordered to attend the EM club activity that afternoon. There was a one-star general present, many officers and enlisted men, and two very well-mannered Turkish soldiers. There was a lot of toasting and drinking, but I was impatient for the day to end. Since I didn't drink, I found this activity all the more frustrating. Thoroughly aggravated with the morning's events—the unrelenting burning sun causing me to sweat and the dragging day progressing uneventfully—to my relief the day finally ended and I was glad to be released. I then somehow managed to escape from the compound to other interests.

THE CAVALIER ANNOUNCING THE REFLAGGING FROM THE FIRST CAVALRY TO THE SECOND INFANTRY DATED JUNE 28, 1965

Within the next few days, however, we were all hit with the monumental task of changing our First Cavalry patches with the Indianhead patch of the Second Infantry Division on *all* our uniforms at our expense. I felt sorry for the guys that ended up physically responsible for exchanging, painting, and replacing symbols, crests, and lettering for each unit, battalion, brigade, and division. The new division brought with it ribbons earned during World War II that went with the adopted uniform. Now, I proudly wore two fourrageres, the blue fully braided infantry along with the green and orange plaid Belgian, one on each shoulder. As I fixed them on my uniforms, I recalled how I had proudly also displayed two others on my ROTC uniform: the color guard white, and the speckled blue and white for the Drill Team. As I pinned the unit's awards, I recalled my own high school that among others was the Highest Grade Average ribbon. This was one boon of serving in the infantry; we got to flaunt respective unit awards the *earlier* soldiers, the heroes in past wars, had earned with their blood, sweat, and lives.

Although reflagging was another of those parades that once thrilled me in high school, the "magic" of "soldiering" had vanished and was replaced with military reality at this Far East corner of Asia.

Adventures on the Imjin

Field gear, rifles, and live rounds
Ghosts, shadows, and muffled sounds
Dark hooches mid starry skies
Seeking joy before moonrise

"The Imjin! The Imjin River!" I exclaimed to myself in high spirits upon receiving the news from the first sergeant. I was going to pull guard on the fabulous Imjin. The river partially separated our Korea from communist North Korea. The two orderly room clerks eyed me curiously because I was behaving as through as I would be attending some yachting excursion. I could not have cared less; I really looked forward to the night river duty and the possibility of firing live rounds at some enemy craft! If not, it was my chance to fetch a sample of this Asian river of Korea.

WE STOOD STAKEOUT GUARD DUTY ALONG THE IMJIN RIVER BANKS MUCH LIKE ON THIS PHOTO WHICH WAS TAKEN DURING A PERSONNEL FORM 20 RUN.

Following guard mount, the trucks heading for the Imjin could not roll fast enough to satisfy my adventurous spirit. I had always been fascinated by the river that I had once crossed while visiting the line troops with their

Personnel Form 20s. I had passed by it countless times on my way to Seoul via the Munsan-Ni Depot and now I would finally get to camp on its banks! The truck rolled for what seemed like hours, so we arrived at the river at dusk. I had no idea where in the division sector we were. Upon arrival we discovered some boy scouts cooking rice camped at the river bank. The crackling yellow and blue fire under their covered pan for a split second flashed me back to my Boy Scout second class cooking requirement. The sergeant told the KATUSA to let them know that they had to leave. We unloaded our equipment and set up our stakeout consisting of guard shifts. We knew we were sitting ducks each posted about twenty paces from the next soldier along the river bank. I was fascinated by the distant lights along the opposite bank of the river. The reflection on the passing waves made flotsam highly visible. The night turned cold and one of the KATUSA loaned me his jacket. Following my shift, I fell asleep to the sound of the sergeants' muffled bawdy jokes, experiences, and incidents with loose women. It was still dark and just before dawn when the sergeant kicked my boot. We all quietly collected our gear, jumped aboard the approaching truck, and headed back to the BLV. To my dismay no military confrontation occurred during this trip.

Another time it was one of those moonless nights when I was again on detailed guard duty on the Imjin River. We were never advised where we were, all we knew was that we were assigned stakeout duty. My adrenalin shot skyward one night when the sergeant's whispering brought me back from dead sleep. We were all ordered up and to fix bayonets. In a whisper the sergeants ordered a line skirmish and we proceeded to systematically jab the brush in search of possible agent infiltration or crossing. We were ordered not to open fire. I wasn't about to take chances so I chambered a round. I figured that I'd shoot first and ask questions later. Four decades later I reflected that in my naïveté I did not realize I could have returned home in a pine box. However, to my disappointment after a few zigzagging maneuvers, we were recalled, and we resumed sleep or guarded post.

On my third night on Imjin stakeout duty, something interesting happened. I lay to sleep lengthwise between two rows in the middle of a furrowed field. I had fixed my bayonet, so it lay flat on my nose. I seriously cautioned the guys not to tease me because I *was* jittery. Well, later during the night two big white wide eyes awakened me, so I quickly snapped my rifle in bayonet stance while lying down. The bayonet was aimed straight up at the apparition and if it hadn't called out in familiar English, I would have probably stabbed him. All I could see was the whites of his Afro-American eyes and teeth. He asked me if I wanted to go for a walk. I wanted to resume my sleep but the possibility of an unusual midnight adventure beckoned me, so I consented, and we crept silently into the pitch black curtains of darkness.

In the cool of the night we walked for what seemed like miles when we finally approached a tiny sleeping village. It had to be a farming hamlet because there wasn't an army compound nearby and thus, no obvious brothel edifice. There was also something that was not there: barking dogs. Suddenly, we were on firm ground after plodding through plowed rows. As we silently closed in, the dark outlines and silhouettes of the hooches were visible against the starlit skies. The black overhanging straw eves from roofs and the black posts that divided the porches against the midnight blue sky reminded me of a Nopae Dong twilight observation while seated at a porch. I reveled in the moonless night that was pitch black, and only the starlight enabled us to slip about at will. Some hooches we passed by were black and formless. As we quietly sneaked about and *vanished* among the hovels, I clearly remember discerning, but not touching, the hooch walls by the dimly available light. We just noiselessly glided all around looking for I didn't know what, other than night-time adventuring in dissimilarity to my preteens at backstreet adventuring.

There was something exciting about this night prowling without notice or opposition, as if we were involved in some great clandestine and unopposed espionage mission. It was one of those noiseless windless still nights where any sound is magnified and would echo loudly so we were extra quiet and careful. This was one of those quiet and exciting ventures where my tinnitus, my symphonic sounds of silence were at their sweetened loudest. I was paradoxically experiencing an orchestrated sonorous but pianissimo composition. A wavering arrangement of hissing and humming within my hearing senses reverberated throughout this dark and silent vacuum. Heart pounding, I enjoyed the moment of excitement at being the outsiders, of not belonging, but invaders ensconced safely within one of those dreamscape safe fantasies. Under the stars, I noticed a road in southerly direction (traversing Orion), so I concluded the village was located north of the road but south of the Imjin and of our perimeter. After we had lurked around the stone-quiet village, my companion decided to return to our sector. I never understood why I agreed to go on this nocturnal wandering; to me it just seemed like a stimulating unscheduled midnight venture, something different. Perhaps my dare-devilish curiosity kicked in as to the possibilities of what could happen. It wasn't until decades later that I realized my companion was in the mood for a beer or a woman and that's what he was searching for. We were never discovered by barking dogs because their absence was caused by the stew pot at large. This was one midnight adventure that could have resulted in disaster; as dereliction of duty was a grave offense and thus punishable if we had been discovered away from our duty posts at this Far East corner of Asia.

Birthday Suits
July 1965

With open eyes my view beheld
The female body thus was weld
All curves and corners now unshelled
All dreams of paradise now gelled

It was during the broiling summer days of 1965 that troopers from Blue Lancer Valley pulled week-long bunker guard duty and I was one of them. The pillbox faced North Korea from the BLV's western mountain that faced Spoonbill across the Imjin River. We were standing around wilting and cussing at the sweltering heat. It was as hot as a boiling caldron under the searing sun and even hotter inside the concrete "vault" occupied by the guards, despite the slotted windows for gun barrels.

During one such blazing afternoon, two lovely prostitutes strolled by selling their favors. Hormones jumping, we eagerly came back to life. We chatted with them in street language. Suddenly, the second *josan* stepped back a few paces and us soldiers turned curiously at her. Feeling no compunction about what she was about to do, she nonchalantly slid her slacks and briefs down below her knees, squatted, and clearly and fully exposed herself to our view. For the first time in my life, *gaping and wide eyed*, I experienced a breathtaking view of an until-then-only dreamed wonder of the fair gender. Then, *saucer eyed*, I gazed at the downward steady golden jet-stream violating mother Korea's sweet earth. Just as naturally, she stood up, fully completing *to my now popped-out eyes* her second wondrous dark V-contoured revelation as she slid up each layer of her clothes. She returned gracefully and chatted a bit more. Since no business was to be had, they both continued their way.

Back at camp I wandered about, aimlessly walking around in demented fascination, but delightfully enchanted for days. Repeatedly, I envisioned her well-defined asset amid limited dark revelation on youthful silken paleness, plus satin-smooth paled moons before my amazed eyes, and frankly, it blew my nineteen-year-old mind. Cold showers and my comfortable sack eased the sweet pain. I knew tomorrow would bring more adventures and unexpected wonders. As I sank sleepily into oblivion, I marveled, with the great complacency of my youth, at *the* greatest of all solved paradisiacal mysteries.

It was on another one of those scorching days, that Blue Lancer sustained a drought with unavailable water except for cooking. The latrine was limited to solid waste. Pebble-filled pipes extending from most hillsides all over the company area provided for bladder relief; we all lined up awaiting our turn, with no privacy expected and none requested. We survived on soft drinks and rapidly depleted the PX stock. Finally, we were obliged to seek the cooling cleansing comfort of her majesty's waters right at her feet below her skirts.

The rushing stream was located at the camp's southeastern sector within the barbwire fence among huge smooth boulders. Her Majesty was first startled at such an invasion at her skirts, but kept her back to us with one eye shut as she stole peeks with the other. With about thirty skinny-dipping infiltrators from HHC, she had her pick on whom to spy, or perhaps she relished an orgy of flesh. We all lined up at the stream's edge and stripped in her presence sporting white, brown, or black birthday suits. We washed, shaved, and pottied.

WE STRIPPED, BATHED, SHAVED, AND POTTIED AT A RUSHING STREAM WITHIN THE CAMP ON A SCORCHING DAY DURING A WATER SHORTAGE.

Whole companies followed, with all new comers consistently claiming the cleaner waters farther and farther upstream. I would later wonder what the down stream waters contained! I took several pictures, and in my youthful naïveté never realized until years later via my girlfriend (subsequently wife) an amazingly revealing discovery of the embarrassing power of obvious buoyancy *and I had sent duplicates to my entire clan!*

Nudity was second nature in the service. I wondered if the unusual echoing male chatter attracted any of the young rural female population; so that conceivably, her majesty was compelled to share her male wealth with them. It wouldn't be surprising to suppose they peered through the dense brush giggling and gawking. As if innocent, perhaps they, too, wandered delightfully around in demented fascination for days in their Far East corner of Asia.

STONE POST DISPLAYING ENTRANCE TO THE KYUNG GUK SA TEMPLE. NOTE TEMPLE NAME IN KOREAN (SHADE) AND CHINESE (SUNLIGHT), AND SWIMMERS IN STREAM.

A Momentous Call at a Picturesque Temple
July 1965

Pink monocots mid leafy greens
Alone among three lovely queens
Gold images, a green dragon
Burned in soul to ne'er abandon

On one of my solo adventures in Seoul during the summer of 1965, I took a Korean bus in search of the Kyung Guk Sa and Pul Guk Sa Buddhist temples. The sun bathed my way with its golden yellow light as I boarded, transferred, and reboarded the Korean Kimchi buses all over Seoul. It never crossed my mind that I was an easy target for an assailant in need of a few Korean won or perhaps American dollars, even if they were mere military certificates. My goal was one of those private and off-the-beaten-path havens I happened to find on a map. I had no idea where it was other than somewhere in the northeast quadrant of Seoul. I was as excited—probably wide eyed with flared nostrils—about what unknown adventures I would encounter when I took my first bus ride, aged eight, in downtown San Antonio. All directions were in Korean, some of which I could read, and some of which I asked along my way.

I stepped off the bus and read the temple name in Korean on a square post at a distant secluded area off the main road. I scrambled up a cobbled walkway that boasted dense foliage on both sides up to the top of my head. Dozens of huge pink flowers emitting an intoxicating scent dotted the brilliant green-leaf wall that led toward the entrance. The ascending walkway curved left at a U-turn. A great sense of peace enveloped me as I felt the quietude and stillness away from the loud street traffic of Seoul when I walked amid that sweet fragrance. As I wandered through this maze-like flowering shrubbery, I experienced a similar enthusiasm as when I ventured the back streets, alleys, and backyard byways overgrown with flowering greenery of San Antonio. I seemed to be venturing under the tree branches that arched over those alleys which, in my boyhood, were a passageway into another realm of adventure. As I approached another curve to the right, I encountered another U-turn that led into a flag-stoned courtyard. A long building of typical Korean style, like those straw-roofed, plaster-walled, and paper-windowed structures at the division sector, greeted me. A smooth well-worn wooden porch extended all along the wall, and for a moment and only a moment I experienced a flashback of my sunny front porch back home. In front of me and a little to the left sat the temple. A two-story-high frondescent wall covered with the ever-present fragrant pink flowers surrounded the entire sunny flag-stoned courtyard.

I SCRAMBLED UP A COBBLED WALKWAY THAT BOASTED DENSE FOLIAGE ON BOTH SIDES UP TO THE TOP OF MY HEAD.

Three smiling and attractive young novices came out of the hooch and greeted me. My legs weakened and my soul faltered amid the stimulating floral scent and their girlish sweet chatter and soft giggles. My head swam in the presence of this Oriental porcelain doll trio, while my rampant hormones and my wicked mind visualized not three innocent novices but three charming teenagers. I had no idea what they were saying but I remember three pairs of hazel sloe eyes smiling as they focused on me, attesting to their angelic naïveté. They wore loose tunics with buttonless cuffed long sleeves and snug ankle-cuffed slacks. The fabric was a fine tweed, or broadcloth, with more gray thread than black. I could see that their clothing was not fashionable street wear, but somber and "of the cloth" in nature.

I finally addressed them in my broken Korean and a bit of English, and the adorable trio again broke into a soft girlish but subdued laughter. My head was swimming with all this female purity and attention at which I must have been displaying facial ecstatic weakness when a *papasan* emerged and the girls became silent and serious. I asked him about the temple grounds and he proceeded to rattle off a long speech in Korean of which I understood very little. I listened respectfully and attentively, however, but caught only a few understandable words. It seemed he was explaining the history of the temple. The girls observed in respectful silence as he looked about and pointed around. At the end of his sermon, I motioned if I could take pictures, and the *papasan* nodded. I dared not ask to photograph the girls. They all went inside.

The temple was of the usual Oriental structure with colorful walls, and tiled roof with upturned corners. It was completely enclosed by the foliage and pink flowers. As I approached it, the familiar scent of the ever-present burning incense, typical of all temples in contrast to the flower's fragrance, permeated the hushed and grave atmosphere. As I peaked in, the usual seriousness, reverence, and respect due to the Buddha's sacred presence as always, overpowered me. I took pictures of its outside and of the colorful temple ceiling. The ceiling crossbeams bore extended carved open-mouthed dragons and decorations predominantly in green, with red and yellow, all outlined in black. Despite the lack of sufficient light, I managed to photograph these unique dragons within this dark haven. In the center of the ornate altar sat the Buddha in meditation surrounded by a multitude of Buddha images. Significantly, these multiple images were gold-leafed whereas all others I encountered in Korea were in ceramic or wood and painted, with usually only one seated Buddha at any one altar. I strolled about the flag-stoned courtyard in reverential silence, absorbed in the peaceful environment. The quaint overall architecture was so unlike the buildings I had seen thus far in the *modern* Seoul of 1965. I found it hard to tear myself away from this restful retreat and return to the bustle of the city. When I exited the grounds, I was humbled by the fact that, henceforth, I could die happily knowing I was living my dreams of visiting the Orient and visiting an actual Korean Temple. Aahhh! but I had ascended to nice nebula Nirvana, at a penny's cost to me!

THE TEMPLE WAS OF THE USUAL ORIENTAL STRUCTURE WITH COLORFUL WALLS, TILED ROOF WITH UPTURNED CORNERS, BUT COMPLETELY ENCLOSED BY THE FOLIAGE AND PINK FLOWERS.

THE CEILING CROSSBEAMS BORE EXTENDED, CARVED OPENED-MOUTHED DRAGONS WITH DECORATIONS PREDOMINANTLY IN GREEN, RED AND YELLOW OUTLINED IN BLACK.

IN THE CENTER OF THE ORNATE ALTAR SAT THE BUDDHA IN MEDITATION SURROUNDED BY A MULTITUDE OF BUDDHA IMAGES, ALL GOLD-LEAFED, UNLIKE OTHERS I HAD ENCOUNTERED, WHICH WERE MADE OF CERAMIC OR WOOD AND PAINTED.

I STROLLED ABOUT THE FLAG-STONED COURTYARD IN REVERENTIAL SILENCE, ABSORBED IN THE PEACEFUL ENVIRONMENT.

I then searched and found that the Pul Guk Sa temple was no more, but only a draped altar remained, which was uncovered for me by the complacent worshippers. I loved losing myself in such out-of-the-way dreamlands and encountering the indigenous population under genuine circumstances—their own habitats.

Thirty-seven years later while reminiscing, I flattered myself with the thought that maybe the three novices were peeking at me through the papered windows all the while. Having breached their lives of recluse perhaps I, a rare foreign intruder from faraway America, became the subject of an occasional conversation. Perhaps for a moment, but only for a moment, youthful romantic thoughts may have entered their innocent lives. No decent girl, under Korean tradition, would even consider addressing a non-Korean, much less an American serviceman in occupation of their country. Perhaps an exception could be made occasionally with random citizens, but never with girls *of the cloth*. I had intruded a rare realm of unusual circumstances because these young women actually smiled, and within limits, communicated, perhaps in their naïveté even *flirted* with me. "So this is one of those 'Yankees' we have heard whispers about regarding the American Army occupation of the North Country," they could have reflected later, "and he wasn't blond or blue eyed as in American films!" Still, I would like to have known that they admired this lone soldier, maybe were even dazzled by his military decorations. I really wondered what they thought of this stranger, who sought out and found interest in their remote safe haven and how their remote temple could be of interest to him, in their sphere. I would have liked that the three young novice priestesses actually cherished this intersecting minute fragment of my life—as I did of theirs. Leaving behind their sacred off-the-beaten-path sanctuary within the vast bustling city of Seoul, I felt privileged to have shared their Far East corner of Asia.

Her Majesty, the Queen
July–September 1965

If I could only kiss her skirt
'Cause I was just her lump of dirt
But then her charms were mine to glean
My dearest curvy earthy Queen

In the course of my numerous clerical duties at Camp Blue Lancer Valley, I found myself ambling around from the Headquarters Company Orderly Room to the Brigade Headquarters offices or to Battalion Headquarters offices or anywhere in the company area as necessary. When off duty, I rambled on to Hooch Ten, the PX, the dispensary, and anywhere to and from the main gate. I always felt the sunshine brightly illuminating my way. I was perpetually comfortable, happy, and unperturbed, and yet, I was always conscious of someone or something watching. I sensed an observer to my every movement during all my activities. I excluded chaperone or parental eye, and I was doing my military duty and attending church services, so what was the quandary? Then, it finally dawned on me that her majesty, the Queen had stood by me through my entire tenure in Korea.

I was enchanted when I first laid eyes on her that wintry day of November in 1964 from the indoctrination Quonset. She stood tall in all her royal majestic composure in her doe-brown radiant blush behind Camp McGovern, sloping from ground level to sheer cliffs at her crest. Because of military gossip regarding her overrun situation, I remembered I had dreamed of taking her—of having her yield all of her ravished assets to me alone, and of how she had taunted and flirted with me while at Guard Tower Four. I recalled how I craved to ascend her skirts, to scale her high and mighty tantalizing bluff, and triumphantly conquer her lofty summit.

I bore in mind how she had retained her dignity and evasive composure, yet smirked at me as I rode away the day I lost her in March of 1965 when

PSC#3 relocated to Ross. It wasn't until June through November of 1965, when reassigned at Blue Lancer Valley, that all my dreams came true. She was dressed in all her green finery, but vulnerable from her assailable backside. I then realized she was all helplessly mine to enjoy and hopelessly obliged to reveal all her hidden secrets and mysteries to me alone. Then followed our many wild rendezvous and escapades where no secrets of nature, exposure, or fatigue existed between us. She allowed me to fully creep and wander all over her curves and attributes. I was able to view every curve, nook, cranny, corner, and protrusion of her from every angle from the backside of her skirts. We relished a carefree half-year open relationship, oblivious of observers or warnings from buddies to include my company commander—my heart was totally devoted to her. My Queen never questioned my meandering or direction on her spacious realm, and she always granted me her unlimited time and freedom. She observed my duties, miseries, and tears, and shared in my joy and happiness, as she maternally beheld me mischievously develop from late boyhood to early manhood. Then one day I tearfully bade her farewell and did so more the wiser, fully mindful of her beckoning coquettishness and charming beauty. I openly wept shamelessly because I had freely given her my all, yet I acknowledged that I had not been or ever would be her only lover. Still, I thanked her for indulging me by sharing her affections—her every all! I knew too well that she would enrapture another GI, she could not help herself—she had all the time in the world.

Mount Easy Queen was the strategic title of a precipitous mountain during the Korean conflict and thus labeled on military maps. Easy was a gradual ascension from the north (and west), and Queen was the lofty summit. It towered 1.6 miles from the demilitarized zone (DMZ) on its north, and geographically separated Camp McGovern (eastside) and Camp Blue Lancer Valley (westside).

MOUNT EASY QUEEN WAS THE STRATEGIC TITLE OF A PRECIPITOUS MOUNTAIN DURING THE KOREAN CONFLICT AND THUS LABELED ON MILITARY MAPS. EASY WAS THE GRADUAL ASCENT FROM THE NORTH AND WEST AND QUEEN WAS THE LOFTY SUMMIT. NOTE SKOSHI NOPAE DONG AT LEFT AND ROOF OF GUARD TOWER TWO ABOVE LEFT QUONSET. (SEE PHOTO P. 415)

Because of the mountainous landscape that surrounded me, I really had no concept of geographical sectors or distances within the division or anywhere. All I could see were mountains and mountains with villages and compounds amid rice paddies connected by paths and major roads. All along, my comfort zone was limited to McGovern and the church in Seoul via the bus route. During my tenure at McGovern, I maintained the payroll of the First of the Twelfth. Unknown to me the First of the Twelfth was quartered in a beautiful valley named Camp Blue Lancer Valley below her majesty, my elusive Queen's western slopes. Then, while stationed at Ross, and having to call on the line troops with the 201 Personnel Form 20s, we visited Blue Lancer Valley. When finally stationed at the camp, I suspected that McGovern was just over the puzzling mountain.

I reminisced how Private First Marvin Garcia and I explored and climbed all over the Queen and happened upon her numerous secrets through our adventures. By this time, I was more familiar with the military sector as I had wandered unconcerned all over the division area such that I never took notice of time, distance, or whereabouts. My senses kicked in and I just seemed to time or accommodate all adventuring to my day. I believe I was gifted with a natural sense of direction and time unconsciously reckoned by sun position, and somehow I always seemed to find my way around. The summer sun still shed its warmth that glowed all over the rugged and green panoramic mountain scenery despite the cloudiness announcing the upcoming monsoon season. The partial overcast created a tolerable cooling effect despite the humidity. Curiously enough, a surprise shower never caught us.

As I mused over her majesty, the Queen, I appreciated that she had become my natural backyard. All of her supposed puzzles unlocked before me—as did those of my earliest childhood when I alone first stepped out of the house and into the backyard. Her majesty's stately conceit lessened as I increasingly became familiar with her much as when I recognized the entire yard surrounding my home as I grew up.

Although I roamed from Blue Lancer Valley all the way to "modern" Seoul, it was the Mount Easy Queen locale where I feasted on the open-air unspoiled and preserved medieval treasures touching on ancient Korean life and culture of this Far East corner of Asia.

Chapter 13

Exploring Queen's Treasures

There comes a time in every rightly constructed boy's life that he has a raging desire to go somewhere and dig for hidden treasure.
—Mark Twain

O'er her hills and o'er her dales
Up and down her curvy vales
In and out and round each day
Oh what ventures crossed our way

Prologue

    Private First Marvin Garcia, a medic, and I struck a close friendship immediately upon crossing paths. We discovered that we both shared the same adventuring spirit and goal of not only clambering all over our beloved Queen but we were also shutterbugs. We always checked the duty roster and advised one another of nonduty Saturdays concurring our day to assault our lady. Each climb on our sovereign was a different adventure limited only by the duty roster and our remaining tenure in tours of duty.

Ghostly Visitation
Summer 1965

I love to go a'wandering
Along the mountain track
And as I go, I love to sing
My knapsack on my back
—The Happy Wanderer

On one of those splendid sunny mornings in the midsummer of '65, I excitedly readied my harness with pack and canteen for our first scale up Easy Queen. I had long planned an extensive ascent all the way to the summit. I had craved to set foot on the Queen ever since I first caught sight of her from Camp McGovern back in November of '64 from Number Four, and today was that day. My best new-found friend, Marvin, a medic, and I headed for the main gate after breakfast.

From early morning the day promised to be superb; but during the ascent it became cloudy gray. Humid, yet just breezy enough to comfortably scale its rugged inclines. Puffed-up clouds with the light-gray flat bottoms of summer hinted at the anticipated monsoon rains and obscured the sun. There was not much conversation as we ascended, just the sounds of Marvin and me setting a steady but brisk upward pace. Although we were conserving our energy, I felt as if I could not climb up fast enough. I was anticipating viewing my previous elusive duty station from the peak I had always dreamed of conquering.

Coming across a brook whose clear endless running waters tripped and stumbled over smoothed rocks and boulders, we paused. We were stopping only long enough to rest ourselves and soak our feet, but the beckoning pool was too inviting to pass up so we decided to strip and dip. The pool's welcoming cold waters were refreshing as they were invigorating. After a few moments of splashing palms-full of water wars, we settled as we lay flat in the pool, floating, deaf with water to our ears, observing the blue patches of sky between the overwhelming puffs of clouds—all amid lush greenery. We pottied, air dried, dressed, and trekked on.

WE WERE STOPPING ONLY LONG ENOUGH TO REST OURSELVES AND SOAK OUR FEET, BUT THE BECKONING POOL WAS TOO INVITING TO PASS UP SO WE DECIDED TO STRIP AND DIP.

Continuing upward, we carefully crossed Easy's tricky ravines and cautiously scaled her rocky cliffs. My camera froze a stone in midair that Marvin flung from a cliff. We took numerous pictures of each other among the abundant green foliage; our poses included the gray cliffs and the very distant Blue Lancer. On one particular steep ascent, Marvin, who was behind me and feeling the fatigue, clung to my pack. This annoyed me and provoked a start of playful war games. Feeling like a pair of mischievous schoolboys, we continued willy-nilly in our silliness all the way up Easy.

A much fresher free-flowing breeze greeted us at the skyline. As we progressed toward Easy's apex (the Queen), I experienced an optic phenomenon. As the summit lessened at my feet, the hazy distant mountains along with the vast expanse below suddenly seemed to loom up—all rapidly rising and opening before me.

I finally stood on the Queen, conscious of the sheer drop to the valley. Sure enough, Camp McGovern extended below me in all her magnificence. Marvin took a picture of me mere millimeters from the very drop, breathlessly conscious that one puff of wind would have sent me down her majesty's peak. My mind struggled to encompass all her majesty's breathtaking splendor. There at the top, I was surrounded by dense mountain greenery facing McGovern with the BLV at my back (both paying tribute to me *on the Queen*). I stood there as "King of the Mountain," having conquered her majesty's lofty and high crest. I was in sheer ecstasy as the mountain breezes filtered through my hair and dried the beads of perspiration cooling my forehead and cheeks. The vastness of the spacious Korean skies was randomly graced with huge white flat-bottomed cumulous clouds. I felt as small as a gnat, hardly visible on a measureless ocean of endless alpine greenery. I could not help but mindfully harken to Vince Guaraldi's soothing piano sounds of "Cast Your Fate to the Wind" I had been listening to on the AFKN radio station. Aahhh! but how I was pleased in this green glorious garden, another army perk. I would not trade this splendid half-year dream, even as time doubly added to my life span. I reminded myself that *this* was only one instance of why I had joined the army.

(PFC) MARVIN GARCIA TOOK A PICTURE OF ME MERE MILLIMETERS FROM THE VERY DROP, BREATHLESSLY CONSCIOUS THAT ONE PUFF OF WIND WOULD HAVE SENT ME DOWN HER MAJESTY'S PEAK.

As I stood above McGovern, my spirit visited my old stomping grounds. I scanned the panoramic length of McGovern, Nopae, Koom-Shi, First of the Seventh, the rice paddies, villages, and paths where I once bunked, worked, walked, visited, and frolicked. A haunting shadow peeked up at me from the back door of the indoctrination hooch where I had first gazed longingly at Queen's summit, back in late November (see photo p 77). As Guard Tower Four caught sight of me, we both reminisced of its bygone glazed-eyed sentinel, and my freezing guard duty memories lost in all these progressively materializing wonders (see photo p 92). My gaze followed the barbwire fence from Number Four right to Number Three where one night I fell victim to Al Martino's crooning of "I Love You Because," the colonel's tower, then Number Two where I became one with those twilight and dusky guard duty evenings, and finally, Number One where I photographed Nopae, finishing half circle at the main gate.

Then it happened. The entire valley became a cold doe-brown winter wonderland. My entranced gaze focused on two ghostly olive-green clad soldiers approach the vill via the wide dirt path across the road from McGovern. One was ecstatic at the curiosity of gallivanting in Nopae for the first time and of all the wonders therein. Then the scene gradually faded as a fuzzy mural simultaneously materialized and cleared, of the same apparitions on a cold and dreary afternoon evolving into an evening lost on a wild adventure on the town. Just as rapidly the picture dissolved and my magical mural revealed an early summer frolic where my eyes traced and mentally followed the steps of two khaki-uniformed translucent silhouettes again crossing the road from McGovern toward Nopae. My heart skipped a beat as these ghosts sauntered along the wide earth path and then disappeared into the village. I focused on one phantom as it dallied here and there, roaming about absorbed in sightseeing and picture taking. Suddenly, it emerged on the left, strolling merrily as it laughingly paused midway between the rice paddies while aiming its camera toward my position on the Queen's apex (see photo p 294) with further picture taking. All the while, it exultantly cruised across the rice fields that spilled miniature water fall synchronizations under the warm Korean sun. The phantom was totally unconcerned of the unbearable stench as it made its way toward Koom-Shi at the extreme left. There again, it tarried until it reached First of the Seventh at Camp Coursen. Very soon, it appeared at the main gate where it flagged and boarded a deuce-and-a-half. The ghostly truck appeared to inch its lethargic way clear across my cloud-patched panoramic landscape. The truck could not roll fast enough for its exhilarated passenger as it disappeared behind a mountain at my right. It was heading toward Pobwan-Ni and marvelous Yongju-Gol, transporting the rollicking wide-eyed nose-flared young figure to yet another carefree adventure.

I lightheartedly turned away from this tri-scenic spectacle and ghostly visitation entirely absorbed in childlike happiness. I eagerly descended Mount Easy Queen and joyfully continued on my way ever mindful of future wonders, adventures, discoveries, escapades, and explorations of Easy's unlimited secrets. Marvin, however, descended quietly, probably impressed with our panoramic vision and retreated to his own world of private thought.

It was not until decades later that I recalled this whole scenario as if freshly occurred. Blinking back tears, I smilingly recalled my happy-go-lucky experiences filled with youthful innocence. Sentimentally, I sighed contentedly while simultaneously encouraging tender flashbacks of my long ago carefree past at this Far East corner of Asia.

I FOCUSED ON ONE BUST IN PARTICULAR AND LIFTED IT FOR CLOSER INSPECTION. THEN I ASKED THE MAN IF I COULD HAVE THE SCULPTURE.

Easy Queen Encounter
Summer 1965

I wave my hat to all I meet
And they wave back to me
And blackbirds call so loud and sweet
From every green-wood tree
        —The Happy Wanderer

On one of our Mount Easy Queen adventures before the monsoons of 1965, my best buddy Marvin and I began our descent from the summit on a glorious golden sunny day. Puffy, cumulous, flat-bottomed clouds randomly spotted the blue heavens. The color of the azure skies enhanced the horizon with a richer blue as it touched the green woodland foliage.

Heading northwest, we stumbled into a tiny one-family plot. An impressively neatly swept dirt courtyard greeted us, but what attracted my immediate attention was the ground-level stone stove emitting smoke. Since it was close to midday, I guessed the residents were cooking lunch. It might have been rice but there was no definite smell of food in the air. A Buddhist temple and an L-shaped dwelling with a porch all along its length, characteristic of village style, greeted us. The abode enclosed half the yard east and north, respectively. Both buildings were constructed of typical plastered walls and papered windows on flat, pencil-thick, lattice-like wooden screens. The dwelling was roofed with straw thatch, and the temple boasted a partial roof of concrete tile. At the southwest corner of the patio was a clump of vegetation in front of some trees that just seemed to attract attention. There was an improvised rack with stone sculptures. Two girls went about attending to the cooking.

I immediately began taking pictures. In my dusty jump boots, I was like "The Ugly American," disrespectfully clopping on the restricted discalced temple floor to photograph the Buddha. However, within the soft shadowy walls of the unlit temple, I immediately felt a serene atmosphere of reverence and deep quietude praiseworthy of a house of worship. The meditating Buddha sat on an altar with the ever-present aroma of incense filling the sacred and quiet chamber, adding to this solemn ambience. Prior to visiting the temple in Seoul, I had only beheld such a sanctuary in *National Geographic* magazines, my American Geographical Society's *Around the World Program* monthly booklets, and documentaries on television. The silence was broken when a man suddenly poked his head into the temple. I immediately bowed in reverence to the Buddha, and as the man stared, I quietly retreated into the brightness of the day.

THE BUDDHIST TEMPLE WAS CONSTRUCTED OF TYPICAL PLASTERED WALLS AND PAPERED WINDOWS ON FLAT PENCIL-THICK LATTICE-LIKE WOODEN SCREENS, AND BOASTED A PARTIAL ROOF OF MASONRY TILE.

I IMMEDIATELY FELT A SERENE ATMOSPHERE OF REVERENCE AND DEEP QUIETUDE PRAISEWORTHY OF A HOUSE OF WORSHIP.

The man then calmly greeted Marvin and me, introducing himself as the girls' father. He was quite friendly and more so when I answered in my broken Korean. We asked about his life. He reminisced about his time with his parents on Easy Queen and the conflict which was still recent in his memory. As a little boy, he recalled the North Korean *infiltration*, seeing soldiers swarming all over the mountain, hearing shots and aircraft fire.

I directed his attention to the rack with the stone sculptures. He said that they had been in the family for as long as he could remember and were once objects of worship, but that some had been damaged or destroyed during the war. I focused on one bust in particular and respectfully lifted it for closer inspection. It was beige in color, crude and pitted with exposure to the elements, and the head was half broken off. He said they were made of volcanic rock. (Three decades later an examination at the Geology Department of the University of Texas at El Paso disproved it was lava.) Impulsively, I asked if I could have it. To my pleasant instant surprise, the man nodded with a "*Ne.*" It called for a monumental effort for me to contain my surprise and emotion. Here I was in a remote mountain of East Asia not only beholding but now, after his gift, actually owning an authentic object of worship! I owned a miniature jewel fulfilling my daydream during my indoctrination spiel at McGovern! Aahhh! but I was about to swallow this solid stone sculpture, my first authentic blessing from a native gentleman directly to me! I was floating on cloud nine as this genuine family-graven icon exceeded *all* my wildest dreams and expectations—the crowning apex of my adventures among these temples, a genuine freebie! In gratitude, I took pictures of the man with the icon, and of him and me with it. I then very reverently wrapped the sculpture in my fatigue shirt and placed it in my pack. As we departed, I gathered the courage to motion to the girls if I could take their picture. They giggled and nodded as they posed. We then bid the family farewell and proceeded down Easy.

I GATHERED THE COURAGE TO ASK THE GIRLS FOR THEIR PICTURE; THEY GIGGLED, NODDED, AND POSED.

As we descended, Marvin marveled that the man would even consider parting with such a family treasure and more so to a non-believing total stranger. Still stunned, I agreed as we headed down Easy in a northerly direction to another adventure under the warmth of continuous marvelous sunshine. Aahhh! but I was flying and clawing cumulous clouds, and all thankfully at taxpayers' expense.

Later, I would wonder at my good fortune at this unexpected experience during this Easy Queen jaunt; I knew I would always cherish this one object of worship. This gift was not only made to a non-Buddhist foreigner, but a GI! I was perplexed at destiny since I simply happened to stumble upon this place, this family haven. I finally concluded that the Korean man bestowed his gratitude to a soldier representing the army that had defended his ancestral home in this Far East corner of Asia.

Nature's Gifts to Easy
August 1965

I love to wander by the stream
That dances in the sun
So joyously, it calls to me
"Come join my happy song."
   —The Happy Wanderer

"The monsoons, what in the world are the monsoons?" I quietly wondered to myself. I did not consider asking anyone, as I was accustomed to the humidity and thunderstorms of the Texas Coastal Plains. Still, the very word "monsoon" sounded so Oriental and mysterious. What aquatic adventures awaited me in the upcoming season? What new vistas would I be photographing? Little did I know what was to come!

It was during an infrequent rain lull in the middle of the monsoon season that Marvin and I decided to survey Mount Easy Queen. We looked forward to find an undiscovered secret or perhaps rare artifacts, or a surprise find. As we climbed, we were endlessly overwhelmed at the remarkable quantities of swirling pools, singing brooks, and bubbling cascades that abounded on Easy during this monsoon trek. In my delighted adventuring, it never crossed my mind to question where all this downward running water originated, because we were so close to the summit of Queen. The cleansing waters appeared as a myriad of bubbling watercourses surging all over the mountain wonderland. Decades later I realized perhaps this clean and uncontaminated water from the heavens was suitable for emergency drinking. The humidity caused torrents of perspiration to drip down my forehead as I excitedly wandered all over my Queen. My fatigue shirt, wet with sweat, stuck to my back and later resembled a huge pond surrounded by salt residue. However, I was accustomed to the high humidity of San Antonio and thus oblivious to the moisture that ran in rivers down my body. Now and then, we circumvented churning pools where we once hiked through basins bedded with dry broken boulders and pieces of rock. We also came across glass top pools that were so still and clear that the rocks and wood debris were transparently visible at the bottom. The ravines' beds, we once descended littered with dry brush, now gushed downward forming rushing foaming streams. We stopped long enough to gaze in wonder and appreciate the endless sparkling trickles seeming to hang in droplets from high to lower brush. The drops, like silver marbles, bounced and rebounded to puddles below. As we trekked, the silence was broken only by droplets that tinkled and trickled ever downward from leafy overhangs and mini-cascades to boulders or ledges, and pushed gently downward swishing into pools below. We achingly attempted to preserve this marvel in the painstakingly-taken photographs of many spills that seemed to leak in sheets and rivers from every rocky shelf. The whole scenario was an animated water symphony from droplets, trickles, gurgles, gentle flows, and bubbling pours, to crashing splashes, and deafening waterfalls. Aahhh! but I was elated as my mind swam in my sparkling wondrous water world, all made sweeter by my favorite relative, my Uncle Sam.

THE WHOLE SCENARIO WAS AN ANIMATED WATER SYMPHONY FROM DROPLETS, TRICKLES, GURGLES, GENTLE FLOWS, AND BUBBLING POURS, TO CRASHING SPLASHES, AND DEAFENING WATERFALLS.

NOW AND THEN, WE CIRCUMVENTED CHURNING POOLS WHERE WE ONCE HIKED THROUGH BASINS BEDDED WITH DRY BROKEN BOULDERS AND PIECES OF ROCK.

As memories of my teens flooded my mind, my singular middle school adventures surfaced as I mentally sidestepped the similar dancing waters of the *Alazan Creek* on my way to middle school after a good San Antonio *norte* (northern wind or storm). Then my mind raced back to the almost still waters of some slower streams, namely the Riverwalk where the San Antonio River flowed peacefully through the city. Observing the cascading waters of Easy recalled similar tumbles the San Antonio River splashed on its course through the Brackenridge Park woodlands toward the downtown Riverwalk following those "northerns" that I chanced to observe during my high school years.

The thick gray-white overcast sky provided to the pregnant atmosphere as we meticulously ventured down the rocky declines from the Queen. Newer horizons rewarded our northerly pace. We came across another of the many private-family Buddhist temples scattered all over The Land of the Morning Calm. (These charming places of worship reminded me of Virgin Mary or Patron Saint altars in many of the shady Mexican front *patios* of San Antonio.) We did not encounter any family dwellings however, but we were met by a father and his young son who tended the temple. The temple was of better construction as customary with a typical altar where the Buddha was seated in meditation and with relevant wall paintings and icons of the religion. The friendly Oriental duo eagerly showed us around the rugged grounds. Marvin and I strolled within a rock garden exhibiting bizarre human faces painted on stones. The man explained his belief that the faces scared demons away.

The temple and the rock garden were adjacent to a water flow ingeniously diverted and converted into a blasting outdoor bathtub. This clamoring and rushing deluge from the mountain highlands came swooping downhill into the concrete shower-size tub fashioned like a stall, crashed, swirled, and then wound its way down the mountain. The Korean had engineered his bathhouse so that the unceasing and deafening gush prevented body height overflow by use of a shoulder-high channel. Just above the tub's water level was an inset box made of concrete that housed a crude stone sculpture. This was the Korean's protection and blessings which came with the mountain's natural gift. With naive joy, Marvin and I marveled at the ingeniousness of this cleverly constructed and directed monsoon overflow, though we wondered what happened to the baths during dry spells.

WE CAME ACROSS ANOTHER OF THE MANY PRIVATE-FAMILY BUDDHIST TEMPLES SCATTERED ALL OVER THE LAND OF THE MORNING CALM.

MARVIN AND I WERE MET BY A FATHER AND HIS YOUNG SON WHO TENDED THE TEMPLE.

WE STROLLED WITHIN A ROCK GARDEN EXHIBITING BIZARRE HUMAN FACES PAINTED ON STONES WHICH SCARED AWAY DEMONS.

AN INSET BOX MADE OF CONCRETE HOUSED A CRUDE STONE SCULPTURE THAT WAS THE KOREAN'S PROTECTION AND BLESSINGS WHICH CAME WITH THE MOUNTAIN'S NATURAL GIFT. THE BUDDHA WAS SEATED IN MEDITATION WITH RELEVANT WALL PAINTINGS AND ICONS OF THE RELIGION.

We lingered a few moments more, long enough to photograph the temple, rock garden, and the man with the little boy. Bidding the Korean farewell with polite traditional bows, we proceeded by a westward decline. As we ascended a nearby ridge, we turned back to see the father and son still seeing us off with a second bow and thus a double farewell. At this, we both returned to bow in unison. I noted that as we advanced farther west, the father and his son had ascended the temple's highest step to continue seeing us on our way. Returning one last farewell bow at another crest, we descended gradually so that the temple sank out of sight. My heart wondered what thoughts could be passing through their minds regarding the two young "Yankees" of Latin descent who had accidentally stumbled upon their sanctuary. As we continued adventuring westward, nimbus clouds approached and darkened the already subdued skies. We increased our stride to avoid the upcoming rain, and looked forward to returning to camp to await the next adventurous outing.

The natural splashing waters of Easy provided a pleasant distraction for us from the not so pleasant paperwork that personified our military duty during the monsoon miseries. Her majesty freely showed us all her natural gifts—the Koreans skillfully and proficiently domesticated nature's gifts from Easy. I stood in awe as my beloved queen disclosed yet one more wondrous secret within another seasonal change beyond the numerous revelations already granted to me at this Far East corner of Asia.

IN MY EXHILARATION TO DOUBLE UP MY PACE ON THE MUDDY ASCENT, I SKIDDED, AND WHEN I REACHED THE MOUNTAINTOP I WAS REWARDED BY THE HOLLOW EYES OF A BUDDHA STATUE STARING AT ME.

Chapter 14

Uncovering Queen's Mysteries

Prologue

Oh, but the joy of wandering all over Mother Korea's hills and valleys. The scaling of inclines, searching for war relics, locating cultural jewels, and viewing distant murals of endless fields under nimbus and cumulous skies, amid mountain greens with a silver ribbon backdrop was a never-ending rapture.

Gravestones, Temples, Buddhas, and Bunkers
August 1965

Silent eyes from ancient wards
Vigil ranks as trusted guards
Tend their masters laid to rest
Time aft' time have stood the test

It was in the middle of the 1965 monsoon season during another rain letup that Marvin and I descended Easy via a different route on our way to the Camp Blue Lancer Valley Main Gate. The sky's entirety was an ominous gray, heavy with rain and the pea soup air was thick with humidity. Although my forehead was constantly beaded with perspiration, I could not get enough of clambering all over the mountains of Korea. I knew there was always another adventure waiting over the next rise.

As we approached the camp, we noticed that a few burial mounds and gravestones paralleled the road along Easy's skirts. The stroked Asiatic writing on a rectangular granite-like gravestone and two pillars, one on either side, especially attracted our attention as well as our curiosity. There were many other older, more humble, single gravestones that time and the elements had weathered away. We photographed the monuments with one another in the picture. Then we decided to cross the road and head west in search of new places to explore at the foothills located far north of Radio Hill but outside the compound and close to Nullo-Ri.

THE STROKED ASIATIC WRITING ON RECTANGULAR GRANITE-LIKE GRAVESTONE AND TWO FLANKING PILLARS ATTRACTED OUR ATTENTION.

THERE WERE MANY OLDER, MORE HUMBLE, SINGLE GRAVESTONES THAT TIME AND THE ELEMENTS HAD WEATHERED AWAY AND FLANKED BY STONE PILLARS.

The road from Camp Blue Lancer dead-ended (T-boned) at the main road at Nullo-Ri. On the left of the T-bone was the Blue Diamond Store and to the right was the village of Nullo-Ri. As we crossed the BLV road, I recollected a Buddhist temple that I had seen on my way to the camp just a few months earlier while carrying the detested Personnel Form 20s. Just beyond the T-bone's crosspiece at an irrigation ditch by a tree, was one of the three most colorful, picturesque, and stunning Buddhist temples I had beheld in my entire year in Korea. It was located just beyond heavy military and local traffic, yet unspoiled, quiet, and picture perfect. It just seemed to emerge from a book of ancient history. The overlaid tile roof was upturned at the corners. Of important note was that a tiny fence, no more than two feet high, contoured with the sloping mountain's incline surrounded the tiny building. It served more like a boundary marker to keep out intruders, and fronted by three gates, each about four feet high. I found it quite perplexing that this sanctuary was closed and inaccessible, unlike any other I ever encountered. Perhaps it was a community temple with scheduled worship, unlike those of private families and the public ones in Seoul. I was so impressed as well as awestruck by all its miniature majesty that I always cherished the picture I took of it.

ONE OF THE THREE MOST COLORFUL, PICTURESQUE, AND STUNNING BUDDHIST TEMPLES I BEHELD IN MY ENTIRE YEAR IN KOREA WAS LOCATED CLOSE TO THE VILLAGE OF NULLO-RI.

As we climbed the foothills on the road's western inclines, my excitement grew in anticipation as to what lay ahead. In my exhilaration to double up my pace on the muddy ascent, I skidded, and when I reached the mountain top, I was rewarded by the hollow eyes of a Buddha statue staring at me. We actually stumbled across the Buddha statues I had always dreamed of! I scrambled on to find a few more Buddhas. Like a sleepwalker or a delirious man half dead with thirst, approaching an oasis, I plodded deliberately toward the goal. I could not believe my luck! I had finally located the statuary I had lived ten months to discover in this headland of Asia! Once while daydreaming of this moment, I had fantasized that their sightless eyes had observed and beckoned me since earlier in the spring when I was visiting the line companies north of the Imjin and at the BLV on a Personnel errand. I insisted that these statues magnetized me, and since then I had lived for this moment in time since I received the indoctrination spiel back at Personnel hooch upon arrival in November 1964. I felt a reverence to actually be laying a hand on, examining, and standing next to a genuine Buddha grave guardian—one of many jewels scattered all over this remote mountainous corner of Asia. Here was the sentinel of an Oriental religion silently standing vigilance over an Oriental burial mound of a once live Asiatic human! Ecstatically, I imagined a farmer that once tilled and sowed the rice paddies lying under this hollowed soil below, flanked by these two guardians. We noted that the two statues which faced one another were both weather-beaten by time and with partial pieces broken off, stood in front of the burial mound. One had a bullet indentation on its back, probably from the war. Under the Korean monsoon skies, Marvin took pictures of me with my camera as I took some of him with his camera, all amid this mountainous medieval splendor.

We stood there taking in all this grandeur while the breezes cooled us as it dried the perspiration beads off from our foreheads and faces. As we continued a little higher to survey our skyline find, a whole new breathtaking panorama opened before us. The road to Munsan-Ni, the Imjin River, Spoonbill, and the distant mountains of North Korea on the horizon greeted us. A little to the right we spotted a village that met a bridge traversing the Imjin. My heart must have skipped another beat as I realized the full view of the road I had long traveled yearning to find this Buddhist statuary that I had not discovered, and that all along I imagined had gazed out at me. Decades later I identified the vill as Changpa-Ri and the bridge as Libby.

I SAT ON A GRAVESTONE AMID THE BUDDHA STATUARY I HAD SUSPECTED FROM THE MUNSAN-NI ROAD AND YEARNED TO DISCOVER. BOTH FACED ONE ANOTHER GUARDING THE BURIAL MOUND BEHIND THE HEADSTONE WITH A BUNKER ABOVE AT SKYLINE. NOTE BULLET HOLE ON THE BACK OF THE GUARDIAN.

A WHOLE NEW BREATHTAKING PANORAMA OPENED BEFORE US: THE ROAD TO MUNSAN-NI, THE IMJIN RIVER, SPOONBILL, AND THE DISTANT MOUNTAINS OF NORTH KOREA.

We then noticed a strange protrusion at a higher rise at our left along the skyline. The closer we approached it, the more we identified it as a bunker. Although I had stood bunker guard, this find was within an adventure. It was a hollow sandbag-topped earth-sunk cube of concrete with horizontal slots to accommodate weapon barrels that faced north toward Spoonbill across the Imjin. We approached it from the rear by means of trenches, some of which were lined with sandbags and floored with monsoonal sludge. We did not enter the muddy structure but took pictures. We did notice several farther down the skyline but decided that one represented all. This was one of the numerous bunkers visible from the road that ran from Nullo-Ri to Munsan-Ni that gaped at me on every bus ride on my way to Seoul (see photo p 263). Decades later, Specialist Fourth George Gustavson related to me that he had built these bunkers back in 1963.

THE BUNKER WAS A HOLLOWED SANDBAG-TOPPED EARTH-SUNK CUBE OF SOLID CONCRETE WITH HORIZONTAL SLOTS TO ACCOMMODATE WEAPON BARRELS AND FACED NORTH KOREA TOWARD SPOONBILL ACROSS THE IMJIN.

How fascinated I had been and how I had longed to explore these mountains and inspect these menacing strongholds that defiantly faced North Korea! I stood there feeling king of the mountain, struck dumb by the impact of the scene before me. From below the cliff where I stood, the rice paddies extended to the Munsan-Ni road lined with telephone poles and paralleling the river. I was taken aback by the majesty of the mile-wide shimmering Imjin River which flowed like a silver thread as viewed from the Queen (see photo p 329). I did not know then that the silver ribbon before me flowed south from North Korea, across the thirty-eighth parallel and the DMZ, and that it looped a half circle northward within South Korea (Spoonbill). From there it flowed southward again on its way to the Yellow Sea below China. It was no wonder why our views from the Queen revealed the gleaming river in three separate processions amid the mountains.

My head was swimming with excitement as I continued gawking and surveying this glorious river's meanderings, contrasting from among newly discovered medieval, perhaps ancient, artifacts, and modern military defenses. I stood in awe, further captivated by the North Korean mountain backdrop, which furthered my spectacle of this Far East corner of Asia.

DUMBFOUNDED, WE BOTH JUST STOOD PETRIFIED, AND IN SILENCE STARED AT OUR FIND.

Skeleton Find on Easy Queen
September 1965

High overhead, the skylarks wing
They never rest at home
But just like me, they love to sing
As over the world we roam
       —The Happy Wanderer

During a monsoon lull on a Saturday in September 1965, Marvin and I were strolling down a path on the west Easy slopes following another escapade on the Queen. We just could not seem to get enough of clambering all over *Mother Korea*. We were approaching the compound when a small round plate embedded on the earth attracted our attention.

At first we thought it was a mine from the war and decided to fling rocks at it. We then jumped into a huge nearby crater expecting an explosion. After several attempts we bravely approached and began knocking on it. Since there was no response, we began digging around it with a stick. We then excitedly forced our working fingers round and round not knowing what we would find. The deeper we dug, the more we found what we identified as an apparent steel helmet. Filled with adrenalin, with about two inches of earth to go, I wiggled my fingers deeper in the mud around the steep pot and secured its edge with a good grip. As I pulled it up, we heard a "*shwop*" sound as the earth's suction finally gave up the helmet. To our great shock, a human skull rolled out of an attached well-preserved helmet liner. Marvin crossed himself and exclaimed, "*Dios mio!*" (My God!). Dumbfounded, we both just stood petrified and, in silence, stared at our find. Decades later, while viewing the Sam's full-frame photos, I discovered that in my excitement I had lost a little control over my urinary system. After we recovered our faculties, we began to examine our find.

THE DEEPER WE DUG, THE MORE WE FOUND WHAT WE IDENTIFIED AS AN APPARENT STEEL HELMET.

Some brown straight soiled gritty hair had remained stuck to the inner liner fabric straps when the skull rolled out. For this one split second in my life, I forgot all about my camera. However, upon our recovery, I began to take pictures of the skull in the liner, with and without the hair. Bravely, Marvin and I then picked it up and took more pictures of each other with it. Oddly enough, all teeth were intact with no fillings or cavities. Disrespectfully, I pulled out a molar and a bicuspid lined with stain that appeared to have belonged to a once healthy body. I carefully hid them and told no one. Marvin and I continued digging and uncovered some corroded 30 mm shells; some were hollow, some contained tiny pellets, and all showed greenish-bluish rust.

TO OUR GREAT SHOCK, A HUMAN SKULL ROLLED OUT OF AN ATTACHED WELL-PRESERVED HELMET LINER.

SOME BROWN STRAIGHT SOILED GRITTY HAIR HAD REMAINED STUCK TO THE INNER LINER FABRIC STRAPS WHEN THE SKULL ROLLED OUT.

UPON OUR RECOVERY, WE CONTINUED TAKING PICTURES OF THE SKULL AND WITH HAIR.

Excitedly, after covering our dig, Marvin and I continued our descent of Easy Queen heading to the main gate. The following Monday we reported our find to Captain Baker, CO of HHC Second Battalion Thirty-eighth

Infantry. He called some unit in Seoul and two GIs came around a few days later. We all then hiked up Easy to the skeleton's location—it was still there, untouched. We continued our dig and unearthed a complete human skeleton with well-preserved bones that displayed traces of sinew and cartilage within a three-foot depth. The bones were cream and off-white in color. The only item of clothing remaining was the pair of boots on its foot bones. They were remnants of green canvas uppers that were once attached to rubber lower quarters. Chinese characters were visible on the soles right where the molded rubber sole joined the almost flat heel. We placed the bones and artifacts in a black body bag that was taken to Seoul for examination and identification.

Upon further inquiry, Sergeant Morgan of S-3 confiscated all our pictures. I managed to retain a few that I had hidden. The stolen teeth haunted me for the next twenty-plus years until I finally drove to Concordia Cemetery here in El Paso. I buried them with a small prayer pleading forgiveness of the Almighty for having disrespected one of his children, though perhaps a once rival brother-in-arms.

Aware that the artifacts and the high cheek-boned skull we unearthed pointed to remains of a Korean or Chinese, we could not help but reflect upon the life and duty of this Asian soldier. He could have been either one of us, of a different time and, perhaps, loyalty. We wondered how many more bones were littered all over this war zone whose remains had yet to be found. Why hadn't someone else found it? We knew that *papasans* traversed these paths unceasingly—perhaps the rains uncovered the helmet.

Sadly, because of this epic unearthing, Marvin and I talked about the MIAs and KIAs in the Southeast Asian country of Vietnam (where a war was going on during our present tour of duty), and of future unearthing and finds. For days, Marvin and I could not help but reflect that we had truly unearthed and handled bones and artifacts of a once live Korean War combatant. Personally, I felt privileged that destiny had singled me out to uncover the remains of a brother soldier at this Far East corner of Asia.

Instruments of Destruction
Late summer 1965

Oh, may I go a wandering
Until the day I die
Oh, may I always laugh and sing
Beneath God's clear blue sky
   —The Happy Wanderer

"Martinez, why are you going around looking for things?" Captain Walter M. Baker angrily roared. I had never been approached by the company commander in such a manner. I could just imagine the snickers the first sergeant and the clerks were casting at me.

"Hunhhhh?" I replied.

"Where's that mortar missile you found?" the commanding officer of Headquarters and Headquarters Company Second of the Thirty-eighth demanded as he glowered at me, "I'll have to post a sentry at it."

"S-s-somewhere up on E-E-Easy Queen," I stammered.

"Oh, for heaven's sake," retorted the captain petulantly as he stormed back to his office and slammed the door.

I acknowledged certain gratitude for my healthy excretory system. Thirty-five years later I concluded that Captain Baker probably chuckled to himself at this trivial caper. However, I really could not fault the CO for being so upset. Only a few weeks earlier two Koreans had found a bomb from the *conflict* and tinkered with it for metal salvage. A loud explosion reverberated through the village. The battalion ambulance rushed out and returned with the two badly burned bodies. My buddy Marvin, the medic, reported that he knew nothing more of their whereabouts or recovery.

It was during the last days of September that Marvin and I had been roaming all over Mount Easy Queen. The 1965 late summer sun graced a beautiful golden yellow light, occasionally subdued by the few post-monsoon clouds that darkened and enhanced the color of the surrounding green brush and wood and gray boulders. The rains had saturated the entire Korean mountain world with a richer green. Although the monsoons had ended, the mountain still boasted cascading waterfalls, pools, and rushing brooks.

A SILVER WATER WALL DESCENDED AND SPLASHED ONTO A SPILL BELOW, AND A CASCADE DROPPED ONTO A CLEAR POOL.

THE MOUNTAIN STILL BOASTED RUSHING BROOKS, FALLS, AND POOLS.

Marvin and I could never tire of investigating her majesty. To our excitement, we came across the conflict-era abandoned tank we had heard about. Climbing the tank's height, we could clearly see the distant winding silvery Imjin River circumventing Spoonbill, and the farther mountains of North Korea. In my naïveté and youthful excitement, I thrilled to just know how close I was in sight of the enemy. The tank had received many visitors from its heyday to the present. Snapshots of a Blue Lancer on its deck immortalized the tank with the shimmering Imjin like a silver thread in the background. It again experienced curious visitors carefully examining and climbing all over its thick and solid metal body searching for yet unrevealed secrets. Some enterprising native had sawed off the barrel for scrap metal. It still showed some olive green color which time had flaked exposing rusty spots. It displayed traces of a once colorful triangle of the artillery insignia. As we departed, the lonely tank's gaping barrel seemed to glance and follow us, but it was assured that in time others would come, seeking secrets—they always did.

As I hurried to catch up with Marvin, who had departed earlier, I impulsively commenced skipping down Easy. After a few seconds of progressive bounding momentum, my pace could not keep up with the advancing decline. I panicked as I increased my leg rate to keep up with my advancing body. I felt a chill or two as if a few of my nine lives slipped skyward. I was about to bounce the remainder of what seemed a mile when only by Divine intervention was I able to safely descend. I almost killed Marvin who, having watched my unorthodox descent, rolled with laughter saying he thought I would somersault all the way down Easy. Recalling later how my descent must have likened a Road Runner cartoon's gyrating moves with my legs almost torn off, I felt I must have aged a year or two.

CLIMBING THE TANK'S HEIGHT, WE COULD CLEARLY SEE THE DISTANT WINDING IMJIN RIVER LIKE A SILVER THREAD CIRCUMVENTING SPOONBILL, AND THE FARTHER MOUNTAINS OF NORTH KOREA. THE FEW SCATTERED CLOUDS UNDER THE BLUE SKY ENHANCED THE MOUNTAIN GREENERY AS THEIR SHADOWS ADVANCED ACROSS THE VERDUROUS HILLS AND VALLEYS.

TO OUR EXCITEMENT, WE CAME ACROSS THE CONFLICT-ERA ABANDONED TANK WE HAD HEARD ABOUT.

In the interest of "undiscovered territory," we decided to explore in a new southerly direction toward South Queen. The few scattered clouds under the blue sky enhanced the mountain greenery as their shadows advanced across the verdurous hills and valleys below us. Their edges seemed waving like stingrays, as they rolled over the landscape contours. Like a thirsty man, I drank it all as I observed my generous Korean mountainous scenery. Aahhh! but I was shadowed beneath a pearly cloudy cobalt cover, all made possible with my tax-free dollars. I chuckled with delight as I reminded myself that *this was what it was all about*, world travel at the earth's remotest corners. Oh yes, and aahhh! but how I lingered beneath continuous cumulus cloud nine, all a freebie by the U.S. Army at this PCS. We headed southwest toward the rear of the compound. We paced down the treacherous novel declines carefully observing every step on the rough rocky slopes. Gazing back to the skyline, the heavens appeared a richer, enhanced royal blue where the sky touched the mountain greenery. It was then that we came across the rocket within the dense vegetation but had sense enough to leave it alone. The first sergeant later identified it as a 50 mm rocket-launcher missile. Strangely enough, since Captain Baker never again mentioned the missile, neither did I.

WE CAME ACROSS A ROCKET WITHIN THE DENSE VEGETATION.

This was the last of our numerous adventures on Easy Queen. Only by Divine Providence did I survive near misses that could have resulted in disaster had I not paired off with Marvin, who shared in the same adventurous spirit of this Far East corner of Asia.

Epilogue

In addition to being in a war zone with relics and artifacts along with native finds, just the existence of the mountains alone justified their exploration. Since the Texas coastal plains were void of mountains, simply climbing the Queen was an adventure as climbing the pecan trees at the house. I cannot express enough how much I enjoyed climbing all over the Queen and the Nullo-Ri area. We made the most of our tour accommodating our time as available and will always reflect what more we could have found, and what other adventurers would, like us, have discovered, and perhaps their story is being written.

Chapter 15

Sopping Wet Monsoons!

August-September 1965

A pessimist sees only the dark side of the clouds, and mopes; a philosopher sees both sides, and shrugs; an optimist doesn't see the clouds at all—he's walking on them.
—Leonard Louis Levinson

Prologue

Someone once said that there was a silver lining in every cloud. I found platinum in the misery of every day life and duty beneath the darkest heavens. Under a waterproof covering, I experienced the hot humidity and drenching streams of the Korean monsoons along with the blessings of camaraderie, family, and the pure love of total strangers.

Monsoon Miseries

Water, water, and mud, mud, mud
A splish, a splash, a slip, a thud
Where soldiers and officers trod
A boot, a knee, a butt with crud!

I was accustomed to the year-round, rarely weeklong, *nortes* ("northerns") and rainstorms of the Texas Coastal Plains, but I had never before encountered the multiweeklong extended downpours of Korea. I remember the nights of my earliest childhood when I sat at a window with the curtains drawn behind me to watch thunderstorms. The branches of the pecan tree in the front yard swung wildly in the wind. I remember the lightning bolts flashing from far above the heavens down to the earth illuminating the gabled houses across the street followed by loud deafening claps of thunder. I could see the multitude of huge drops of rain when the lightning resumed. And again, a loud thunderclap. Sometimes, I could see that the clouds were puffs of light blue-gray color amid darker clouds where the lightning bolt appeared. I remember the loud pelting of the rain on the rooftop. It sounded as if we were being invaded by an incessant barrage of shot. In retrospect, at different intensities I was reminded of the drum roll I heard once, as the prelude to the national anthem in high school. To me, there is nothing greater than watching a thunderstorm at night. I always imagined these storms as God in all His glorious majesty. The August through September skies of Korea in 1965 were continually covered in varying shades of gray. The entire nimbus heaven was so solidified that it freely released its creation in unceasing torrents. How the heavens could sustain so much condensation perplexed me. It continually rained day and night and, oddly enough, there was no lightning or thunder as back home. However, according to Specialist Fifth Bruce Tinker of Hq Btry, 2nd 71st, 38th ADA Bde, Korea, April 1968-August 1969, "... we saw this lightning bolt strike a pole and go down a wire and skitter across the cement area we had for formations and award ceremonies. Shortly, thereafter, came the thunder. You could actually feel the concussion from the thunder. Our eyes about came out of our sockets." It was hard to keep dry within an entire humid world that was drenched, wetted, dampened, or moistened. During lulls or drizzles, I ventured out and was awed by the incessant majesty of multiple waterfalls, the bubbling cascades on Queen, the shimmering Imjin, and once I ran for cover at the phenomenon of an approaching rain curtain. I gawked at the many speeding flashfloods, rivers, and rapids at the field, and the boiling dashes through the BLV "river" and ditches. The foundations of two Company A Quonsets gave way and the buildings collapsed, almost sliding into the ditch under construction that ran the length of Blue Lancer. I diligently attempted to photograph running or waving water sparkling with reflective surfaces.

I GAWKED AT THE MANY SPEEDING FLASHFLOODS, RIVERS, AND RAPIDS AT THE FIELD.

THE FOUNDATIONS OF TWO COMPANY A BARRACKS GAVE WAY AND THE BUILDINGS COLLAPSED, ALMOST SLIDING INTO THE DITCH UNDER CONSTRUCTION THAT FLOWED THE LENGTH OF BLUE LANCER.

As part of the seasonal equipment, the government provided good calf-high rain boots with clip-on ties and ponchos. The rain boots usefully assured dry and comfortable feet. However, the ponchos were not made for six-foot-tall GIs; as rainwater trickled down to soak the blouse (where the fatigues were tucked into the jump boots or rain boots), thus trickling droplets into the dry socks and feet. After experiencing a Korean monsoon season, I was not about to ever again scoff at the mild and welcomed rains of San Antonio.

I recalled a major rain lull on this especially still-drizzling and partly sunny day when raging waters from South Queen splashed through the rear gate of Blue Lancer. The unceasing water rush flooded the entire ditch that ran the length of the camp. The engineers came in and improved the ditch that year. I remembered being detailed to sandbag the torrent at the rear gate along with a few of the KATUSAs. Since I was the third clerk in the orderly room typing pool, and probably the most expendable, I always ended up on the detail roster. I snapped on my rain boots over my jump boots so that my feet remained dry throughout the entire ordeal. Private First Jung (a KATUSA) and I were assigned to fill sandbags, and thwart the flow. In the course of our work, we began slamming and tossing sandbags at one another. Then, laughing and playful with cupped hands, we dashed water at each other. I remember Jung's hazel eyes smiling with mischievous mirth. I noticed that Jung wore Mickey Mouse thermals instead of rain boots. Poor Jung was so amused that he was oblivious to the water continually pouring in and out of his ankle-high boots. The light-hearted banter, a luxury in his poverty-ridden life, caused him to forget his troubles for a short time. Our fun continued all the while until we got the stream diverted and controlled.

Nothing compared with my misadventures as those at the monsoon field problem. That week of field duty was the most miserable of my life. The ceaseless rain kept me sweating under the hot poncho while I either pulled guard duty, set up my tent, or lined up for chow. There was so much mud everywhere that I once slipped and fell, landing my butt on a tree stump. This accident had my tailbone hurting for a week. Finally, after what seemed an eternity, the week ended. We enthusiastically tore down the camp, loaded the deuce-and-a-halfs, and evacuated the detested area.

The convoy slowly made its way down the mountain and finally arrived at the graded road. Along the way to the BLV we crossed lowland. Suddenly, the entire convoy stopped and everyone got off to see a flooded jeep. It had entered a dry wash and a flash flood inundated it. Sergeant Camp and Private First Withee were waist-deep in the water that topped the jeep. Both men had jumped off when it would not start. The convoy members could not do much, but eventually, a deuce-and-a-half drove up and with a cable from its front bumper, hooked the jeep, and rolled it out backward. As the jeep dragged out, a green laundry bag rolled out of the jeep and was soon bobbing in the fast current of the flooding river out of sight.

During this lull in traffic my imagination and sense of adventure kicked in, so I jumped off the deuce-and-a-half. I gazed in fascination as I walked about and explored my immediate surroundings. The graded road was mired with small broken rocks. As I strolled up the bushy inclines, I marveled at the never ending streams that devoured the rolling hills, gouging deep furrows as they splashed down the hills. Eroding newly formed banks, they rushed past me toward some unknown destination within the dense foliage. To my senses, the endless greenery, the bubbling waters, and the smell of fresh damp earth in the thick moist air was exhilarating under the Korean gray skies. Despite the drizzle on my face, the uncomfortable hot poncho and wet fatigues, the wonder of it all overwhelmed me. I could not get enough of this dreary aquatic wonderland and I could not imagine where else I would want to be in spite of these momentary miseries. Eventually, I noticed two guard dogs at the rear of a truck and strolled up. In the drizzle I had a picture taken of me with the dogs and their KATUSA handlers.

A JEEP ENTERED A DRY WASH AND A FLASH FLOOD INUNDATED IT ALONG WITH (SERGEANT) CAMP (LEFT) AND (PFC) WITHEE (RIGHT). A CABLE FROM A TRUCK ROLLED OUT THE JEEP.

I JUMPED OFF THE TRUCK TO MARVEL AT THE NEVER ENDING STREAMS THAT DEVOURED THE ROLLING HILLS, GOUGING DEEP FURROWS AS THEY SPLASHED DOWN THE HILLS ERODING NEWLY FORMED BANKS. NOTE PONCHO BACK SEAM WELL ABOVE BLOUSED RAIN BOOTS.

IN THE DRIZZLE I NOTICED TWO GUARD DOGS AT THE REAR OF A TRUCK, SO I STROLLED UP AND HAD A PICTURE OF ME TAKEN WITH THE DOGS AND THEIR KATUSA HANDLERS.

The truck convoy was continually stopped for one reason or another. At crossroads other convoys claimed right of way, as did the tank caravans that had priority. The flash floods were a continual problem. At times the deuce-and-a-halfs rolled over damp grade and at other times water flooded to the tops of the four-foot wheels but never quite reached up to the bed. I got the illusion we were riding low on the water in a river boat. Once while fording such a "river" someone yelled out, *"A mermaid."* We all rushed up and crammed at the truck's back. A bedraggled feminine figure occupied a precarious position on an isolated boulder in the middle of the flood plain. The foaming rush slapped, parted, and merged around just below her precarious perch. Her face, streaming with rain, appeared framed by her hair stringing down to her shoulders and below a drenched blouse that barely concealed her well-endowed assets. The swift flow slapping around the boulder, compounded by rising and falling waves made by the advancing trucks, prevented her from maintaining her balance. Her legs and now-and-then visible bare feet continually seemed to rise and dip to the rhythm of the trucks' swaying roll. As she fought to preserve her dignity, all efforts to prevent her saturated black skirt from riding above her knees proved fruitless. As our fleet sailed by, she regally ignored the entire pack of wolves cat-calling at her. I felt somewhat apprehensive as she slipped out of sight behind the following truck as the procession rolled on. Forty years later I reflected that a low ranking driver on independent duty would have probably offered rescue, but because the convoy was on official duty—supervised by senior sergeants and officers—no driver dared to do so. Strangely enough the girl did not appear frantic, but rather apprehensive of the passing soldiers. Perhaps the arrival of the convoy had disoriented her; and I hoped that in a matter of time she would have waded out. The water rush did not appear dangerously turbulent.

Nature endowed Korea with seasonal downpours. The monsoon cleansing cycles perpetually assured the yearly laundering of the land. All human, animal, and vegetative debris washed away toward the seas and an eternal rebirth resumed. Where Korea once surrendered to the monsoon torrents, she now prepared to maternally yield her life-rendering rice seed to nourish her children. I felt it my privilege to reside for a little while in this solid world of seemingly perpetual deluge, while I was able to assess the land's rebirth during its freshening lulls, at this Far East corner of Asia.

MOTHER KOREA NOW PREPARED TO MATERNALLY YIELD HER LIFE-RENDERING SEED TO NOURISH HER CHILDREN. I ALWAYS ENJOYED THE QUIET SCENIC TREKS BETWEEN THE RICE PADDIES. I SQUATTED ON THE EIGHTEEN INCH-WIDE PATHS WITH RICE SHOOTS AT ABOUT ONE-FOURTH GROWTH ABOVE THE RICE PADDY FLOOD LEVEL. EVERY FEW YARDS OR SO, ANCIENTLY TESTED DIMINUTIVE WATERFALLS CALCULATED THE DESCENT OF FLOW FROM THE UPPER FLOODING FIELD TO THE LOWER ONE (SEE PHOTO P. 218).

Monsoon Guard at the Turk's Compound
Monsoon Season 1965

Soldiers near and soldiers far
We were from across the Mar
They were from an Asian side
Across their continent thus wide

It was during the wild and wet monsoons of '65 that I was detailed (assigned) to stand guard at Camp Amahie. The Sixteenth Turkish Company had replaced the Fifteenth, and the BLV troops (GIs and KTUSAs) were honored with securing their compound while the Sixteenth settled in. It was disheartening to experience some of what our Far West Asian brothers may have felt as they were simply dropped off at a strange compound surrounded by mountains, unlike the desert flatlands in their own home across the continent. There were only traces of occupancy left behind by the former occupants. No one from home greeted their arrival or welcomed them, or made their arrival a pleasant transfer or indoctrination. The Sixteenth Turks were just dumped off in Korea *cold turkey.*

I was overwhelmed but welcomed this opportunity to mingle with yet another culture within a culture in this Far East Turkish outpost of Asia. The soldiers from the extreme end of Asia opposite Korea had always fascinated me. I had heard many wild stories of their propensity toward intruders and deceivers.

In the words of an eyewitness:

> "I recall a Turkish Rifle Company near Pobwan-Ni and the 2nd Field, 20th Artillery compound at Camp Snow where I did my tour '60-'61. Lots of Turkish soldiers frequented the "clubs" and "houses" in Pobwan-Ni, and we used to "hoist a few" in allied comradeship. They were a robust—dare I say—"formidable" lot, folks that I certainly wouldn't have wanted to tangle with. We would frequently see their formations headed off across those rugged hills, shouldering their machine guns, mortars, and gear while we Americans cruised up to our alert positions ensconced in jeeps, three-quarter ton trucks, and deuce-and-a-halfs. Their compounds did not display the barbed wire fences, coils of concertina wire, and guarded towers of the typical American army compounds, and shortly after my arrival at the 20th Arty, I found out why. They caught a hapless and careless "slicky boy" on their compound, and after due Turkish "justice" (censored) as I recall, they had few problems with "slicky boys" unlike the constant problems that we experienced in our compounds."
>
> —SP4 Bruce Miller,
> 2nd Field, 20th Arty, 1st Cav Div,
> Korea, 1960-1961.

Before this adventure I had only entered and immediately exited this compound solely by military bus. I noted foreign words on posts and signs. On one of those few bus entries I noticed team sports, the playing of a game by kicking a ball away from one another. I was intrigued and fascinated by this foreign ballgame. Also, they wore lighter khaki uniforms with curved pockets. A few visited the EM club along with their officers following the reflagging ceremonies in July 1965. A Turk soldier in a GI bus once conversed with me in Spanish.

We were driven to Camp Amahie and although I had always wanted a picture of the Fifteenth Company welcome sign, it now had the Sixteenth. I managed to take a picture of the "16th welcome" sign from the far back of the deuce-and-a-half in spite of the truck's motions over the graded road. As we arrived, there were crowds of Turkish soldiers emerging from their Quonsets to greet us.

The Turkish soldiers were just as curious of us as we were of them. All our English speaking efforts were met with apologetic smiles. I spoke in Spanish and in my broken Korean but was met with equally regretful smiles. Then Private First Ray bridged the gap when he spoke German, as did a senior ranking Turk. In their conversation they discovered that they had both attended school in Germany. We all communicated through them until we realized that the lines of messaging dragged by slowly. Some of the Turks brought the thumb and index finger close together and toward their mouths which immediately rewarded them with cigarettes from our troops. Since we were all crowded around busily shaking hands and exchanging names, and due to the lack of individual conversation, I jumped on a concrete embankment and shouted. When all of the Turks turned toward me I began taking pictures of all within range. I pointed my camera at smiling groups and sat with them while Marvin took our picture. Later, I noticed that one or two of them appeared in every picture with broad smiles.

The Turks were as full of fun and mischief as schoolboys. They shoved or climbed on one another piggy back style, or "wrestled." They stopped long enough to smile and fully displayed their fresh youthful faces to pose for the camera. Since all units of all three armies were commanded by junior sergeants and senior privates, all the ranks were involved in the great deal of mirth, laughter, and general gaiety. We were all having so much fun that discipline was temporarily overlooked.

Then a small black sedan of a foreign make arrived and an officer got off. He said something to the Turk sergeants and they all immediately fell into formation. The officer left the scene, but I continued taking pictures of them in formation. Some saluted and others crowded the front rank to be in the picture. The Turk sergeants again lost control when the soldiers turned away from the formation and faced the camera to be in the picture in the absence of their officers.

Suddenly it started to rain in torrents, so the Turks were dismissed and they ran toward their barracks, subsequently appearing by poking their heads wearing T-shirts and drawers—the humidity being very high in contrast to their desert homeland—from windows and doors toward us. Later I saw a Turk soldier without a poncho stand at attention in the rain while an officer railed at him from within the comfort of his car. We all stood around like a bunch of idiots because the compound lacked a guardhouse. During guard duty the rain poured down my hot sweaty poncho, soaked my bloused fatigue pants, and ultimately seeped into my rain boots. After a while we finally got settled into an empty Quonset without bunks. The KATUSAs slept anywhere—on the bare concrete floor or on each other. How anyone could sleep in wet fatigues was beyond me. Finally, bunks were provided but we all slept in damp discomfort anyway.

SIXTEENTH TURKISH COMPANY WELCOME SIGN TO CAMP AMAHIE. (PFC) RAY CONVERSES WITH TURK SOLDIER.

I JUMPED ON A CONCRETE EMBANKMENT AND SHOUTED; WHEN THE TURKS TURNED TOWARD ME I BEGAN TAKING PICTURES OF ALL WITHIN RANGE.

I POINTED MY CAMERA AT SMILING GROUPS OR SAT WITH THEM WHILE MARVIN TOOK OUR PICTURE.

THE TURK SOLDIERS STOPPED LONG ENOUGH DURING FORMATION TO SMILE AND FULLY DISPLAY THEIR FRESH YOUTHFUL FACES TO POSE FOR THE CAMERA.

THE TURK SERGEANTS AGAIN LOST CONTROL WHEN THE SOLDIERS TURNED AWAY FROM THE FORMATION AND FACED THE CAMERA TO BE IN THE PICTURE IN THE ABSENCE OF THEIR OFFICERS.

One day during a rain and duty lull, I was afforded the rare opportunity to independently roam around the innermost recesses of this otherwise "forbidden city" and without restraint photographed everything of importance. I photographed a large crescent moon and star high on a prominent hillside. An oversized Quonset improvised to serve as a mosque with a prayer minaret fascinated me. As I wandered around I came to realize that Camp Amahie and Camp Blue Lancer Valley were both obscured from the main road that connected them and distant from each respective village, in effect both were "hidden valleys." The officer's club was identified with a red-framed triangle bearing the Ursa Major constellation of white stars on a black field. Another hillside identified a subunit with white rocks. Eventually, I drifted toward the camp's entry. Their main offices boasted four poles each with small, barely discernable flags on this windless monsoon day. At the main gate, I borrowed the MP's shoulder ID to have my picture taken. I took other pictures of the main gate and at a one-way sign. All this time the Turk soldiers were confined to quarters but I saw them lounging carefree in their bunks as I passed their Quonsets.

I FREELY WANDERED WITHIN THE INNERMOST RECESSES OF THE COMPOUND AND WITHOUT RESTRAINT PHOTOGRAPHED EVERYTHING OF IMPORTANCE.

AN OVERSIZED QUONSET IMPROVED TO SERVE AS A MOSQUE WITH A PRAYER MINARET ALONG WITH THE OVERGROWN COUNTRYSIDE ROAD CONDITIONS LIKE BACK HOME COMPLETELY FASCINATED ME.

THE OFFICER'S CLUB WAS IDENTIFIED WITH A RED-FRAMED TRIANGLE BEARING THE URSA MAJOR CONSTELLATION OF WHITE STARS ON A BLACK FIELD. ANOTHER HILLSIDE IDENTIFIED A SUBUNIT WITH WHITE ROCKS.

THE MAIN OFFICES BOASTED FOUR POLES EACH WITH SMALL, BARELY VISIBLE FLAGS ON THIS WINDLESS MONSOON DAY.

AT THE MAIN GATE I BORROWED THE MP'S SHOULDER ID TO HAVE MY PICTURE TAKEN.

In my wanderings, I came across a rain gutter littered with discarded uniforms bearing the white star and crescent moon on red shoulder patches and repaired footwear that had seen far better days. It crossed my mind to tear off a few as souvenirs, but regretfully I refrained due to the odors of unwashed clothes emanating from them despite the rain flow. Perhaps soldiers decided to leave one last souvenir by saturating the uniforms with body fluids. I was also tempted to collect a better pair of holed shoes of the many scattered around for salvage replacement, but all were so worn out they were beyond usefulness that no supply sergeant would accept them. However, I found and successfully redeemed a pair of damaged gloves.

I CAME ACROSS A RAIN GUTTER LITTERED WITH DISCARDED UNIFORMS BEARING THE WHITE STAR AND CRESCENT MOON ON RED SHOULDER PATCHES AND REPAIRED FOOTWEAR THAT HAD SEEN BETTER DAYS.

We pulled guard duty at Camp Amahie for one week or less. It was the longest week of my life. At the end of that time we were ready for the showers and the mess hall of the BLV. We sadly and gladly bid farewell to many of the Turks who crowded us for cigarettes and handshakes.

A few weeks later, two Turks visited the BLV and looked me up. I was pleased they remembered me. I had a shot taken with them in Hooch Ten, along with Marvin and Pak Bok Dong.

TWO TURKS VISITED THE BLV AND LOOKED ME UP. I HAD A PHOTO TAKEN WITH THEM IN HOOCH TEN, ALONG WITH (PFC) MARVIN GARCIA AND PAK BOK DONG.

I would always cherish this rare "changing of the guard" experience. It was a rare piece of shared history with the Sixteenth Turkish soldiers—and of exploring their taboo compound at this Turkish Far East corner of Asia.

Prologue

At each of the four seasonal maneuvers, I paused long enough to observe my favorite landmark—the farmer's hooch. During the dreaded and unwelcome monsoon field problem of August 1965, I stood at the northwest corner of the camp bluff absorbed in scanning the valley below. As in previous field exercises, I was again burdened with my harness and pack, protective mask, slung M14 with barrel downward, and canteen, but this time I was sweating within my poncho beneath a momentary drizzling lull after a heavy deluge under a dreary world of gray. This would be my fourth and last field experience in Korea. The distant rice paddies resembled dragon's scales and were leveled with monsoonal flow reflecting the pregnant gray clouds above. As I scanned the distant fields, I finally caught sight of my faithful farmer's hooch, but this time under a showery panoramic scene that brought back memories of my former wanderings. The ancient home had faithfully withstood all the punishing elements during all of my almost completed one-year tenure in Korea. Deeply lost in thought of field problems past while gazing at the familiar agrarian scene, I recalled my last ten months of seasonal experiences as a U.S. Army soldier.

A Charming Farmer's Hooch
November 1964; January, February, August 1965

Strolling through the woods at dawn
A charming hooch my eyesight won
Every season brought a change
In time therein I was not strange

I strolled through the forest just within the sector's perimeter on a chilly sunny Monday morning of November 16, 1964. As a newly arrived from the States buck private, my adventurous spirit wondered what I could possibly find of interest in this remote backwoods mountaintop at this

Asian country in the Eastern Hemisphere. Pleasantly at peace with myself, I strolled amid the pure and fresh pine scent of the novel woodland. I inhaled deeply of the crisp, cold, and pure "morning calm" mountain air in hopeful anticipation of some initial encounter with the Korean people or artifacts. I rambled confidently and warmly secure in my army cold weather clothing. As I wandered, I felt the Korean sun pleasantly warm and inviting as it filtered through the shade of the pine needles warming my cold face. Not until decades did I realize that I had stumbled onto a burial mound that are scattered all over Korea.

I STROLLED AMID THE PURE FRESH PINE SCENT OF THE NOVEL WOODLAND WHERE I INHALED DEEPLY OF THE CRISP, COLD, AND PURE "MORNING CALM" MOUNTAIN AIR. NOTE BURIAL MOUND IN FOREGROUND.

I was soon rewarded as I caught sight of a charming farmhouse. It was my first glimpse of a close-up Korean dwelling, as this was my first week on overseas duty. The straw-roofed mud-plastered abode with latticed windows and paper panes was both strange and fascinating. A stream of gray smoke emerged from a tubular chimney suggesting the family was present therein. The tiny, cozy, slap-dash cottage seemed so inviting, that I craved to meet the occupying family. I imagined and envied the Mom, the Dad, and the children warmly and happily nestled inside—their feet warmed on the hot floor. At the left of the yard was a huge cupcake-shaped straw-stacked pile overlaid with a seemingly Chinese hat-like top. The tiny earth yard was neatly swept and surrounded by a makeshift fence of brush sticks. This entire scenario held me captive as I stood gaping from the corner of the gateless rectangular lot. My attention was caught by this cozy picturesque dwelling because it was my first exposure to nonmilitary Korea.

Thrilled at this chance-meeting and hoping to chat with country folk, I had a snapshot taken of me by another bypassing soldier in the foreground with my Instamatic 126 camera when I finally became aware enough to snap this precious moment for posterity.

THE STRAW-ROOFED MUD-PLASTERED ABODE WITH LATTICED WINDOWS AND PAPER PANES WAS BOTH STRANGE AND FASCINATING. A STREAM OF GRAY SMOKE EMERGED FROM A TUBULAR CHIMNEY SUGGESTING THE FAMILY'S PRESENCE WITHIN. THE TINY COZY SLAP-DASH COTTAGE SEEMED SO INVITING, THAT I CRAVED TO MEET THE OCCUPYING FAMILY.

I HAD A SNAPSHOT TAKEN OF ME IN THE FOREGROUND OF THIS PRECIOUS MOMENT FOR POSTERITY.

I then summoned to mind the unwelcome snows of January 1965 that brought the scheduled winter field problem. Personnel was again stationed at this same campsite as last November. The whole forest was now a snowy wonderland. The entire ground, layered with about three inches of snow crunched under my thermal boots as I privately walked through the woods. The entire scene appeared like a picture of snow-laden pine trees on the white earth as on the Christmas card I once saw as a little boy while I rummaged through my mother's picture box. Wandering through the now familiar woods comfortably alone, I privately enjoyed the chilly, crisp, and stinging clean air. Intent on observing, listening, and searching for new panoramas, I paused surrounded within the whispering and frosted woodland. A steady subdued pattering caught my attention. I discovered a myriad of melting and trickling snowdrops dripping and patting like falling crystals resembling a chandelier, dropping from needle to needle making the tapping noise. Being from South Texas, I was unaccustomed to the freezing temperatures and snowstorms of these latitudes. As I ambled along, after a while I came across the same farmer's hooch that I found so charming back in chilly November. The white roof reminded of the sugar icing on a graham cracker house where the little gingerbread boy lived that ran away. I stood entranced as I viewed the stream of white smoke lazily ascending again from the chimney attesting to the cozy family snuggled there. I recalled the imagined family circle composed of an elderly gentleman, the lady of the house, and a few children all at play, maybe enjoying an Asian folk game. How I longed to bond with the family inside! Perhaps they were kowtowing in prayer at an indoor Buddhist altar. How I longed to worship with them—I could count on my fingers the number of family prayers in my Christian chaotic home. Maybe the Mom or Dad was telling a folk tale with a moral encouraging their good behavior, unlike the horrible pinches my mother gouged on my upper arms and buttocks. On that chilly afternoon in a Korean snow land, for some reason I considered myself part of the invisible family, though I was just an unknown passing stranger on the outside frozen world looking in. Later, I realized that I had imagined this family as I would have hoped exemplified mine.

Fortune smiled upon me that morning as I passed by the only attraction that I looked forward to during seasonal field duty. My heart leaped that chilly snowed morning as the family I longed to encounter, chanced to be in the yard. A sweet little girl carried her sibling baby on her back, wrapped Korean style, happily smiling at the camera. The lady of the house was busily bent, sweeping the yard with a makeshift brush broom close to the gate. I gambled as I called out to them for a picture. To my pleasant surprise the Mom looked up, displaying a friendly smile as I snapped the picture. Instantly a ray of happiness flashed through me. I felt a sense of family, a sense of a loving Mom with happy children, and surely a loving husband and father—I subconsciously yearned to enter the spherical glow of their happiness. It was my privilege that she allowed the snapshot. It was the crowning peak of all four seasonal field problems because most Korean folk frowned and turned away from cameras. I had captured a natural moment of Korean life and tucked this cherished incidence away like a treasure.

MY HEART LEAPED THAT CHILLY MORNING AS THE FAMILY I LONGED TO ENCOUNTER CHANCED TO BE IN THE YARD.

Then I recollected the trucks rolling up to this mountain post again toward our familiar bivouac campsite last February of 1965. The Asian snows were succumbing to the chills of the year's early months. The sun shone weakly through the defrosted pine needles and gently warmed the Korean earth, and my face within my parka hood. Amid the misery caused by these field problems, my sole recompense was looking forward to a pleasant stroll through the woods.

My gaze remained on the farmer's hooch and farmyard as I continued to recollect on that gloomy August monsoonal day from my lofty roost. From this higher vantage point, the farmer's fields appeared like a nubby yellow carpet studded with rice stubble. The flooded fields continued to reflect the gray, eternally swollen heavens. Evidently, the Korean farmer had successfully completed the harvest following the growth season since my February visit and was waiting patiently in his hooch for the monsoon cycle to end.

MY GAZE REMAINED ON THE FARMER'S HOOCH AND FARMYARD AS I CONTINUED TO RECOLLECT ON THAT MONSOONAL DAY.

As I stood there staring and studying my agrarian landscape on that hot humid cloudy day, I thought of the young naive soldier gaily and nonchalantly spending his off duty hours roaming in the woods on his first few November days in Korea. How excitedly and how eagerly I had snapped seasonal pictures those days and pictures of the hooch at each visit. I knew that my assignment in Korea had reached full circle and this would be my final encounter with my adopted family. Teary eyed, while reminiscing years later, I regretted not having taken them a copy of the family photo, and perhaps a can of sour ball candies to the children at this Far East corner of Asia.

Epilogue

My soul haunted this charming hooch where not only did I visualize the young soldier snapping that February photograph, but who now imagined himself in the courtyard as their *boysan*. I was then on the inside looking out at a wandering American soldier strolling by his dad's woods. He must have likened the soldier to an occasional passerby at opening a two-dimensional world outside his three-dimensional surveyed dirt yard. He may have paused to wonder who these strange combat-clad foreigners were and what their business at infiltrating his world was. Perhaps he smiled and waved at them as he sat on the porch. Then it happened, I was transformed. I pictured myself henceforth in the bosom of my new family playing folk games surrounded by my mom, dad, little sister, and brother, snug within the cozy hooch—with onlookers from faraway lands wandering about the outside frozen world looking in. Later, I realized I had all along adopted myself into the family that I once so busily visualized and henceforth too, during the upcoming winter snows—confirming that a part of me did indeed remain in this Far East corner of Asia.

Monsoon Lull at a Remote Village
Monsoons 1965

Flashing colors from the sky
Monsoon deluge flowing by
Meeting fam'ly by the well
Trace of time when raindrops quell

The Second Battalion of the Thirty-eighth Infantry was on one of those field problems at the usual campsite somewhere in the Second Infantry bivouac sector during the monsoon season of 1965. We were experiencing the end of this downpouring station of Asia, though the humidity, heat, and the now incessant drizzle created a frustrating ambience that drove us mad. When the sun rarely broke through the overcast, the unceasing heat only suffocated us all the worse. All were continually cussing on duty in full field regulation gear.

One afternoon during a duty lull, H. and I decided to hike to the nearest village for Seoul Cola. A cool soft drink would bring a nice change to the flat potable water amid the maddening duty. This Korean cola was stronger than our American coke. The drink fizzled where the soda touched inside the glass bottle a lot longer after a swig. As we descended from the wooded camp, an expected view of terraced flooded rice fields extending to the distant mountains opened before us.

This time, however, I was astounded by the difference in the view. A colorful rainbow made its way from a height of about twenty feet into a nearby rice paddy that was in flood. The dazzling scene seemed to vanish into the lagoon-like field that our footpath circumvented. As we walked, the rainbow remained to our right, so I was continually in awe at how close I was looking at the rainbow's end! The multicolored wonder was huge, maybe about six feet wide, and it appeared so close, I estimated about twelve feet distant, as it vanished into the waters of the rice paddy. (Thirty years later a professor at the university explained that such rare phenomena occurs only under exceptional given conditions, such as at "a body of water nearby" [sic] where I was fortunate to have been present right time right place.) I wondered why the rainbow did not appear flat. (The professor promptly replied that given the precipitation and atmospheric conditions, rainbows are flat or cylindrical.) I was disappointed, however, of not having discovered a legendary pot of gold at the end of it! Come to think of it, maybe that was OK, because the gold was beneath the water and so deep in a mire consisting of fecal concoctions which had been brewing there for decades, if not centuries. Although H. noticed the rainbow, I did not comment on it to him. He probably would have dismissed it with a shrug, or merely say that it was simply a water prism reflecting light. H. was a five-year college man who declined an officer's commission. Thus, he was drafted and became a great soldier and administrative clerk, but because he was a pragmatic being, he never was impressed by anything as astonishingly phenomenal as a beautiful rainbow on an overcast dreary day.

As H. and I continued down the narrow path between the shimmering flooding paddies, we met an oncoming *ajema* (woman). She carried a load of bread rolls on a circular metal tray that sat on a coiled cloth balanced on her head. Inquiring about the village, she and the tray as one turned around facing toward the village and responded, "Choooooogie," expressing "faaaaaaar away." To this day, I had no idea where we were in The Land of the Morning Calm, but we both felt comfortable and safe as usual.

A widened well-worn path finally led us to a tiny farming village that bustled with its tiny population. It boasted an artesian well at ground level. The well was a minute contributing origin of irrigation for the rice paddies. Water was controlled such that it flowed continuously at just above ground level onto and through several channeled concrete washbasins (resembling a cartwheel) continuing on, thus onto the rice paddies. A young Korean girl squatted as she was washing rice seed at one of the basins. She looked up, gave us a short note, and resumed her task. Elderly Koreans were seated near the well or by their hooches. They were taking full advantage of the day's rain lull and engaged in phonetic chat.

The well water seemed so cool and refreshing that I removed my steel pot and confidently rinsed my face at one of the nearest basins. At the moment an elderly lady brought out a plastic dish familiar to all military toilet kits that contained the remaining thin sliver of her precious soap. I thanked her, and then committed the greatest military blunder. I trustingly slung off my M14 and placed it on a nearby bench. After that, I slipped off my burdensome harness with pack, canteen, poncho, and protective mask. I got down on all fours, dipped my whole head into the basin, and lathered my face and rinsed. To my pleasant surprise an elderly gentleman approached me with a noticeably clean and thread-bare towel. It hung on his forearm as he politely paced toward me—his eyes smiling with loving kindness. After thanking him, I proceeded to dry my dripping head and clean face. Aahhh! but I so felt finely refreshed, at the generosity of my indigenous family! All the while H. stood by patiently observing the whole caper, and never said a word—the charitable Korean folk obviously impressed an unimpressionable soldier. Then I donned my cumbersome equipment and we both proceeded to the tiny general store. I retained the cola bottle and later removed the label as a souvenir of my sweet mom-and-dad encounter.

Decades later, I realized that these were the feudal country folk that had suffered the full brunt of the North Korean infiltration. This was a time when the last of these gentle agrarian inhabitants of these isolated communities still embraced the occupying *Meegook* (American) army. In their own humble and reverent manner, they rendered appreciation to a GI who represented their liberators.

I horded this spiritual experience along with so many others during my tour of duty. I acknowledged the overwhelming and inadequate feeling of the GI who happened to be present in place of the real heroes. I found myself in a comfortable solemn spiritual sanctuary. I felt greatly humbled yet proud of the privilege that Providence had elected me to represent and thus honor *all* GIs at this remote village at this Far East corner of Asia.

SEOUL COLA BOTTLE LABEL

Chapter 16

September 1965

A cloudy day is no match for a sunny disposition.
—William Arthur Ward

Prologue

It was one of those rare moisture-laden September nights during a monsoon lull that I lay in my bunk lethargically sleepless and absorbed in deep thought. The clean night air was thick with refreshing moisture. In a blink, I became conscious of myself as a tiny entity resting in my hooch surrounded by the freshly cleansed mountain basin of the Blue Lancer Valley. I imagined having a bird's eye view consisting of the vast mountain clusters that roofed this calm Far East Asian country. I felt myself enveloped in a dreamscape within the twilight of sleep and persistent wakefulness. Light gray clouds provided a canopy under the Korean heavens. The pleasant stillness and muted night sounds made it a pleasure to reminisce. I lay cuddled within a darkness that seemed peopled by black shapes against a weakly filtering light. My body did not feel prone as a sleeping person, but more like a spectator in a two-dimensional array of grays along with black. The tattoo bugle call had sounded off one hour earlier, and all lights were out—now that taps had pealed at ten. The pungent odor of insect killer, provided by the army in dark olive-green spray cans, still lingered within the confines of my mosquito net. After showering a little earlier, I lay in my skivvies under my mosquito net thoughtfully recalling my most recent adventures.

I ENCOUNTERED NUMEROUS GREATER-THAN-LIFE-SIZE BUDDHA SCULPTURES SEATED IN MEDITATION ON PEDESTALS.

Kyung Bok Ku
July 1965

Under the Asian skies I lay, Reliving ventures of my day
I strolled the walks, the yards and halls; I saw the bridge, the lake, the walls
Of kings and queens on royal thrones, All dressed in silks with precious stones
All for me to enjoy alone, All for me to enjoy alone

With eyes accustomed to the Quonset's darkness and attracted by a gentle breeze being admitted through the Quonset's open door, I glanced across the black-contoured bunk to the silhouetted sleeper at my left. The breeze flowed pleasantly though the Quonset and exited at the opposite entry. I reveled in its pleasant cooling caress on my freshly showered body in the humid air of the barracks. Through the open door, the clouds displayed varying shades of gray. Closing my eyes, I recalled the stroll I enjoyed earlier at Kyung Bok Ku on a day self-tour.

It was one of those very hot summer days when I strolled under upturned tiled roofs and through oversized wooden gates and entered the wonderland of pagodas and pavilions of Kyung Bok Ku. Alone, I had had the whole park to myself, as not even light pedestrian traffic existed during my entire visit. The grounds and gardens contained the ancient palace of the Korean kings and stood behind the Japanese-built capitol in Seoul.

I walked into a quiet extended yard of geometrically arranged flagstones that completely surrounded a pagoda-like building. It was intricately designed with gorgeous geometric patterns in red, gold, and yellow outlined in black.

Another pagoda-like pavilion of many pillars with a red facade rose from a pond covered with green floating pads and yellow lilies like those at the Chinese Sunken Gardens of San Antonio. The buildings boasted overlapping tile roofs which curved up at the corners.

I STROLLED UNDER UPTURNED TILED ROOFS AND THROUGH OVERSIZED WOODEN GATES.

IN A QUIET EXTENDED YARD WITH GEOMETRICALLY ARRANGED FLAGSTONES, I SAW A PAGODA-LIKE BUILDING THAT WAS INTRICATELY DESIGNED WITH GEOMETRIC PATTERNS IN RED, GOLD, AND YELLOW OUTLINED IN BLACK.

ANOTHER PAGODA-LIKE PAVILION ON MANY PILLARS WITH A RED FACADE ROSE FROM A POND COVERED WITH GREEN FLOATING PADS AND YELLOW LILIES.

I wandered silently down a shady multi-pillar dark red, gloomy, almost spooky, inner hall that surrounded one of the courtyards where I encountered numerous, greater-than-life-size Buddha sculptures seated in meditation on pedestals. Their meditating expressions added to the grave and silent atmosphere. I could not help but feel the pervasive ambiance of reverence and respect caused by their presence alone. As I strolled about the grounds, I was attracted by a weather-beaten gate with a fascinating ancient tube and chain security device. Noiselessly, I peeked into the empty throne chamber where I read a note explaining that the Korean alphabet was created therein.

I TOOK A PHOTO OF THE PARK'S ENTRANCE BILLBOARD WITH A MAP OF THE GROUNDS. I WANDERED SILENTLY DOWN A MULTI-PILLAR DARK RED, GLOOMY, ALMOST SPOOKY, INNER HALL.

I PEEKED INTO THE EMPTY THRONE CHAMBER.

I ENCOUNTERED NUMEROUS GREATER-THAN-LIFE-SIZE BUDDHA SCULPTURES SEATED IN MEDITATION ON PEDESTALS. I WAS ATTRACTED BY A WEATHER-BEATEN GATE WITH A FASCINATING ANCIENT TUBE AND CHAIN SECURITY DEVICE.

At the southern part of the sunny grounds, I came across a lake traversed by a bridge. The red upward curved bridge had lattice-like handrails and posts. On a walk around the lake was a colorful hexagonal pagoda, also with upturned tile roof corners. I remembered the cloudless day and the heat of the superbright sun—its clarity made outdoor picture taking much easier and shadows trickier. I was fascinated by the quietude of this "forbidden city" treasure in the middle of the bustle of Seoul. Chuckling with glee, I remembered sitting under a shady tree feeling privileged to be taking in this entire ancient Oriental spectacle in absolute privacy. Aaahh! but I was basking below brightness, and all at below poverty wages.

I closed my eyes reflecting that I was enjoying yet another ecstatic carefree adventure, alone and far away from all care with no thought of home. My cup was full, this was my life, and I was living it to its fullest extent, and knowing that Uncle Sam was paying for it made it all the more sweeter.

I opened my eyes and gazed across the Quonset where the few windows lined the barrack's length. They allowed just enough light to make out the black bunks quietly occupied by tranquil and undisturbed silhouetted sleepers. For a second and a second only, I wondered what they were dreaming of. It never occurred to me that I too was simply one of those (sleepless) sleepers this night in this hooch! With the available light I made out the sparse furniture against the curved walls, while the windows revealed weather changes. My gaze turned to follow the electrical wiring running along the curved joints and molding across the ceiling above me. Again, my eyes gravitated toward the open door examining the distant, now dark-gray, sky. Faithfully, it displayed all the signs of the promised and unceasing downpours, humidity, and drudgery of the continuing monsoons of this Far East corner of Asia.

The Capitol
July 1965

Through gardens green I strolled
Past columns topped and scrolled
A span for notables so vast
Echoing sounds of now and past

It was on one of those cloudless, superbright, and sunny days that I exited the Kyung Bok Ku Palace, the ancient capitol of Korea, and strolled down the Seoul Boulevard with the intention of exploring the modern capitol building. The building and grounds were adjacent to Kyung Bok Ku on the southern perimeter of the ancient palace city block. It was built by the Japanese upon invasion, purposefully fronting (in effect covering) ancient Kyung Bok Ku, to humiliate the conquered Korean people. These government buildings and grounds were open and available for random touring. There was no one about, and the building was seemingly abandoned and devoid of life—I again had the entire historical site to myself alone.

I entered the open ground to find myself next to the gigantic columns and walls of an impressive civic building. I was met by two protective lion statues that flanked the entrance. The columns bore Corinthian-like capitals where they met the eves. The entire building was constructed of what appeared to be white marble. To me, the architecture of this office building hardly had a hint of Japan, and even somewhat unlike the Greek triangular facades I had thus viewed in the States or history books. I strolled through front gardens where I saw a tall spire that resembled a thin pagoda. I stood in the center of many floral bushes.

I STROLLED THROUGH FRONT GARDENS WHERE I SAW A TALL SPIRE THAT RESEMBLED A THIN PAGODA. I FOUND MYSELF NEXT TO GIGANTIC COLUMNS AND WALLS OF AN IMPRESSIVE CIVIC BUILDING WITH TWO LION STATUES THAT FLANKED THE ENTRANCE.

I walked through the grounds toward the capitol's portico. Facing south from the building's steps, I was attracted to the majesty of the entire Seoul Boulevard by the vehicular clamor. The wide boulevard extended as far as the eye could see with all its heavy oncoming and ongoing, seemingly ant-like, traffic on multi-lanes, and bustle of city life amid the odor of diesel and gasoline exhaust pollution. I knew that somewhere along the street was the USO on the left, the train depot on the right, and that farther down traffic bypassed South Gate. Both oncoming and ongoing traffic bypassed the building in its own left. The sight was a spectacle!

I freely had the walk of the building. I entered into a huge silent chamber with two curved flanking staircases meeting in the center of a second story. My mind refused to envision Japanese public figures in "roaring twenties" dress hurriedly trafficking back and forth conducting government business. I felt rather violated as a soldier assigned in the defense of Korea where, at this time, my loyalty lay. As I raised my head, I saw a colorful glass dome that admitted limited light. I lay on the floor's center and took a picture of the glass dome's interior. It was too hot, and I did not care to climb the stairs to the second floor which consisted of a walk with pillar and rail banister that surrounded the entire building within.

FACING SOUTH FROM THE CAPITOL'S STEPS, I WAS ATTRACTED TO THE MAJESTY OF THE ENTIRE SEOUL BOULEVARD IN A RARE MOMENT OF QUIETUDE.

AS I RAISED MY HEAD, I SAW A COLORFUL GLASS DOME THAT ADMITTED LIMITED LIGHT.

I ENTERED INTO A HUGE SILENT CHAMBER WITH TWO CURVED FLANKING STAIRCASES MEETING IN THE CENTER OF A SECOND STORY. ROAMING THROUGH THE QUIET GROUNDS, I TOOK A PHOTO OF THE CAPITOL FROM THE PARK'S SOUTHEAST CORNER.

Exiting the stone-quiet building I found I still had the grounds all to myself, now oblivious to the bustle of the boulevard. I was lost in thought reflecting in the irony that these noble columns of supposed Greek architecture were not worthy of the Japanese harsh occupation of Korea during the Japanese Imperial Period of 1910-1945.

I stood only for a moment, sun-burning on the unshaded capitol steps, on one of several visits on that hot summer day somewhat agitated under the unyielding sizzling sun—perhaps upset at the foreign aggressive occupation of my Korea that this bare building represented. Yet, I took in this splendor: the capitol building was all mine, as were the gardens, the structures, and the bustling boulevard—all paying homage to me from my vantage point at this Far East corner of Asia.

Inchon Adventure
July 1965

Tapings and whisperings and moisture too
Puffings and huffings of dampness do
Enter and freshen and exit through
My still wakeful world of thought and view

The mellow downpour on the Quonset's roof soothed my mood during that September monsoon sleepless evening of 1965. I felt the slight sway of my protective mosquito netting as the cooler refreshing breezes entered through the small windows and door of the barracks. As I opened my eyes to distinguishable shapes and shades, outlines of dark wall lockers against the lighter curved walls greeted me. Available light imparted progressive shadows of graduated grays. Complacently, I rolled over and settled into a more comfortable prone position. Mentally, I began retracing my adventure to Inchon on the west coast of Korea.

Sneaky as usual, I remember I went to a business in Seoul and used their Underwood typewriter to enter Inchon on my pass to validate the outing. As company typist and originator of the only document, I could do so without question. The train ride was rather pleasant, but the scenery was unattractive with increasingly deteriorated buildings and no countryside or rice paddies to alleviate the depressing view. The Inchon Train Station was a plain windowless concrete plaster structure with many wet spots on the bare concrete floor. A short stroll away from it led one to the deserted beach. As usual, the sun displayed its midday brightness and warmed the entire paradisiacal panorama. Here, I was gratified to discover I had it all to myself! I saw no humans or animals, not even sea gulls! This view was like a sci-fi scene after life has been extinguished from earth leaving only a panorama bared of living things. The cloudless aquamarine-blue sky above graduated to a sapphire blue where it blended with the sea at the distant horizon. And perhaps the searing sun compounded by the sea's reflection magnified the broiling ambiance. From faraway, the Yellow Sea's approaching swells slowed down to white foamy ripples and tiny bubbles at the sandy seashore. The waters that lapped toward me were reflected on the partial mirror shine of my now sandy low quarters. An empty, somewhat bluish, bright world spread before me, not unlike the scenic Polynesian Islands described in *The Bounty Trilogy*. I gazed across the expanse of water toward an island in the distance with tropical vegetation that displayed a weak semblance of the tropical paradise I read about in my childhood pirate and navy books. If the two lackluster black and white ships farther out were examples of the navy, I was thankful I had joined the army after all.

IF THE TWO LACKLUSTER BLACK AND WHITE SHIPS FARTHER OUT WERE EXAMPLES OF THE NAVY, I WAS THANKFUL THAT I HAD JOINED THE ARMY AFTER ALL.

So this was the beachhead from where General Douglas McArthur had launched his famous amphibious landing that turned the tide in favor of the United Nations' forces during the Korean conflict! I imagined gray destroyers (at the present ship's distance) slowly looming from the blackened night. Then suddenly, the confident North Koreans caught totally by surprise, awoke to the horror of thunder. From the darkness, the colossal multi-barreled battleships' guns erupted flames as they burst the silence with repetitive missiles. The screeching tracers streaked and lit the glorious starlit night, all amid the thickness and acrid odor of sulfur and gunpowder. Suddenly, all the deafening rumble quieted to stony silence as I imagined hundreds of ghostly infantrymen in seeming slow motion spill from hundreds of troop carriers. I pictured terrified troops—some silently yelling and shouting from hollow mouths and others stumbling and falling upon the quiet waters. I visualized their empty eye sockets and grim faces under steel helmets all thoroughly drenched as they swallowed and slapped the salty water before reaching the sandy shore—the beach resembling a stirred ant's nest, all racing in one direction, inland. I sensed their mixed emotions among fear, laughter, and sobs, in this death-gripping scenario—myself among them. Then the startling thunderous gunfire resumed and the accelerated beach assault continued with the predawn heavens tearing themselves apart with cross fire. Suddenly, a vendor of huge concord grapes broke my bubble of dreams rudely intruding on my images.

Buying a cluster of oversized berries from the vendor, I found a bench under a weatherworn paint-flaked white canopy. Despite this less-than-heavenly scenario, I self-indulgently imagined a scantily leaf-clad maiden from Polynesia peeling and dropping the fleshy dark purple juicy grapes into my mouth one by one, as I lay back on the bench in self-pampered delight indulgently leaning sideways to spit out the seeds. Then, succumbing to further delusion, I partially realized my life-long dream of having the company of that alluring maiden at some paradisiacal island as I fantasized with a drop-dead gorgeous hula girl—her long jet-black hair with blue reflection flowing down her perfect physique. I had always dreamed of chasing a light-brown haired well-endowed scantily draped fairy in white transparent gossamer around some crystal pool of water or around trees in the coolness of a grassy forest somewhere. Aahhh! but this was excitable ecstatic Eden, all duty free and free of duty. The thought never crossed my mind, if only my friends and family could see me now! In fact, I was a universe away from home and, this was one more adventure I freely pandered to and treasured for its audacity. The perfect seashells I had picked up broke up into little fragments and did not survive the trip back to camp.

Returning to earth with eyes again into the darkness (and visions of sweet fairies disappearing), I glanced around to the other sleepers' silhouettes through the blurry obscurity of the net oblivious to my imaginary escapades. My sleep-blurred vision traced the indistinct gray shades, shapes, and shadows in this dark stone-quiet world as I desperately tried to regain the delicious details my earlier musings.

The gentle whisper of the fine drizzle, however, was unable to lull me to sleep because my unyielding excitement gave me no relaxing rest or deep sleep in this quiet night at this Far East corner of Asia.

I REMEMBER LEISURELY MEANDERING THROUGH THE GARDENS AND MUSEUM AT THE DUK SOO PALACE LOST IN WONDER AND COMPLACENCY TAKING IN SO MUCH AND REMEMBERING MUCH LESS!

Duk Soo Palace
July 1965

Walking up and down the halls
Wand'ring round the outdoor stalls
Crowns of gold and cats of stone
Buddha statues reverent zone

I resumed my adventures as I recalled a very pleasing tour of the popular Duk Soo Palace in downtown Seoul. I strolled through extended grounds with pagodas and a huge modern museum of Greek architecture. In the museum, I saw ancient stone doorknockers, vertical cylinder locks, gigantic two-story or multi-armed Buddhas, royal 24K gold jewelry and crown, freestanding statues, ancient lion's heads, gate/door guards, and more. Then I caught sight of a row of antique cars exhibited under a tiled porch in the open grounds. Another palace of great proportion that I visited was Changduk. The extensive flagstone courtyard via extended walkways led to a huge palace also with tile upward-turned roof corners. Interestingly, small statutes of roaming monkeys topped the roof. The walls were intricately designed with more red than yellow and gold, and all outlined in black. Would I ever again come across these wonders? I remembered leisurely meandering through the gardens lost in wonder and complacency—taking in and photographing so much and remembering less of this Far East corner of Asia!

GREEK ARCHITECTURAL ENTRANCE TO DUK SOO PALACE MUSEUM

I SAW A MYRIAD OF BUDDHA SCULPTURES AND A STONE DOORKNOCKER AT THE DUK SOO PALACE MUSEUM.

ANTIQUE CARS WERE EXHIBITED UNDER A TILED PORCH IN THE OPEN GROUNDS.

ANOTHER PALACE OF GREAT BEAUTY AND PROPORTION WAS AT CHANGDUK.

SOME OF THE STATUES WERE MEDIEVAL WARRIORS CLAD IN ORNATE ARMOR WITH INTRICATELY CARVED SWORDS, HELMETS, AND MESH CHAIN MAIL.

Keum Kok Royal Tomb
July–August 1965

Armored warriors of sculpted stone
Lined with beasts from faraway zones
Grotesque bizarre they all appeared
To a foreigner all seemed weird

I was rudely returned to the present from pleasant memories by the stomping boot steps on the damp grade outside the Quonset. I was still wakeful under the monsoon drizzles and lost in deep thought. Subsequently, I became aware of the increased rain and a fresher breeze-flow that filled the Quonset. As I lazily lifted my eyelids and rolled my eyes toward the open door, I caught sight of the passing sentry. Glimpsing his poncho as it covered his torso from his helmet and draping downward, I chuckled at his probable soaked blouse and socks. Too involved in my reminiscing world to give the sentinel further attention, I let him amble past without a passing thought.

My mind raced back to an adventure somewhere in East Seoul. It was under one of those overcast premonsoon Korean skies that I attended a tour sponsored by the Yongsan Service Club where I visited the Keum Kok Royal Tomb. As I exited the bus at a grassy park, I caught sight of a double line of human and animal stone statues before a grove of towering trees. The oversized sculptures stood facing one another as if in respect to a procession. Some of the statues were medieval warriors clad in ornate Oriental armor with intricately carved swords, helmets, and mesh chain mail. Some animals were fashioned like horses, camels, lions, tigers, and elephants. All the animal statuary appeared somewhat bizarre and unearthly, but perhaps this was the Korean influence at reproduction of mid-Asian and African animals. I could best describe this menagerie as a combination of astrological figures and grotesque animal sculptures, fashioned like a fanciful chess set from memory by alien visitors. Perhaps these sculptures were an impressive royal introduction of foreign beasts to this remote Asiatic country. Yet all were finely crafted and fascinating, and of contemporary concept.

AS I EXITED THE BUS AT A GRASSY PARK, I CAUGHT SIGHT OF A DOUBLE LINE OF HUMAN AND ANIMAL STONE STATUES. SOME ANIMALS WERE FASHIONED LIKE HORSES, CAMELS, LIONS, TIGERS, AND ELEPHANTS.

ALL THE ANIMAL STATUARY APPEARED SOMEWHAT BIZARRE AND UNEARTHLY.

AT THE END OF THIS HONOR GUARD WAS A PAVILION AND BEHIND THE PAVILION WAS AN EXPANSIVE GRASSY MOUND.

At the end of this honor guard was a pavilion and behind the pavilion was an expansive grassy burial mound. The burial hill was about twenty-five feet in diameter within a finely lattice-patterned sculptured stone and quality masonry embrasure. A few stone posts about two-feet thick topped with oversized box-like receptacles and portholes for flames with upward curved corners once illuminated the imposing shrine. The well-preserved structures and gardens were so authentic that I felt transported back in time. The gray stone common to Korea resembled granite or rough marble, and appeared somewhat porous in nature. The entire royal burial ground was an enchanting Oriental setting, remote and peculiar, yet unique in nature and time. I stood in the midst of this ancient splendor under light gray, occasionally sun-lit, skies, reminding myself that I could never recompense Uncle Sam with enough tax revenue to cost-effectively realize another of my childhood dreams. Sighing, I took another deep breath as I reminisced my night away. As a naive youth I had no responsibilities waiting stateside, not a care in the world. Aahhh! but what silent stone statuary, and to think that my Uncle Sammy paid me to be here!

THE BURIAL HILL WAS ABOUT TWENTY-FIVE FEET IN DIAMETER WITHIN A FINELY LATTICED-PATTERNED SCULPTURED STONE AND QUALITY MASONRY EMBRASURE.

A few weeks earlier I had made a short trip to another pagoda at a grassy park. My picture was taken next to a statue of what appeared to be a Chinese or Japanese samurai-like soldier in a standing guard position. Both hands held his sword with the hilt at his chin and the point in the ground, yet he seemed asleep or in meditation. The meaning of this unusual, perhaps surrender, stance is still a mystery to this Latino. The Oriental soldier stood before a medium-size, red, temple-like building. It uniquely featured a portico with round columns, and a tile roof with upturned corners. It was not a burial chamber; but perhaps the Chinese or Japanese built it during the occupation.

A STONE SCULPTURE OF A JAPANESE SAMURAI SEEMED ASLEEP OR IN DEEP MEDITATION. A MEDIUM-SIZE TEMPLE-LIKE BUILDING BORE RED FACADE AND COLUMNS, WITH A TILED ROOF.

Sleepily, I regained awareness of the pleasant beating of the preautumnal rain as it tapped on the Quonset. I finally sank into delicious slumber of unconsciousness amid the gratifying pitter-pattering sounds though I clearly remember reflecting, "September nineteen sixty-five, the happiest month of my life." Aahhh! but I was in happy harmonic heaven, the month of September... Sep*tem*ber... Sep... tem... ber... Sep... zzz—*poof!*—And *ah* yes, zzz, the anticipated *thrill* of next month's prodigies in The Land of the Rising Sun: Japan, *Tokyo!*—Another dream coming true!... zzzz. Oh, but woe was me!... zzzzzz. How I suffered in The Land of the Morning Calm!... zzzzzzz.

Inclusion

Sometime in my childhood, I viewed the motion picture *Buck Privates* with Bud Abbot and Lou Costello. This army-themed film especially impressed me with the Andrews Sisters' lively rendition of "The Boogie Woogie Bugle Boy of Company B." The trumpeter played a short jazzed version of the reveille bugle call which sounded off each morning from the loudspeaker on the pole just outside my hooch Number Ten. But, most nights in the darkness of the hooch lost in reminiscing thoughts, I never ceased imagining that the peal was performed by *our* Company B bugler, a stone's throw down the BLV at the foot of Easy Queen.

Epilogue

Ah, but it was on such transcendental nights that I greedily gorged on delightful encounters and experiences and wonders in this exotic Far East corner of Asia.

AT KAMAKURA, JAPAN, I DAWDLED BY DAIBUTSU, WHERE I STOOD AT THE EXACT SPOT WHERE CANTINFLAS STROLLED SUFFERING HUNGER PANGS IN THE EPIC MOTION PICTURE *AROUND THE WORLD IN EIGHTY DAYS* OF 1956.

Chapter 17

The Land of the Rising Sun

October 10, 1965

I might have been born in a hovel but I am determined to travel with the wind and the stars.
—George Eliot

Prologue

Thr-r-r-r-r-BANG! Thr-r-r-r-r-BANG! Thr-r-r-r-r-BANG-BANG went the Pacific Stars and Stripes cargo airplane repeatedly over the Sea of Japan on its way from Kimpo AFB to Tokyo. At every bang, the ten-passenger little Army newspaper propeller transport plummeted what seemed a mile to my stomach. My dinner, which was controlled by my equilibrium, was about to regurgitate. The stewardess approached me and asked me if I was sick. All I could do was nod. She brought me a cup with two pills and some water. After taking the medication, I felt better. I was on my way to *Tokyo! Japan!* And if my stomach had to pay this price for flying me there free, it was well worth it. A double cheer for Uncle Sam and my fellow tax payers!

Flying o'er the Chosen skies
Eastward where the sun doth rise
Different culture 'most the same
Thrilled at travel t'was my aim

I was walking from childhood dreams into reality! And here I was, realizing one of those television travel programs. I cannot remember landing in Japan, only that I began scheduling my tours at the Kishine Barracks Service Club. All were ten- or eleven-hour tours. I had no idea where to go or what to see but I knew that whatever I signed up for would be of superinterest because this was *Japan!*

PLANE TICKET

STATION

ARMY HOUSING

The first tour available was of Tokyo. I remember, the streets were crammed with vehicles and traffic was heavy. We got to ride up the Tokyo Tower where I heard a description via a telephone in Spanish but was so garbled, it sounded like a girl's comical voice through a bottle. I took a picture of the panorama and another by a mosaic. We were turned loose on the *Ginza*, the greatest business street in Tokyo. I wandered aimlessly around and ended up in a *Mikimoto* pearl jewelry store. There were thousands and thousands of pearls on gold jewelry set on black velvet backdrops within glass counters and enclosures. At a store, a pretty Japanese girl beckoned me, took my hand, and with a pencil-thick fabric emery-shaped board, smoothed and then buffed my nails without polish. I thanked her and walked out. We took a short tour of the Olympic stadium where the competitions took place only the year before. A bunch of plump preteen girls surrounded me for pictures and I gladly complied. We went to a castle where the emperor resided. It was a white pagoda-like building with crossed rooms and floors, and raised corners that arose from a moat. Then we went to the Meiji Shrine where I saw so much Japanese arched architecture that after a few moments all appeared similar. I cannot remember more, other than I took many photos, as usual. I remember my picture buddy and I took a cab to a sex drug store that night. Well, being nineteen and full of mischief, he purchased a tiny tube of ointment that he thought would not work, but which alarmed him. The following morning he reported that he had a scare all night, that the application kept him up all night with his manhood in full prep—I chuckled the entire morning until he receded by midday!

THE STREETS IN TOKYO WERE CRAMMED WITH VEHICLES AND PEDESTRIAN TRAFFIC WAS HEAVY AS WELL. COMPARE 1950S BUS AT LEFT WITH LATE MODEL AT RIGHT.

VIEW OF TOKYO SKYLINE AND TOKYO TOWER

IMPERIAL PALACE GROUNDS

GATE TO IMPERIAL PALACE

OLYMPIC STADIUM, TOKYO

INTRICATE COLORFUL ARCHITECTURE, A BUDDHIST PRIEST, AND ME ACTING CRAZY.

ENORMOUS TORII ENTRY TO SHRINE

MEIJI ROOF ARCHITECTURE AND PAGODA FRONTED WITH BUDDHA STATUE

MEIJI SHRINE DWELLING, COMPARE ANCIENT STONE LIGHT BOX WITH MEDIEVAL WOOD.

We attended a musical stage show at the Kokusai Theater consisting of several different performances. The entire production was about a two-hour duration by an all-girl cast. An overwhelming performance began with the curtain opened to reveal a fantasy-like scene of gigantic people-size mushrooms and colorful fruits of all kinds. It was the girls dressed as this produce and they sang and danced so many international numbers but I can only remember the South American carioca. The dancers' heads were adorned with fruits including yellow bananas and pineapples draped with purple grape clusters. The music and the dancing accelerated to the ecstasy of the audience—I was overwhelmed with the music, dancing, and costumes. Then some centered the stage and performed the maypole game entwining and untwining pastel-colored silk ribbons on a pole. The entire performance was a colorful spectacle on grand scale!

The curtains opened to a scene of a quiet very well decorated life-like village in a colorful medieval Japanese setting like in the motion picture *Shogun*. Villagers were going about fishing, mending nets, others keeping house, raking ground, and about their daily life. All of a sudden, samurai warriors attack, the villagers scatter, but are chased, captured, and enslaved, with their possessions taken. The next scene is of an Oriental throne room with an emperor, his retinue, and people, all sporting kimonos and contemporary silks as in the movie *Geisha*. Colorful silks hang from the ceilings, and the walls are opulently decorated with silk paintings. Some village folk approach the emperor, seemingly petitioning their plight. The throne room is assaulted by the samurai, and a great battle scene ensues of defenders and aggressors displaying fine swordsmanship with their clashing samurai swords each time ringing out sparks of fire. Tongues of flames spew everywhere, and back stage smoke arises and emerges into the audience creating an involvement of the viewers. The stone walls fall and silk hangings wave down to the floor as the defenders defeat the attackers, and the curtains close to a thunderous applause.

Then the theater lighting was subdued and the stage was an entire black scene. With spotlights from each end of the stage entered two girls dressed as bugs, one in a white lacey sizeable evening dress and the other in a tuxedo, each with white wings. Walking toward center stage, they hugged and held hands so that the spotlights merged and then proceeded strolling to the stage's right. A spotlight lit another girl bug at the stage's left, and as she began singing *"Stardust,"* the couple began dancing and ascending a hidden arch always upward toward the upper left ceiling corner through the duration of the song. As the song and dance ended, both spotlights slowly diminished to a roaring applause. I can only say that I was overwhelmed and awestruck by the entire production. I regretted taking few photos of best quality due to distance and limits of my flash.

ALL GIRL DRAMA THEATER

At Hakone, we drove to a place in the mountains where there was much steam arising from the waters of the lakes and boulders. Then we rode extendedly on a cable car for what seemed like miles, but it was very enjoyable looking down at the rising steam. Someone bought and ate a boiled egg. I met a bunch of schoolgirls that surrounded me, and being the oddity they insisted taking pictures with me. I could not make myself understood in English, Spanish, or Korean, but we did understand picture taking. They clumped around me taking turns photographing me with the group. While they were only aged around fourteen, I could not help but giggle with flattery. Aahhh! but I was at a jovial Japanese jubilee, with most expenses absorbed by my favorite rich Uncle Sam. I remember, we next took a subway to Gotemba, and then boarded a ship that took us around a lake and we got to see the distant peak of Mount Fuji which was partially hidden in the mist.

ON HAKONE SHIPPING LINE BOUND FOR KAMAKURA; AFT OF SHIP HOLDING JAPAN FLAG.

SCENERY FROM SHIP DECK WHILE BOUND FOR HAKONE AND KAMAKURA

SCENIC FOREST VIEW WITH TORII IN CENTER WITH MOUNT FUJIYAMA IN BACKGROUND OBSTRUCTED BY MIST

I MET A BUNCH OF SCHOOLGIRLS THAT SURROUNDED ME, NONE SPOKE ENGLISH, SPANISH OR KOREAN; AND BEING THE ODDITY, THEY INSISTED TAKING PICTURES WITH ME. WHILE THEY WERE ONLY AGED AROUND FOURTEEN, I COULD NOT HELP BUT GIGGLE WITH FLATTERY.

The crowning tour was my visit to *Daibutsu*, the giant Buddha at Kamakura. I cannot express how excited I was, as here was where *Cantinflas* in the 1956 motion picture *Around the World in Eighty Days* wandered while lost in Japan. I had my picture buddy take a photo of me at the exact spot where the movie actor enters the scene just in front of the giant Buddha. Aahhh! but I was in elated East Eden as I dawdled around the grounds; behind, beside, and below the sculpture—probably open-mouthed with flared nostrils as I just could not get enough of the attraction—all at a grand total cost of eighty dollars (and in reality, Uncle Sam footing the entire bill)! There were hundreds of Japanese children on excursions and tourists. It was at Kamakura that I rambled down a street with antiquated shops seemingly in a turn of the century setting like in the movie *Geisha*. Then down the street came a procession of boys in similar attired silk black shirts and gold shorts carrying a decorated box. They seemed to squirm and rotate all over the street as if they were inebriated. Following them was a comical figure dressed in long red robes with long hair and a mask with a long nose. They passed me by and made their way down the street.

STREET SCENE IN KAMAKURA, JAPAN

A PROCESSION OF BOYS CARRYING A DECORATED BOX WAS FOLLOWED BY A COMICAL FIGURE DRESSED IN LONG ROBES, HAIR, AND NOSE.

Epilogue

I cannot stress enough the excitement I experienced on this unique treasured adventure. There was so much to take in that it was impossible to remember unless preserved on photo paper. This was one of four main reasons for joining the service. A dream come true; three cheers for Uncle Sam and the United States of America from this Far East Land of the Rising Sun Island of Asia!

Chapter 18

Camp Blue Lancer Valley

June 16-November 19, 1965

Prologue

Blue Lancer Valley just seemed to bring elated closure to the remaining five months of life and duty to my tour in Korea. To my free from care spirit, the BLV was paramount of all camps where the majority of my dreams materialized. It was here where I also experienced the best of daily life the army had to offer.

My Commanding Officers
Korea, 1964-1965

Prologue

I was blessed with fine commanding officers from the very start of my arrival in Korea, namely, First Lieutenant James R. Daniels and Captain Walter M. Baker, who approved every pass I applied for. Officers were usually involved with command-level business leaving the Noncommissioned Officers (sergeants) in charge of the lower ranks. The less we had to do with our commanding officers the better, as it usually involved some kind of serious disciplinary action or promotion, but I have fine experiences to relate.

Silver bars on shirts and caps
Men who ruled from Rev to Taps
Kindest hearts I ever met
Must have thought of me a pet!

Lieutenant James R. Daniels was the commanding officer of Personnel Service Center Number Three (PSC#3) at Camp McGovern and later at Personnel Service Center Number Two (PSC#2) at Camp Ross when we relocated on March 1965. The way I understood it, Lieutenant Daniels rose from the enlisted ranks to commissioned officer status. His gray eyes smiled through his glasses and seemed to kindheartedly peer into my very soul. He was the kind of man that immediately earned one's respect and I for one, could not help but like him. Even though he freely volunteered Personnel for increased guard duty, he was not disliked. It was just one more "added hardship" duty we had to endure in this tour of duty.

I was first introduced to Lieutenant Daniels at PSC#3 at McGovern when I was called "on the carpet" at CO's office. Instead of remaining in camp to help unload the trucks from the November field problem on my week one in Korea, I had run off to the recreation center. Terrified upon entering his office with crossed unit flags behind his desk and the familiar division crest, I stammered whatever words came out of my mouth, this being my first experience before an army officer for disciplinary action. I knew I would be heard and justly disciplined unlike accusations at home along with undeserved floggings without explanations. After a short lecture, Lieutenant Daniels waved me away saying, "Consider yourself reprimanded." Taking my reprimand with a healthy excretory system, I waddled out on shaking legs that felt like wet noodles on a slippery floor. Recalling the incident decades later, I recognized the amusement in his kind whimsical eyes—I believe he quietly chortled at my terrorized expression and demeanor.

"*Very nice, is this all you have to do?—Lt. Daniels,*" the commanding officer wrote beneath the rough pencil sketch I had left on my desktop. The CO had conducted a surprise inspection while I was away. I was designing a photo album cover that I wanted custom made in Yongju-Gol.

I examined the smear-rubbed pencil sketch closer to see exactly what the CO had viewed. On an arch across the top I had: "ADJUTANT

GENERAL CORPS" and drawings of the cross sabers with 15th Admin Co, the Personnel crest, and the Cavalry crest just below. Across the middle I had written, "PERSONNEL SERVICE DIVISION," next "JULIO A. MARTINEZ," while the fifth line bore, "EIGHTH UNITED STATES ARMY FAR EAST PACIFIC—KOREA," lastly, with my years of service "1964-65" at the bottom. I took it to Oggie at Miss Lee's Variety and Souvenir Shop in Yongju-Gol. A few weeks later it was delivered for a whopping price of twelve dollars!

Lieutenant Daniels never mentioned the sketch again and I never reminded him! It was all part of goofing off in Personnel on government time.

I DESIGNED A PHOTO ALBUM COVER THAT I HAD CUSTOM MADE IN YONGJU-GOL.

"*Allllright*, let's get back to work," Lieutenant Daniels raised his authoritative and well-known voice as Colour Sergeant Bourne's growl at the British soldiers gazing at the departing "Durnsford Horse" (cavalry) in the motion picture *Zulu*, starring Stanley Baker and Michael Cain. Similarly, all of us returned to life from our trances when we as one turned toward him. Privates and even the sergeants, had swiftly emptied the offices at PSC#2, Camp Ross, when, like kids chasing a fire engine speeding to a fire, we had all rushed outside to observe the airplanes. At the sound of his voice though, everyone immediately complied and returned from our skyward trance "to the salt mines." The CO must have chuckled, realizing a normal reaction from his command that had not seen jets for about half a year.

A FLIGHT OF JETS THUNDERED OVERHEAD, A RARE SIGHT THIS CLOSE TO NORTH KOREA.

"Why was that light turned off?" Lieutenant Daniels, roared as he entered our hooch for Saturday inspection. Terrified, I had just clicked it off in order to partially darken the hooch so as not to reveal imperfections. All the guys had barked at me to turn it off before his arrival but I had hesitated. The CO walked down the hooch and around every bunk inspecting every foot- and wall-locker. In some cases, he overturned improperly made bunks. Then I trembled as he drew closer. Approaching my bunk, he picked my Book of Mormon from the footlocker and hummed, "Um*humm*," indicating what I took to be approval. I breathed a sigh of relief as he continued to the next bunk, and left through the back door.

Captain Walter M. Baker was the commanding officer of the First Battalion Twelfth Cavalry. Since I worked in the orderly room under his direct supervision, I sensed he acknowledged my awkward and blundering personality and tolerated me. The captain always seemed so understanding and pleased with me that I fell in immediate disfavor with Top and the other two clerks plus the recreation sergeant. These four soldiers seemed envious of the captain's friendliness, and ridiculed me mouthing off stuff like, "You walk around this orderly room thinking you're better than the rest of us." I really had no idea what they were talking about. I was oblivious to their comments as I reveled in my own world of tourism rather than that of soldiering. Even though I was ham-fisted with my typing and my documents, the captain made no comment on my mediocre performance and allowed me to slide through by the seat of my pants without incident.

"Who the hell do we have here, Gypsy Rose Lee?" exclaimed the commanding officer as he inspected the assembled troops dressed as-is following a bungled alert. I reported to the orderly room, my duty station, in drawers and field jacket. Only ten minutes earlier, the alert sirens wailed all over the compound on an unexpected alert. Most of the year, we had known of the upcoming field problem and maneuvers—but this night the troops were caught totally unprepared necessitating a *fadeout* (cancellation). Before the ever-ready equipment could be donned, the blackout occurred. Needless to say, chaos ensued. The CO announced on the PA system that all troops report to duty stations as they were—so I showed up in my underwear and field jacket. One soldier showed up for duty in complete field attire including his protective mask! *That* was one for the books!

"Sir, I was able to add Hong Kong to my orders for my R&R next week," I happily informed the CO in the orderly room.
"How did you come by these orders? How did you swing this?" bellowed the captain as I stood smiling undaunted by his yelling.
"I telephoned Specialist Fifth Laboy in Personnel," I replied.
"Specialist Fifth Laboy," he roared, "I'll have to take action."
"You signed my 1049, Sir," I uttered, pretending puzzlement.
"What? Here, take your orders," the captain responded, "you make a mountain out of a molehill." He shoved the papers into my hands, turned to his office, and slammed the door.
I turned back to my desk undaunted but never-the-less bewildered as to why the captain had gotten so wound up.
"Martinez, why didn't you go on R&R to Japan prior to this assignment since you had more time in Korea than the rest of us?" Specialist Fourth H. annoyingly demanded of me, "now some of us can't go because of your absence." Unresponsively, I went about my business.

One morning there was great excitement in the orderly room. I overheard that several rare allocations were received for the advancement to grade Specialist Fourth. I heard that Top was promoting the two orderly room clerks, I was not included. Instinctively, I walked into the captain's office and—in what I realize today was in naïveté—flatly asked him if he would advance me to Specialist Four from Private First. I remember he smiled the entire time and I couldn't understand why. A few moments later as I sat at my table typing away, he walked out of his office and I overheard him telling Top, "Put Martinez on the promotion list." I just kept on typing nonchalantly as if nothing had happened and in time I did receive my promotion along with everyone else.

"Now, where's Martinez?" The first sergeant asked annoyingly.
"On three-day pass, sergeant" the orderly room clerks responded.
"Again? MAN!"
So Private W. interned in the orderly room advised me later.

MULTIPLE DAY PASS CERTIFICATE FOR 0600 HOURS 7 AUGUST '65 - 2300 HOURS 9 AUGUST '65 ALLOWING ME TO VISIT SEOUL AND THE DIVISION AREA

Epilogue

I remember a curious and kindhearted look in their eyes as if they were expressing amusement at my every word, request, or explanation, even as I ignored the chain of command. I felt the same way in the presence of either man; each independent and unknown to one another and at separate occasions. I sensed a comfortable feeling somewhat like Oliver under the tutelage of Fagin, *favorably* portrayed by Ron Moody in the 1968 musical motion picture *Oliver Twist*. Somehow or other, I felt that I was doing something right amidst all my imperfections and deficiencies. I always felt comfortable in approaching or telephoning them directly without my immediate sergeant supervisor's authorization. Perhaps they saw straight through my naïveté, which may have reminded them of themselves at one point in their own lives while growing up. It could be argued that the Korea hardship duty tour tolerated more of this type of "casual insubordination" than stateside—a somewhat sweetening of the existent camaraderie. In any case, I was always granted my requests and in some cases, maybe, I overrode my immediate sergeant's recommendation if indeed I had asked for at it at this Far East corner of Asia.

Our KATUSA Brothers
June-November 1965

KATUSAs serve their time as due
As many times without a clue
They augment the USA
Without protest without delay

"*Pocho-nun chun-dae pom-buro o-ship-shee-o*," followed by, "Guards, fall in by the Orderly Room," I announced on the PA system that was heard all over the company area. My fellow clerks resented and criticized me as I summoned the KATUSAs (Korean Augmentation to the U.S. Army) to guard mount in their native language. I was unconcerned; I even broadcasted my Korean brothers by their first names and initials. Not even the first top sergeant could silence me, until the captain in a mildly annoyed voice asked me to "call out the guard" in English.

The Republic of Korea (ROK) surely selected their finest mild-mannered soldiers to augment the U.S. Army. I immediately noticed that the ROK soldiers were teenagers serving their time just as us GIs. These brothers were sharing the same hardship as their American buddies, only with an occupying force within their own country. However, they never seemed to have a life. They always seemed to be on the guard duty roster. I saw the KATUSA as gunners on jeeps most of the time during field problems. I encountered but very few KATUSA soldiers at McGovern and still even fewer at Ross.

I SAW THE KATUSA AS M60 GUNNERS ON JEEPS MOST OF THE TIME DURING FIELD PROBLEMS.

From the very beginning, I took a fondness to these guys. I knew that I could learn from them—their culture, language; perhaps visit their homes, that it simply would be the beginning of fine friendships. I remember I always respectfully addressed them with the suffix "*Shi*," meaning Mister. In return, I was unexpectedly addressed as Mr. Martinez. I felt somewhat uncomfortable as I experienced a high respect for them, so I would not dream of claiming the appellation in return.

The monsoon maneuvers found me worn out from weeklong duty. Upon news of loading the trucks for departure, I found the tedious and tiring duty so disagreeable that I begged with a pleading frown like a kid with a tantrum to my KATUSA buddies for help. I kept repeating "*Oshipshiyo. Oshipshiyo*," meaning, "Please, please," whereupon two of my Korean buddies loaded my personal gear and field cabinets. I remembered some negative comments from my fellow workers, but I could not have cared less.

One summer night on Imjin stakeout, I left without my field jacket and became chilled to the bone. I asked my KATUSA buddy if I could borrow his jacket and he immediately wrapped it around me. I felt so relieved, my chills subsided. I felt as comfortable and safe as when I was with my older brother Beau, back at San Antonio as a preschooler. I recalled a night at the *Arroyo Alazan* (see photo p 29) when we bravely camped overnight. I awoke from the sound sleep of a four-year-old to a very loud croaking of bullfrogs. They filled the atmosphere and alarmed me so much that I began crying uncontrollably. Although my brother tried to comfort me explaining that it was only a bullfrog, nothing could convince me that it was not a giant monster which might dash out of the creek and swallow us up whole. Although I felt safe and secure with my brother, my hero, I was terrified that for my entire older brother's omnipotence, the monster might easily overpower even him. Since nothing could quell my terror, we left for home. My chills over, no monster emerged from the Imjin River, and I slept warm wrapped in my brother KATUSA's jacket.

Everyone liked Private Pak Bok Dong, he was the life of the party. He had an easy way about him. He was an excellent representation of the Korean soldier and youth. He was bubbly, full of life, and seemed to be everywhere laughing and carefree.

Corporal Kim Kap Jin was a clerk at the Battalion Headquarters. He was further into his service time. He had been looking forward to promotion to sergeant and was upset when he was passed up. I remember teasing Kap Jin as I had not been promoted to Specialist Fourth either due to lack of allocations at Personnel (I did fare better in the infantry). While Kap Jin was one of the wiser and more mature soldiers, he would have been happier had he been promoted. I looked to Kim for advice on Korean civilian matters.

Private Lee Soo Moo was a withdrawn soldier. Word came up one day to the orderly room that a GI had beaten him up. I remembered that Kim Kap Jin had typed a statement in English and Lee Soo Moo was signing it. It seemed that this super mild-mannered guy had crossed some big GI the wrong way and the big dude beat him up. I could not fathom what Soo Moo could have said, since he was such a docile soldier. Apparently, the more aggressive GI found Soo Moo an easy target. One has to remember that some GIs were draftees and hated not only Korea but thought little of the population, especially a Korean soldier of equal rank.

Kim Ahn Yang hardly spoke. He seemed spaced out and robotically turned his head left and right. He had a constant blinking problem. He was one of my favorite buddies. He never questioned orders or suggestions, and always did as he was told.

Jung was just as jovial and light-hearted as Pak. His hazel eyes that danced with mischief betrayed his youthfulness. He was always ready for tomfoolery. He and I got along fine during the monsoon season while sandbagging the river flowing from Radio Hill and South Queen. I once asked Jung if I could visit once the service was over, and Jung replied that he lived in Yong Dong Po.

FRONT ROW: JUNG, KIM; SECOND ROW: MARTINEZ, MOO, PARK, KIM.

Despite bunking, chowing, working, and enjoying certain of the U.S. Army's privileges, the Korean soldiers seemed to understand "their place." They never seemed to have a life. The only exception was when they attended the Blue Lancer Playhouse to enjoy an English movie. I never once knew of any of them smoking, drinking, or cussing. In fact, other than early chow designated for guards, I never remember seeing any KATUSA in the chow line or at the mess tables—soldiers or sergeants! They kept a low profile but were always there. They were always on the duty rosters. They never argued or complained. Rarely, only twice, could I remember a KATUSA acting dumb about being detailed to guard duty (detail differed from scheduled guard duty). I once remembered Captain Baker commenting something about sending "him back to the ROK Army." They freely accepted their plight and always seemed to "hold back." Perhaps *it was* a privilege to augment the American forces rather than serve their time in the ROK Army. Although their duty appeared double that of an American soldier, their salary was reported at one dollar and sixty cents a month! It was not a wonder that they could not afford the American luxuries they observed daily, those that their equivalent ranking U.S. brothers enjoyed. Perhaps something of the American lifestyle rubbed off on them that led some to higher goals. I felt privileged and overwhelmed that I served and shared in the hard-knock life equally with fellow soldiers from this Far East corner of Asia.

Prologue

It was a beautiful sunny morning in late summer following the monsoons and before the November "browning" fall season that I tuned my radio to the military channel upon my arrival at the orderly room. "Good Morning," the disc jockey announced, following the introductory trumpet peals of "The Mexican Shuffle." "Good Morning," he repeated with the instrumental sounds diminishing as his cordial voice continued, "This is your AFKN, American Forces Korean Network, Morning Report." I complacently yet absentmindedly lent ear to the news and programs. It was the memorable music of the classical sixties that made the late summer heat and humidity of 1965 tolerable all the time I stayed in Korea. As I reflected on the *songs of the day* via radio Tomahawk during that Indian summer, I reflected on my tour of duty. It was in that quiet moment lost in the gripping songs, while charge of quarters and the staff at chow that my thoughts raced back to a 1964 November morning.

Cavaliers and Tomahawks
November 1964–November 1965

Songs of sixties round the clock, News and time by disco jock
Mail from Home from Howze to Z, Tuned by comp'nies A to C
'Cross the Cav all lent an ear, Made the difference the whole year

♪ "DOWNtown, where all the lights are bright, DOWNtown," ♪ went the captivating lyric that held me in a hypnotic trance upon my arrival at PSC#3 Camp McGovern, that morning of November 1964. The keynotes, "DOWNtown," by Petula Clark's mesmerizing voice would forever haunt me. The lyrics resounded clear across the atmosphere, and the attention-grabbing melody reverberated from the nearby radio clearly visible on a desktop. The music enveloped the entire silent Quonset. The sun's rays filtered through a tiny protruding window and cast pale yellow sunbeams on the First of the Twelfth's 201 Files. My eyes were fixed on the sunspots that appeared like white blotches contrasting with the florescent lighting that momentarily bleached the print on the Leave Records. Mesmerized by the song, I was to always associate that emotional instant with my newfound military culture shock on that chilled Friday November morning. Thus did Radio Cavalier greet me on *day one* at Personnel.

While stationed at Camp McGovern, I recalled that the voluble ambience suddenly ceased on that chilly day in the office tent during the November field problem—Bobby Vinton's wailing falsettos of loneliness rent the air with "Mr. Lonely."

♫ *"Loan-LEE, I'm Mr. Lown-LEE*
I have nobaah-DEE, four my owe-OWN" ♫

Suddenly, the field cabinets ceased slamming, the staplers stopped snapping as did the staple pullers, the paper shuffling ceased as did the hole punching, and the typewriter clicking died away. The chitchat and jesting came to an unforeseen halt and it became as quiet as a graveyard, each mind on the memories the song triggered. Curiously, I turned to catch my peers withdrawn, remembering, reflecting human need for others and still others hypnotically entranced—their eyes staring into the air—by the feelings the songs revealed. I felt sorry for the melancholic guy singing on the radio, but was far sorrier for my fellow clerks absorbed in the privacy of their own thoughts. Strangely enough, although I mostly ventured out alone, I never felt lonely.

Then I remembered the November night at the end of my first weeklong field experience, that I stood air guard on the deuce-and-a-half in the pitch-black night. Despite this detested duty, I took my turn at the truck's rear with my head above the canvas cover, while the chilled wind of fecal stench, blasted and froze my face. My heart leaped as I caught sight of distant lights that twinkled against the black night. It seemed to me that the truck could not roll fast enough as I rode in anxious anticipation of the approaching wonders. I later learned it was the ever-popular village of marvelous Yongju-Gol. In my naïveté, the bright lights immediately echoed the song "Downtown."

♫ *"Where all the lights are bright, DOWNtown"* ♫

The radiantly lit mom-and-pop scrapwood slapdash pigeonholes that clustered along both sides of the road overwhelmed me as my sense of adventure kicked in. Open before me lay diverse wonders that awaited my buying pleasures in a land that was exotic and foreign to my hometown of San Antonio, Texas. Asiatic people swarmed and trotted along the earth-packed side paths and brightly lit shop canopies. Children ran wildly chasing the trucks—all amid diesel exhaust and the continual fecal stench. The Asiatic strokes that appeared on vertical signs as well as across the tops of the shack-like shops and on wood-framed storefronts all amid yellow lighting fascinated me to no end. My head turned left and right, and left and right as again the windows skipped by or blurred at every turn. The numerous canary yellow twenty-four karat gold rings behind a jeweler's glass window momentarily held my hurried attention. I was attracted to a blue silk kimono embroidered with yellow dragons at a back wall, while the sight of a stars-and-bars red, white, and blue Confederate battle flag overcame me. What Asiatic souvenirs in gold, silk, wood carvings, ceramics, lacquered wood with inlaid mother-of-pearl that I caught glimpses of and bargains were not mine as keepsakes? The truck rumbled along faster than my capability to devour the splendor of *downtown* Yongju-Gol—I had found places to see and things to do.

I STOOD AIR GUARD AT THE TRUCK'S REAR WITH MY HEAD ABOVE THE CANVAS COVER. THE MOM-AND-POP SCRAPWOOD SLAPDASH PIGEONHOLES THAT CLUSTERED ALONG BOTH SIDES OF THE ROAD OVERWHELMED DIVERSE WONDERS THAT AWAITED MY BUYING PLEASURES IN A *"DOWNTOWN"* THAT WAS BOTH EXOTIC AND FOREIGN. A MOMENT'S BREAK FOLLOWING ARRIVAL AT FIELD JUST PRIOR TO SETTING UP FIELD FURNITURE INSIDE OFFICE TENT WITH RADIO SOUNDS IN HAND.

"Did you know that you must meet weight requirements to qualify for reenlistment?" the DJ broadcasted, "see your reenlistment counselor for further information before your anniversary date."

"Who the hell was considering reenlisting while serving at this duty station," I chortled as I recollected the announcement while at Ross's tower by the water tank.

♪ *Dzeene, dzene-dzene-dzene, dzene-dzene,* **DZENE DZENE***, dzene,* ♪

Filled with instant emotion upon hearing the introductory organ buzzing sounds, and being alone in the orderly room with no one to oppose me, I raised the transistor's volume as my favorite song filled the empty Quonset.

♪ *"There she was just a WALKING DOWN the street, singing (Dooo wah diididdy diddy DUM DIddy do)"* ♪

"Do Wah Diddy Diddy" brought back to mind the sunny and chilly December day when I froze with emotion as I drank in the lyrics of Manfred Mann's song. In the romanticism of my youth, I had dreamed of a cute girl walking up to me like in the song and simply promenade around *downtown*. Now more than ever, I longed to stroll down the lane with a sweet "Do Wah Diddy" girl hanging at my forearm throwing me off balance. But not like the homely strumpets that walked up, clung to my arm, saying, "*Hooch hooch*" while I strolled through the greater villages of Pobwan-Ni and Yongju-Gol. The pulsating ascending and descending chimes vibrated my eardrums as my legs trembled. This particular haunting song along with the accompanying drums, choral singing, and organ background moved me so much that I decided to purchase a radio. I wrote home and requested my savings bonds be sent. I would then personally enjoy all the programming and popular songs I yearned to hear at will.

That December I rushed to the Bank of America at Camp Pelham to cash the bonds. I rushed to the Post Exchange and selected a Sony stereo AM FM radio that featured the luxury and privacy of white wired earplug. I then proudly joined the ranks of the radio-toting elite. I could count on both hands how many GIs owned radios during my entire tour of duty. I remember hurling my wailing radio strap across one shoulder and slinging my camera on the other, so that both straps crossed my torso and I was ready for another world of adventure.

My thoughts then wandered back to the freezing winds of 1964 and how they rolled into the cold conditions of 1965 at Camp McGovern Guard Tower Four. My eyes watered within my parka hood as the monotony of guard continued. It was the sole purpose of this overseas duty—"Guarding Freedom's Frontier," as the indoctrination brochures read, and for which the army paid me fifty-three dollars a month. The days cooled to February such that the fatigue jacket and Korean pile cap sufficed to ward off the occasional chills.

FIELD JACKET AND PILE CAP KEPT OFF THE FEBRUARY CHILLS WHILE ENJOYING MUSIC FROM RADIO IN AMMO POUCH PRIVATELY VIA THE LUXURY OF A WHITE EARPLUG.

From Guard Tower Two I scanned the nearby Personnel Quonsets as I recalled the indoctrination that took place there three months earlier. My mind flashed further back to the galvanized barbwire fence, the dusty road, a silver bus, and the alluring landscape which seemed alien months ago but which was now familiar territory.

One night I spied an uncommonly lit Personnel Quonset, and as duty warranted, I proceeded to investigate. Cautiously, I entered without first removing the radio's white earplug wire which extended from my ammo pouch. I found Mr. D., a Personnel Warrant Officer working late, and rightfully so, was not thrilled to view me with the radio's earplug. As he proceeded to berate me for it, he growled, "If you were on my guard mount,

I'd have you court-martialed." Duly chastised, I returned to the tower in a foul mood.

I called to mind a subsequent guard mount in the early spring, when I again stood at my favorite post, McGovern's Guard Tower Two. I glanced up, down, and over the barbwire fence—and then south across the rice fields toward Skoshi Nopae Dong that extended toward Queen's foothills at my extreme right. Thirty-five years later, I learned of a high-rise apartment complex at Skoshi's right, next to the Queen. Number Two was located by the Personnel offices between the colonel's tower and Number One. It was one of those pale-blue cool twilights turning into a classy blue-black evening over the calm land when AFKN aired the *Mail from Home* program. Ah, but "*Mail from Home!*" I sighed. This program featured the *day's* songs dedicated to soldiers from their stateside wives and sweethearts. I found myself jealously absorbed in their sometimes-suggestive messages. My arms crawled with bumps in Number Two at Andy Williams' "Dear Heart" dedication as I observed my post. I descended from the tower to walk the fence to break the monotony. Despite Andy Williams through the earplug, a rustling of foliage by the fence caught my ear as my boot touched the ground from the last rung. In full panic, I felt an adrenalin blood-rush to my head via my temples, as my heart palpitated wildly. With the swiftest single movement of my life and with the high rush of adrenalin I unslung the shotgun, aimed at the foliage and at the top of my lungs yelled, *"Halt!"* (I forgot all about the official painstakingly drilled challenge.) My panic reached a height of terror as an animal swift as lightening, turned and raced in the opposite direction screeching like a banshee. It was a cat, which was just as terrified of me as I was of it. I had only seen two cats during my entire year in Korea: a sickly white one on a leash in Seoul and this one. How it escaped the stew pot bewildered me. So much for sweethearts, "Dear Heart," and my still palpitating heart, I gasped!

The late spring found me one evening again at my preferred Guard Tower Two quite shaken following guard mount. "I'm gonna have your ass, Martinez," snarled Mr. D., the Officer of the Day, with menacing eyes, "if anyone filters through your post tonight!" He was the same Personnel officer who had threatened me about the radio sometime back. The night before, a back door to Personnel by Number Two appeared forced open and several Underwood typewriters were missing. The responsible guard was punished under Article Fifteen of the Uniform Code of Military Justice. I recalled a recent night when I crept upon Number Two's sentinel and startled him with a shove. The guard turned, cursed me, and resumed his beat. He was concentrating on his minitransistor, which made him an easy infiltration target. Why the guys did not take guard duty seriously was beyond my comprehension. It never occurred to me that "There but for the Grace of God go I."

Still quaking from Mr. D.'s threats, I stood sulking for a few minutes at my post. Then the land became stony quiet, not even crickets' singing rent the hushed atmosphere. It was that special moment of moments when my tinnitus, my sound of silence, was at its loudest. In due course, a girl's voice from the distant village broke the still twilight as she customarily sang, ♪"Yo SO so soo."♪ I relaxed—the OD's roaring now seemed unimportant, far away, and long ago. Only then did I feel reasonably comfortable to take out my radio from my magazine pouch. The clapping of the village generator further broke the evening's silence over the calm land.

♪ *CLAP-CLAP-CLAP-CLAP-**CLAP-CLAP**-CLAP-CLAP* ♪
♫ *"Bay-bee, bay-bee-baay-bee don't leave me"* ♫

Diana Ross's voice awakened new sensual drives and others I hadn't known existed. I visualized sparklers and meteor showers clear across the skies. Oh! But The Supremes' feminine voices, echoes, and lyrics of "Where Did our Love Go?" were liquid music that opened up passions and other sentiments I had never before experienced. Then yellow lights randomly dotted the hooches at the distant village that appeared snuggled along the mountains as the dusk brought in the darkness. I continued gazing toward Nopae Dong and pictured the tomfoolery within The Imjin teahouse and The Tavern. I imagined I could hear the merriment flowing across the cultivated rice paddies as surely as did the unholy fragrance of fecal matter.

EASTWARD FROM GUARD TOWER TWO, I VIEWED THE INDOCTRINATION QUONSET AT LEFT AND THE WINDOW THROUGH WHICH I HAD FIRST SEEN THE *KIMCHI* BUS ON THE ROAD THROUGH THE BARBWIRE FENCE. DISTANTLY WAS THE VILLAGE OF NOPAE DONG. A CAT SCREECHED LIKE A BANSHEE AS IT RACED OPPOSITE THIS VIEW AT LOWER RIGHT CORNER THAT GREATLY TERRIFIED ME, I BEING ALREADY ON EDGE. (SEE PHOTO P. 294)

FACING SOUTH FROM GUARD TOWER TWO WAS THE VILLAGE OF SKOSHI NOPAE DONG, WITH THE UNHOLY STENCH OF RICE PADDY FECAL MATTER PREVALENT. I WAS FOREVER MESMERIZED AT VIEWING THIS MURAL FROM NUMBER TWO.

Sundays I tuned to *The Crossroads of the West*, a religious program, when unable to attend services at Camp Pelham. I found great consolation during bunker, tower, and walking sentry duty while listening to the sermons by the Elders of the Church of Jesus Christ of Latter Day Saints. The fifteen—or twenty-minute inspiring sermons were taped broadcasts from Salt Lake City, Utah. The discourses were like purifying water to a thirsty man in an alien desert.

One time, I stood at Guard Tower Three, a stone's throw from the dreaded Number Four on my left and the colonel's tower on my right as I faced the camp. Again, I was lost in observing full circle the concertina fence, the Officers Mess, and the compound's recesses from Queen's skirts.

VIEW OF CAMP MCGOVERN FROM GUARD TOWER THREE, WHERE I TUNED IN TO THE AFKN *MAIL FROM HOME* PROGRAM TO THE CROONING VOICE OF AL MARTINO.

♪ *"EYE Lo-ve you because you understand dee-r*
Every single thii-ng I tra-eye to do," ♪

crooned Al Martino loudly through my earplug. His quavering emotional voice singing "I Love You Because" accompanied by the harmonized choir and female voice floored me in Number Three. Oh, but how the female soprano's voice liquefied my bone marrow that sent my hormones raging, skyrocketing, exploding with fireworks ranging higher than flying stars and comets!

While stationed at abhorred Camp Ross, I remember an early summer evening that the Officer of the Day discovered me with the radio on full blast less the earplug. However, the OD was the band director and perhaps because he was a professional officer of the arts, dismissed the radio by commenting that I had enough company in the camp's rear-most tower. Relieved, I chuckled having narrowly escaped an Article Fifteen punishment under the Uniform Code of Military Justice had he been an infantry officer. My favorite program that night was Lawrence Welk's *Champaign* music. At other times, *The Sod Busters* brought a pleasant old-time radio cowboy feature, and *Gunsmoke* provided further western adventures. I detested *The Tonight Show* with its mind-numbing presentations of weird celebrities.

Then while at Blue Lancer Valley, my thoughts prevailed upon the midsummer of 1965 and the joy it brought me with my transfer to the BLV; the radio station resumed the *romanticism* I previously experienced at McGovern. "This is your AFKN, American Forces Korean Network—Cavalier," the disc jockey's mellow voice broadcasted. His announcement was previously introduced by Kai Wynding's rendition of apparent guitar thrumming and of Jean-Jacques Perry's ondioline pulsating sounds of "More." The wavering music tapered and I remember complacently looking forward to one last full hour of pleasing programming.

"This is your AFKN, American Forces Korean Network—Tomahawk," the DJ announced. I noted that following reflagging from the *Cavalry* to the *Infantry* on July 1, 1965, the AFKN Radio Tomahawk had replaced Radio Cavalier.

I finally stood atop the Queen's summit absorbed in her breathtaking entirety that summer, 1965. The skyline breezes evaporated the beads of perspiration from my forehead. Pleased with myself, I removed my cap allowing the free flowing breezes to filter through my hair. I closed my eyes and deeply filled my lungs inhaling the windy mountain freshness. I continually rotated my head left and right to receive its full effect. The early monsoon droplets that lay on the abundant green foliage blanketed Easy. I basked in her resplendent windswept mountainous panorama of woody green hills and valleys that extended to the sloping far-flung circumventing western and southern horizons. I fantasized that all frondescence kowtowed to my Queen. I stood proud, envisioning all her vassals, consisting of visible military camps, surrounding rice paddies, and villages on her eastern and northern flank, kneeling at her skirts in reverent homage to me—who had ascended to her high and mighty bluff. She was all mine, my conquered Queen, my long-elusive lover. Despite the humidity, the cooling breezy effect was invigorating after the long ascent of Easy. I closed my eyes amid this lofty mountain grandeur as my nineteen-year carefree life swooned to the soothing piano sounds of Vince Guaraldi's "Cast Your Fate to the Wind" on the AFKN Radio Station.

I BASKED IN HER MAJESTY'S RESPLENDENT WINDSWEPT MOUNTAINOUS PANORAMA OF WOODY GREEN HILLS AND VALLEYS THAT EXTENDED TO THE SLOPING FAR-FLUNG CIRCUMVENTING WESTERN AND SOUTHERN HORIZONS TO THE PIANO SOUNDS OF *"CAST YOUR FATE TO THE WIND"* VIA AFKN RADIO STATION.

> ♪ *"[Sand in my shoes]*
> *Oohhh, Brings memories of the salty air*
> *[Sand in my shoes]*
> *Oohhhh, the blanket that we used to share"* ♪

The lyrics of "Sand in My Shoes," the falsetto up- and down-swings of The Drifters' male lead singer along with the haunting electric guitar sounds all accompanied by classic violins overwhelmed me. Oh, how I wished to have been with a "Do Wah Diddy" girl trembling and holding me "so tight down by the sea."

♫ *"[Under the boardwalk]*
People walking above
[Under the board]
We'll be falling in love" ♫

Ah, but the lyrics of "Under the Boardwalk" also by The Drifters sent crazed flares through my circulatory system. How I romanticized with that "Do Wah Diddy" girl at the Inchon beach where I gazed out at the distant Yellow Sea's horizon just dreaming with that elusive South Sea island girl. There were no French fries or hot dogs to be had but I did get to drop peeled concord grapes down my throat by that scantily clad nymph I always dreamed about if only in fantasy on that hot sweltering sunny summer day.

Switching from ear to ear, my eardrums again sensed the earplug's buzzing and reflected I could just take so much discomfort. Every night by ten o'clock while on guard, following all worthwhile programming, I called it a night. I turned off my radio, brought closure to another day, and resumed my undivided attention to my duty station: whether it was the broiling or freezing wind-sliced guard tower, or the tramping over crunching snows, or sloshing through the monsoon mud. Tuning in to AFKN was taboo on guard because the programming distracted from responsibility as with the startled guard at Number Two at McGovern. Yet, it was radio Cavalier, then Tomahawk, that maintained an emotional song of the classical mid-sixties in my heart day in and day out. It was the only luxury that made *guard duty*, the sole purpose of service in Korea *bearable*. I often wondered if the voice within the transistor ever sensed the emotional impact it had on the listeners all over the Western Corridor.

In the words of a disc jockey:

> "For almost a year I did the *Mail from Home* program of songs (mostly rock and roll) dedicated to 1st Cav troopers by wives and loved ones back in the States. The entire agenda lasted about an hour and a half Monday through Friday evenings at seven. Once in a while I had a Red Cross girl (Donut Dolly) to help read the dedications. The show was very popular and I could not play all the requests I got. The Shirelles' "Soldier Boy" was the most requested. Our radio station was

a compound of just five U.S. soldiers with a Specialist Fifth as the "station commander." One was an engineer and kept the station running with the help of a Korean National engineer. The other four of us each worked a six-hour "board" shift seven days a week. Most of the time I worked the 6:00 p.m. shift as PFC Dave Hagen. During the off time we spent a few hours preparing our next show. We always wondered if anyone was listening to us. I am glad you appreciated what we did. It makes it all worthwhile."

—PFC Dave Hagen, AFKN Radio Cavalier,
8th Army, Sonyu-Ri,
Korea, 1963-1965.

Inclusion

Once back stateside at Fort Bliss, Texas Radio Station KELP filled the El Paso air waves with the popular love song "Somewhere My Love." The melody moved me as the lyrics hit home and lingered in my hearing senses all day. My entire chest bounded and I experienced blood rushes to my temples as I was still foolishly romantic enough to continue visualizing myself again over the Queen with *songs to sing* at either Nullo-Ri or Nopae Dong, but especially at Blue Lancer—that something perhaps someone *somewhere a hill blossoms in green and gold*. I realized that although Korea was now a *dream all that your heart can hold* of the past, Korea was still in my system and the song emotionally carried me back. Needless to say my quixotic emotions kicked in such that I fantasized with a *dove of my own*—that *someday we'd meet again my love*, yet mine again only in my memory banks. Those were now yearned paradisiacal *out of the long ago* days that were once filled with my sweet mischief and wild adventures. Although I knew we'd never *meet again my love*, all was brought back to mind by way of "Somewhere My Love" by the Ray Conniff Singers. Significantly, but for this musical work, all combustion and celestial phenomena were snuffed out. The noisy barracks with apathetic soldiers suddenly became stone silent at the sounds of "Coming Home Soldier" and especially "The Green Berets" as many of our bunk buddies had shipped to Vietnam.

ENJOYING THE AFKN SOUNDS DURING GUARD DUTY AT THE TURK'S COMPOUND ONE-WAY SIGN DURING THE MONSOON SEASON

Epilogue

The troops returned from chow and resumed their administrative duties. Overwhelmed with my dreamy music, I walked out into the sunshine and humidity leaving the comfort and privacy of the orderly room behind. As I headed for the mess hall, my head reverberated with lingering melodies and lyrics. Aahhh! but I was swooning in the sweet sounding sixties, all with paid expenses. I reflected that throughout the freezing snows, drenching rains, or sweltering heat during my entire tour of duty at the Turk's and all camps' towers, the Imjin, wandering on pass, or clambering all over the Queen, it was the AFKN radio station monitored by the gallant disc jockeys that made *all* the difference. I must admit that during my entire romantic hitch in Korea, I was forever haunted by Ray Peterson's rendition of "Corinna, Corinna," recalling that the humming violins liquefied the very marrow in my bones, *but* with my own amorous words in substitution—*poof!*—

♪—*Blen~n~n~n~n~ng!*—♪
♫ *"I left Ko-re-AH, way across the see-e-e, (oh me)*
I left Ko-ree-ah, way across the see-e-e" ♫
. . . . at this Far East corner of Asia.

IT WAS NOT UNCOMMON FOR CLOSE BUDDIES TO SHARE MAIL FROM HOME, SINCE THE RECIPIENT AS WELL AS THE BUDDY WERE GRATIFIED. HERE (PFC) ABILIO MENDIOLA (RECLINED) SHARES MAIL DURING A SWEEP DETAIL BREAK.

Mail Call
November 1964–November 1965

Through rain or shine or hail or sleet
The names rang out with ours a treat
To know from home a written sheet
To share with pals without discreet

"SINCLAIR," Specialist Fourth McClain, the postman shouted. "Sinclair," the troops responded in unison. This repetition went on for several days as Sinclair would not collect his mail. Then someone shouted back, "If Sinclair won't take his letter, I will." A chuckle was heard throughout the congregated troops.

One would have to be away from home, *far far away* from home, across the world with only the comfort of a message in writing whether flying or sailing to and from home to understand the impact "mail call" had on a soldier in Far East Asia. We airmailed our letters at eight cents for a flight across the Pacific patiently waiting, as a five-cent stamp would take a message a month to cross the ocean. (Alexander Graham Bell and Uncle Sam were not yet synchronized as to the availability of long distance calling common to the average pocketbook). Our return address was our name, service number, our unit and the destination was APO San Francisco 96224. I located all my letters home so that I am able to publish my return addresses from all three camps where I was once recipient of mail from home with respective postmarks.

BEAUTIFUL AND COLORFUL STATIONARY WITH HISTORICAL KOREA SITE. I WAS STATIONED AT PERSONNEL SERVICE CENTER NUMBER THREE, CAMP MCGOVERN. POSTMARKED JANUARY 14, 1965.

ENVELOPE POSTMARKED APRIL 11, 1965; STATIONED AT PERSONNEL SERVICE CENTER NUMBER TWO, CAMP ROSS.

STATIONED AT CAMP BLUE LANCER VALLEY, POSTMARKED ON OCTOBER 7, 1965.

ON PASS DATED DECEMBER 25, 1964 BILLETED AT THE USO, DOWNTOWN SEOUL.

This was a time when long distance calls were sold dearly by the minute, and international long distance was an impossible dream to a soldier of the lower ranks. The average soldier hardly received enough spending money for health and comfort needs, let alone extra for telephone calls; and calling home was for the senior sergeants and officers. Suffice it to say a letter from home, from any home, from any person from across the Pacific was indeed *mail from home.*

The joy of one's name being called and being handed a letter was like water to a man dying of thirst. To hold the letter with both hands to ensure its reality, head for the warm Quonset, turn on the head lamp, and nestle on the blanket covered bunk was a delicious ritual. Then the rite of slowly ripping it open at a snail's pace, reading and savoring each word, each line, each curve, each dot, and each crossed t. At other times, impatience to savor the message would cause one to rip it open there and then, outside the mail room, and devour it. It was all part of the soldier's personal ceremony. Aahhh! but mail call, what sweet sour sounds, at the cost of a mere eight-cent stamp: a candy bar, soft drink, or a pack of chewing gum.

There were times when letters from sweethearts were the joys of some and the distress of nonrecipients. It was not uncommon for close buddies to share mail, since it gratified the receiver as much as the other reader who in turn shared in the recipient's happiness; and in effect, allowed him to read mail from home.

I had a newspaper subscription of the San Antonio Light delivered to me. About each week I would receive about six rolled-up newspapers. Although my mother went through the hardship of paying for a subscription, I hardly read the papers once they were delivered. They were not delivered to the camp; I had to go to Camp Howze Mail Room, about ten miles distant, to pick them up. The only importance they had to me was because it was constituted daily mail from home. I told the postman to throw them away, but he said he couldn't. He had to deliver them to me personally. Once I got them, I got an idea of how to get rid of them. I remember that I'd wrap my arms around a bundle of them and hop on the next truck going my way. From the truck's bed, I took particular enjoyment out of hurling them on the graded road and watch the Korean people pick them up. The other hitchers and I got a chuckle out of this as I rode all the way back to camp. The only newspapers that really choked me up were those of downtown San Antonio during the Christmas holidays, 1964. Oh, but how I missed the downtown streets where I used to cruise around especially the Wolf and Marx Clothing Store and the Joske's window. The Joske's Department Store, next to the Alamo, boasted a Christmas window that was an attraction all in itself. It was a seasonal tradition to visit and view it. There was always a crowd there. I remember a display, once, of many affluent children, seemingly of the twenties, with a Santa, gifts in hand, turning left and right in the motion of handing them to the children. Still, just having to catch a ride to far off Camp Howze to pick up the newspapers was an adventure in itself—especially seeing the people picking them up. I never once realized that to these Korean pedestrians it was like acquiring something valuable and foreign, and of use in their daily lives; paper, free paper.

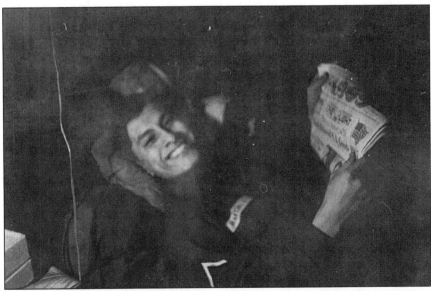

THE ONLY NEWS ITEMS THAT REALLY CHOKED ME UP WERE THOSE OF DOWNTOWN SAN ANTONIO DURING THE CHRISTMAS HOLIDAYS COMPRISING MY STOMPING GROUNDS DURING MY TEENS. THIS FRONT PAGE HERALDS THE 1965 NEW YEAR.

Once I received a letter from an Ester Martinez who wrote about her daily routine, but it wasn't until the end of the letter that she informed me that earlier that week they had laid flowers at grandmother's grave. My grandmother was alive, so I knew the letter wasn't mine. Anyway, I then wondered how many of mine were lost or delivered to another soldier with the same surname. To this day I am fascinated by Ester Martinez; God bless her.

It cannot be said enough that amid all the daily trials and tribulations experienced during the hardship tour of duty in Korea, one awaited that one hour that one lived for when one would approach the mail shack to hear the mail call. Just the trip to the mail room was medicinal. The hope of looking forward to a return letter was tonic. Upon one's name called, the relief that one had been thought of from home was life itself, and the envy of those who walked away with a fallen faces and glassy eyes with unshed tears at our Far East corner of Asia.

Wildlife of Korea
November 1964-November 1965

Cumulus puffs on cobalt skies
Mountain greenery extends and lies
Naught a snake or bee to sting
Ne'er a creature, foot or wing

Throughout my year of adventuring, I noticed something that was not. The entire striking Korean panorama and scenery was breathtaking. The colossal Buddha statues were astoundingly impressive. Seoul, with its hustle and bustle of human and reeking vehicular traffic diesel exhaust, was as busy as any major city in the United States. The people were of a different culture and as much a people as the Americans or Latinos back home. The villages, camps, rice paddies, mountains, and skies were void of something. It was unseen from buses, trucks, and trains. The military life had its ups and downs, yet there seemed an absence of what was obviously unaccountable. Something was not there that should be, unmissed sounds of nonappearances, unseen existence of absent objects. The absence of wildlife—normally taken for granted—was shocking, although some soldiers reported seeing and hearing rats in the village. Other than mosquitoes, and a few dogs that avoided becoming a meal, I had very little occasion to encounter animals in the ecosystem of Korea. Specialist Fourth Tinker reports that "In the summer months on the hill, we would run into huge moths! I could not believe how big these suckers were! We had to wear mosquito netting over our steel pots to keep them out."

As I wandered and traversed the picturesque mountain greenery of the Queen, I never once encountered the fauna of Korea. In my naïveté, I felt as safe from crawling or swarming potentially dangerous animals as under the house floorboards or at the Alazan Creek that I explored during my preteens. I had heard reports of snakes slithering about, and I did find a snake skull, but I never encountered any. According to Specialist Fourth Lynn Zolnoski, 122nd Signal Bn, TDY Blue Lancer Valley, Korea, 1966-1967, "There were a lot of big rocks around and I saw a brown-colored snake moving toward a rock. Not too far from there I saw a grey lizard sunning himself on another rock. I also saw some hawks flying overhead looking for prey and a few magpie birds sitting around too. I thought that was interesting as we had those black and white magpies back in Montana some eight thousand miles away. Maybe they originally came for the Orient? That was all the wildlife I ever saw in Korea as I am sure the Koreans kept the wildlife down." The DMZ brothers reported accidentally shooting deer that ventured into their perimeter. One would consider that water life would emerge during the monsoon downpours, perhaps croaking frogs, or maybe across the clear skies. However, according to Specialist Fourth Bruce Tinker ". . . it started to rain hard filling the flood control ditch up in front of the hooch. I don't know where the frogs came from, but it reminded me of the movie *The Ten Commandments*, when Moses called for a plague on Egypt. We had frogs up to our eyeballs; we were throwing frogs out the front door." Nesting fowl suddenly taking flight upon human approach could surprise one, but I saw none. Once, only once, did I chance to sight two pheasant ambling on Queen's foothills from the back of my Personnel office hooch at McGovern. Blue Lancer Valley's Captain Baker purchased two hunting dogs that he supposedly used for hunting pheasant, but I never learned of any success.

I only saw two cats in my entire year. One cat was a sickly white one on a leash in Seoul, and probably someone's status symbol or nonstew pot pet. The second encounter was while on guard duty one night at McGovern's Tower Number Two. The rustling sounds I heard that had terrified me, turned out to be a cat, which screeched away just as frightened.

On one of my adventures somewhere in the cavalry area, I came upon a pond with a flock of ducks swimming happily in the postwinter cold. On another occasion while on a *hopsan* to Seoul, a flock of huge white birds resembling swans emerged from a distant paddy causing delightful expressions from the vehicle's occupants.

I CAME ACROSS A POND WITH A FLOCK OF DUCKS SWIMMING HAPPILY IN THIS POSTWINTER COLD. NOTE *HOPSAN* AT PHOTO RIGHT.

At Camp Ross, I crushed a carpet of black beetles under the lampposts while at Tower Number One close to the main gate. These were more of a nuisance than wildlife.

Once in a while a GI would bring in a puppy from the village and feed it table scraps. Cecil, a Hooch Ten mascot at Blue Lancer, was such a camp dog that noticeably responded to anyone, once his master had DEROSed to the United States. I remembered that upon my arrival at McGovern I chanced to observe a litter of about eight puppies and mother. At Ross, Dagger gave birth to Lucky, fathered either by Chingo or Lifer.

The armistice had only been signed ten years earlier, and within that time it was conceivable that the fauna population would have survived off the fat of their war-torn land. It could not be surprising that in view of the extended poverty, the hungry human population would consume all available meat while awaiting the annual rice harvests. At the time of this writing, many rumors circulate that the Demilitarized Zone, the military-free zone separating North Korea and South Korea, could become a wildlife preserve once the borders are open. This no man's land has become a natural safe haven where all the native fauna, the wildlife of Korea, have been free for fifty years to abundantly repopulate this Far East corner of Asia.

Hi Bob, *Hello, Dolly!*

Left the camp to see a show
Lost mid soldiers, trucks, and snow
See a show to Seoul and Go
A sweet drag, sweet bore, so slow

On one of those cold shivery days in the late winter months of 1964-1965, some of us were trucked to Camp Beard to see the Bob Hope show. I remembered him as a kid when I collected lids from dime ice-cream cups from the ice-cream man's truck that upon saving twelve, I could trade for an eight by ten full-color picture of my favorite star. My very first picture was of Bob Hope. Although I wasn't crazy about Bob Hope, I always knew his overseas tours were loaded with pretty women and a few jokes, that were always welcomed by soldiers during my first few weeks in Korea and I would be one of them. I had also heard from time immemorial that Bob Hope was a treat as he was always visiting troops all over the world. I remember that I climbed onto a deuce-and-half at McGovern and trucked to Beard, who knew where? At Beard, all the guys and I jumped off the trucks and found a place among what were thousands of equally olive-green attired GIs.

I saw Bob Hope crack a bunch of jokes with a soldier named Love. Then he introduced a few lovely women, all in summery attire: Miss World and a singer, who was wearing a mink coat, took it off and revealed a white sparkly low-cut dress. She sang what the Stars and Stripes later claimed as top performance. I didn't think so. In the middle of the show it began to snow and we all huddled up. Then all the girls began singing "Look Me Over" and we all thought the show was over, so our entire troop of thousands of soldiers got up.

Bob Hope called out, "Hey, where are you all going?" So we all laughed and continued to stand under the snow flurries 'til the program ended. After a few jokes, he was presented with a *kimchi* jar on an A-frame. He cracked a few more jokes, and we all knew it was time to leave.

Suddenly I found myself lost in what seemed a tsunami of men all dressed alike. I could not tell who belonged to what unit even when I detected the strange heraldry crests on their uniforms. I panicked because when I approached the massive number of trucks, all appeared cloned, all lined up, all belonging to some camp somewhere, and I had no idea which truck belonged to which unit camp, or any of the soldiers from my camp, being new to Korea. Then by the grace of God I saw 3RD BDE (Third Brigade) stenciled in white on the bumper of one and I immediately recognized that the Third Brigade was housed at McGovern. With my heart almost leaping out of my mouth, I jumped in and eventually ended up at my barrack. After that near fiasco, I was able to relax enough to reflect on the enjoyment of seeing Bob Hope live, and especially those lovely dressed ladies that we had all left behind stateside.

CAVALIER NEWSPAPER DATED JANUARY 4, 1965 REPORTING THE BOB HOPE SHOW

It was on one of those days, sometime in the fall of 1965, that there was subdued excitement in the camp. Rumor had it that we were invited to attend a drama in Seoul. None of us were especially excited by it but it was something different, something to do one of those evenings where we were expected to attend. Army Greens was the attire of the evening. The entire Headquarters Company was somewhat withdrawn, silent, but we all thought it best not to fight the system. I remember that we were bussed to the Munsan-Ni Train Station. We arrived at the depot around dusk. None of us had ever been together as a company group and much less in greens. It was dark by the time we arrived at the Seoul Train Station, boarded another bus, and were dropped off at the Korea Music Hall somewhere in Seoul.

We wound up in the balcony. We had all been given a ticket which said the Broadway musical being performed was *Hello, Dolly!* None of us were overly excited, but accepted this outing as something different and far better than walking guard back at camp. As always the national anthem preceded the curtain rise and the performance began.

HELLO, DOLLY! WAS PERFORMED ON OCTOBER 28, 1965, SEOUL.

There was a sign painted on a fence in the backdrop with the words of a city in New York titled Yonkers. What a nutty name—it reminded me of a soldier from Yonkers whose marriage paperwork I prepared when he married a *josan*. Quite a few dancers swung, swayed, jumped, glided, and rolled all over the stage. Colorful signs and backdrops adorned the stage representing a city at the turn of the century, I supposed. I remember the plot consisted of a girl who was seventeen and who wanted her inheritance. She met up with a guy, and that's all I recall. At the end of the show we all applauded. The officers in front began to stand up so that the rest of us from the lower echelons and caste system, like idiots, followed their lead. The trip back was unexciting. We left the hall as a group and were all bussed back and railed to the BLV. Actually, it turned to be a nice unexpected evening, albeit uneventful, at this Far East corner of Asia.

Wonderland by Night
November 1965

Midnight lighting within the camp
Strewn with flecks from hardly a lamp
A flash in time a speckled sight
A glorious wonderland by night

The chilly winds of November 1965 blew down the Queen across Camp Blue Lancer Valley and westward toward Radio Hill. A ghostly silence reigned over the compound—the troops were at the field on the weeklong seasonal bivouac. The whole compound was darker without the customary Quonset lighting, human bustle or vehicular traffic. A skeleton crew had remained to secure the entire camp.

Although fatigued, cold, and sleepy at this postmidnight hour, I stopped on second walk (first guard) at the road behind the hooches that paralleled Radio Hill at the camp's southwestern corner. I paused long enough to rotate full circle walking my *post in a military manner* assuring observation of *everything within sight or hearing.*

Facing southward, I lowered my wet gaze toward the rear gate and scanned my stomping grounds panning left from the Orderly Room facing east toward the entire Headquarters Company area. I spied the shadows of my hooch Number Ten as my eyes continued northeastward toward the guard shack. The faint sound of the wire cable halyards clanging against the flagpoles made their way across the brigade offices to my ears. I rubbed at my runny eyes as they focused and adjusted on the northeast distance, such that I could make out the contours and shapes of the farther buildings. There were gray shadows and then there were lit shadows. I recognized the outlines of the Blue Lancer Playhouse and the gym. The line company's Quonsets at the farther distance catty corner from my post were all faintly lit under their own random light specks.

I imagined the main gate guards were ever alert although no traffic passed at the northern-most end of the compound. I envisioned the added absence of military gaiety at outlying Nullo-Ri in the unseen horizon. The customary babble of Pyongyang Patty wavered by the whims of the wind with the usual white flares visible on the northern skies signaling the presence of North Korean propaganda at the DMZ.

In the words of a DMZ veteran:

"White flares were ignited for illumination, red for contact with North Koreans, and green signified all clear. Most flares were normally used along the Barrier Fence positions and viewed all over the division. The nerve-racking loudspeakers blared day and night 24/7. At times they mentioned a GI's name; for example: 'PFC Ross of Charlie Company, we know that you are in the DMZ and afraid—tonight you die.' Then they played a tune that we referred to as "The Death March." It was a very depressing organ type composition. More likely than not, when it played, somewhere on the Zone a firefight broke out."

—PFC Dale A. Patton,
Co C, 3rd Bn 23rd Inf, 2nd ID,
Korea, 1967-1968.

I continued panning left and in a straight line facing due north from this post, imagined the Motor Pool and the 702nd Quonsets, all invisible behind the PX silhouette. Fronting the PX I could make out the Battalion Headquarters offices and the Mess Hall back having observed half circle from my post.

PHOTO CREDIT: (SP4) FELIX CASTRO, MEDIC, HHC 1ST BN 12 CAV 1ST CAV, 1965
THE HHC COMPANY AREA WITH MY ROAD GUARD-POST (AT BASE OF PHOTO) PARALLELED THE SIX HOOCHES WITH RADIO HILL BEHIND VIEWER. THE ORDERLY ROOM AT RIGHT SHOWS THREE WINDOWS, THE MESS HALL IS THE LONG BUILDING AT CENTER, AND THE GABLED LATRINE LEFT OF MESS HALL. THE THIRD QUONSET ACROSS WHITE ROAD FROM THE LATRINE WAS HOOCH NUMBER TEN AND THE HALF QUONSET AT LEFT OF PHOTO WAS THE GUARD SHACK. BUILDINGS AT EXTREME LEFT ARE BRIGADE HEADQUARTERS WITH HALYARDS OUTSIDE PHOTO.

SCENE OF BLUE LANCER'S SOUTHWESTERN QUARTER AREA FROM SOUTH QUEEN. I WALKED THE ROAD VISIBLE BETWEEN THE HOOCHES THAT PARALLELED RADIO HILL AND HEADQUARTERS COMPANY. ROAD LEADING TO TOP OF RADIO HILL VISIBLE ON LEFT WITH IMJIN RIVER ACROSS AT UPPER FOURTH OF THE PHOTO WITH NORTH KOREA AND PROPAGANDA EQUIPMENT AT HORIZON.

The ice-cold wind buffeted my windproof parka as I continued down the road in the northerly direction toward the mess hall. I glanced left (westward) at the barbwire fence and skirts of Radio Hill and then faced right (eastward) toward the lined Quonsets below me; then strolled southward, then northward, then southward again and again—the quarter mile walk—in execution of my walking post. All was quiet, safe, and sound in the chilly, windy, and bitter cold world of Korea. Then, while strolling northward, I was attracted by the entire length of dimly lit Blue Lancer—the limited lights seemingly brighter in contrast with the unusual darkness. I marveled from this vantage point as the entire camp's extent opened before me. Although the lamppost lights glittered and wavered through my windswept watery eyes, I was awed by the vision of the brilliant wonderland that lay before me.

From this post at the southwest corner of the compound, the whole of Camp Blue Lancer Valley lay open before me in all its windswept twinkling glory. I could clearly see the whole spectacle clear to the main gate and gave me the appearance of glitter sparkling on tilted black paper edged at eye level. I then noticed that the camp's lighting was augmented by celestial sparkles as I raised my eyes skyward. The whole array of the speckled heavens suddenly opened above me. I had previously observed the starry skies but not until tonight did the twinkles become apparent and numerous. The whole chilly, moonless, black sky suddenly became a multitude of hundreds of thousands of blinking flecks through my watery view. In my eyes I saw a complete union of the sparkly overhead and the Blue Lancer lights creating a conglomerated atmosphere of sparkles from pedestal to heaven.

PHOTO CREDIT: (SP4) LYNN ZOLNOSKI, 122ND SIGNAL BN, TDY, BLUE LANCER VALLEY, KOREA, 1966-1967

I WALKED GUARD ON THE ROAD AT THE LEFT AND FROM THIS POINT AT THE SOUTHWEST CORNER OF THE COMPOUND, THE WHOLE OF CAMP BLUE LANCER VALLEY LAY OPEN BEFORE ME. PHOTO TAKEN FROM SOUTH QUEEN.

Amid a myriad of celestial twinkles, I recognized the Ursa Major constellation. I then located the pointers directing at Ursa Minor as I gazed northward above the main gate. The Little Dipper appeared as faint as always. I remembered that my favorite constellation hung in the southern Texas skies. I turned a half circle south and sure enough, there was the faithful and beautiful Orion, bright and prominent as usual in the midst of numberless stars under the southern Korean skies. The oversized constellation's two lowest stars stood halfway between South Queen's horizon and overhead so that the constellation occupied a full fourth of the southern heavens. Orion's tri-star belt twinkled as brightly as I remembered as a preschooler back in San Antonio. As usual, the jeweled knife was visible among the numberless stars. As a child I had been fascinated by those jewels. I had imagined those gems set in a silver dagger lying in a pirate treasure trove as plunder.

Two-and-a-half hours earlier—I reflected in my weariness—I was warm and asleep during my five-hour seemingly short break following first walk in the comforts of the guard hooch. After a rude sergeant's awakening kick, I paced zombie-like into the chilly night toward this second walk. There was a bizarre, yet comforting, feeling of approaching my remote guard-post knowing that a fellow guard, restless and chilled to the bone, awaited me. I had caught sight of the strolling dark green bundle barely discernable against the dark background of Radio Hill. Again, I reflected as numerous times before, that guards were sitting ducks, and probably posted more so to keep our soldiers within the compound rather than the *slicky boys* out. Acknowledging the challenge with the proper password, I relieved the sentry who handed me the shotgun along with the three shells, and envyingly watched his dark-green bundled body drift back to the guard hooch.

Recalling myself to duty, I still stood awed by the mile-long stretch of the camp and then continued patiently walking to and fro my two-and-half-hour outpost. Aahhh! but each time glancing at my magnificent midnight mural all at the expense of post midnight fatigue. Calculating that my second walk was nearing completion and elatedly anticipating my relief sentry at any time, made the spectacle all the more charming. Then I caught sight of a dark-green bundled apparition approaching me—my relief, concluding my second walk and thus ending my guard evening. Following the challenging procedure fully fatigued and worn out, I trudged back to the guard hooch while the heavens through my wet wavering eyes seemingly flowed as they moved with me.

Then it happened! In my fatigue, I found myself in continual approach entering that conglomeration of combined light effect. I drifted within the sparkling array of the celestial lights that blended with the myriad of Blue Lancer. Being enveloped in this wonderland by night would forever burn in my memory. It was during this starry night surveillance where my tinnitus experienced another ambience filled with silent explosions of skyrocketing fireworks including falling stars, comets, and crashing asteroids. With watery eyes, I sighed deeply as I drank in all the delicious splendor and majesty of this augmented universe that was all mine alone to privately relish, at this post midnight chilly and windy hour, at this Far East corner of Asia.

In the words of a fellow guard:

> "When I walked guard duty, the only thing I imagined was 'Joe' or a slicky boy sneaking up on me and the most strenuous thing I did was hold on to my bladder when I heard a strange noise. We read this chapter, and I'm fascinated; I never knew you had such poetry in your soul. Wish I could have had your attitude."
> —SP4 Tom Jeffrey, S1,
> Ed Ctr, HHC 1st Bn 12th Cav, 1st Cav Div
> Korea, 1965-1966

The Case of the Slickied Camera
Fall 1965

Now you see it now you don't
Now he has it now he won't
Gave his cam'ra for the bill
Checked his pocket all was nil.

"Do not play their game," Master Sergeant O. had advised us at the indoctrination spiel upon our arrival at Camp McGovern that November of 1964. He was referring to all the confidence games the Korean low life play on the unsuspecting soldier. However, did I listen? *No*, I had to learn the hard way!

Early one evening, my buddy Specialist Fourth George Sellers and I went to Pobwan-Ni, one of the "greater" business villages in the division, and made it known I wanted to sell my Yashika Lynx 5000 camera. I approached a shop, made my sales pitch. The dealer offered me ten dollars. I notified him that the camera was brand new and would take no less than forty dollars. I added "I can get more for it on the black market." Cordially, the shopkeeper replied that he was a businessman and could not do business otherwise.

On the street once more, I was approached by a man who asked how much I wanted for the camera. I replied "forty dollars," which was the PX price.

The Korean man promptly ushered us into a recessed corner of a back Pobwan-Ni street. Being with George, I wasn't overly concerned. The man counted and proffered four blue ten-dollar Military Payment Certificate (MPC) bills which I accepted and firmly grabbed in my left hand within my fisted tightened thumb and curled index finger.

(SP4) GEORGE SELLERS, ONE OF MY TWO BEST BUDDIES AND ME, CLOWNING AS USUAL.

    I folded and placed the bills deep in my left pocket and gave the man the camera. The man took the camera in his right hand. He hesitated and wouldn't leave. Casually, he placed his left arm around my shoulders so that his left hand was on my left deltoid. We were then standing side to side. I removed his arm and with my hand threatened to clip him a chop. He walked away. Quickly, I reached in my left pocket and was relieved to feel the wad of bills still there. George and I hurriedly left and stopped a speeding taxi to Yongju-Gol for which the chauffer asked two hundred won (about eighty cents).

    As George and I arrived in Yongju-Gol, I reached in my pocket for the taxi fare, and withdrew the wad of bills I was given for the camera. *Two hundred won*! No four ten-dollar MPC bills! I realized I had paid with a forty-dollar camera a one-mile taxi ride from Pobwan-Ni to Yongju-Gol!

    How did slicky man rip me off? The old switch game, *but how? When?* Perhaps by the old flip wrist switch. All I could think of is that the Korean must have flipped his hand, thereby releasing the *won* from his little finger side of the hand rather than the proffered MPC from the index finger side of the hand. *But*, I remembered that I had clenched my curved index finger and pressured thumb on the *blue MPC in full light*, because I was suspicious of any slicky routine. Perhaps, this is why the Korean hesitated—the sport, the old con game, was about to begin—with his arm on my shoulder.

    Was it that, the left-hand-in-the-pocket scam? But the Korean never reached into my pocket! His right hand held the camera and his left hand was on my left shoulder all the time. Maybe he had three arms and hands. Perhaps then, it was real magic! I never knew ... mumble ... mumble ...

    I remain puzzled, can anyone explain the scam? If not, I realize, I'll go to my grave bewildered at this perfect crime at this Far East corner of Asia!

Chapter 19

Departing the Pacific

It is astonishing how short a time it takes for very wonderful things to happen.

—Frances Hodgson Burnett

Prologue

I could not believe that one full year, composed of sweet and sour sweat, and tears of joy and misery, had lapsed. I sported my short-timer swagger stick and flaunted my clipboard with clearing documentation at the lifers. It seemed like only yesterday the short timers and seemingly arrogant senior privates teased us as lifers. I felt that my time left in Korea was as between a wall and the point of the sword. I still had much I wanted to explore but not enough time or money to spend. My tour of duty was up, time to rotate stateside. I was emotionally mixed, part of me wanted to depart and the other yearned further adventure though I was maxed-out at this Far East corner of Asia.

Bathhouse Spectacle
November 1965

Dame Venus, love's lady, was born of the sea
   —Thomas Jordan (1612-1685), *The Careless Gallant*

Rub a dub dub
Three in a tub
Boiling waters, glances, sways
As Venus rises from the waves

One cold morning in early November 1965 with thoughts of returning to the States, I decided to have one last overwhelming adventure. I proceeded to find a bathhouse in Pobwan-Ni. I had heard of these but I never entered or really knew.

I wandered down the main drag of Pobwan-Ni until I located a bathhouse. For the life of me I had no recollection of how I found it, entered, or where exactly it was. I walked into what was a private accommodation. I found myself solo in a room about twelve by twelve feet with a gray concrete wall-to-wall tub about two feet high and about three feet from the entry. A rusted brown faucet with a plus-shaped handle emerged from the concrete wall and I noticed an equally rusted drain receptacle with a once white, now creamy, worn, cracked rubber plug. I noticed that steam hovered just above the still hot water. The floor and the tub were finished of rough concrete, probably to avoid slipping and accidents. At the tub's rail lay a stack of cream-colored worn washcloths and at an oblong indentation was a huge rectangular bar of brown soap. Some bath but "whiter" towels hung from a row of equally corroded nails that extended from the concrete wall. Upon closer examination I noticed the towels were worn almost thin with little thickness of absorbent properties.

Although the outside temperature was about forty degrees Fahrenheit, I perspired as I removed my army greens in the steamy room. I remembered hanging my uniform on rusted nails, and then concealed my skivvies beneath the greens as I stripped down bare-naked. I remembered that the floor was wet and warm. I placed one foot in the half boiling water and slowly stepped into the eighteen-inch high water level. There was an absence of a showerhead and I could not decide whether to sit, lie, or soak, as I had this spacious luxury all to myself. As I stood calf-deep, I slowly scooped water with the small metal scum-caked washbasin and scalded my legs and torso as I progressively splashed myself. Then I picked up the bar of soap that immediately reminded me of my poverty conditions as a little boy back home. The family used Octagon, a huge block base soap for both washing clothes on a washboard and for bathing. I lathered a threadbare washcloth and began soaping my body. As I scooped up water to rinse my suds-covered body and head, I felt a cool gush of air as the door opened. Being in the army and unaccustomed to privacy, it took me a second or two to react that I was supposed to be alone. As soon as my eyes cleared, I saw a young couple closing the door behind them. Although I pretended to be accustomed to this "normal practice," I immediately, but with care, hurriedly sat and burned my butt in the boiling water. I remembered how my God-given gifts burned too, to the unaccustomed high temperatures. I decided that if this duo was oblivious of me, I would be just as oblivious of them. I had heard of such communal bathing, but I had never given it any thought.

THE BATHHOUSE WAS LOCATED SOMEWHERE AT THE BUILDINGS ON THE LEFT. NOTICE *KIMCHI* BUS ALMOST SEEMINGLY OF EARLIER MAKE THAN OF 1965.

They did not seem concerned about my presence. They appeared pleased with one another "in their own world" and somehow in good spirits such at what I guessed was the luxury of "the bath." I heard them chatting in soft low tones, almost reverently. Momentarily shocked, I knew they must be aware of my gawking, but they also knew that I was the "guest" and thus the "observer" of their culture.

He wore a top coat over a white shirt and tie along with black slacks. She wore a blue tweed almost terry cloth two-piece suit, a knit light blue beret-type hat and black flats. They both unashamedly disrobed with their backs to me. From her purse she took out a clear piece of plastic which opened up into a cap and during what seemed like a ceremony did up her long black hair, and covered it completely within the cap. With smiling eyes they both turned toward me as they approached the tub, and never made an effort to conceal their anatomies. I took full note of the opposite gender who was nicely endowed and unspoiled. Girlishly giggling (and to my delight), she lifted her leg and slowly dipped her foot in the water while he affectionately held her oppositely by the arm. Finally, they slowly and fully set foot in the tub, entered, and slowly sat, savoring what I realized were the "bathing comforts of hot waters." They crept toward one another, still smiling and happily embracing as if in performance of some ritual.

I continued lathering my upper body in a sitting position. I found that I had over lathered to the point that suds were swimming on the water. The couple glanced at me and the soap. I then replaced it on the indentation. The man reached for it and they both rose from the water as if in performance of a ceremony. They stood and hurriedly lathered their washcloths, themselves, and then each other's back alternatively. They dipped and rose again several times. Then they submerged until only their heads were visible and sat quietly. They did not use the basin, but all along contently smiled in what appeared to me as ecstasy.

I remember I reached for the basin to rinse myself to maintain body temperature with the tub water. The couple arose and scrubbed their bodies and each other with their rinsed and wringed washcloths, rolling off tiny scrolls and ringlets of lifeless tissue. Then they dipped again. To my alarm, not only were suds floating on the water, but also tiny oily specks and tissue scum augmented them. I arose and reached for a towel.

Then everything happened so fast. The pair stepped out, took my towels and tenderly patted one another dry, and caringly uncovered their underclothes from the nails. I decided I was not ready to evacuate the premises, so standing buck-naked I pulled the plug to replace my hot water. As the water rapidly drained, the couple, donning their clothing, turned to view the lowering water level and me. At that point, the door opened with another cool gush, to admit an open-mouthed chubby girl displaying bucked gapped teeth with questioning eyes. On impulse I wrapped the forgotten towel around my butt from this non-bather and stood dumbfounded, "freezing" in the now ankle-deep hot water. She glanced at the water level, the couple, and me. The couple turned their faces looking toward me. The intruder advanced toward me and plugged the drain, but I immediately opened the faucet to more scalding water, as I was not to be cheated out of *my* hot water or a clean rinse. Gaping and seemingly bewildered, the girl just looked at the gushing scalding water, slowly turned around staring into the air and walked out. All the while the amused couple wearing a semblance of a smile completed their dressing and stepped out with another cool gush of air.

I continued dipping and rinsing and then wiping in continued frustration at missing out on viewing a woman "doll up." I could not remember dressing or leaving the bathhouse, but I did enjoy this unexpected bathhouse spectacle, especially of Venus rising from the waves, at Pobwan-Ni at this Far East corner of Asia.

The Ring
November 10, 1965

Turning left then turning right
Flashing scenes by village light
Frozen face via slicing cold
Fixed my gaze on yellow gold

It was late in October 1965 that I wandered around the BLV always with the word "gold" nagging me in the back of my mind. I had always been fascinated by the bright yellow color of the numerous gold rings I had seen in a show window that night on road guard during November, last year. During my year of duty, I had seen a few Korean folk wearing rings with a thin shank with a thin face that weighed two don (3.75 troy grams). Since I wanted a bigger ring, I preferred one with a greater square face which weighed three don, creating a masculine macho look on my ring finger. I noticed that Korean rings were designed with varied geometric etchings.

I was aware that I had overspent my budget by $80 on last month's ten-day tour of Japan. I had lavished almost two month's pay in Kamakura, Hakone, Tokyo, and a few tours of palaces and shrines around the Tokyo proximity. I attended two theaters featuring female performers and dancers. Then I conveniently got myself solo lost on Tokyo's main drag namely, the Ginza.

For the longest time I had been debating whether to splurge eighteen of my measly Specialist Fourth dollars for a ring of pure gold. For the entire length of my one-year tour of duty, I had been fascinated by the gold of Korea without giving in to temptation. Korean gold was unlike the gold of the United States. It was pure gold, of twenty-four karats fine and stamped 999. I had only known of karats in diamonds and of 10K stamped on an onyx initial ring I had once purchased at Gordon's at the corner of Houston and Broadway Streets in downtown San Antonio back in 1963. But this gold of Korea looked yellowier, a fascinating yellow that one would need to behold in order to understand. This gold was more of a brilliant amber color, all aglow, perhaps fiery, and definitely radiant in a refined but lightly buffed state. And my entire life had been spellbound by the 120-karat (fantasy) gold barrel I once read about in my childhood comic book *Uncle Scrooge* by Walt Disney. Scrooge McDuck melted a roof of pure gold in Indo-China as payment for a furnace intended to warm airplane hangars in Alaska. Then I reflected back to that one night in November 1964. I recalled that night newly arrived in Korea, when the truck rolled on the mud-packed road through the village. My face froze and my eyes watered as I stood road guard on the deuce-and-half's bed, but I was so awestruck that I ignored the slicing wind. As the lit shops flashed and blurred past me, my attention was locked for a split second on the bright yellow gold rings displayed at glazed show windows. I would forever be haunted by the unique color of the pure gold set in a black case so unlike that of the fourteen and ten karat I had known stateside.

It was one of those cool days in November 1965, the tenth day of the month to be exact, and as many from payday that I finally decided to take the plunge. I headed for Yongju-Gol with the sole purpose of this one last investment. *Gold!* I arrived at Yongju-Gol in the late morning and walked along the shops on the west side of the street beneath the mountain. I did not bother to glance into Camp Beard to my left. I passed the road that T-boned east toward the river, and continued at a brisk pace passing the shop where, during my earlier carefree days, I had purchased the lacquered albums for my many photos. I nonchalantly passed by another shop where I had bought other souvenirs and a custom-made photo album. Somehow the sun seemed cold as it cast long black shadows amid the solidly dirt packed walks and dirt street—unlike the wonderful brightness it once cast and warmed my face at bygone times. Neither the noisy traffic nor the chant of the populace or the presence of fecal matter caught my attention. I never once remembered my former flame, *Oggie*, and didn't even remember her shop as I evidently passed it. Finally, I approached a gold jewelry shop and viewed all the rings in the show window. There were about thirty rings resting in their slots, all staring at me just begging to be selected from their black velvet bed.

I entered the shop and was greeted by a middle-aged man who was sitting on a straw mat in the middle of dirt floor which centered his tiny shop. I bowed upon entry addressing him as *ajoshee* (Mister). The man immediately stood up and slipped into his sandals—the kind with a thong that separates the big toe from and four others and in return bowed at me, giving his full attention. The man was not dressed in business or in casual attire. He wore a thick T-shirt and white trousers that were somewhat stained and had seen better days. I pointed at the ring tray in the show window. The jeweler removed the gold tray and presented it such that I carefully lifted the ring I wanted from its secure slot. There were hardly any words exchanged. All the while the man kept a serious and friendly business-like facial expression and demeanor. Both of us were probably equally excited but I was more so as I had never owned 24K before.

Once I had selected the ring, the man produced a small wooden tray with many bezels and after two or three tries, found one that fit my left ring finger. Having found the proper fit he slid the gold ring into a long tapered metal rod and began gently tapping all around the shank except the face. Every few taps he placed the ring on my finger, which only reached to my most recessed knuckle. After a few repeated taps, when the ring slid clear to my palm, was he satisfied that the ring was of proper size.

Upon the ring fitting my left ring finger, the man sat on the matted floor. He then took out a small wooden rod from his workbench about the length of a pencil and about as thick. The dowel had one mark of black on one end and a few other colored marks on the opposite end. Three fine colored and silk-like strings extended from the rod, one on either end and one from the center. He hooked the ring onto the string at the black spot and a counter weight on the opposite string adjusted to the correct color. Then he held the rod by the middle string and the gold ring went up.

The jeweler then lit a torch which he adjusted to a blue flame. From another box at his workbench he produced a small wooden tray with tiny ribbons, squares, and particles of the yellow metal. He selected a ribbon and placed it lengthwise on the shank of the ring that he held with a pair of steel tweezers. He applied the torch to the ribbon, and it lightly hissed and spackled as it disappeared into the shank and became part of the ring. After a few moments, he replaced the ring on the same hook, held it up by means of the middle string, and the dowel leveled. He rubbed the ring with a cloth and proffered it to me, and requested payment of five thousand one hundred won. (The army had an exchange table among many others at the mess hall on payday so that GIs could buy W270 per dollar rather than W250 on the black market.) I proffered the man fifty-one of my crisp one-hundred won notes, about eighteen dollars. The *ajoshee* then took out a small salmon printed paper, filled in the blanks, and handed me the receipt. I took the paper and bowed as I thanked the man and left. I had to admit I was very much impressed at the professional service I received at the jewelry shop. I happily sported the ring as I rambled on down the streets of Yongju-Gol to perhaps a last adventure at this Far East corner of Asia.

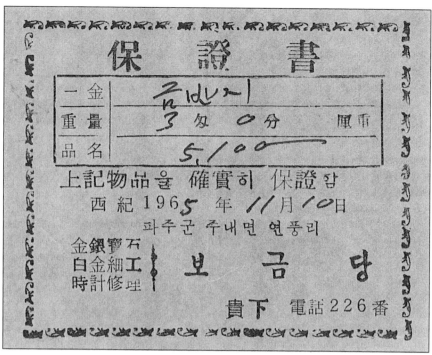

THE *AJOSHEE* TOOK OUT A SMALL SALMON PRINTED PAPER, FILLED IN THE BLANKS, AND HANDED ME THE RECEIPT.

Certificate

Price   Gold Ring
Pound *(weight)* 3 Don 0 Pun Pound *(weight)*
Item   5,100 *(won)*

We guarantee this gold ring 99.9 percent intrinsic pure gold

Anno Domini 1965 Year 11 Month 10 Day
Paju gun Juneh myon Yeon poong lee

Gold, Silver Jewelry
White Gold Design   **BO**   **KOOM**   **DANG**

Repair Watch

(Name of significant)   **To Dear**   **Telephone Number 226**

Explanations:

Paju gun Juneh myon Yeon poong Lee: The name of the political district such city, county, and state in our country.

Bo Koom Dang: The name of the business.

Rate of Exchange: At the time of the date indicated Korean won traded at 270 per dollar at the pay table at U.S. Army installations. The amount I paid was $18.89.

Cost of the ring: 1965 gold market was $36 per troy ounce or $1.16 per gram. Three don or 11.25 grams was valued at $13.05. The fine gold or intrinsic value of the ring was $13.05. The merchant's margin was $5.84 or 1,500 won.

Note that the goldsmith erroneously entered *gold ring* where the *price* belongs and *5,100* where the *item* belongs.

A note on Korean precious metals weights and measures: In world markets precious metals trade gold in troy ounces. Most bullion merchants trade in troy ounces consisting of 31.1 grams per troy ounce. Pound is the closest word in English to the Chinese word weight. In the Korean metals market gold trades in Dons, Puns, and Ris. These weights and measures stem from Chinese systems. 1 Don = 3.75g, 1 Pun = 0.375g, and 1 Ri = 0.0375g. In some ancient civilizations wheat was used as a unit of weight, such as 480 grains equals one ounce, perhaps the Chinese once used rice grains.

Regret at Munsan-Ni
November 1965

Throughout their hist'ry and their years
By brows that stream with sweat and tears
On ancient backs are burdens born
O'er land rebuilt that war had torn

An early day of November 1965 found me eagerly packing my baggage for hold shipment to the States. It was a wooden box (that I had been lugging from camp to camp) loaded with all the souvenirs, clothing, and junk that I had purchased and that could not be taken on board the homebound jet. The supply sergeant inspected the contents. He hassled with me the GI-issue rain boots that I had purchased at the Blue Diamond Store by Nullo-Ri until I produced a receipt. No other stuff was contraband, so the sergeant approved and sealed the crate for shipment.

The box was quite heavy, so I convinced my houseboy to carry it for me. He obligingly shouldered it down to the main gate. At the main gate, I caught a three-quarter ton truck that dropped me off at Nullo-Ri. I was able to load it aboard a Korean bus headed for the train depot in Munsan-Ni. The hostess wanted an extra thirty won (roughly thirty cents). I did not want to pay it but she pointed to the crate and demanded "*SOMEshee*," so I paid it. When I arrived by Munsan-Ni, I found I could not carry the heavy case by myself to the train depot.

As luck would have it, two Korean gentlemen were sitting and chatting by the wayside each with a homemade pushcart. I motioned if they could take the crate. One agreed to take the job for thirty won. The *papasan* squatted and easily lifted the box and placed it his cart and we continued to the train station. As we approached our destination, the conglomeration of so many rails that crisscrossed the yard obstructed our way such that he could not roll his cart farther. Amazingly enough, he stopped and slid the case to the end of the cart, carefully stood it up, and walked it off the cart so that half was tilted on the cart's edge as he leaned it onto his back. The folds of his hands then acted as flanges as he dexterously worked his fingers backward so that the fold of each hand ended up at the far corners of the box. We then continued rail hopping for what seemed another mile and all the while the *papasan* never complained or so much as groaned. As we arrived at the military window, he squatted ever so skillfully but not without effort, and settled the crate on the floor.

I thanked him as I handed the gentleman two bills of Korean currency, which might have been a five won and a twenty-five won note. The old man took the two notes, focused on them, and as if cherishing a great prize, very carefully patted them together as if straightening a sheaf of bills. He then folded them with infinite care and placed them in his pocket. As I observed the consideration he gave his earnings, utter shame overcame me. I wished I had had more money. This was not the way I had ever anticipated of dealing with my Korean family. With despairing regret, I watched the gentleman (who could have been my dad had he remained in Mexico) walk away.

Although Koreans are used to hard work, and perhaps thirty won was a decent earning for this chore, he had really merited more according to stateside standards. Unfortunately, my funds happened to be extremely limited since I had just blown eighty dollars in Japan one month earlier. I had also bought a gold ring in Yongju-Gol, which further lightened my wallet. Although I had just been paid, my budget did not allow me the luxury of being more generous. I badly needed the money for things other than souvenirs for the family. As the matter of fact, when I arrived in San Francisco, I only had six dollars. A bus ride from one airport cost another four dollars, so that I arrived in San Antonio truly *busted*!

Still, deep in my conscience, I harbored a mental snapshot of this gentleman and how he cherished his meager earnings in a way that shamed me. I was to always recall this incident with a regret that pierced my heart and cleaved my spirit because this *papasan*, the thought haunts me to this day, could have been my dad in postrevolutionary Mexico. Despite my impoverished status at the end of my tour of duty, I would not find peace knowing that my last transaction could have ended on a more charitable note at this Far East corner of Asia.

Eligible Date to Depart the Pacific
November 19, 1965

Chip eecanda
Hanguk oopseemneeda
Megook kuneen ilyun
Nauy Hanguk ilyun

It was November 19, a cold and chilly morning of 1965 just before the Korean snows, that I prepared for final departure. How could I forget the date that all the troops looked forward to? My day had finally arrived. I had completed my tour of duty and thus reached the Cavalry's Eligible Date to Depart the Pacific (EDDPAC) or Date Eligible to Depart Overseas (DEROS), as the Second Infantry Division termed it.

That predawn morning differed from all the others. I awoke instantly alert and with my towel wrapped around my butt under my field jacket headed to the latrine for one last body wash and shave. Then I quietly proceeded to dress in the darkness of Hooch Ten. All the troops were still asleep as I donned my greens. The night before I had sold my gooseneck lamp and *eedeewah* stand (night stand), and packed my clothes and uniforms. I had carefully placed my fatigues, khakis, and second green uniform at the bottom of my duffle bag followed by the light brown dress shirts all neatly folded. My skivvies, low quarters, and boots followed. My AWOL carry-on bag held my toiletries, one skivy change, and miscellaneous items. This was major packing. This was farewell! Although this day was different from all others, my mind was in turmoil, there seemed to be what, regret? What was my problem?

Sighing, I exited the stove-warm hooch and in the chilled morning proceeded to the lit Mess Hall. I was the only soldier there, so I sat down quietly to eat my breakfast. Then I proceeded down to the familiar orderly room for my final signature on the company roster. I greeted the charge of quarters at the brightly lit office, presented my orders to the sergeant, and signed out. The charge of quarters smiled as he bade me farewell saying, "You lucky dog." I smiled back and went to Hooch Ten for my gear.

All the troops were still asleep upon my return from the mess hall and orderly room since it was still before the reveille bugle call. The silence seemed deafening as I looked around Number Ten, my home for the last five months. I had seen troops come and go before—what was happening? I paralleled the duffle bag against my right leg, and with one swift movement catapulted it over my knee up my torso and onto my right shoulder where it rested in balance. I put on my flying saucer hat and picked up my AWOL bag. Silently, I turned to face my empty wall locker, footlocker, and checked the neatly stacked linen and blanket on the half-folded mattress on my bunk. With one last turn, I glanced around the hooch and saw myself in hundreds of flashbacks as I momentarily relived my quarter's experiences of the last five months. I saw the shades and shadows of my monsoon wakeful evening, Cecil our canine mascot that chewed and crapped all over my leather sandals, listening to the annoying beer parties, hearing the nightly bugle calls, reading mail from home, the Turk's visit, etcetera, etcetera, etcetera. Sighing again, I passed through the door from the warm shelter into the dark cold morning under the starry skies of The Land of the Morning Calm. The military day had not yet begun.

As I sauntered out, I met my houseboy at the door and convinced him to carry my duffle bag down to the main gate about three-quarters of a mile distant. Carefully descending the Brigade Headquarters' steps in the predawn facing north, I turned back facing south for one last look as I intently scrutinized my domicile one last time. Continuing my way, midway while crossing the parade ground, I again turned back (south) for one last look toward Brigade Headquarters. The starlit sky silhouetted South Queen, the faraway mountain background with the descending rows of hooches in the foreground enabling me to spy on Number Ten. As continued northward, I almost killed myself as I stumbled over the pipe sunk in concrete where its cannon fire sounded off between the Retreat and To the Colors bugle calls every evening. The houseboy proceeded down the dark parade ground carefully and sure-footedly ahead of me. I would never return to this moment or the place that was my "neighborhood" for one-half year. Still facing south, I panned from my right observing the PX, the message center, the mess hall, the distant orderly room (where I once typed and emotionally reminisced oldies on AFKN), Brigade Headquarters, and flags, then finally came half circle to my left as I made out the shape of the Playhouse against Easy's starry heavens where I had enjoyed many movies, and the gym. For a split second, my legs faltered as numerous flashbacks crossed my vision as I gazed at my stomping grounds for the last time. My entire environment suddenly filled with ghostly sounds and shadows of GIs and KATUSAs, trafficking, crossing one another, the reflagging ceremony, jeeps, the helicopter landing, sandbagging the flooding monsoon waters—with me in greens, khakis, or fatigues among them. I made out the houseboy at the end of the field before descending by the tank and watched as he dexterously lifted the duffle bag to his head so it balanced lengthwise along his neck and bent back. I followed, but before descending the field and onto the street, I took one last glance at the tank at my left and I hurried downhill to catch up with the advancing houseboy.

Down the torn-up street I sauntered, taking care not to get killed stumbling over the Corps of Engineers' quarter-mile long construction site on my way to the main gate. No more would the BLV undergo flooding once the channel was completed which in effect, the channel along with reflagging, became a meridian of times at the BLV. Catching up with the houseboy, we quietly continued down the torn-up street while I made out the silhouettes of the C Company hooches on my left and of A and B at my right against the dark starlit sky and the Queen. We walked along the concrete canal under construction. No longer would Blue Lancer be flooded with monsoon waters gushing through the rear gate by the orderly room, I again reflected.

At the lit main gate, I thanked my houseboy who in turn thanked me profusely for his daily hire, and trotted back to the rear of the BLV heading to Number Ten. I displayed my ETS orders, and handed the guard a picture of the two girls from one of my Queen's adventures and trustingly asked him to have them delivered. The guard acknowledged and accepted them. A three-quarter ton truck coincidentally approached the main gate as I had anticipated and hoped for, from the POL (Petroleum, Oil, and Lubricants, i.e., the Motor Pool). After the driver checked at the main gate and acknowledged my thumb, I threw my duffle bag on the truck's bed and climbed on with the AWOL bag. A lone soldier, who quietly sat behind the truck's cab, eyed me envyingly all the while knowing of my EDDPAC. As we rode by, we were bombarded by the renewed stench of the rice paddies, whereupon we spied a woman pacing down the dark abandoned road. The lone soldier suddenly broke the silence and pointed to me as he yelled out to catch her attention, "*Chip eecanda*" (going home). She nonchalantly glanced at the two soldiers in the emerging twilight as she resumed her way involved in her own world.

I quietly reflected and realized that every soldier must have understood this departing solitude. I was the only one involved in this solo but unique experience. I was done with flashing my clearing documents and moreover, *I* sported my "short" swagger stick that uniquely boasted a projected carved green dragon coiled around it. The army would continue on duty, the earth would continue its course in occupied Korea, and the indigenous life and that of my families would go on—all without me, as before my arrival at this Far East duty station. My bunkmates knew of my departure, as did my orderly room peers, but suddenly I felt unimportant—alone. No one would miss me as I never missed anyone who rotated stateside, it was just a given. It did not even cross my mind to bid farewell to Marvin or George! Perhaps, others after yelling out "short" began their "shortness" by purchasing rounds at the club, or shaking the hands of pals at the hooch. Maybe someone special waited for them back home—but for me, this was not the case. Then I reflected that I was going home, but to what? I did not leave a girlfriend behind, a job, a Mustang, or anything. I was going back to San Antonio because it was there, because it was a pit stop and a launching pad to other adventures in my next Permanent Change of Station—at Fort Bliss—out in the West Texas town of El Paso. Little did I know that one year and a half hence would see me wed my eternal beloved, a lady with green feline eyes. Yes, I would spend Thanksgiving and Christmas of 1965 at home, but somehow I looked back at Thanksgiving in the chilled winds that blasted me at McGovern's Number Four, and the Christmas of 1964 at a grand church conference and party in Seoul.

Lost in departing sentiments, I hardly noticed that the truck had rolled into the Nullo-Ri community and turned right at the T-bone, advancing east toward the Turk community and the pale-blue light of daybreak. The road curved south where I supposed my heart would leap with strong emotion as I rolled by the Koom-Shi, Camp McGovern, then Nopae Dong communities—all now clearly visible with signs of life in the first daylight—with all its bygone memories of wild adventures and sweet mischief, but I remained lost in hypnotic reality. As the truck continued through the rice paddies before the Mickey Mouse Corners at the Pobwan-Ni community, I continued my observations somewhat disoriented with a faraway gaze. However, I did not take note of the golden disc now rising in the eastern sky that had always brightened my way through all my adventures. The truck dropped me off at Camp Beard in marvelous Yongju-Gol; I could not remember seeking Number Twenty-five, the

Seoul-bound bus. My remembrance resumed upon my arrival at Kimpo AFB, with a complete loss of all incidents in between. Still, my subconscious continued ringing with, "I'm going home, Korea is no more, I served as an American soldier for one year, and Korea was mine for that year." I made one last telephone call to Brother Han In Sang at the Mission Home from the airport, and then boarded the Northwest jet, bound stateside and to "The Land of the Big PX." With mixed emotions, I flew away from the fully lived year-long habitation I called "home," where I spent my one year growing up in 1965, my once Far East corner of Asia.

PART III

Our Korea

> *There was a brotherhood in arms—one might almost say a brotherhood of blood—between them, something that divided them off sharply into a caste utterly different from the ignorant civilians here.*
> —C. S. Forester, *Hornblower During the Crisis*

Prologue

Imagine for a moment that you are an eighteen-year-old soldier fresh out of high school and basic military training from earth assigned to planet Mars. After an extended space trip you arrive, and through a porthole view a red dusty surface against a darkened sky littered with rocks, pockmarked with craters, protrusions, and glassy domes resembling half bubbles bearing military crests and emblems. Near each glass enclosure are settlements of huts constructed of sandstone and rock, all oxide red in color. Much of the surface is plowed and prepared with moistened fields which evidently were once craters and protrusions, and now brimming with mushroom-like growths—the staple of Mars. As you exit the space port and enter a jet-fueled capsule that speeds you to your bubble-camp, an overwhelming intoxicating odor of corrosion, like a chemistry laboratory coupled with airport-like superstrong fuel exhaust, reeks the atmosphere and assaults your nostrils. You are totally disoriented, momentarily dazed with lost equilibrium, dumbfounded with jet lag, and blasted ears still hearing the humming of the space craft's drone. However, the senior privates assure you that the field vapors and fuel exhaust are non-lethal. As on earth, billboards and signs with pictures greet your eyes, but with lettering resembling loops like the Olympic circles scripted in different arrangements. As you observe the Martian population, you see them all somewhat smaller in stature with light green complexions and hazel eyes, and except for gender, all appear similar, with Earth-like clothing. You catch a bit of their language which sounds musical, almost "cartoonish." Martians are humans in all respects with their own history, language, religion, cuisine, clothing, traditions, and customs. In time you are allowed privileges and exit your glazed dome to freely intermingle with the indigenous population without your interplanetary passport or visa—your uniform is your pass. Although you had been provided with a booklet to acquaint you to Mars and the inhabitants, you are still experiencing a culture shock; and regardless of your views, you are the guest on Mars. Perhaps my readers will understand the impression that Korea made on the impressionable me at my arrival on that November 1964.

The Military Sector

Wand'ring o're the entire Cav
Like county sector ours to have
To come and go and at our will
The Cav, the camp, the field, and vill

While the anthropologist might only focus on the villages for human observation, the agriculturalist would concentrate on the rice fields for agrarian improvement, a military commander would scrutinize strategic sectors, but an infantryman would spotlight the military complexities and challenges that the Korea hardship duty demanded.

After extended time, I recognized that the military sector was composed of three entities which began at the MP checkpoint approximately five miles north from Seoul and within about the twenty more to the DMZ, being the North Korean border. To my mind, the whole of this division or the military sector would be categorized as homes within neighborhoods, neighborhoods within communities, and communities within a county. Being so far from the comfort zones of home, family, and familiar surroundings resigned one to accept the barrack or Quonset as home with the rank and file as brothers or family; the neighborhood as the camp; the community would compose the immediacy of the camp along with the adjacent rice field and village; and the county would be the entire military sector. There were as many "communities" as there were neighborhoods (camps) with random overlaps. Intermingled within the county (military sector) were stationed three army divisions with an average of two thousand soldiers each: the First Cavalry (later the Second Infantry), the Seventh Infantry, and the I Corps.

As time went by and I had settled in the camp that November 1964, I developed an awareness and familiarity of the division area and began my wanderings. We all confidently roamed around anywhere and everywhere in the division at will as we would within our respective counties back home, thoroughly in the knowledge that in effect we belonged. My uniform was my passport to anywhere within the community, the division, or as far away as Seoul. I was never once asked to produce my Military Identification Card, liberty pass, or three-day pass. I was never stopped or questioned by the authorities; in effect I believe that our Military Police were the authorities in the division. I boarded local public buses, trains, and flagged Korean privately owned trucks and vehicles, which always stopped to give the soldier a ride. Still, my orders on plain paper without a passport was all that I needed to hop a flight on the Stars and Stripes airplane from Kimpo to Tokyo later in October 1965 with a Hong Kong option. Again, despite this Uncle Sam's blessing of disbursing all my traveling around expenses, I continued being a pawn bearing my time in a dormant war zone that could potentially erupt anytime during my 1964-1965 tenure.

Having an adventurous spirit since childhood, Korea was no exception. The northern military sector (county) from Seoul to the DMZ consisted of a conglomeration of military complexes, villages, and rice fields. The realization that most "camp soldiers" frequented the local or adjacent village traversing the immediate rice field created a "community"; so in effect, the mind-set of the soldier was within "the community." Once I became aware of the surroundings outside my "camp neighborhood," the whole world of the adjacent rice fields and of the village opened before me for exploration. It just seemed to be understood that Nopae Dong was "the village," that it was "our" (Camp McGovern's) village, and the adjacent rice fields along with our camp was "the community."

While there was no dividing line between these imaginary communities, perhaps two or three camps shared the same village and thus augmented the community. It was just a matter of crossing rice fields that separated two villages to enter another community. This could account for one reason why some *josans* accompanying a soldier at the EM club or camp theater from an adjacent community were not recognized—as each *josan* conducted business in her own village or community. While at Camp McGovern I acknowledged soldiers from adjoining Camp Paris, Camp Harris, Camp Johnson and Camp Coursen, at our greater EM club when major entertainment such as a floor show, live music, or dancing was to be enjoyed. I remember seeing crests from First of the Seventh (Gary Owen) on their caps from Coursen, and others, all sharing in the merriment and brotherhood that drinking and entertainment provided. Only once did I hear of an altercation during the winter of 1964-1965 of two units when the MPs came and broke it up. I wasn't told too much of what happened but some inebriated soldiers had began a punching bout, when more joined in, and even our own guards from the guard house were called out. It is my understanding that it didn't last long as "punches hurt," or so I was told. I never knew of *josans* joining in the altercations as I guess they could lose their VD cards or ID (Medical) Cards and camp privileges.

Notably, the *mamasans* and village *josans* within each community developed an awareness of their own "regulars," and soldiers trafficking from other communities were always welcomed though immediately recognized as visitors or perhaps as newly arrived "lifers." The rest of the population were fully aware of all soldiers among the indigenous residents and were tolerated whether as continued liberators or government guests.

It was customary to freely enter any community at will or camp for that matter. We were free to roam through all the earth packed paths, and even navigate through private backyards because we knew that the uniform alone was welcomed by the *mamasans* with their smiling *josans* at any time whether trading was to be had or not. I loved to walk up and down, around and through the tiny paths, and up the back mountains of any village to take pictures. I guess I subconsciously felt right at home as in my own barrio community. I remember walking by the brothels with the foul odor of beer reeking from the doors. I strolled through back paths hearing *josans* giggling, and "carefreely" offering their wares to all bypassing soldiers. The agrarian neighbors lived in their own world indirectly insensitive to the American soldiers. We were also welcomed at the tiny shops and general stores that these tiny rural villages boasted as the Military Payment Certificate (though illegal) was always well received. Not very many soldiers ate in the village. To begin with, other than Seoul Cola and OB Beer, the food was not acceptable to the soldier's stomach. I learned of a few bouts with hepatitis despite all immunizations and warnings at orientation. Curiously enough I never saw a chapel, fire station, police station, utility buildings, etc. as in the average stateside community. The villages only provided scant necessities to sustain the rural community life.

The overbearing stench of human fecal matter permeated the entire community, but the stench of human fluid waste was prevalent at back windows and doors and highly evident when passing by. I guess all communities were self-sufficient or perhaps undeveloped at this time.

I had always heard of army installations in the United States historically known as forts, as in the movie *Fort Apache* and as in the *Rin-Tin-Tin* television series during my boyhood. I also recalled the sign "FORT S.H." on buses in bustling downtown San Antonio while growing up and of Fort Polk and Fort Harrison where I trained in the army.

Passing through the cavalry sector, I immediately noticed the differences. The expanse of the Korean country open before me was a complete opposite to the military setting I had experienced in the States. Fort Sam Houston, Fort James Polk, Fort Benjamin Harrison, and Oakland Army Terminal were all self-contained subdivisions or perhaps "sub-communities" within a city. In effect, each military post was one autonomous community. Army "forts" in Korea, on the other hand, were barbwire enclosed camps secured with strategically spaced guard towers and an identifying sign posted over a main gate, and sometimes a rear gate.

As a youth the term camp was a thrilling recollection of sleeping in a recreation tent under open skies as my one rare experience at Indian Creek Boy Scout Camp in Ingram, Texas the summer of 1957. The word *camp* had a dissimilar meaning in Korea. "Camp" identified our compounds as indeed camps in existence from the time of the war. A "camp" in time of war was a "temporary location" that remained in place through the armistice but the term continued because the war never officially ended. Hostilities ceased during a ten-year armistice or ceasefire in 1953 so that in consequence the war was still in effect as were the camps.

To my observations, a camp or compound in Korea paralleled a stateside neighborhood. The smaller basic and perhaps specialized camp offered the billeting Quonset as bedrooms equating a bunkhouse or barrack. The Quonset or barrack itself was home, with fellow bunk mates, family. A row of barracks constituted neighbors' homes with a communal restroom with bathhouse nearby. The single mess hall building would be the kitchen with sit-in dining area. A motor pool with vehicles constituted a garage, while the orderly room would be the business office governing the compound with the company commander being the administrator and division representative.

Among other facilities common to many compounds was a chapel, a pub (EM Club), and barber shop. These camps housed units of tanks, artillery, infantry, mortar, dog handler's units—each with its own unit, orderly room (commanding officer's office) and independent in specialty and duty or combinations thereof.

The entire military was dependent on the four recreation centers for greater entertainment and leisure pursuits that, with one exception at Camp McGovern, were independent and separate compounds. These Recreation Centers or camps were also referred to as cultural centers (CCs) or wittily termed concentration camps that boasted a service club, recreation facilities, and a theater; an EM, NCO, and CO club; a better stocked PX, added hobby and leisure facilities consisting of a photo lab, gym, bowling lane, and woodcraft shop. RC#1 was located by Camp Beard at Yongju-Gol, RC#2 within Camp McGovern, RC#3 at Spoonbill, north of the Imjin close to Camp Wagner, and RC#4 by Camp Pelham and the greater village of Munsan-Ni and Sonyu-Ri. Thus, the neighborhood was a "modernized" or "permanent" though ironically a "temporary" camp remaining as such following the Korean conflict.

In the words of a recreation center commander:

> "In 1967-68 Camp Pelham was occupied by the 1st Bn 15th Arty as well as HHB 6th Bn 37th Arty, and, was also home to the Red Cross Donut Dollys. Camp Pelham was the same area the United Nations Command had set up their HQs during the armistice negotiations. The final signing by General Clarke took place in the compound movie theater, a semi-permanent building that later became known as Armistice Hall. Also in the Camp Pelham area was the AFKN broadcast studio, the village of Sonyu-ri and Recreation Center #4. RC#4 housed a movie theater, a PX, a bowling alley, a gymnasium, a library, a service club, a softball field, a taxi stand, and a branch of the Bank of America. It was also home to the Kiowa Skydivers club."
>
> —1LT Ken Leighty,
> Compound Commander, RC#4,
> Korea, 1967-1968.

It was the place itself, it "grew" on you. It was in the line of walking guard where I maximized time for reflection and thought. I discerned a peaceful ambience over the dawning land where I stood vigilant. The dark predawn hours under the lampposts limited my view beyond my post, thus demanding my full attention to duty. But then, a phenomenon occurred that distracted me from duty and jarred my very soul in harmony with the land: the first soft glow of dawn, the blush of bluishness, the advancing whiteness of light, and the progressing yellowish beams heralding the brightness of morning light. The play of light mesmerized me as the phenomena of the quiet and still earth spectacularly opened before me. I felt assimilated, digested, and now flowing within the circulatory system of silent Mother Korea. Calm and still described this dawn as well, thus the name The Land of the Morning Calm. Perhaps the mountainous landscape of the geography contributed to the stillness of the land. In effect, the land became one of those picture-perfect paintings capturing the viewer's gaze and rendering the yearning to enter and savor the place and moment, like those Chinese gum-drop mountain misty scenes with vertical stroke writing painted on silk. Perhaps too, the stillness was due to this being a military sector located in a postwar buffer zone not ready for "modern" infrastructure. This zone was an agrarian culture prevalent in a developing country prone to invasion, markedly perhaps not enabling investment in the technology of the sixties, thus appearing in the European Dark Ages.

In the course of my duty tour, I experienced many a twilight evening just as calm and serene. In the quiet moments standing guard duty I became acutely conscious of the stillness in the summer and winter evenings, but more so in the spring and fall. As available light progressively diminished during sunset, and dusk to darkness, I experienced a vacuum, a settling of movement, moments of privacy that involved me in the midst of the whole of the land. Tranquility of the evenings became a universal embrasure, harmonious and still, which overpowered me as I became one with the land. It was a special moment when my tinnitus, my sounds of silence prevailed and were at their loudest. It was as if the whole world had stopped, just for me to enjoy my daily fresco. I felt like I belonged to the land and the land belonged to me, particularly in those two segments of day.

This third world farming country was reduced to the use of human feces for the fertilizing of the eternal yielding rice fields. The stench was prevalent all over this northern sector. In time one became accustomed to it, lived side by side with it, and became part of the inhabitant. The rice paddies were established throughout the division area, so the rice paddy, the nearby village, the passing road, and the surrounding mountains were our habitation. A few times after a night in the village the guys crossed the familiar paddies like a backyard on a shortcut route back to camp to elude the authorities.

The war had now officially resumed in 1964 following the end of the armistice scheduled to July 1963. As occupying forces, the division area was actually the war zone such that our trucks and tanks rolled, and soldiers trafficked, without restraint, anywhere, any place, anytime, at will in our Korea at this Far East corner of Asia.

Our Crossed Cultures

I drank it in, I drank it all
Nook and cranny, street and wall
Palace, temple, museum and hall
One great place my dream at call

In retrospect, as I rambled through all the Cav and Seoul during my entire duty year, I studied the contrasting cultures. I was fascinated by the chanted language and perplexing script; the sloe-eyed people and their peculiar dress; the Buddhist religion and solemnity of their temples; the geography and agricultural country; and the infrastructure and edifices of this new and different country in the Oriental hemisphere known as Korea. I cannot stress enough that upon my initial commute through Seoul, everywhere and all around, my stateside languages were bombarded with the peculiar symbols of the Korean brushed writing. Accustomed to our alphabet on all signs, I was mystified. It didn't take me long, however, to decipher the meaning of their advertised products or services due to the accompanying related sketches or drawings.

I really should have realized earlier that I would be completely taken aback, being that this new land with a diametric language would be totally different from mine. Not only did I encounter a new language but a wholly new *written* language. I mean, it was happening! I loved to hear the population chatting and I was reminded much of my primary language, Spanish. The phonics and accents were similar, and there were times in San Antonio when I switched from English to Spanish, I automatically did so here in Korea. No way! No one understood Spanish. Some barely understood English. I realized then that if I was to mingle with the people I would have to learn their language as they would not understand my "Spanglish" or "Mex-Tex" English. I knew that this, the local military jargon was like my "Spanglish."

In Seoul or elsewhere in the interior of Korea, Korean mixed with English or vise-versa would be totally ineffective.

Taking in this entire new wonder, I found, that not only was one of my travel dreams now a reality, but here was a rare opportunity for me to learn not only the spoken language, but also to read and write this perplexing script! This was already an unexpected blessing on top of touring the world while in the U.S. Army! Despite my shock, within a few miles down the road I was already anticipating the writing and seeking adventures ahead in this new land of baffling inscriptions.

We were "confined" by our language. Despite the military jargon and street language, Hangul, being Korean language, was the actual oral communication. English being *our* language, further caused our dependency upon one another thereby further strengthening our camaraderie. To some extent, this language hedge further contributed to our comfort zones so that we did not roam about at large as we would in any city stateside.

The Oriental people fascinated me. Their language, their customs, their mode of dress, and even where they lived was interesting. To begin with, I was fascinated to see so many Oriental people. On the army bus from our ride from ASCOM through Seoul to Camp Ross, I saw their mode of dress different. Among westernized dress, the difference was highlighted by elderly men who wore white blown trousers, jackets, and in some cases, with mini top hats while the elderly women wore white long bell-shaped dresses with tight vests. As viewed from rail rides and roads all over the cavalry, being the agrarian countryside, I saw Asiatic people walking along the road—men with the A-frames and women with jugs, trays, or baskets on their heads—a contrast to the United States of 1965, where it was customary to carry burdens against the chest with hands accommodating the bottoms of packages. Sloe eyes and petite height was another evident difference that fascinated me.

In the States we are accustomed to see chapels in every neighborhood in the community. These are identified with cathedral colored glass windows, a simple sign, a cross or steeple, or a combination of either. We also have cemeteries where we lay our loved ones to rest that are identified with headstones. It is our custom to have funerals in commercial homes, vehicle processions, and burial ceremonies. Some of us observe the Sabbath with a day off for rest and houses of worship are always crammed with worshippers in their Sunday best. In effect, it is a given that Sunday is set apart for worship and rest at large.

In contrast, I never noticed a chapel or altar for respective Christian or Buddhist worship in any community in my extensive wanderings in the Cav. I did come across private and family Buddhist temples while clambering all over Easy Queen. In Seoul I came across a huge beautiful multicolored Buddhist temple, the Kyung Guk Sa, when I visited the northeast quadrant of Seoul while solo touring, and a picturesque temple north of Nullo-Ri. One day while touring Pobwan-Ni, I noted a funeral procession composed of a huge colorful ovular case born by side straps on men's shoulders. I saw mourners—professionally dressed hirelings in woven basket-like fiber tunics—actually shedding tears at a funeral. Unlike our dead buried in orderly rows in selected cemeteries, the Korean dead were buried randomly on hillsides—their place of rest specifically and purposefully chosen by each family. During field problems and while scrambling all over the mountainsides, we accidentally stumbled over burial mounds and tombstones overlooking the valley and rice fields below (see photo p 350).

A FUNERAL PROCESSION AT POBWAN-NI. NOTE CARRIER AT HEAD OF MARCH.

A NUMBER OF MEN BEAR DECORATED COFFIN. NOTE HIRED MOURNER IN WHITE AND CHILDREN BEING SHOOED AWAY.

The U.S. Army never held back on the availability of ecclesial assistance for any denomination at the camp chapel, though attendance was usually minimal. I am sure that at specific chapels denominational services were conducted such as my LDS services at Camp Pelham, yet I remember Catholic and nondenominational services prevalently posted at chapel marquees. I noted that the chaplains' branch crests of 1965 reflected their denomination: a plain cross identified a Christian (nondomination) minister; a cross with a crucifix, a Catholic minister; and a Star of David above a Ten Commandment double tablet symbolized the Jewish faith. It must be understood that the average age of the soldier was in the late teens or early twenties with other interests, and far away from any parental supervision of the Sundays in home.

The Korea of 1964 was still under a third world agrarian economy. As a result, the whole of the mountainous division area, every available piece of land in *our county*, was cleared and terraced for the planting of rice. Everywhere were signs of poverty as the population was recovering from the war. Unless one was from the country accustomed to fields and shacks, one would, more than likely, feel right at home—except for the fecal stench.

This scenario was nothing like what I had just left behind in the States: rice paddies, poverty everywhere, hovels made of mud-plastered sticks or of scrap brick and crate wood, hovels, mountains, in a supposedly war zone as opposed to brick or wood residential houses and mansions, and commercial modern infrastructure with the poor and rich living accordingly. I had just left behind cities with homes.

The animal drawn carts and electric street cars I saw in Seoul threw me back in time, at least, to the Great West and the Roaring Twenties, respectively, in U.S. history (and which contrasted with the ox and plow I saw in the Cav). I was stunned when I saw South Gate, a medieval structure that our Alamo, back home, could not rival by decades, let alone by centuries. The avenues were broad with noisy traffic, the overpowering smell of diesel, and buses with curved backs likened to those I remembered from my childhood in the early fifties. Eventually, I rode the train system which impressed me with the panoramic countryside. I had only traveled by train to California as a four-year-old child—the mode of travel in my time being Greyhound buses with airfares just beginning to be affordable to middle class America. Seoul being the capital would seem to have at least bettered the concrete open-windowed buildings that I barely remember and I grew up with in downtown San Antonio of the late forties and the fifties inclusive. Looking at Seoul in 1965 was like viewing the matted postcards circa turn-of-the-century in my mother's picture box. It somewhat resembled the reconstruction of the South following the Civil War, this Seoul of our Korea in this Far East corner of Asia.

Epilogue

I realized that I was journeying through living history—that the armistice had only been written eleven years earlier and that I was present in the year where hostilities could resume anytime. Decades later I realized I had been so involved in just the thought of travel that I had completely neglected to consider local culture, thus my dreams were truly doubled within this Far East corner of Asia.

The Camaraderie

Prologue

It could be argued that a brotherhood is composed of members having a common bond, interest, or experience. The military unit, the division, in this case the First Cavalry Division succeeded by the Second Infantry Division, geographically covered as much land as its subunits or as many compounds as were scattered all over the Division Area. The members of this Army Division, as with any other group, instantly formulated a sense of belonging, especially when all wore the same insignia. A few subunits of other divisions sharing the same uniform in our area were warily and merely glanced at, yet all well accepted. It may be that camaraderie is indefinable, but must be experienced within a relative state of affairs so that each man feels a sense of debt and association. Perhaps, it is the love of one's fellowman to defend one another with their lives knowing always that for a soldier in the field, death is part of that life.

Shoulder to shoulder there all stood
Every man knew and understood
One for all and all for one
Standing tall second to none

I experienced a sense of belonging from the very beginning as I immediately sensed a dependence upon one another. Living in a foreign land with indigenous people, a different language and script, dissimilar religion or philosophy, money and pricing, a contrast of living conditions, yet all sharing the hardship of duty under the possibility of invasion in this war zone did indeed create a sense of camaraderie. A trust within the same Quonset became greater as brothers bunking under the same roof often took natural responsibility for care of one another. Although each soldier's work-specialty differed, it was a trust within a trust as all subconsciously shared in the common concern in Korea and the sole purpose of occupation: the remote possibility of open hostility and resumption of the war! We were under the auspices of the government and bonded by camaraderie contained like a religious order, an extended fraternity, a specialized society within a foreign element, like the Foreign Compound in the motion picture *55 Days at Peking* with Charlton Heston and Ava Garner. One of the most binding factors was the cross-culture represented such as religious denomination, former occupation and education, race and perhaps ethnic background that was respected and unquestioned which created a stronger bond and esprit-de-corps. The existence alone of a fellow soldier—whether lifer or short timer—justified his membership in the brotherhood. The division worked as if we were a specialized group under one roof, moving as one consequential function. Our duty posts were generally located within a stone's throw inside the compound much like a self-contained beehive or an ant colony. Duty just seemed to me that each one of us had a purpose and a common denominator; that is, an occupation within company.

The KATUSA performed all duties right along with us. Although they were serving within the limits of their country, they walked guard, dug ditches, ate food, wore our military patches and crests, handled the M60 on jeeps, all for a reported salary of $1.60 per month. I never knew that these Korean soldiers ever complained, they must have been well indoctrinated or interviewed by their commanders as well as ours. I heard following my departure from Korea that many were killed alongside with our own soldiers all along the length of the Demilitarized Zone during the "DMZ War" and "Cold War." It would not be surprising that some took a bullet for our men as our men took a bullet for them. Following my tour of duty, two hundred eighty-plus soldiers were killed along with uncounted Korean soldiers we may not be aware of. At the time of this writing, the American public is not aware of these casualties. The way I understand it, these 280-plus dead were not properly noted at the time in order to avoid drawing notice from the Vietnam conflict or that the Korean armistice was expired. Today, many mid-60s thru mid-70s Korea DMZ veterans afflicted by exposure to the Agent Orange chemical, yes *Agent Orange* are experiencing difficulty in recognition and thus therapy. These Korean soldiers walking the DMZ fence shoulder to shoulder with our soldiers were surely cemented with a stronger bond or a brotherhood of blood.

Our Turkish brothers, although one company of about four platoons strong, were also right there along with us. None of us entered their compound not only because of the many stories we had heard, but mostly because we really had no business there. They were a unique military force and we were all only too glad they were on our side. Although numerous stories circulated about their contact with the Korean population, there was less regarding contact with our soldiers. These men were highly respected and their presence was greatly appreciated. The way I orally heard it decades later at DMZ veterans' reunions and from *the* veterans who had worked in their compound, should invasion arise the Turk soldiers declared they would zealously stand shoulder-to-shoulder, man-to-man with their protégés and us, and without hesitation receive and return fire, bullet for bullet. They were seen on their own maneuvers climbing over the rough Korean terrain shouldering their weapons and artillery, while we were rolled around on deuce-and-a-halfs.

Although we all shared in the spirit of charity—gladly giving out our rations and loose change—to the needy or children, the population looked upon us as sources of a quick dollar from vendors. It wasn't so much that we had money; it was the fact that we were a source of money. Despite the few money lenders, many of us gladly loaned money without interest to comrades, even to the newly arrived soldiers, whether short timers or lifers, with absolute trust strengthening the camaraderie even more.

We shared trust in knowing that upon relieving a sentry during guard duty, another would be there and we were confident that our relief would be on time. One would have felt disheartened, frantic, perhaps betrayed, had the relieving soldier not appeared. The post could not be abandoned without a relief guard. The brothers at the DMZ surely depended more on one another as lives were at stake.

The army provided the best it could under the circumstances to make free time and life as comfortable as possible for the troops. The recreation centers had more facilities, including sightseeing, than the smaller compounds to entertain or detract from the duty of "hardship." Although

I mostly ran around alone, I was never lonely. I was never bored; I always found something and there was a whole never-ending world of Korean wealth to attract and retain my interest. Decades later, I learned that many of our comrades did some serious drinking which probably created "drinking buddy" company. Since I am not a drinking man, I did not experience the closeness that develops among drinking buddies. I suppose that the trust and confidence grew "experientially" as the alcohol flowed! If such was the case, then the brotherhood more than likely extends to *oneness*, indicating the harmony of *an understanding*, or a confidant. This chapter will need to be written by one of those comrades. The guys I'd hang around with, my two best buddies, Marvin or George, were also nondrinkers. Marvin and George were two of four "bosom buddies" with whom I formed a closer friendship (N.E. and Abilio at McGovern and Ross)—but distant due to the nature of scheduled duty that governed our common interests. This buddy partnering was further limited by tour of duty tenure as very few soldiers' tours of duty coincided. There was always the thought in the back of the mind that we lived only for the moment, knowing that our best buddy or either one of us would rotate stateside ending this camaraderie segment from this Far East corner of Asia.

Epilogue

Companionship was a given, it was a fact of life, an understanding, a natural almost creed, a faith, or conceivably, a new formulated religion, if I may say; clearly though, water sought its own level. The phonetic chat and company of the *josans* and leisure moments accessible in this overseas component were a sure addendum to the comradeship. Wearing a required uniform, enclosed with a compound, surrounded by mountains, limited to village life ("community") within a foreign element compelled us to that dependence on one another—and *that* was *our life*. It was this camaraderie that got us through our days in this Land of the Morning Calm and that made it a life apart with its own norms and values.

Camaraderie Lost

Prologue

The greatest kick serving one's tour of duty in Korea for any soldier was looking forward to the departure date, especially days in the single digits, the DEROS, the Date Eligible to Depart Overseas. Several times a day, from somewhere in the compound, the shout *"short!"* was heard, meaning fewer days to departure date. All of us looked forward and lived for this day, and teased others unmercifully, especially the new in-coming lifers. One relished the anticipated clearing, turning in all equipment just prior to departure and flaunting clearance papers. The others just cast a forlorn glance and went about their duty. On the departure date the soldier dressed up all happy with all out-processing completed, flight ticket and reassignment orders in hand, not giving his buddies further thought, but filled with the anticipation of returning to the States and to an American life. Yet, all left something behind that we were virtually never to recover, the camaraderie.

Left behind were times gone by
Now manic unknowing why
Returning home at one year cost
Mesmerized at comrades lost

Subsequent to all my out-processing, and solo flights across the Pacific, at Travis Air Force Base and at San Francisco in the Western United States, I arrived in San Antonio to spend Thanksgiving through Christmas and New Year. I walked the downtown streets of San Antonio, more so parading my greens, showing off my fourrageres and military ribbons of the Second Infantry Division (unit awards not personally earned), rather than my civilian clothes of high school. I got many a side-glance from pedestrians, policemen, and girls who mainly glimpsed at my decorated coat, not at me. I attended dances at the local hangout and recognized many former girls who were seniors during my year in Korea. Many of these girls had blossomed into beautiful young women, now lovelier than the high school sophomores and juniors I remembered. I had forgotten the radiance of our Latin-American girls, their warm feminine bodies, and their daring innocence which I hadn't experienced since the dances at school. Newly arrived from Korea, I foolishly rediscovered the girls of my culture just as pretty as those I had just left behind except that they fluently spoke both languages, Spanish and English. I so enjoyed my leave such that I had even forgotten I was in the army until I counted the days and realized I had to report at Fort Bliss in El Paso, Texas within two days. I packed up my duffle bag and AWOL bag, headed for the airport and back to army life.

As soon as I arrived on post and duty at Personnel, I noticed a great change from what I had previously experienced. In 1966, the Civil Rights Act of 1964 began to bloom in government offices and especially in the hiring of clerks in Personnel. Whereas before male soldiers dominated the office, now women civil servants, retired military and civilians served side by side with our sergeants as supervisors. Aside from the retired military, I found supervisory employees rather arrogant in their attitude toward the work and especially egotistical toward us returning and experienced veterans. I despised the nonmilitary connected supervisors because of their pomposity as they were not experienced veterans as I or my returning buddies from Korea or Vietnam. It was the young and single girls that sweetened the work force. We wore greens or khakis to the office unlike the daily attire of fatigues in Korea. The Finance and Accounting Office complex functioned as an open business administrative center under one roof in contrast to the individual Quonset offices of Korea. My job as Personnel Administrative Clerk enabled me to browse through the records for buddies from Korea. However, I personally found them by accident.

I came across Virgil, and my best buddies Marvin and George, who all seemed to have a purpose. Virgil, whom I only spoke to once or twice and was family in Hooch Ten while in Korea—a draftee and therefore an older soldier—was in his own world and evidently unaffected by the camaraderie. George, a supply clerk somewhere, bought a red car and was always going somewhere; and curiously enough, he neither invited me nor did it cross my mind to tag along—I guess I was still stunned and within a period of adjustment. Marvin, shortly, was wrapped up with a Latin girl. I was soon involved too, with my Latin girlfriend so that we all had a life in the civilian sector of the city, and outside of the fort, so the dependence or camaraderie of Korea was nonexistent—we each had (or resumed?) an *American* life. Because of the nature of our job specialties, my buddies and I bunked at multi-story ceramic barracks clear across Fort Bliss away from one another. This, too, was way unlike bunking within one or two one-story Quonsets a stone's throw away from one another as within the camps of Korea. Thus, we lost all track of a sense of belonging, inadvertently desensitized, with the brotherhood vanished.

Fool and romanticist enough that I was to compare the local tail end of the Rocky Mountains with Mount Easy Queen and that Blue Lancer was just over Mount Franklin—from Camp McGovern, it wasn't. The mountainous terrain of Korea had limited my peripheral to life within the compound (the neighborhood and community) which was the closest association to home. To my comparing mind, *now* the neighborhood was the entire military installation, the city had become the community, and the whole nation was the county! As we assimilated within the city of El Paso, Texas, there was no longer a dependence on one another; the comradeship of Korea was absent! All bunks were void of soldiers whose only purpose was for sleeping and not for "dwelling" as in the Quonsets. In the past the Camp PX held mementos of Korea and extended needs while the local (at barracks) Fort Bliss PX simply held corner store needs like the small Korean camp PXs which likened to the American neighborhood corner grocery stores back in my barrio. I was forced with slow realization which my soul rejected to accept that I was back in my environment and that Korea was a segment of the past.

Duty in Korea was a restricted way of life, limited by military duty but still *our life*; in effect the military was our life and our peers were our family whereas in the States, back in our elements, *we had a life*. Here at Fort Bliss each and all GIs *had a life* away from the fort.

The sun shone as a brighter hot unrelenting searing disk under the blue cloudless southwest desert sky burning my very skin and pouring out precious water from my every pore. Fort Bliss was so spread out that all facilities were seemingly miles away requiring extended walking causing fatigue. Again, as in Korea, I experienced unscheduled army buses with no public transportation within the vast fort other than expensive taxis. I unconsciously missed the frequent reliable and inexpensive kimchi transportation of Korea. I also missed the immediacy of the community back in Korea on more than one occasion. For the first time in my life I felt alone in this vast environment that required either bus rides or independently driving a car—which is probably what George recognized immediately upon his arrival. I realized my sheltered upbringing followed by close communities in Korea left me unprepared to assimilate into the big city life without feeling alone. Yes, alone, never lonely, but had I had yet to meet my girlfriend, I admit I probably would have experienced true loneliness for the first time in my life. Yes, I was adrift amidst an ocean of independent soldiers who had not experienced the camaraderie of Korea or who had resumed or immediately assimilated into the stateside lifestyle.

One evening one of my buddies excitedly returned from a dance where the famous Sonny and Sunglows pop group from San Antonio performed saying that the place was crammed with an overabundance of girls—"*muchas, y muy bonitas*" (many and very pretty), he kept repeating. I silently reflected that there were pretty girls everywhere. I further reflected that, in part, prior "loneness" was alleviated by the open conviviality with the *josans* of Korea. And that some of the local girls and some of the soldiers were advancing toward a final commitment. All local girls were indeed marriageable candidates, in contrast to those in whose "company" capacities were left behind in Korea. I was not ready for any kind of commitment, and although I was serious with my sweetheart, I was not ready to be tied down. A whole new life crossed my mind—marriage with no more travel or reenlistment and travel, I nixed both!

Within a few months I had explored all that there was to explore and all the interesting places in El Paso—the missions, Mount Cristo Rey, the tri-state corner pyramid boundary monuments, old Fort Bliss officers quarters, the UTEP Centennial Museum, the cable car ride up the mountain, etc. From a Korean viewpoint, I was reminded of Seoul each time I crossed Rio Grande and visited Ciudad Juarez in Mexico. In fact, it was George that didn't like Mexico because it was "too much like Korea." I was ready to move to another Permanent Change of Station or in the least take a bus south to explore Mexico City with all its Aztec museums and archeological wonders—only problem was that Uncle Sam didn't cover the expense. Yet, the mere fact of being on the border with Mexico opened my mind to the reality of travel to the interior—it was doable, but not on my current army salary. Fool enough was I to once consider a short-term reenlistment in Korea (following a one-year tenure) to see more of the world when I would end up at a similar ghastly PCS such as this desert city with remaining tenure limited to a handful local sites—unlike a whole overseas country like Korea or Japan (and Europe had I reenlisted). To me, longing for another assignment as epic as Korea, reenlistment, and the opportunity to travel would have been my sole purpose for rejoining the army. I soon realized I had outgrown part of my late youth and naïveté.

I still experienced apathy for the local military life and doggedly longed for the camaraderie and duty of Korea. Decades later, I learned that the Korea I knew and toured was no longer the same. Camp Blue Lancer Valley was no longer swarming with soldiers as in my day: green cavaliers attending my princess; it had become a ghost town with a skeleton crew. Many soldiers bound for Korea were diverted to Vietnam as were many transferred out from Korea to Southeast Asia. The Korea I yearned for no longer existed.

In the words of a Communications Specialist:

> "When I arrived in Korea on February 1966, though the units were at field duty, the second of the thirty-eight was nonetheless woefully short of manpower and equipment. The BLV was a ghost camp with a skeleton crew pulling guard duty and charge

of quarters constantly besides taking care of downed commo wires. The whole second battalion, all four (HHC, A, B, C, and other support) companies was under 500 men with my platoon undermanned having 6 GIs and 3 KATUSAs. When my secret clearance came through, I went into the message center to learn the job before Sergeant Tomzack ETS'd. Well, for the rest of my tour there were 2 of us running the message center 24/7 and was never left without one of us being there, it got very tiring at times—we didn't have enough manpower to really do anything. My very first impression of the situation was what Custer must have felt at the Little Bighorn."

—SP4 David Pechtold, Message Center Specialist,
HHC 2nd Bn 38th Inf, 2nd ID,
Korea, Feb 66-Mar 67

I had to accept that gone were the days of gallivanting around wearing the Olive Greens with pile caps and camouflaged scarves, with trousers bloused above our spit-shined jump boots by the houseboys. Left behind were the days of looking forward to seeing sloe-eyed ebony-haired China dolls with sweet Oriental accents. Vanished were those days where our stomping grounds were narrowed to our camp and village community. Spent were the days when we were limited to the AFKN radio station and sweet lovey-dovey dedications and dreams with a waiting sweetheart, or just of home stateside atop a freezing guard tower. Left behind were flashes of Marvin and I clambering all over the Queen, and of George and I childishly horse playing and wrestling or of wandering through Pobwan-Ni, Yongju-Gol, or Munsan-Ni. I resumed stateside dress "norms" consisting of civilian clothes (now webolene or dectolene (polyester) shirts) not worn for one and half years since "zero week," day one in Basic Combat Training, or high school teen fashion scene. New were the days of girl's fashions of miniskirts, fishnet hose with Nancy Sinatra's sexy voice blaring "These Boots were Made for Walking" on the radio. Then Staff Sergeant Barry Sadler's "The Green Berets" hit the radio waves and each time all fell silent at the office or at the barracks—especially quiet were the new recruits of which many were being shipped to Vietnam. All military news centered on Vietnam, nothing of Korea where I had served and which continued to be "forgotten." Oh, well, the news goes where there is war and Korea was peaceful in the year 1966, or so it was thought. However, I used to always sing "Coming Home Soldier" by Bobby Vinton to my sweetheart and subsequent wife declaring that I had returned "home" to El Paso solely to meet and marry her.

Those of us who enlisted in the army following high school graduation, and had experienced a continued life in Korea, returned to an updated or novel American way of life. Perhaps, some of us relearned or continued a life unlike that which we had left behind prior to enlistment or draft. I felt I had to catch up with a world I had left behind as an adolescent and returned to as a man. I had awakened from a pleasant dream in a medieval setting, having slept while the rest of the world had rolled on. I realized that I had left behind my one year growing up in 1965 Korea, never to be retrieved, in the esprit-de-corps of our Korea solely in my pestering memory of my once Far East corner of Asia.

Epilogue

The lack of solidarity was not apparent until I was at stateside duty. Once back at a military fort within a stateside city, perhaps driving a car enabling absolute independence, the sense of the close ties had physically vanished. We were surrounded by the English language and stateside environment; meeting and dating American girls became our life—a single man's life behind, with thoughts of marriage. We experienced a life, a "new" life, or simply resumed a life. However, we had changed. That one year as a soldier in Korea had changed our spiritual composition. Our original place of departure, the United States, felt like being reborn, like growing up. Like a snake shedding its skin, we left behind a unique unified military way of life, a foreign culture in a limited environment, and an outgrown sense of brotherhood that only those who were there could understand.

PART IV

Close

When I joined the army . . . it was the fulfillment of all my boyish hopes and dreams.
                              —General Douglas MacArthur

Alas, good things come to an end
With all my roads my way they wend
By ways, back ways, all my ways tend
My Far East year my wish naught end

Epilogue

It was May 24, 1967, that I so looked forward to that finally arrived. *It* was my Eligible Date to Terminate Service (ETS) or my discharge from active military duty. The mustering out spiel at the CO's office, the A Battery Service Group Orderly Room at Fort Bliss, Texas, to look into benefits met with my response, "I am a veteran of the Korea hardship duty tour, there is nothing in the army that can make me reenlist, and I have seen so many fresh acting-jack corporals give me orders who have yet to know the army's gray side." I also related adverse experiences with civilian "supervisors." Without further a due, I turned in all my military materials and walked away from the post a free man!

During my last week in the army I applied for a position as a State Trooper with the Texas Department of Public Safety at El Paso. I took aptitude, physical, and other exams, but at my final interview, a captain, a lieutenant and a sergeant would determine my hiring. Following general questioning all three became incredibly serious, as the last point was made. My background investigation disclosed that I had lived a "sheltered" life and that immediately upon graduation I had enlisted in the army. My interviewers clearly mentioned that I had applied for the department in El Paso, when I could have returned home to my family and applied in San Antonio. Three incredibly grave pairs of eyes resembling a firing squad pierced right through me. I had no reply for that unexpected shotgun blast which struck at my tender-most of feelings, and if they were trying to break me, they succeeded. I broke down and cried, I was told to go and wash my face. Upon my return, the captain and the lieutenant were heading out the front door. With my heart choking my throat, knowing I had botched up, I was making a run for it, when the sergeant called me, smiling. He motioned me back to his office. I expected a death blow when he said to report Monday in trainee uniform! I was floored with elation! My guess was that the department could not have a vindictive officer with unresolved problems who would not represent the commissioned officer's badge honorably. He said the interview was a complete success. I attended the academy in Austin, Texas, and after one month's training decided that a law enforcement career wasn't for me. From Austin I headed for San Antonio, and after one month with the family, though lucratively employed, I announced I was departing for El Paso. Upon announcing my departure, my ever critical sisters concluded that I would more than likely become a lost soul (probably to drink, tobacco, women, unemployment, indebtedness, etc.) and that eventually one day return home crawling on bended knees begging my mother's forgiveness for some imagined fault. Standing around, like cloaked judges at a Spanish inquisition court, they would all witness my mother's extended arm magnanimously granting me absolution while they smirked at my repentant soul. And my daughter commented: *"So there was dead silence at the opposite end of the line when you announced your Celestial Marriage with Mom to the family!"*—Rebecca M. Smith, Army Wife, Mother.

I was employed by the El Paso Civil Service Commission as a clerk in four separate departments for eighteen years. In my first year I met a wonderful lady, a return missionary at church, teaching a Sunday school class whose sparkling green eyes under the sunshine that filtered through the sculptured cathedral glazed window, dazzled me. (Curiously enough, we both simultaneously served during the years 1964-1967, she as a missionary in Mexico, and I in the army.) Two months later she accepted my modest solitaire diamond ring, and the following fifth month a Celestial Marriage united us for all time and eternity at THE HOUSE OF THE LORD,

Mesa Arizona—a family first. The following decade saw us blessed with four wonderful children, and fourteen grandchildren to date. That all our children successfully dated and married members of our faith; that our son labored in Lord's vineyard of Germany as a missionary for the church; that during my last three years employed with the El Paso Civil Service where I obtained a night position enabling me to attend day school, and graduated from the University of Texas at El Paso with a Bachelor of Science in Education, were all family firsts—away from a former inferno. I taught at El Paso public schools where I experienced two gratifying decades working with children from the second through eighth grades and experienced the joy of witnessing a child learn.

I have no regret and I make no apology for my absence or presence in my San Antonio hometown. I never missed the love that was never there. The San Antonio siblings had stood still and solely lived for life with no motivation for self-edification, higher education, yielding limited growth. Most only lived day by day for life itself, on dead-end jobs and never rose above the second level of Abraham Maslo's pyramid of hierarchal needs. My sisters Magnolia and Gladiola held to the prideful persistent belief that I should "come home and see mother" whom they unconditionally worshipped and who could do or who never did anything wrong, and to whom I owed a "repentant apology." They were apathetic of my emotional sufferings, indifferent, and their denial of my emotional abuse continued with putdowns the times I telephoned, visited, or wrote. Through the decades I never found why only I became my mother's scapegoat or if her incestuous marriage with my maternal uncle or her "incapacitated" children affected her harsh behavior toward me, considering the family's guarded and undisclosed conduct toward her; it has all been a well-kept family secret. My bishops, celestial family, and college and school counselors all independent of one another, concurred that I would have stagnated in the mire of the house or the city, as I would have been "pulled down" had I remained in San Antonio. This was substantiated by the adversity I received in the only two answers to my few letters—but responded to with hatred and rabid anger. I would not have been able to be myself, to grow, to develop, to advance as I did away from the bedlam that was once home. I now realize after a lifetime that the only happiness I ever experienced throughout my youth at any one time was outside the house. I realize that I had survived my childhood by burying myself in the classics, my comic books, adventure, and as actors' roles within motion pictures, and deeply absorbed in the lyrics of the songs of the fifties and sixties. My spirit was never broken—it was my dogmatic belief in God, the rigidity of self-discipline and restraint facilitated, augmented by military regulation, that got me through life and that made me a better person, impossible under my mother's abusive tutelage, or for that matter, in San Antonio.

It was the military that fulfilled most all of my temporal successes from employment skills to education, and travel outside the barrio as anticipated since childhood. I fully enjoyed my tour of duty in Korea. I always felt as welcomed as in the poverty of my barrio, except that all of the division area (the county) was one huge barrio, so I felt very much at home. I also felt comfortable with the language and the people who to me were fellow Latin-Americans. In comparison I learned to appreciate life in the United States and all its blessings—especially when awakened to the plight of my *pueblo* (people) in their obvious conditions of poverty visible immediately across the Rio Grande upon my arrival at the border with Mexico. I realized that as much as a military man that I thought I was or could be as within my childhood gaming and play, I learned of the rigidity in my character, but not a career man. I had experienced only enough military duty to fulfill my emotional and patriotic needs. I learned that I needed God far more than what I ever had before, although under the protection of the government and available denominational worship, I was morally on my own, and spiritually held accountable for all my deeds and actions—especially in the military sector of this Asian country. I further experienced an awakening from my naïveté when I realized that the army was not a tourist agency, and that one was stationed in the world somewhere, was coincidental to the needs of the army; and to tour surrounding sights was an accidental privilege to the venturing individual, and not a given under the benevolence of the COs. When I returned to the States, I was disappointed that the army in which I had perhaps considered serving a lifetime was no longer an army man's army. It was filled mostly with undisciplined civilians with power over us enlisted soldiers though they were not subject to military justice. When we addressed them in military terms they would respond, "I'm a civilian." These "civilians" enjoyed the best of our world, issuing out orders, imposing their authority over senior specialists and sergeants, and never subject to military duty such as kitchen police, guard duty, fatigue details, and etcetera. I concluded that this was not the army I wanted to continue being part of.

I am enjoying my retirement after eighteen years of service with the El Paso City Civil Service and another twenty with the independent school districts of Texas. I have been blessed with lifelong dreams of travel, and thus far toured the countries of Spain, Gibraltar, Morocco, Italy, Israel, Jordan,

Palestine, Egypt, China, Tibet, Peru, Mexico, Belize, England, Wales, Ireland, Scotland, and the nearby protectorate of Puerto Rico. I look forward to the publication of this book made further possible by my included photos taken while "touring" Korea and complemented by my brothers' comments. I thank my readers for allowing me to share my adventures and hope you found my chapters pleasant and enjoyable, especially if you felt you were right there with me—I will have fulfilled my purpose.

I extend my gratitude to this great government of the United States of America, the land of my birth—I neither owe nor claim allegiance to any other flag—for all the resources and benefits extended to my family and me regarding my education and lifelong temporal blessings. I also extend my thanks to my dad who emigrated to the U.S. and for having the foresight of the blessings of this great country. But none greater is my recognition of God Almighty, His Son Jesus Christ, and The Holy Ghost along with my eternal beloved Ines, who have seen me through a lifetime of trials and tribulations and to whom I owe my all, my very essence. I experience great comfort to know that my family and I, while families are not perfect . . . there is love . . . I learned love . . . love initiated by our beloved matriarch and duly practiced by them.

I was gifted with a clear memory so that at some reminiscing quiet solitary moments lost in reflections, I linger therein and thus view and blissfully *relive* that one year. Through the decades' daily and seasonal changes, I could never help but parallel them with similar days and weather conditions that I experienced during my adventuring or duty. Though I keep reminding myself that I was in the impressionable age of barely eighteen, fresh out of home and high school, I cannot help but smile as I sit back in silent contentment—I have no willpower. And still these balmy nights going on six decades as I lay quietly in bed enjoying the summer breezes through my window, my soul races back to September 1965 at Hooch Ten, when I relive the breezes that cooled my body as I dozed away toward slumber land, and ponder how many more of these reminiscing summers are still mine to enjoy. And when I take my walks in the stillness . . . in the quietude of the evening's dusk with silent sounds at their loudest . . . my soul again races back to Guard Tower Two at McGovern where I once became one with the privacy of the quiet, calm, dusky land; and when I listen carefully, I mentally hear a girl singing, ♪"Yo-SO-so-soo."♪ And then perhaps when Valkyrie honors me at the halls of Valhalla, it might be told that on certain cold afternoons at McGovern, sightings are reported of a fresh-faced green-clad sentinel's apparition atop a once existent fourth guard tower with glazed eyes significantly focused at the Queen, haunting his Far East corner of Asia.

Aahhh! . . . but this touching timeless tome of this Far East corner of Asia was my life's first travel experience—all expense paid—beginning in a faraway land, far-flung from the apparently long past inferno of home: my young soldier's memoirs, my one year growing up in 1965 Korea . . . this Far East corner of Asia.

If we ever forget that we are One Nation Under God, then we will be a nation gone under.

—Ronald Reagan

GLOSSARY

AFKN: American Forces Korean Network, our radio station
Ajoshi: a man's appellation
Ajema: a woman's appellation
Alert: Wailing sirens summoning the units to immediate field duty
Alamo: San Antonio, Texas shrine; a cottonwood tree
Arroyo: a creek or brook
ASCOM: In 1945, after the Japanese surrendered to end World War II, the Army Support Command Korea was established at the former Japanese depot. It was at this time that the area of Camp Grant, Camp Market, Camp Tyler, and Camp Haye acquired the acronym.
AWOL: Absent Without Official Leave
Azalea: My third sister and fourth lifelong bed-ridden sibling
Battalion: A unit composed of companies
Battering Parent Syndrome: a set of symptoms and injuries exhibited by a child who has been mentally and/or physically abused by a parent, guardian, or child-care provider
Beau: My second eldest brother, and sixth sibling
Black Market: Any unlawful sale
Bloused: Trousers tucked at boot level, bulged, exposing full lacing up to knot
BLV: Blue Lancer Valley
Bowling Alley: A lowland stretching from Seoul to Pyongyang and the traditional invasion route of the peninsula
Boysan: A boy
Brigade: A unit composed of battalions
Business woman: prostitute, *josan*
CC: Cultural Center; a camp with extended recreational facilities, sometimes overlapping a recreation center
Camaraderie: Brotherhood, a unique, perhaps indescribable, esprit-de-corps experienced by only those present
Camp: The military installations surrounded by barbwire with entry at the main gate

Cantina: Saloon, EM club, a nightclub
Cav: Cavalry Area, the military sector of the First Cavalry Division ranging from the MP checkpoint north of Seoul clear to the DMZ
Charlie Block: A mountain landmark
Chosun: Ancient name for Korea
Chingo: Friend, buddy, pal; mascot dog at Camp McGovern and Camp Ross
Chop Chop: slang for food
Chow: food; breakfast, lunch, or dinner
Chungook: China, people of China
Compound, Camp: The military installations surrounded by barbwire with entry at a main gate.
CO: Commanding Officer
Commo: Communications, the Signal Corps
Community: My definition of the camp, nearest village, and adjacent rice paddies
CONUS: Continental United States
Company: A group of soldiers consisting of squads, about ten men in each squad
County: My definition of the entire division area, the Cav
Detail: Unpleasant chores and duty
DEROS: Date Eligible to Depart Overseas (Second Infantry Division)
Deuce-and-a-Half: A two and a half ton truck
Division: 1. A unit composed of brigades. 2. The military sector of the Second Infantry Division ranging from the MP checkpoint north of Seoul clear to the DMZ.
DMZ: The demilitarized zone
DOD: Department of Defense
Eedeewah stand: Night stand
EDDPAC: Eligible Date to Depart the Pacific (First Cavalry Division)
EM: Enlisted Men: all privates, specialists, and sergeants
Fade out: The canceling of an alert
Family: My definition of the soldiers quartered in the same Quonset or barrack
Fellowshipping: Socializing
Field Problem: Usually one week of camp duty
First Sergeant: Enlisted grade eight, three arches and three chevrons, diamond or triangle at center; see Top
Fourragere: (for JEER) A triple braid with a double strand or a combination of strands, and with or without a loose strand from which a brass tip hangs that is worn around the shoulder attached from the epaulette
GI: Government Issue, a soldier; an adjective to describe anything related to the army.

G. I. Party: An inclusive exhausting clean-up of the barracks by all resident soldiers
Guard Mount: Inspection of guards in prep for duty
Gladiola: My fifth sister, seventh sibling, and my eternal tormentor
Hangook: Korea, People of Han
Hangul: The language of Korea
HHC: Headquarters and Headquarters Company
Hopsan: Small Korean bus resembling a VW van
Hooch: Korean makeshift, sometimes dilapidated, hovels; any building
Houseboy: A man hired to polish foot wear, make bunk, and general cleaning
Iago: A masterful evil plotter. Othello
Ilbon: Japan, should actually be Ilbongook, people of Japan, but because of former invasion brutality, Korea has never really accepted Japan as a friendly power
Ilbon Sea: Sea of Japan
Imjin: The Imjin River that practically traverses Korea
Jody: A marching song for troops to drill in cadence
Joe Ching: A North Korean soldier, equivalent to GI Joe
Josan: Japanese word meaning girl, but meaning prostitute in the Cav
KATUSA: Korean soldiers augmenting and serving with the U.S. Army
Kimchi: A Korean staple dish; also a word to identify anything of Korean manufacture or brand.
Kimchi bus: A large silver Korean bus servicing *all* of the land
KP: Kitchen Police, kitchen or dining room clean up duty.
Land of the Rising Sun: Japan, Ilbon
Latrine: Restroom
Lifer: Career soldier; mascot dog at Camp McGovern and Camp Ross; duty with days remaining in the triple digits
Line company: The infantry
Line soldier: Infantryman on duty at hazardous duty posts
Mamasan: An older woman; a pimp or a procuress
Marigold: My eldest sister and first sibling
Magnolia: My fourth sister, fifth sibling, and my self-proclaimed stepmother
MDL: Military Demarcation Line, the actual border that separates both Koreas
Meegook: American, People of America
Mephistopheles: A speaker and a worker of lucifer. Doctor Faustus
Middle Land: China, Chungu
Mickey Mouse Corners: The crossroads at Pobwan-Ni
Moe: My learning-disabled eldest brother, third sibling
Monsoons: Rainy season sometime from July to October

Motor Pool: The POL building for parking, repairing, and servicing military vehicles
MP Checkpoint: located approximately 5 miles north from Seoul and entry into the military zone.
MPC: Military Payment Certificates, small certificates replacing currency and change
Munsan-Ni: A greater village on the western side of the Cav, south of Libby Bridge
NK: North Korean
Neighborhood: My definition of facilities within the camp
Nogal: Pecan tree
Norte: Dust storm; in San Antonio a *norte* was a regional word for thunderstorm
OD: Officer of the Day, officer in charge of security for the day
Papasan: An elderly gentleman
Pass: a permit to leave the compound
PCS: Permanent Change of Station; a duty station
POL: Petroleum, Oil, and Lubricants; the Motor Pool
PX: Post Exchange, army general store
Pobwan-Ni: A greater village north of Yongju-Gol, known as Mickey Mouse Corners
Private: Enlisted grade one, no insignia
Pyongyang Patty: Female voice on loudspeakers at DMZ
Quonset: A semicircular-shaped corrugated iron barrack
Quarters: Barracks, hooch, Quonset
Raza: Our Hispanic buddies
RC, Rec. Ctr: Recreation Center, a camp with extended recreational facilities, sometimes overlapping a cultural center
Reflagging: The departure and replacement of a unit ceremony
Repple Depple: Redeployment, Personnel Office for Soldiers departing Korea
ROK: Republic of Korea
Rosebud: My second sister and second sibling
Short: Duty with days remaining in the single digits
Short Timer: Duty remaining with days in the double digits
Simon Legree: A brutal earthly slave master. Uncle Tom's Cabin
Skivvies: Underwear
Slicky boy: A thief, usually who infiltrates the compounds
Spoonbill: a long plot of land north of Munsan-Ni bordered on three sides by the Imjin River.
Stakeout: Guard duty with a specific purpose
Stateside: The United States, CONUS

Stewardship: ecclesiastical appointment
Taps: a bugle call at 10:00 p.m.
Tattoo: a bugle call at 9:00 p.m.
Teahouse: brothel, club
The Land of the Morning Calm: Korea, Chosun
Tinnitus: a sensation of ringing or humming only heard by the one affected
Top: General nickname for a First Sergeant, highest sergeant at company level
Tour of Duty: A duty station assignment
Troop(s): a soldier, a GI
Village Rat: Village frequenter
Vill: The village
VD Card: A prostitute's identification and medical card
Western Corridor, The Bowling Alley: a lowland from Seoul to Pyongyang and traditional invasion route.
Won: Korean monetary value. The won varied from W200 to W270 per dollar in the (1964-65) black market and Army pay table respectively.
Yankee: A slang term referring to a GI.
Yobo: girlfriend, sweetheart
Yongsan: A greater military community in Seoul consisting of a bus depot, shopping center
Yongju-Gol: A greater village south of Pobwan-Ni

Army Rank and Grade

Buck Private: PVT, enlisted grade one, no stripes, grade at entry level in the Army
Senior Private: PVT, enlisted grade two, no stripes, a private with two months service
Private First Class: PFC, enlisted grade three, a senior private with one stripe
Specialist Fourth Class: SP4, enlisted grade four, Specialist Fourth, yellow eagle on green patch
Specialist Fifth Class: SP5, enlisted grade five, Specialist Fifth, yellow eagle on green patch with one overhead arch
Staff Sergeant: SSG, enlisted grade six, three chevrons and one arch
Master Sergeant: MSG, enlisted grade eight, three chevrons and three arches
First Sergeant: 1SG, enlisted grade eight, three chevrons and three arches with a triangle or diamond at center
Sergeant Major, SGM, enlisted grade nine, three chevrons and three arches with a star at center
Command Sergeant Major, CSM, enlisted grade nine, three chevrons and three arches, with a star within a wreath at center.
Warrant Officer: WO, warrant officer grade, one bar with multiple squares denoting grade
Second Lieutenant, 2LT, commissioned officer grade one, one gold bar
First Lieutenant, 1LT, commissioned officer grade two, one silver bar
Captain, CPT, commissioned officer grade three, two silver bars

Note:
All five sergeants' enlisted grade five to grade nine are addressed as sergeant
Both Lieutenants' commissioned grade one and grade two are addressed as lieutenant

About Photographs

All photos otherwise credited were taken by me or of me by Marvin. Childhood photos and portraits in the introduction were gifts from my mother's picture box.

I have been a camera buff since I was able to handle a 620 Box as a child. As I grew up in the San Antonio barrio, I moved up to a Baby Brownie Special. Early photos of Korea were taken with a Kodak 126 Instamatic until I finally graduated to a Yashika that I bought at the PX for $40. This was my whole month's salary in the army of 1965, a sacrifice I made willingly.

Technically for you camera buffs reading this, it was a Yashika Lynx 5000 F/1.8 50 mm lens, and I used ASA 100 Pan 35 mm black-and-white film set at 125 ASA. Developing the pictures at the McGovern and Ross PXs where I was stationed, I later used the Blue Lancer Photo Lab when I was transferred there. Thirty-nine years later, I was able to retrieve almost all of my negatives and to order reprints which are published here at 300 dpi. However, while scanning photos, I found that my originals—those I printed in Korea with controlled lighting, paper exposure number, chemicals, and timing, although on matt paper and "pebbly" in appearance—in most cases, were far better representatives of the subject matter than lastly hardcopies on gloss paper.

Most of the pictures of places I saw required my image as evidence of my presence—not that I am so self-interested that many are here printed—and then, this is my story, please bear with me. Some were taken by my fellow adventurer, Marvin Garcia while at Blue Lancer and by Abilio Mendiola while at Ross with my camera. All provided memories for my family of my tour of duty of Korea.

As is usual, photo quality depended upon a number of variables on the single lens reflex (SLR) cameras of the day to include light conditions and settings along with darkroom correction. During severe weather conditions, it was necessary to protect the camera from the elements and becomes evident in the picture. In some cases or by sheer ignorance, I damaged the exposed film when processing. In all cases I carefully viewed, considered, and cropped all photos with the awareness of affording as many features or as much detail of Korean or military life as possible existing within the frame. I have always maintained that all photos are priceless as *each picture justifies its own existence*. It is true that *one picture is worth one thousand words* and that *nothing can replace the picture you wish had been taken*.

Being in a totally new world in Far East Asia, with all its wonders and uniqueness, everything I noticed was worth snapping a shot. I snapped my shutter at just about everything novel or that moved or that was different to me or that engaged my interest. And there was still a whole world of Korea within my reach I did not photograph. If I had to do the tour of duty all over again, I would implore Divine Providence to grant me another year like as my one year of 1965 Korea.

PHOTO CREDIT: (PFC) MARVIN GARCIA OR (SP4) SERGIO MARTINEZ
I NEVER IMAGINED MYSELF TAKING PHOTOS, SO IT WAS NICE TO HAVE THIS PHOTO TAKEN BY MY PICTURE BUDDIES.

Testimonial

Well over two million Americans have served in Korea during the last six decades, and Julio Martinez' book is a "must read" for all of them. Most of us went to Korea when we were very young. Some of us had never even set foot out of our own states, let alone traveled to the exotic Far East. Korea was our first real adventure and Julio Martinez' book is as close as we will ever get to reliving it. Like Julio, many of us went there when Korea was a still a Third World country, and poverty and the ravages of war were blight upon the land. We went there when American GIs and South Korean soldiers were being killed in action in a shadow war that few people knew about, and we went there knowing that the North Koreans could launch another full-scale invasion at any time.

The pages of his book vividly conjure up the sights and smells and sounds of that adventure. Martinez lived it to its fullest, enthusiastically spending every free moment walking and hitchhiking, traveling everywhere, speaking to as many Koreans as he could, taking thousands of photographs, and even teaching himself how to speak, read, and write the language. Nothing escaped his youthful eyes, from ancient temples to rice planting and harvesting to little known facets of the country's rich 5,000-year-old culture.

His exuberance with each of his discoveries is faithfully recorded, as are the familiar things we all felt—homesickness and fear, camaraderie and purpose. If you want to see the Korea of forty-five years ago through the bright eyes of a nineteen-year-old soldier from Texas with a truly remarkable memory for every detail, this is the best way to do it. Above all, this is an intensely honest book, which faithfully records what so many of us thought and felt.

SP5 William Roskey, Intelligence,
United States Army, Korea 1966-1967
Author of *Muffled Shots: A Year on the DMZ*

It's truly a heartwarming account and expresses genuinely who you are and what you experienced.

—SGT Tim Norris,
Corrections Personnel and Provost Marshall,
United States Army, Korea 1973-1975
Author of *Seasons in the Kingdom*

COMMENTARY

IN THE WORDS OF A MOTHER AND GRANDMOTHER:

Thank you so much for the honor of allowing me to read your manuscript. As you know I have started reading a few days ago, but put the book down, (or rather laptop) as it was too much to bear at the time and couldn't read on as I became extremely emotional not only with tears but aches in my heart with grief for you as that young boy. I wanted to take that little boy in my arms and hold him until every bruise dissipated, and the years of it restored to love, pure love, overwhelming love to cover all the pain and memories so that they wouldn't hurt anymore, never again. It brings me comfort to know that now with your family you have that, while our families are not perfect . . . there is still love. Bless you Julio.

—Karen J. Fisher, Mother and Grandmother

IN THE WORDS OF A FATHER AND GRANDFATHER:

The chapters of your early life at home are frank and even shocking. I think they tell an important chapter in your life and it was always clear what you thought and where you stood. As I read it I ached inside for you. It left me with a real sense of admiration for how well you dealt with it then, and what you have made of yourself since. You are an intelligent, generous, kind and gentle man in spite of the constant abuse as a child.

—Command Sergeant Major Jay Fidel,
United States Army (Ret.)

In Memoriam

In memory of our American heroes "killed in action" during the Armistice, the Korean "DMZ War," the "Cold War," and those known but to God . . .

1955-1965

BROWN, CHARLES W.—ANDERSON, DELYNN
DILLINGHAM, JIMMY E.
RIMER, RICHARD J.—JOHNSON, JAMES A.
DESSART, CHARLES T. III
SEILER, DAVID A.—LARION, GEORGE F.
CAPP, RAYMOND JR.
HARLE, JAMES T.

1966

FRANKLIN, CHARLES B.—SCHAAD, RALPH R.
MITCHELL, WARREN E.
LEFRENIERE, WILBERT E.—MOUZON, WILLIAM C.
OAKRES, RICHARD J.
FISH, WARREN R.—PATTERSON, ROY A.—HENSLEY, JAMES
BENTON, JOHN—BURRELL, ROBERT
FISHER, MORRIS—HASTY, LES
RAYNOLDS, ERNEST D.—KUCHARSKI, EDWARD M.
HOLCOMB, MICHAEL S.
SAVORS, GAR R.—SCRUGGS, ROBERT F.—FACULIK, JAMES F.
GRAYUM, ROBERT L.

1967

MEDINE, WAYNE L.—HOLMGREN, EDWARD R.
CARLSON, ROBERT B.
TYLER, PRES JR.—LAVEDA, ANTHONY B.—LOWRY, DANIEL L.
LEWIS, GEROLD L.—MACEK, VALENTIN M.
SHELDON, WALTER M.
GEROME, HOWARD C.—WILLIAMSON, SAMUEL
CAREY, HERBERT A.
DEVRIES, DENNIS L.—ESSON, THOMAS J.—FINE, RICHARD B.
MURPHY, GERALD J.—MUELLER, CARL R.—SMITH, BARON J.
BEHAN, WILLIAM E. JR.—BUTH, MICHAEL T.—DAVIS, DAVID M.
BULLOCK, GEORGE W.—JACKSON, TYRONE W.
COGGANS, LEE F.
COOPER, CHARLES W.—ADAMS, BILLY J.—HUGHS, JACKIE D.
MAYER, CECIL R.—BURCKHOLDER, JAMES—LOSS, GEORGE H.
HIGGINS, WILLIAM A.—PRICE, WILLIAM R.
FLETCHER, WILLIAM H.
PAULING, EARNEST JR.—ASHFORTH, LEONARD
BOYD, TOMMY D.
GIBBS, JOHN L.—SEILER, JOSEPH A.—HAMPEY, RAYMOND
DIRCK, DONALD L.—GARRAHY, DANIEL F.—PUJALS, JAMIE
CARTER, CHARLES—BOUDREAUX, PHILIP
CZAPLICKI, DONALD J.
SKAGGS, JERRY D.—COOK, BILLY J.
VOGEL, MICHAEL E.—RIVERS, CURTIS
COPP, PHILIP N.—LUND, PAUL G.—MCKEE, EDGAR A. JR.
WRINGER, DALE L.—WISE, CLIFFORD D.—ELLIOTT, LAMOUS JR.
CRAVEN, CARL—ABRACHINSKY, VICTOR—GUTHRIE, JOSEPH P.
CARR, LAWRENCE M.—CHUSTZ, BOBBY N.
ARCEMONT, TERRY G.
PONDER, WALTER B. JR.—DAVIS, FREDDIE L.—KROLL, THOMAS G.
NICHOLAS, JAMES H.—LAWLER, DANIEL W.—MCLELLON, NEAL C.
CHOLEWA, EDWIN—GOINGS, JESSE M.
MCCRAY, LEWIS T.
PIERT, FREDDIE L.

1968

HODGES, DUANE D.—BARNHARD, EDWARD F.
BOTTS, GEORGE L.
WHITE WILLIE S.—BRYANT, WILLIAM L.—MARTIN, PAUL W.
MOJICA, SALVATOR T.—SONGER, MICHAEL J.
KNUTSON, ELDON G.
BENNETT, RONALD C.—HOSE, RICHARD D.
ANDERSON, DAVID M.
COYHIS, BRUCE T.—CUNNINGHAM, JAMES A.—HSIE, VICTOR
PEDROTTI, DAVID W.—VENTSAN, CARL P.—THORNTON, KIRK L.
FLANNERY, ALOYSIUS—KRANCE, EUGENE K.
SLAYDON, CHARLES L.
JAKOB, CHAREL E.—ANDERSON, JAMES L.—WOOD, LARRY M.
BISBEE, ROBERT R.—COFFEY, DELMAR L.—SANDS, WARREN M.
KERR, ANTHONY B.—PETERS, ALLAN K.—WILLIAMS, WILLIE L.
ROETMAN, ROGER W.—JOHNSON, RICHARD M.
COLE, ARUNE W.
STEVENS, ROBERT L.—WEEKS, JAMES L.—HOLMDAHL, JAN. S.
RYAMARCZUK, MICHAEL—IRWIN, RUSSEL P.—WARD, JAMES A.
PETERSON, TERRANCE A.—TWITCHELL, RANDY W.
BASS, JOSEPH A.
HOPKINS, JERRY L.—WOODS, ANDREW K.—BURK, JOHN J. JR.
OLIVER, CURTIS M.—WILLIAMS, JOHN T.—GAGE, WILLIAM
GRIFFIN, SAMMY L.—HOUGH, ROBERT E.—SWAIN, JOSEPH L.
CAYER, JOSEPH E.—REYNOLDS, MICHAEL B.
GARONE, RONALD J.
NASSANI, STEPHAN A.—CAMPBELL, RAY V.—MOTTO, EDWARD A.
KRING, MARSHALL G.—ALDERINK, JAMES N.—TURNER, DAVID L.
CZOLACZ, MYRON—EDWARDS, RICHARD V.—HOLZ, GARY A.
INGRAM, JULIUS H.—MILLER, TERRENCE D.—SMITH, WILLIAM L.
VIGIL, ROBERT J.—O'MALLEY, JAMES E.—BOSTIC, BLAINE C.
HARFF, CRAIG R.—LEAVITT, RALPH E.—COOPER, MATTHEW
MCDONALD, WILLIAM K.—PARKER, ALPHONSO
SNYDER, LARRY W.

1969

LUTTER, GERALD L.—RAY, DONALD W.—COMEAU, GEORGE J.
OUTLAW, JESSE T.—CONRAD, TERRY J.—HALL, NORMAN K.
JONES, JAMES M.—LINDSEY, CALVIN LEE—KERN, PETER M.
MCKINNEY, GEORGE T.—PARK, BENJAMIN JR.
ROTHWELL, JAMES
STOLLER, EDWIN L.—ZANCHIA, CARROL C.
ECHOLS, TIMOTHY L.
DELAGRANGE, PAUL—CHAMPAGNE, HENRY J.—OFFICER, NEIL T.
BALDERMAN, LOUIS F.—CHARTIER, STEPHAN C.
COLGIN, BERNIE J.
CONNORS, BALLARD F. JR.—DZEMA, JOHN N.
GLEASON, DENNIS B.
GRAHAM, GENE K.—GREINER, LA VERNE A.
HORRIGAN, DENNIS J.
KINCAID, RICHARD C.—MCNAMARA, MARSHALL H.
MCNEIL, TIMOTHY H.
OVERSTREET, JAMES H—PERROTTET, PETER P.
PRINDLE, RICHARD T.
RIBAR, JOSEPH R.—ROACH, JAMES L.—SINGER, JOHN H.
SWEENEY, RICHARD E. JR.—SYKORA, ROBERT J.
WILKERSON, NORMAN E.
WILLIS, DAVID M.—DUCHARM, GARY R.—LYNCH HUGH M.
MILLER, JOHN A.—POTTS, JOHN H.—RANDALL, FREDERICK A.
SMITH RICHARD E.—SONDBY, PHILIP D.—TAYLOR ROBERT F.
TESMER, STEPHAN J.—WARREN, HANSEL A.
STRONG, JOHNNY M.
BROWN, TERRY—KELLY, ORIE L.—RANDOLPH, MCCLENDON
SHIRCLIFF, DONALD B.—BROWN CLIFFORD R.—COEN, ROGER D.
WILLIAMS, THOMAS E.—TAYLOR, CLIFFORD V.—SIBLEY, DANIEL

1969

MITCHELL, WILLIAM G.—DIXON, RICHARD W.
MAYHER, TERRANCE M.—STEELE, GERALD R.
RABE, DALE R.—LEON, THOMAS
MATHIEU, DURANT V.—RICH, LOUIS D.—GUTHRIE, A. C.
DAUGHERTY BRADY L.—SAGE, ALDEN O.—AUSTIN, CLINTON
BINGHMAN, GARY W.—BOODY, GEORGE E.

JONES, CHARLES A.—CONOSCENTI, FRANK
CHAPPELL, WILLIAM E.
HARRIS, THOMAS J.—GRISSINGER, JAMES R.
TAYLOR, CHARLES E.
MORRIS, JACK L.—GRIMES, WILLIAM E.—WELLS, CHARLES E.
CLATON, ROBERT H.—ROBERTSON, DONALD—PAULK, CALVIN
WHITE, WILSON D.—TOKACH, JOSEPH J.—ALTZ, JAMES R. JR.
GRIM, JOHNATHON L.—BURTON, CHARLES M.
DAVIS, CHARLES D.
SIX, DENNIS R.—PARKER, ARTHUR L.—BENNETT, JOHN
CALHOUN, WILLIAM R.—WESTERMARK, R. T. JR.

1970—PRESENT

BALLINGER, ROBERT M.—BARRETT, MARK T.
BONIFAS, ARTHUR G.
HAYNES, ROBERT—MILES, JOSEPH—WELLS, DONALD
ANDERSON, THOMAS L.—ROLAND—HILEMON, DAVID

Who Were Those KIAs?

"They were troops who answered the call of duty. Troops that just did their jobs for the greater good. Their actions defined our most sacred words, "Duty, Honor, Country."

"Their commitment to Duty, Honor and Country remind us everyday of the self-sacrifice it takes to safeguard the freedoms that come with democracy. Our Fallen Brothers were then, and are still today, 'American Heroes Killed in Action in the Korea DMZ 1955 to Present.' God bless them, their families and keep the memories of them alive for ever."

—Respectfully,
Russ Donovan, Imjin Scout,
Co A, 1st Bn 23 Inf Reg,
2nd Inf Div, 1968-1969

PHOTO CREDIT: (SP4) RON BENSON, COURIER/COMMUNICATION CENTER SPECIALIST, HHC 1ST BDE 2ND INF DIV, KOREA, JUN '68–JUL '69. PROVIDED BY: (SGT) RICK BENSON, FINANCE, 2ND INF DIV, CAMP ROSS, HOWZE AND CASEY, KOREA, JUL '69–JUL '71.

THE UNITED STATES FLAG AT CAMP BLUE LANCER VALLEY WAVES AT HALF STAFF IN HONOR OF ALL POST WAR BROTHERS KILLED IN ACTION FROM THE YEAR 1955 TO THE PRESENT.

This information cannot be modified, altered or changed. Any additions, corrections, or changes must be unanimously approved by Bob Haynes, David Benbow, Mark Hartford, and Russ Donovan.

For obvious security reasons the master list that includes Last Name, First Name, Middle Initial, Rank, Service Number, Unit, Date of Death, and Home State will be maintained and protected by Russ Donovan.

The American Heroes "killed in action," Korea, 1955 to Present modified roster is here published by Julio A. Martinez by special unanimous permission from the custodians. The author expresses deep gratitude for this protected privilege and respectfully stipulates compliance from all interested readers.

INDEX

A

AFKN (American Forces Korean Network), 299, 416-21, 452, 460, 475, 484
  Cavalier, 409, 417, 419
  Mail from Home, 408, 413, 416, 419
  Morning Report, 408
  Tomahawk, 408, 417, 419
AFQT (Armed Forces Qualification Test), 59
A-FRAME, 93, 159, 165, 192, 199, 219, 430
air force base. *See* individual bases
AIT (advanced individual training), 53, 70, 119-20, 126
Ajema, 195, 357, 484
ajoshee, 195, 445-47
alamos, 32-33, 35, 206, 245, 426, 466
Alamo Stadium, 276
Alazan Creek, 308, 428
Alley, 136
American Geographical Society. *See* Around the World Program
Anchors Aweigh, 61
Arch of Triumph, 188, 191
Army Post Office, 14
Around the World in Eighty Days, 62, 170, 385, 395
Around the World Program, 61, 302
Arroyo Alazan, 29-30, 406, 484
ASCOM (Army Support Command), 70, 72, 463, 484

Aunt Ross. *See* Camp Ross
awakened wrath, 39
Azalea, 38, 48-50, 484

B

Baker, Walter M., 121, 271, 275-77, 324, 326, 330, 398, 401, 407
Bank of America, 411, 460
basic training, 53, 70, 76, 86, 97, 115, 119-20, 126, 234, 455, 475
bathhouse, 309, 441-42, 444, 459. *See also under* Martinez, Julio
Battalion Headquarters, 269, 292, 406, 434
Battle of Flowers Parade, 55
Battle of San Jacinto, 58
Battle of the Alamo, 58
Beau (brother), 22, 29, 48, 406, 484
beetles, 71, 237-38, 429
belonging, sense of, 13, 467-68, 472
Ben-Hur, 76
Bird of Paradise, 62
bivouac, 163, 225, 354, 356, 433
black market, 438, 446, 484, 488
Blue Diamond Store, 261, 316, 449
Blue Dragoons, 264
Blue Lancer Playhouse, 123, 270, 407, 433
Blue Lancer PX, 150
Blue Lancers, 263-64
BLV (Blue Lancer Valley) (*see also* Camp Blue Lancer), 150, 167,

206, 260, 267, 270-72, 275, 280, 282, 293, 316-17, 334-35, 348, 417, 428, 452
Bob Hope Show, The, 430
Bold Journey, 61, 170
Bounty, The, 24, 62, 370
Bowling Alley, 206. *See also* Western Corridor
Boy Scouts of America, 54, 459
Brackenridge Park, 308
Bremerhaven, Germany, 227
Brigade Headquarters, 113, 267, 275-76, 292, 434, 451-52
British Navy, 59. *See also* U.S. Navy
Brother Brittain, 102-3, 111, 274
Brother Fountaine, 102, 108, 229
Brother Han, 454
Brother Jeffords, 102-3
Brother Lee, 108
Brother R., 109
Brown, Michael, 168
buck privates, 71, 81, 83, 91, 115, 126
Buck Privates, 383
Buddha, 62, 78, 153-55, 157, 178, 259, 261, 288, 313, 317, 363, 365, 374, 376, 395, 427
Buddhist (*see also* Buddha), 155, 178, 181, 286, 302-3, 305, 308-9, 316-18, 353, 462, 464
burial mound, 92, 317-18, 350, 381, 464

C

camaraderie, 117, 332, 404, 463, 467-74
Camelot Service Club, 152
Camp Amahie, 339, 341-42, 344, 348
Camp Beard, 73, 167-68, 187, 196-97, 212, 239, 243, 430, 445, 453, 460
Camp Blue Lancer, 110-11, 138, 150, 167, 196, 200-203, 225, 261, 263-64, 266-67, 269-71, 292-95, 314, 316, 334-35, 435-37
Camp Blue Lancer Valley. *See* Camp Blue Lancer
Camp Coursen, 91, 95, 145, 216, 224, 300, 458
camp dogs. *See* dogs
Camp Harris, 458
Camp Howze, 228, 239, 275, 425-26
Camp Johnson, 458
Camp McGovern, 74-76, 85-87, 91-92, 109-10, 120, 125-28, 200-201, 213-18, 239-41, 292-94, 297-300, 399, 408-9, 428-31, 457-58, 460
  guard tower of
  no. 1, 161, 163, 215
  no. 2, 76-77, 294, 300, 412-15, 419, 428, 481
  no. 3, 92, 299, 416
  no. 4, 90-94, 128, 237, 292, 297, 299, 412, 416, 453
Camp Paris, 91, 95, 145, 458
Camp Pelham, 101-2, 110-11, 167-68, 203, 411, 416, 460, 465
Camp Ross, 71-72, 110, 119-20, 167, 207-8, 212-13, 230-31, 236, 239, 241, 243, 245, 249, 251, 270-71, 399
  guard tower no. 1, 71, 231, 233, 237, 242, 244-46, 249, 251, 256-58, 429
Camp Wagner, 460
Captain Galbraith, 102-4, 106, 109
Castro, Felix, 434
Cecil (mascot), 429, 451, 498
Centro, 35
chamkansola, 233
Changduk, 374, 377
Changpa-Ri, 202, 318
Chan Ji, Mount, 152

charity, 469
Charlie Block Mountain, 169, 485
China, 14, 60, 73, 131, 142, 168, 208, 251, 259, 320, 387, 485
Chingo (mascot), 238-39, 429, 485
Chosun. *See* Korea
Christmas, 45, 106-8, 131, 243, 352, 426, 453, 471
Chungu. *See* China
Church of Jesus Christ of Latter Day Saints, 102, 109, 416
Ciudad Juarez, 474
Civil Rights Act of 1964, 472
Cleopatra, 122, 125
comic books, 23, 33, 45-46, 60, 233-34, 479
"Coming Home Soldier," 420, 475
communities, 160, 192, 358, 453, 456-59, 473
companionship, 470. *See also* camaraderie
CONUS (continental United States), 117, 485, 487
cottonwoods. *See* alamos
Cristo Rey, Mount, 474
Crossroads of the West, The, 416
Cultural Center
 No. 1, 187
 No. 4, 167

D

Dagger (mascot), 238-39, 429
Daibutsu, 62, 385, 395
Daniels, James R., 109, 256, 398-401
Datsun, 168
David Crockett Elementary, 58
"Dear Heart," 413
"Death March, The," 434
Department of Defense, 68, 161, 485. *See also* U.S. Army

departure date. *See* DEROS (date eligible to depart overseas)
DEROS (date eligible to depart overseas), 429, 450, 471, 485
DMZ (demilitarized zone), 88, 133, 168, 210, 227, 235, 259, 261-62, 268, 270-71, 293, 428-29, 433-34, 456-57, 468-69, 485
DMZ War, 468, 497
dogs, 230, 237-39, 336-37. *See also* individual dogs
Donovan, Russ, 501
Don Winslow and the Navy, 61
"Do Wah Diddy Diddy," 411, 418-19
"Downtown," 408-10
draft, 53, 81, 476
Drawe, Marisol Iris, 53
Drifters, 418-19
Duk Soo Palace, 373-76

E

East Asia, 143, 304
East Gate, 178
East Gate market, 178, 183
Easy and Queen. *See* Easy Queen, Mount
Easy Queen, Mount, 76-77, 91-92, 159, 225, 259, 269, 271, 293-306, 322, 324, 326, 331, 383, 464, 472
EDDPAC (Eligible Date to Depart the Pacific), 146, 450, 452, 485
education, 37, 44, 59, 131, 138, 140, 468, 479-81
Elder Hinckley, 111
El Paso, 110, 304, 325, 420, 453, 472-74, 477-79
El Paso Civil Service Commission, 478-80
EM Club, 115, 117, 145, 227, 244, 246-47, 274, 277, 340, 458, 460, 485

ETS (eligible date to terminate service), 227, 452, 477

F

Fabrin, Edward, 210, 243
farmer's hooch, 349, 352, 354-55
fatigues, 70, 273, 335, 450, 452, 472-73
Fidel, Jay, 141, 495
Fifteenth Company, 339, 341
55 Days at Peking, 468
First Battalion
  Seventh Cavalry, 86, 120, 145, 224, 299-300, 458
  Twelfth Cavalry, 121, 260-61, 270-71, 275, 294, 401, 409
First Cavalry, 152, 168, 275, 278, 457, 467, 485
First Drill Team, 55, 58, 275
First Sergeant Ch, 271
Fisher, Karen J., 495
flash floods, 23, 218, 274, 335-36, 338-39, 356, 428. *See also* monsoons
forbidden city. *See* Turks' compound
fort, 459, 472-73, 476
Fort Apache, 459
Fort Benjamin Harrison, 68, 70, 130, 459
Fort Bliss, 420, 453, 472-74, 477
Fort James Polk, 68, 70, 119, 459
Fort Leavenworth, 273
Fort Sam Houston, 459
fourragère, 55-56, 58, 278, 471, 485
Freedom's Frontier, 115, 195, 412
Fuji, Mount, 394

G

Garcia, Marvin, 470, 472, 475
  climbing Queen with Martinez, 294, 296-98, 300, 302, 304-6, 309-10,
  322-26, 328, 331
  guarding the Turk's compound, 340-48
GI Bill, 37
Ginza, 387, 444
Gladiola (sister), 34, 42-44, 46-50, 479, 486
gold ring, 444-49
gonorrhea, 137
Gotemba, 394
Great Depression, 39
"Green Berets, The," 420, 475
guard duty
  honors of, 71
  horrors of, 15
  purchase of, 115
Gunsmoke, 417
Gustavson, George, 319

H

Hagen, Dave, 420
Hakone, 393, 444
Hangul, 113, 463, 486. *See also under* Korea
Han River, 178, 181
Han River Bridge, 178, 181
hardship tour, 15, 54, 81, 110-11, 121, 427, 477
hepatitis, 458
Hong Kong, 274, 402, 457
Hooch 10, 292, 348, 429, 450-52, 481
hopsan, 167, 175, 188-91, 195, 197, 200, 243, 271, 428-29, 486
houseboys, 118-21, 449, 451-52

I

I Corps, 457
Ilbon Sea, 14, 259, 386, 486
"I Love You Because," 299

Imjin River, 15, 167-69, 259, 261, 279-82, 317-20, 328-29, 486, 501
Immortal Beloved, 63
Inchon, 370, 419
Inchon Train Station, 370
Indoctrination Center, 70
insubordination. *See under* Martinez, Julio
I Search for Adventure, 61

J

jacalitos, 245
"Jamaican Farewell," 273
Japan, 14, 131, 251, 274, 383, 386-87, 395, 397, 444, 486
Japan Sea. *See* Ilbon Sea
Jeffrey, Tom, 437
jet planes, 14
Joe (corner buddy), 34, 437, 486
Joel, Billy, 50
Johnson (community), 145, 458
josan, 116-17, 130-40, 142-43, 145, 272, 282, 484, 486, 488
Joske's Department Store, 35, 426

K

Kamakura, Japan, 62, 385, 394-96, 444
KATUSA (Korean Augmentation to the U.S. Army), 124, 235, 280, 335-37, 404-7, 468, 486
KELP, 420
Keum Kok Royal Tomb, 379
Khrushchev, Nikita, 124
KIA (killed in action), 71
Kim Ahn Yang, 406
kimchi, 167-68, 170, 175, 188-89, 194, 202, 204, 243, 415, 430, 442, 486
Kim Kap Jin, 406
Kimpo Air Force Base, 69-70, 386, 454, 457
Kingston Trio, 84
Kishine Barracks Service Club, 387
Koom Ja, 108
Koom-Shi, 91, 143, 145, 214, 216, 220, 222, 299-300, 453
Korea, 13-15, 68-69, 75-76, 108-11, 145-49, 220-21, 251-52, 398-400, 419-21, 427-30, 434-37, 454-57, 459-63, 470-76, 485-88, 491-94
  agrarian culture of, 461
  conflict in, 293-94, 371, 460
  as a developing country, 99, 134, 163, 461, 465
  gold of, 444
  language of, 112-14, 210, 225, 404-5, 462-63, 486, 493
  poverty in, 130, 138, 140, 163, 165-66, 215, 225, 365, 429, 465-66, 480
  public transportation of, 188, 195
  soldiers serving with the U.S. Army. *See* KATUSA (Korean Augmentation to the U.S. Army)
  wildlife of, 427-29
Korean War of 1950-1953, 15
Koryo Dynasty, 14, 155
Kumkok, 211
Kwang Tan Miruk, 151-52
Kyung Bok Ku, 189, 361, 366
Kyung Guk Sa, 285-86, 464

L

La Joya, 245
Land of the Morning Calm. *See* Korea
Land of the Rising Sun. *See* Japan
LDS services, 465
Lee Soo Moo, 406
Legionnaire, 76

Leighty, Ken, 460
Libby Bridge, 202, 318, 487
library, 21, 32-34, 130
Lieutenant B., 256
Lifer, 81, 237-39, 429, 468, 486
Lifer (mascot), 237-39, 429
Little Dipper, 436
long distance calls, 425
"Look Me Over," 430
Love (soldier), 430
Lucky (mascot), 238, 272, 429

M

M14, 71, 76, 83, 233, 349, 357
M60, 83, 277, 405, 468
Magellan, Ferdinand, 60
Magnolia (sister), 34, 42, 46-48, 60, 479, 486
Majestic Theater, 170
mamasan, 133-34, 137, 139-40, 192, 486
"Mambo Numero Cinco," 24
Mann, Manfred, 411
Marigold (sister), 38, 486
marriage, 110, 478. See also under Martinez, Julio
Mars, 455-56
Martinez, Ester, 426-27
Martinez, Julio
   adventures on the Imjin of, 279-82
   arrival and reception in Korea, 65-72
   assaulting Mount Chan Ji, 152, 157
   bathhouse spectacle of, 441-44
   battered childhood and family of, 37-52
   buying a gold ring as souvenir, 444-48
   dealing with husband hunters, 134-35
   duties at McGovern, 85
   early days at McGovern, 112, 159
   fondness for music, 409-22
   graduating and joining the corps, 53-63
   guard duties of, 99, 231-49, 339-49
   and insubordination, 256-58
   and the KATUSA brothers, 404-8
   and Korea's wildlife, 427-29
   learning a new language, 115
   looking for a Seoul Cola, 356-58
   losing his camera, 438-39
   and mail calls, 423-27
   marriage of, 38, 41, 44, 50, 110, 132, 135, 150, 272, 474, 476, 478
   meeting Oggie, 148-63
   mission of, 111
   money matters and hiring a house boy, 121
   and the monsoons, 332-39
   mother of, 37-52, 54, 63
   and Mount Easy Queen, 292-96
   nocturnal misadventures of, 214
   and nudity, 282-84
   orderly room blues of, 272-76
   playing outside the house, 21-26
   on poverty, 163-66
   on prostitution, 130-34, 136-40
   reassignment to Camp Blue Lancer, 269-72
   reenlistment dilemma of, 227, 227-30
   reflagging in Camp Ross, 278
   and regret at Munsan-Ni, 448-50
   spending Christmas in Korea, 106, 108
   spiritual practices of, 100, 104
   transferring to Camp Ross, 207, 210
   transfer to McGovern, 72-74
   venturing outside the fence, 26-36
   visits of
      Blue Lancer Valley, 259-68
      Camp McGovern, 225

Capitol, 366-69
Duk Soo Palace, 374-78
farmer's hooch, 349-55
Inchon, 370-73
Keum Kok Royal Tomb, 379-83
Kyung Bok Ku, 359-66
Kyung Guk Sa and Pul Guk Sa, 286-92
library, 21, 32-34, 130, 460
Mount Easy Queen, 297-331
Peak Dae, 251-55
Seoul, 206
Tokyo, 386-97
village, 129
watching the *Bob Hope Show*, 432
Martinez, Marc, 225
Martino, Al, 299, 416
Mary Lou (childhood crush), 34
Maslow, Abraham, 44
Master at Arms, 247
Master Sergeant O., 77, 438
McArthur, Douglas, 371
Meegook army. *See* U.S. Army
Meiji Shrine, 387, 392
Mendiola, Abilio, 422
  in Code of Conduct class, 208-10
  visiting McGovern, 214-25
  visiting Ross's Cantina, 246
Mendiola, Aurora, 17
Merciful Buddhas, 151-52
Mexican Revolution, 37, 50-51, 54, 159
Mexico City, 37, 43, 50, 159-60, 227, 450, 474, 480
Mickey Mouse Corner, 188, 200, 453, 486-87
Middle Land, 14, 251, 486. *See also* China
Mikimoto jewelry store, 387
military identification card, 457
Miller, Bruce, 340

Missionary and Servicemen's Conference, 111
Mission Home, 107-8, 161, 454
Miss Kim, 68
Miss Lee's Variety and Souvenir Shop, 149
Moe (brother), 29, 35, 38, 126, 486
money lending, 115
monsoons, 170-71, 218, 274, 295, 297, 306-13, 332-49, 354, 356, 405-6, 408, 419, 421, 451-52
"More," 417
Morgan the Pirate, 62
Mother Korea, 225, 314, 322, 339, 461. *See also* Korea
Motor Pool, 97-99, 217, 269, 434, 452, 459, 487
Moya, Alex, 212
MPC (Military Payment Certificate), 116, 438-39, 458, 487
MP Checkpoint, 167, 195, 456, 485, 487
Mr. Coe, 118-21
Mr. D., 412-14
Mr. Gumercindo, 27
Mr. Montoya, 49
Mrs. Gerodetti, 58
Mueller, Elizabeth, 21
Munsan-Ni, 73, 101-3, 133, 167-69, 202-4, 261, 263, 318-20, 449, 487
Munsan-Ni Train Station, 431
Mutiny on the Bounty, 62, 126
"My Life," 50

N

National Geographic, 154, 302
needs, hierarchy of, 44
New World, 60
New Year, 426, 471
No. 25 (bus), 453
nogales, 24-25, 32-33, 245, 331, 333

noncommissioned officers, 398
Nopae Dong, 120, 129, 142, 148, 158, 160, 200-201, 203, 214, 217, 221, 240, 413-15, 453, 457
Norris, Tim, 494
nortes, 333, 487
North Korea (*see also* South Korea), 77, 206, 208, 261, 263, 304, 318-20, 328-29, 358, 429, 435
nudity, 284
Nullo-Ri, 167-68, 200, 202-3, 315-17, 319, 331

O

Oakland Army Terminal, 68, 459
OB Beer, 458
Octagon (soap), 442
Office of the Provost Marshall, 131
Oggie (Korean crush), 147, 149-50, 400, 445
Onjo (king), 251
Orient, 14, 61, 68-69, 288, 428

P

Pacific Ocean, 68, 423, 425, 471
Pacific Stars and Stripes, 259, 386
Pagoda Park, 106
Pak Bok Dong, 348, 406
papasans, 93-94, 158-59, 195, 219, 221, 225, 287-88, 325, 450, 487
Patton, Dale A., 434
Payroll School, 59, 68, 70, 73, 84
PCS (permanent change of station), 119, 273-74, 453, 474, 487
Peak Dae, 251-53, 255
pecan trees. *See* nogales
Pechtold, David, 273, 475
Personnel School, 68
Personnel Service Center

No. 2, 212, 239, 260, 399
No. 3, 74, 76, 231, 239-41, 293, 399, 408
Peterson, Ray, 421
Pobwan-Ni, 73, 133, 140, 143-44, 148, 163-64, 188, 191, 198-200, 271, 300, 411, 438-39, 441, 464, 486-87
pocho, 93
POL (petroleum, oil, and lubricants), 269, 452, 487. *See also* motor pool
Polo, Marco, 60, 228
poverty (*see also under* Korea; Martinez, Julio), 37, 41, 59, 130, 138, 140, 159, 163, 165-66, 225, 365, 429, 465-66, 480
Princess Blue Lancer. *See* Camp Blue Lancer
Prince Valiant, 23
Private First C., 135
Private First Jung, 335, 406-7
Private First McC, 82
Private First McG, 82
Private First N.E. (buddy)
  visiting Oggie, 150
  visiting the village with Martinez, 109, 116-17, 398-99, 402, 497-501
  and a wild night, 142-47
Private First R. (money lender), 116-17
Private First Ray, 341
Private First Wain, 81, 126, 213
Private First Withee, 273, 403
Private W., 273, 403
propeller airplanes, 14
prostitutes (*see also* josans; streetwalkers), 116, 130-33, 135-40, 142, 145, 272, 282, 484, 486, 488
prostitution, 130-31, 133-34, 138-40

Pul Guk Sa Temple, 178, 286, 291
Pusan, 131
PX, 86, 103, 109, 117, 138, 150, 205, 269, 292, 434, 452, 460, 473, 491

Q

Quo Vadis, 122, 125

R

RA (regular army), 53
Radio Cavalier, 409, 417, 419
Radio Hill, 150, 259, 315, 407, 433-35, 437
rain boots, 71, 334-35, 342, 449
rainbow, 356-57
Ray Conniff Singers, 420
raza, 487
Recreation Center
 No. 1, 243, 460
 No. 2, 460
 No. 3, 460
 No. 4, 167-68, 460
Republic of Korea (*see also* Korea), 131, 168, 191, 213, 259, 282, 318-20, 328-29, 404, 429, 460, 487
Republic of Korea (ROK) Army, 88, 131, 175, 205, 213, 404, 407, 487
Rhee, Syngman, 155
Richard (childhood friend), 29-31, 125, 497-500
Rin-Tin-Tin, 459
Rio Grande, 474, 480
Riverwalk, 308
Roaring Twenties, 37, 248, 367, 466
Rocky Mountains, 472
romanticism, 411, 417
Rosebud (sister), 34, 45-46, 487
Roskey, William, 493
ROTC (Reserve Officers' Training Corps), 53-54, 57-59, 233, 275, 277-78
Ruth (teen crush), 34

S

Salt Lake City, 111, 416
Sam Chung Dong Branch, 107
San Antonio Light, 425
San Antonio Municipal Auditorium, 57
"Sand in My Shoes," 418
San Francisco, 68, 108, 423, 450, 471
Schindler's List, 42
Seattle, 68
Second Battalion Thirty-eighth Infantry, 275, 277, 324, 356
Second Drill Team, 55
Second Infantry, 275, 278, 326, 356, 450, 457, 467, 471, 485
Sellers, George, 438-39, 470, 472-75, 497-500
Seoul Boulevard, 108, 165, 178, 188, 190, 366-68
Seoul Cola, 178, 356, 458
Seoul Train Station, 165, 168, 188, 431
Sergeant Camp, 276, 335-36
Sergeant Ha, 274
Sergeant Morgan, 325
702nd Battalion, 264, 267, 269, 434
Seven Seas to Calais, 62
Seventh Infantry, 457
Shelly Winters (filly), 27-28
Shogun, 392
short reenlistment, 227
Sinatra, Nancy, 475
Sister Fountains, 39
Sixteenth Turkish Company, 339-41, 349
skivvy, 163
Skoshi Nopae Dong, 294, 413, 415
slick hustler. *See* slicky boy

slicky boy, 166, 242, 487
Smith, Rebecca M., 478
Sod Busters, The, 417
solidarity, lack of, 476
"Somewhere My Love," 420
Sonnier (first sergeant), 212
Sonny and Sunglows, 473
Son of Fury, 62
Sony stereo AM-FM radio, 411
Southeast Asia, 474
South Fort Polk, Louisiana, 68
South Gate, 188, 190, 466
South Korea. *See* Republic of Korea
South Pacific, 61-62, 261
South Seas, 62, 126
South Texas, 352
Specialist Fifth Canyon, 102, 256-57, 270, 490
Specialist Fifth Laboy, 402
Specialist Fifth Riley, 119, 258
Specialist Fourth H., 402
Specialist Fourth McClain, 423
Spirit Honor Medal, 54
Spoonbill, 259, 282, 318-20, 328-29, 460. *See also* South Korea
Staff Sergeant Coffey, 270
Staff Sergeant Gilliam, 256-57
Staff Sergeant Horn, 106
Staff Sergeant Teti, 119
straight drill, 55
streetwalkers, 133-34, 137, 139-40
Sun Jong (king), 155
Sunken Gardens of San Antonio, 361
superego, 46

T

tamales, 27
Teahouse, 131, 414
Teal Bridge, 261-62
Ten Commandments, The, 50, 428

Texas Department of Public Safety, 477
Thanksgiving, 45, 453, 471
"These Boots Were Made for Walking," 475
3rd BDE. *See* Third Brigade
Third Brigade, 145, 259, 430-31
38th parallel, 15
Tinker, Bruce, 333, 427
Tokyo, Japan, 14, 68, 75, 383, 386-88, 444, 457
Tokyo Tower, 387-88
Tonight Show, The, 417
touch-dancing, 131
Travis Air Force Base, 471
Turk compound, 271, 274, 365
Turkey Farm, 139
Turks, 205, 339-44, 421, 451, 453, 469. *See also* Sixteenth Turkish Company

U

Uncle Benny's Rest Home, 70, 72, 82
"Under the Boardwalk," 419
Uniform Code of Military Justice, 414, 417
universal military jargon, 113
Ursa Major, 344, 346, 436
Ursa Minor, 436
U.S. Army, 13, 59, 62, 68, 73, 75-77, 82, 87, 104, 124, 131, 154, 170, 195, 234, 330
U.S. Navy, 59, 61-62, 126, 261
USO (United Service Organizations), 108, 165, 167, 178-79, 187-88, 367, 425
UTEP Centennial Museum, 474

V

Van Clyburn, 124

VD cards, 137, 488
Vietnam, 59, 81, 135, 272, 325, 420, 469, 472, 474-75
Vikings, The, 36, 62
vill, 212, 214, 216, 300, 318, 456, 488
Vinton, Bobby, 409, 475
Virgil (friend), 472

W

Walker Hill, 178-79
Welk, Lawrence, 417
Western Corridor, 13, 73, 206, 259, 419, 488
West Texas, 48, 453
"When Irish Eyes Are Smiling," 27
Williams, Andy, 413
Witmer, Michael, 88
Wolf and Marx Clothing Store, 426

Y

Yashika Lynx (camera), 438, 491
Yellow Sea, 261, 320, 370, 419
Yong Dong Po, 407

Yongju-Gol, 136, 148-50, 167, 243, 271, 399-400, 439, 445-46, 449
Yongsan, Seoul, 138, 150, 167, 178-79, 187-88, 270
Yongsan PX, 106, 138
Yongsan Service Club, 138, 148, 178, 187, 379, 387, 460
Yung Su, 143-46, 148, 221

Z

Zolnoski, Lynn, 428, 436
Zulu, 400

CPSIA information can be obtained at www.ICGtesting.com
232517LV00001B/2/P